CONTENTS

PART FOUR · Pakistan, Al-Qa'ida, and the Wider War

88 DAYS TO KANDAHAR

A CIA DIARY

ROBERT L. GRENIER

Simon & Schuster Paperbacks

NEW YORK   LONDON   TORONTO   SYDNEY   NEW DELHI

Simon & Schuster Paperbacks
An Imprint of Simon & Schuster, Inc.
1230 Avenue of the Americas
New York, NY 10020

First Simon & Schuster Paperbacks trade paperback edition January 2016

For information about special discounts for bulk purchases,
please contact Simon & Schuster Special Sales at 1-866-506-1949
or business@simonandschuster.com.

The Simon & Schuster Speakers Bureau can bring authors to your live event. For more information or to book an event contact the Simon & Schuster Speakers Bureau at 1-866-248-3049 or visit our website at www.simonspeakers.com.

Interior design by Paul J. Dippolito
Maps by Paul Pugliese

Manufactured in the United States of America

1   3   5   7   9   10   8   6   4   2

The Library of Congress has cataloged the hardcover edition as follows:

Grenier, Robert (Robert L.)
88 days to Kandahar : a CIA diary / Robert L. Grenier
pages cm
Includes index.
1. Grenier, Robert (Robert L.) 2. Afghan War, 2001—Campaigns. 3. Afghan War, 2001—Personal narratives, American. 4. War on Terrorism, 2001–2009—Personal narratives, American. 5. Intelligence officers—United States—Biography. 6. United States. Central Intelligence Agency—Biography. 7. Taliban. 8. Afghanistan—Politics and government—21st century. 9. Pakistan—Relations—United States. 10. United States—Relations—Pakistan. I. Title. II. Title: Eighty eight days to Kandahar, a CIA diary.
DS371.413G76 2014
958.104'78—dc23   2014036555

ISBN 978-1-4767-1207-9
ISBN 978-1-4767-1208-6 (pbk)
ISBN 978-1-4767-1209-3 (ebook)

For Paula and Doug, who shared the adventure

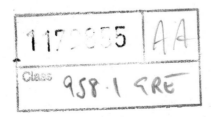

PART FIVE · Postscript: Once and Future Wars

CONTENTS

AUTHOR'S NOTE

On December 7, 2001, eighty-eight days after 9/11, Gul Agha Shirzai seized the Governor's Palace in Kandahar from the fleeing Taliban, as Hamid Karzai, fresh from negotiating the Taliban's surrender, prepared to travel to Kabul to assume his duties as head of Afghanistan's interim government. Just weeks earlier, both events had seemed highly improbable, if not impossible. On that extraordinary day, I knew I would write this book, and what its title would be. I began making preparations.

After my return to Langley in 2002, I was able to review official cables I had sent and received from 1999 onward, and to make cryptic notations to aid my memory. These notes provided the backbone for much of the book. During my subsequent time in Washington, from 2002 to 2006, I was able to document events more easily. My calendar diaries, though very brief, included lists of participants in interagency meetings and the general topics discussed.

When at last I sat down in the middle of 2012 to write, over ten years had passed since 9/11. Many of my recollections from my time in Pakistan were still utterly clear, involving scenes I had mentally stored up and reviewed in the intervening years. I found that my earlier notations brought back a wealth of vividly detailed memories. My habit of saving almost everything I laid hands on while in Islamabad also proved a blessing: official visitor schedules, clippings from the Pakistani press, invitations to official events, even dinner menus, helped me, along with extensive open-source research, to tie the details of recalled events to specific dates.

The book contains reconstructed dialogue. Many of my recollections of key conversations in which I was directly engaged, or which were recounted to me soon after the fact by one of the participants, are available to me upon consulting my notes. My recognition at the time of how extraordinary some of them were served to imprint them in my mind. Conversations where I remember the burden of what was said, but not the specific words, I have related without quotation.

As one might expect in a book written by a former spy, the names of some characters appear as aliases, or as partial true names. In some cases, I have done this in deference to the wishes of the individual concerned; in others, I have done so on my own account; and in some cases I have acted in deference to requests from CIA. Any time I do not identify an individual by his or her full true name, I place quotations around the name in the initial instance of its use. The need to maintain anonymity leads me to withhold some identifying details from my accounts of certain individuals, but in no case do I falsify either their positions or their descriptions.

There were a number of books that greatly helped me to put my recollections into proper context. Particularly useful here was *Prisoners of Hope*, by Heather Mercer and Dayna Curry, the two young American women who were among the eight Taliban captives from Shelter Now International. Eric Blehm's *The Only Thing Worth Dying For* provided an account of Hamid Karzai's campaign from Uruzgan to Kandahar, told from the perspective of the Special Forces A-Team accompanying Team Echo. It helped me to understand strictly military aspects of the operation. *Company Man*, former CIA acting general counsel John Rizzo's account of his thirty-four years at CIA, served me with an optic different from my own on the tumultuous events affecting CIA's detention and interrogation program during my time as director of the Counter-Terrorism Center.

I also have benefited from a number of authors whose experience, research, or analysis have generally informed the thinking reflected here. In *My Life in the Taliban*, Mullah Abdul Salam Zaeef, one of the founding members of the Taliban and its former ambassador to Pakistan, has provided useful insights into the reasons for Taliban actions and attitudes. I have also had the opportunity to meet and speak with Zaeef at some length. These discussions between former adversaries have helped to shape my thoughts about possible future outcomes in

Afghanistan and the potential post-conflict role of the Taliban. In _War Comes to Garmser_, Carter Malkasian, who impressively fills the roles of both scholar and practitioner, provides a very useful "micro" view of how Coalition missteps and local Afghan politics have led to the Taliban's return in a representative part of Afghanistan. Peter Bergen and Katharine Tiedemann of the New America Foundation have edited _Talibanistan_, a collection of analytic research pieces that, among other things, provide useful insight into the reasons for the Taliban's abdication of power and subsequent return, as well as the increased post-9/11 radicalization of the Tribal Areas in Pakistan. And _Duty_, Robert Gates's memoir of his time as defense secretary, offered helpful insights into the attitudes, assumptions, and reasoning behind the formulation of Obama administration policy on Afghanistan.

Finally, the accounts contained in this book benefited greatly from the recollections and insights offered by former colleagues. Barry McManus, lead interrogator of the Pakistani scientist Dr. Bashir, the head of UTN, provided a richness of detail concerning those tension-filled days. During that time, Barry was the embodiment of grace under pressure. Similarly, "Marco," the senior JSOC representative in Islamabad, who would prefer to maintain in retirement the selfless anonymity he chose while on duty, was most helpful in supplementing my recollections of the rescue of the Shelter Now detainees. "Jimmy Flanagan"—who risked his life on many occasions, along with the other members of Team Echo and their uniformed brothers-in-arms, to guide and protect Hamid Karzai—shared his first-person accounts of Karzai's exfiltration from Afghanistan; Team Echo's return; and the decisive battles of Tarin Kowt and Shawali Kowt. "Dave," my redoubtable deputy, was characteristically generous in providing his reminiscences, particularly about the capture of Abu Zubayda. He is an unsung hero of that time.

Any errors or omissions that remain despite the assistance catalogued above reflect my failings alone.

LIST OF MAPS

CAST OF PRINCIPAL CHARACTERS

NB: Names entirely in quotations are either aliases or partially true names, employed to protect the identities of the individuals concerned.

CENTRAL INTELLIGENCE AGENCY

Charlie Allen, Assistant Director of Central Intelligence for Collection

Gary Berntsen, chief of Team Juliet

Cofer Black, Director of the Counterterrorist Center (CTC)

John Brennan, acting Director, National Counterterrorism Center (NCTC)

David Cohen, Deputy Director for Operations (1995–97)

"Dan," senior military targeting officer, CTC

"Dave," Deputy Chief of Station, Islamabad

"Detroit," CIA team leader in Faisalabad

"Duane," member of Team Foxtrot

John Ferguson, senior CIA officer in New Delhi

"Jimmy Flanagan," member of Team Echo

Kyle "Dusty" Foggo, Executive Director of Central Intelligence

Porter Goss, Director of Central Intelligence (2004–06)

"Greg," leader of Team Echo

Pat Hailey, CIA representative to U.S. Central Command

"Hank," chief of CTC/SO

"James," junior reports officer, Islamabad

"Jeff," senior reports officer, Islamabad

"Jim," CIA case officer, Islamabad

Steve Kappes, Deputy Director for Operations (2004)

"Kate," senior communicator

"Jim M," senior paramilitary officer

"Mark," leader of Team Foxtrot

John Massie, deputy chief of CTC/SO

John McLaughlin, Deputy Director of Central Intelligence

Barry McManus, senior polygrapher and interrogator

Pat Murray, chief of staff to DCI Porter Goss

James "Jim" Pavitt, Deputy Director for Operations (1999–2004)

"Colonel Pete," senior CIA representative to JSOTF-N, "Task Force Dagger"

Jose Rodriguez, Deputy Director for Operations (2004–07)

Gary Schroen, chief of the "Jawbreaker" team in northern Afghanistan

Gary Spitzel, chief of the South Asia Task Force

George Tenet, Director of Central Intelligence (1997–2004)

"Tom," Farsi-Dari translator

Dan Webster, former Deputy Chief, Near East Division; senior annuitant, Islamabad

AFGHANS

Tayyib Agha, office director for Mullah Omar, leader of the Taliban

Mullah Abdul Jalil Akhund, "Mullah Jalil," Taliban deputy foreign minister

Mullah Abdul Ghani Baradar, Taliban deputy chief of Army Staff

General Abdur-Rashid Dostum, militia leader, Northern Alliance

Abdul Haq, opposition leader

Hamid Karzai, Afghan tribal opposition leader; president of Afghanistan

Mullah Akhtar Muhammad Mansur, Taliban minister of aviation

Mullah Wakil Ahmed Muttawakil, Taliban foreign minister

Mullah Naqib, Afghan tribal leader

Mullah Mohammed Omar, "Commander of the Faithful," founder and leader of the Taliban

Mullah Akhtar Mohammed Osmani, "Mullah Osmani," Taliban commander, Southern Zone

Mohammed Yousaf Pashtun, "Engineer Pashtun," advisor to Gul Agha Shirzai

Gul Agha Shirzai, Afghan tribal opposition leader; governor of Kandahar

Mullah Abdul Salam Zaeef, Taliban ambassador to Pakistan

PAKISTANIS

Lieutenant General Ehsan ul-Haq, Director-General, Inter-Services Intelligence (2001–04)

Colonel Sultan Amir Tarar, "Colonel Imam," Afghan expert, Inter-Services Intelligence

"General Imran Zaman," senior officer, Inter-Services Intelligence

"General Jafar Amin," senior officer, Inter-Services Intelligence

General Ashfaq Pervaiz Kayani, Director-General, Military Operations; Director General, Inter-Services Intelligence (2004–07)

Maleeha Lodhi, Pakistani Ambassador to the United States

Lieutenant General Mahmud Ahmed, Director-General, Inter-Services Intelligence (1999–2001)

General Pervaiz Musharraf, president of Pakistan

"Brigadier Suhail Majid," Afghan expert, Inter-Services Intelligence

DEPARTMENT OF DEFENSE

General Jerry Boykin, Deputy Under Secretary of Defense for Intelligence

General Ron Burgess, Director for Intelligence, "J-2," on the Joint Staff

Steve Cambone, Under Secretary of Defense for Intelligence

Douglas Feith, Under Secretary of Defense for Policy

General Tommy Franks, Combatant Commander, U.S. Central Command

"Marco," senior representative of Joint Special Operations Command in Islamabad

General Stanley McChrystal, Commander, Joint Special Operations Command

Chief Warrant Officer (CW3) Poteet, Special Forces liaison to Islamabad Station

"Greg R," "Captain Greg," Special Forces liaison to Islamabad Station

Donald Rumsfeld, Secretary of Defense

Paul Wolfowitz, Deputy Secretary of Defense

DEPARTMENT OF STATE

Richard Armitage, Deputy Secretary of State

Robert "Bob" Blackwill, U.S. Ambassador to India; deputy national security advisor for Southwest Asia

Chat Blakeman, political counselor, Islamabad (2001–03)

Wendy Chamberlin, U.S. Ambassador to Pakistan (2001–02)

David Donohue, U.S. Consul-General, Islamabad

William "Bill" Milam, U.S. Ambassador to Pakistan (1998–2001)

Nancy Powell, U.S. Ambassador to Pakistan (2002–04)

John Schmidt, political counselor, Islamabad (1998–2001)

Michele Sison, deputy chief of mission, Islamabad

FEDERAL BUREAU OF INVESTIGATION

Dave Falco, FBI special agent

Jenny Keenan, Assistant legal attaché, Islamabad

Christopher Reimann, legal attaché, Islamabad

WHITE HOUSE

J. D. Crouch, deputy national security advisor (2005–07)

Stephen Hadley, deputy national security advisor (2001–05); national security advisor (2005–09)

Zalmay Khalilzad, National Security Council

Dr. Condoleezza Rice, national security advisor (2001–05); Secretary of State

Fran Townsend, Homeland security advisor

OTHERS

"Akbar," unofficial Afghan-American facilitator between the U.S. government and the Taliban

Dayna Curry, American member of the NGO "Shelter Now International" in Afghanistan

Heather Mercer, American member of "Shelter Now International" in Afghanistan

Georg Taubman, head of "Shelter Now International" in Afghanistan

Part One

INFLECTION POINT

Chapter 1

THE PLAN

S USPENDED IN THE HAZY netherworld between sleep and wakefulness, I gradually became aware of an irritating sound somewhere near my head. It took a few seconds to orient myself. I was in my bedroom, safe behind bolted steel doors. The sound was coming from the secure phone on the nightstand. The clock indicated I'd gone to bed just four hours before.

"What in God's name do they want now?" I thought. I raised the receiver and managed a raspy "Hello."

"Did I wake you up, son?" It was the unmistakable voice of George Tenet.

I wasn't much in the habit of being awakened by the director, but what caught my attention was being called "son." George wasn't all that much older than me.

"No, Mr. Director," I lied. "I was just getting up."

"Listen, Bob," he began, after our encrypted phones had synched up. "We're meeting tomorrow morning at Camp David to discuss our war strategy for Afghanistan.

"How should we begin?" he asked. "What targets should we hit? How do we sequence our actions? Defense is telling us that there are almost no military targets available." We can see from overhead reconnaissance, he added, that the Arab al-Qa'ida fighters, whom we called the "Afghan Arabs," had evacuated their camps. "Should we bomb empty camps?"

These questions had been troubling me for the twelve days since

September 11, while the situation in Afghanistan rapidly evolved. As the CIA station chief in Islamabad, the capital of Pakistan, for the past two years, I was responsible for all U.S. clandestine intelligence activities in both Pakistan and Taliban-controlled Afghanistan—fully 90 percent of the country. For two years, it was my job to lead the men and women charged with ferreting out the region's secrets and penetrating its mysteries. I had devoted nearly every waking minute to understanding problems: the rivalry between India and Pakistan over Kashmir; Pakistan's covert support to terrorist groups; its construction and proliferation of nuclear weapons and long-range missiles; the plans and intentions of Pakistan's military dictator, General Musharraf; and, most important, the terrorist enterprise of Osama bin Laden and its relations with the Taliban, the Afghan religious student movement that dominated the country and provided him with safehaven and support. Now, after 9/11, I knew that it would no longer be enough to report on problems. As the senior CIA officer on the scene, I would have to try to solve them.

For a few days after 9/11, CIA Headquarters in Langley, Virginia, had gone silent. The normal flow of secret message traffic had dwindled to a trickle. It was as though the American giant had been staggered. Then, in the days immediately preceding George's call, the giant had come back to life, and Langley was pummeling me with questions and demands.

We were facing the imminent prospect of a U.S. invasion of Afghanistan. I had visions of large numbers of U.S. troops operating in a vast and difficult terrain, trying in vain to find and strike an evanescent enemy, with no defined targets and no clear long-term objectives. This seemed like a prescription for a Soviet-style Afghan disaster.

Just a few days before, on September 19, one of my officers had gathered our first piece of "smoking gun" evidence of al-Qa'ida's responsibility for the 9/11 attacks. Our best source on the Afghan Arabs—an agent who had been carefully vetted and whose information had been fully corroborated dozens of times—had attended a meeting of over 100 Arab fighters hosted by bin Laden near Jalalabad, in northeastern Afghanistan. Contradicting his previous public denials of responsibility for 9/11, in this private gathering Shaykh Osama had taken full and triumpant credit for the attacks. He exulted over what he said was an imminent U.S. invasion of Afghanistan, which would at last draw the Americans into open combat and surely lead to their defeat. I shared the desire to deal with bin Laden once and for all; but I also feared that if we acted carelessly, his prediction could prove accurate.

As George was talking, my mind was focused on President George W. Bush's State of the Union speech three days before, on September 20. Speaking before the joint houses of Congress, with British prime minister Tony Blair in attendance, the president had laid the cornerstone of a conceptual framework to guide the way forward. The speech had been replete with demands and ultimatums for the Taliban: Turn over Osama bin Laden; close the terrorist training camps and subject them to international inspection; deliver all terrorist fighters associated with bin Laden to competent foreign authorities. Failure to do so, Bush said, would condemn the Taliban to share the terrorists' fate.

Hidden in that hard message, however, was a ray of hope and the possibility of redemption. The president was drawing a line in the sands of time. As of 9/11, he was saying, the rules of the game had changed. Henceforth, nations and subnational groups who acted as sponsors of terrorism would be held to account. There was an implicit opportunity for erstwhile terrorist sponsors to reject terrorist tactics and those responsible for them. That opportunity was the message I thought we should extend to elements of the Taliban, and to all Afghans willing to break with the Taliban policies of the past. Reinforced by the international solidarity which had immediately manifested itself after 9/11, that positive message would guide our policy, and provide the justification and the rationale we would need as we took what would most likely be the tough military actions necessary to bring al-Qa'ida to heel and to deny it safehaven.

"The President has set the policy for us in his speech," I said. "In effect, he has invited the Taliban to join the international coalition against terrorism.

"We shouldn't think about this primarily in military terms. What's important is for us to focus on our political goals in Afghanistan. We can't permanently rule the country ourselves. Everything we do should be consistent with the long-term need to create a new political dispensation in Afghanistan, one willing to drive out the Arabs and to keep them out. Any military means we employ should be designed to serve and to reinforce our political objectives.

"We begin with Mullah Omar. Our initial demands focus on him. If he refuses to change policy, to break with bin Laden, we hit him. That serves notice on the others in the Taliban leadership, who have never much liked bin Laden or the Arabs anyway. We extend the promise and the ultimatum to them, and if they refuse, we have the rationale to hit them too." George stopped me with questions.

"Mr. Director," I said, "this isn't going to work. I need to write this all down clearly."

"That's a good idea," he said. "It's 11:30 PM here, and I'm meeting the helicopter at 6:00 AM tomorrow for Camp David. I need to get some rest. Can you get something to me by 5:00 AM?"

I told him I could. As I sat at my desk to write, it was as if I were merely transcribing something I could see plainly in my head.

This was breaking all the rules. No one knew that better. Every CIA officer is taught that we are never to be "policy prescriptive." CIA's job is to inform policy, never to make it. I had just spent three years as chief of "the Farm," the Clandestine Service's equivalent of West Point for the Army and Parris Island for the Marines, where it was my job to make sure that the next generation of CIA officers knew its proper place in the world. And yet here I was, purposefully violating one of the cardinal rules I had spent a career upholding.

There wasn't an approved format for the piece I was writing. I framed it as an "Aardwolf," CIA's code name for a chief of station field appraisal. Such appraisals, analytic pieces from senior CIA representatives abroad, are relatively rare, prepared only in response to watershed events. They get a lot of attention from high levels in the executive branch. I knew the senior reports officers at CIA Headquarters, who normally reviewed all incoming intelligence reports for conformity to format and adherence to the rules, would not be pleased when they saw a field appraisal specifically intended to prescribe policy. Their ranks traditionally dominated by women, the senior reports cadres were sometimes waggishly referred to, *sotto voce*, as "the Sisterhood." To me they were the Vestals, the guardians of the flame.

But they wouldn't get a vote. They would see this chief of station field appraisal, but only after the fact: it was going directly to Tenet, outside normal channels, for his own use with the cabinet principals.

I banged out the piece, eight pages, in three hours. By the time I was finished, all my senior guys were in the office, and I circulated the draft to them, made modifications based on their comments, and sent it on to the director's security staff with instructions to hand it to him as soon as he awakened.

It would be days before I learned of its fate. George had reviewed it at five in the morning and had immediately sent copies to the full War Cabinet, who used it as the point of departure for their discussions, held without the president present, that Sunday morning. The principals presented their conclusions to the president in the White House Situation Room the following day and, after more discussion, the eight-page document was approved by President Bush as the conceptual template for the war effort. Tenet was directed to put me in touch with General Tommy Franks, the head of Central Command (CENTCOM), and the senior combatant commander charged with leading the Afghan campaign, to make sure his war plan conformed.

Later that week, at a meeting with a UK official in Islamabad, he told me that my report had been briefed to the British Cabinet. "You've got the silver pen!" he said.

I regard that cable as the best three hours of work I ever did in a twenty-seven-year career. The mere fact that a CIA field officer was asked to write it, to say nothing of the fact that it was adopted as policy, is extraordinary. Despite its flaws, it anticipated many of the problems with which the United States and its allies are struggling now in Afghanistan, over a decade on, and it suggested remedies—some followed, some not; some effective, some not. Adopted at an early point when opinions were still malleable, it established many of the key assumptions that governed the conduct of the early campaign in

Afghanistan—sometimes, admittedly, to an extent more literal than was helpful. But those assumptions reflected the eternal verities of Afghanistan, as America has subsequently learned to its cost.

Thirteen years have passed since 9/11. The improbably quick victory won by small numbers of CIA and Special Forces operatives allied with anti-Taliban dissidents in what we might call the First American-Afghan War has nearly faded from memory. Our "victory" proved short-lived. After a pause of perhaps three years, the United States again found itself at war with the Taliban in what we might call the Second American-Afghan War. Only this time, the comparatively modest objectives of the first war had been replaced with an over-ambitious set of millennial nation-building goals which Americans could not achieve and Afghans could not sustain.

Many of the principles of my cable, which guided the American effort in the first war, had long been abandoned by the start of the second. The original plan postulated that while the United States should support the Northern Alliance—the collection of Afghan minorities who traditionally opposed the Taliban and were locked in a civil war with it—we should strictly avoid the perception that we were entering a civil war on their side. To do so would cause the restive and more numerous Pashtuns, from whom the Taliban was drawn, to coalesce firmly against us. Instead, any effort against the Taliban must include dissident Pashtun elements, beginning if possible within the Taliban itself. I asserted firm rules of conduct: America must keep its military footprint in Afghanistan small; it should eschew permanent bases; the U.S. effort should always be in support of Afghans, rather than the other way around; most important, the American quest to deny Afghan sanctuary to international terrorists should conform to the political culture of the country, rather than fall into the trap of trying to change it.

The second war is coming to an end. There will be no victory in this war, illusory or otherwise. Having concluded, correctly, that the prospects for success in the terms it had originally defined are too remote, and the associated costs far too high, the Obama administration has decided to withdraw substantially from Afghanistan.

This recalibration of the U.S. posture in South-Central Asia would be welcome if it were conducted in support of a viable and sustainable long-term American engagement in the region. Instead, the planned post-2014 American military posture in Afghanistan is merely a cover for what the U.S. government actually intends: the abandonment of Afghanistan.

If America's problems in South-Central Asia were confined to Afghanistan itself, the situation would not be so dire. But the U.S. invasion of Afghanistan and its aftermath have unleashed forces within neighboring Pakistan that have further radicalized that country and undermined the political and social underpinnings of a nuclear-armed state of some 180 million people. America's obsession with Afghanistan has put our country's far more important interests in Pakistan in serious jeopardy. Now, having caused more harm than good by trying to do too much, we are set to compound our errors by doing too little.

The challenges that confront us today are remarkably similar to those we faced in the immediate aftermath of 9/11. Afghanistan is again reverting to civil war, and the religiously inspired radicalism that provided an incubator for the 9/11 terrorists is, if anything, stronger in both Afghanistan and Pakistan than when we were attacked. As it has done before, America is trying to wash its hands of South-Central Asia. As before, that may not be so easy, and we may not be able to live with the consequences of our abandonment.

For those who will be charged with future U.S. policy in the region, greater acquaintance with the history surrounding America's first direct military involvement in Afghanistan, and the reasoning that led to our initial successes there, might well usefully inform their—and our—judgments as we prepare for the possibility of yet another phase of our Afghan adventure. It is my hope that a grasp of the practical lessons learned by this writer and his colleagues in the First American-Afghan War, and an understanding of how our distraction from those lessons led to the failure of the Second, will yet prove to be of use as and when America and its allies are forced to embark upon a Third.

Chapter 2

THE SUBVERSIVE

A PLUMP, MIDDLE-AGED WOMAN perched on the edge of a battleship gray metal desk. Her expression conveyed intelligence, confidence, humor, empathy—and something else I couldn't quite put my finger on. Call it an unusual form of detachment: Here was someone who could evaluate you clinically, but do so with such charm that you weren't put off. She seemed both intrigued and faintly amused by me.

With a three-by-five file card in hand, I had literally wandered in off the street into this unprepossessing, unmarked government office in Rosslyn, Virginia, just across the bridge from Washington, D.C. I had no clear idea what I was there for. A series of appointments had been made for me, and this was simply the next one on the list, neatly typed by my congressman's legislative assistant. Joe Early, Democrat from the Third Massachusetts District, was my wife's second cousin. My brothers-in-law were precinct captains; my father-in-law had worked in Early's last election. In a transaction recognizable to those familiar with old-fashioned Massachusetts ward politics, the congressman had done a favor for the loyal extended family of a rather clueless, long-haired twenty-three-year-old.

Long-haired and clueless though I was, "Dotty," the CIA recruiter, seemed to have all the time in the world for me. She asked questions about my background. I really couldn't fathom why; there was little remarkable about it. The dutiful eldest son in a Catholic family of seven children, I had grown up in a comfortable house in a comfortable suburb of Worcester, Massachusetts. My childhood had been simple and relatively happy. The nuns who taught me in the local parochial school may have been self-congratulatory in their virtue, but they offered a marvelous education. My summers were spent playing baseball, running through the woods, swimming with friends in our pool, and voraciously reading the biographies of American explorers and military heroes. Unsurprisingly, my instincts growing up were both conservative and deeply patriotic.

In something of a departure for my family, but perhaps reflective of American upward mobility, at least as it's sometimes expressed in the Northeast, I was sent away at fifteen to Williston Academy, an old-line brick-and-ivy New England boarding prep school, the sort of place where, in those days, the teachers were still called "masters," and the boys dressed in jacket and tie for dinner. Although the student body was liberally salted with the names of ethnic Catholics like me, and even a few Jews, the history and tone of the place, symbolized by the Episcopal chapel whose spire dominated the campus, was pure New England WASP. It was an environment that suited me. The sense of social privilege and corresponding obligation that subtly but thoroughly permeated the culture of the school felt comfortable.

Even Williston was not immune to the social and political ferment of the late sixties and early seventies, but the radical student activism of that anti–Vietnam War period left me cold. The university protesters of my generation, for all their proclaimed idealism, struck me as anything but altruistic: it seemed obvious to me that they didn't really care a fig about the Vietnamese; they simply didn't want to be shot at. The supposed vanguard of my generation appeared to me to be transparently self-serving, self-indulgent, and largely ignorant of the American institutions they denigrated.

Ever since my boyhood brushes with John Paul Jones, Stephen Decatur, and General Douglas MacArthur, I had dreamed of attending one of the military service academies. During my "Upper-Middler" (Junior) year at Williston, I got a pair of nominations to Annapolis, and went with my father for a guided tour of the campus during Plebe Summer. The evident discomfort of the Plebes notwithstanding, I was intrigued by the culture of the place, and by what I perceived as the necessity to simultaneously embrace and resist its heavy authoritarianism. That, too, suited me. I was ready to go ahead with my application.

Neither the antimilitary spirit of the times not the attitudes of my classmates could dissuade me, but my father could, and did. Ours was a highly independent family, and I can count on the fingers of one hand the number of times my dad tried directly to influence me on anything. But this was one of those times. "Just remember," he said. "If you join the Navy, you won't spend your career doing what you think is best for you; you'll do what someone else thinks is best for the Navy." That gave me pause; I opted, instead, for a civilian education. But as I look back, I can see a young man instinctively primed for a life of public service, even if he was largely unconscious of the reasons for it, and had no idea where his proclivities might lead.

In those days, and particularly among the prep school set, it was expected that if you did well, you would naturally go to one of the "good" schools. For me, reflecting typical New England parochialism, that meant the Ivy League. When I arrived at Dartmouth, though, something changed. I had worked so hard to get there, but now, to my surprise, it felt like I had merely traded a small prep school for a bigger one. Going to college was supposed to be moving on; this felt like treading water. I rebelled, at least after a fashion. Rather than focusing on my studies, in my first year I set about addressing what I felt were the real gaps in my education. I spent much more time than was prudent hitchhiking around New England to see friends. I learned to drink, was introduced to recreational drugs, and began seriously dating girls. My grades slipped badly. My parents were shocked.

The summer after that first year, my dad pulled me aside for one of our rare little chats. A successful contractor, he framed the problem in straightforward business terms: "When I agreed to pay for your college education, I saw it as an investment," he said. "Right now, this isn't looking like a good one." My grades improved thereafter, but I remained naive, idealistic, and wildly impractical. I had no idea what sort of career I might want, and while I understood the need for money, its pursuit held no interest. College, it seemed to me, was a time to discover fundamental truths: I became a philosophy major.

The Philosophy Department at Dartmouth did not prove a good fit. With few exceptions, my college professors were a disappointment to me. I had expected to find earnest seekers of truth. What I generally found instead were smart, glib fellows who knew a great deal about what other people thought. Hanover, New Hampshire, is a beautiful place, and I enjoyed the company of an eclectic group of characters in the ramshackle, countercultural fraternity I joined. But they and the few compatible professors I found were a limited antidote to the college experience itself. For reasons that said more about me than them, many of those around me seemed self-satisfied, conventional, and oddly anti-intellectual. Eager to get out of school, I managed to complete my studies in three years, which left me with the suddenly acute problem of what to do next.

I had loved boarding school and was eager to return. It may sound strange, but within what some might perceive as a straitjacket of form and tradition, I had encountered far greater freedom of thought, and far more interesting people, than I ever encountered in the supposedly freewheeling intellectual ferment and drug-fueled hedonism of 1970s eastern academia. The economic downturn of the mid-1970s had hit many private secondary schools hard, however, and there were few jobs to be had. In response to the many letters of introduction I sent out, I received only one invitation for an interview.

The position on offer at Concord Academy, outside Boston, was not at all what I had in mind. Concord had for years been a small, exclusive girls' school, the tone set by the many socialites who sent their daughters there. Caroline Kennedy had graduated a year earlier, before going off to Harvard; the student body was dominated by old-money eastern establishment families, leavened with the offspring of film, television, and theater people. The school had only recently become coeducational, and was looking for a dorm parent for one of its few boys' residences. It wasn't a teaching job, but it was a foot in the door. Only slightly older than the charges I was to supervise, I was offered the position.

The following year, which would otherwise have been my last in college, was idyllic. My dorm parent's stipend was tiny, but came with free room and board. I supplemented my income by substitute teaching in the local public schools, and helped coach the cross-country and baseball teams. I made terrific friends on the Concord faculty, and spent off-hours in the bars and cafés of Boston and Cambridge. It would all have been a good first step toward realizing my goal of becoming a latter-day Mr. Chips, but there was just one hitch: barely out of adolescence myself, I found I had little patience for the emotional trials of younger adolescents. School would be a terrific place, I thought, if it weren't for the damned students. I was going to have to come up with something else.

That summer, a friend and I formed a house-painting company, and landed a couple of contracts to paint old colonial residences in Cambridge. Lounging in paint-spattered clothes, poring over the newspapers during meal breaks in seedy, working-class diners off Harvard Square, I found myself increasingly drawn to the international pages. I became fascinated by Middle East politics, the post-1973 emergence of the oil-rich sheikhdoms of the Persian Gulf, efforts to settle the Arab-Israeli dispute, and the Cold War struggle for post-colonial influence in Africa. I followed the maneuvers of Robert Mugabe, Joshua Nkomo, and Ian Smith in Rhodesia as though I were reading a weekly serial. I had always had an interest in international politics, but had never really taken the time to develop it. Now, my partner had trouble tearing me away from my reading to get me back on the job. On the basis of nothing more than that and a few romantic movies I'd seen about the Middle East, I decided to get a graduate degree in international relations.

There was just one holdup to the pursuit of my latest enthusiasm. While at Dartmouth, I had fallen in love with a Boston College nursing student, one year my junior, from a large, extended Irish family. Paula and I wanted to get married as soon as possible, but it would be another year before she could graduate. Not wanting to assume in bad faith the responsibilities of a proper, entry-level position I had no intention of keeping for more than a few months, I took a cheap, walk-up garret apartment in Boston's Back Bay area and embarked on a series of dead-end jobs while waiting to hear back from graduate schools. When it got too cold to paint, I sold household smoke detectors door-to-door. I later became manager of a twenty-four-hour gas station, employing minimum-wage roustabouts in a tough section of Dedham, Massachusetts, while working a sixty-hour week. That year provided an enormously valuable education. Among other things, it strongly reinforced the lessons I had gleaned during summers working for my father's construction company, where I had developed an appreciation for the ennobling qualities of hard manual labor. It also taught me that I had a knack for developing close, empathetic relationships with people who did not begin to see the world as I did.

In the spring of 1977, on a Sunday afternoon, Paula graduated summa cum laude from Boston College. We were married the following Friday, in a large Irish wedding attended by 200 people, most of whom I'd never met. Within weeks I was a kept man, studying at the University of Virginia while my wife supported me as a neonatal intensive care nurse at the University Hospital. I was twenty-two, and she twenty-one.

All that led me, some ten months later, to Dotty's door. After about an hour of amiable but seemingly undirected conversation, she asked: What did I think I was applying for? Somewhat taken aback, I replied that I guessed I'd be interested in working as an intelligence analyst. This was my first encounter with a CIA field operative, a "case officer" in agency parlance, and so it was also the first time that one would lie to me. "We don't have any openings for analysts," she said. "But have you ever thought about how the U.S. government goes about gathering secret intelligence overseas?" Without any reflection, I answered truthfully. "No ma'am," I said. "I've never given it a moment's thought."

Laughing, she told me about her own career. She, too, had married young, but to a considerably older man, a former ambassador who was one of the State Department's original "China hands" from the 1950s. Eventually recruited and trained as a case officer by the CIA's Directorate of Operations (now called the National Clandestine Service), she had moved in her husband's wake, able to take advantage of his contacts with senior foreign government officials and others with access to secrets of interest to the U.S. government. Her job had been to find such people, assess their motivations and their suitability to be spies, and convince them to cooperate, in secret, with the CIA.

We had spoken minutes before about the young French couple I had lived with as an exchange student in Toulouse, France. "What motivated the husband?" she asked. "What did he want in life? Was he happy with his career, with his marriage?" In truth, although I could speculate, I really wasn't sure. Like anyone, I had lots of idle thoughts and insights into the character of friends and acquaintances, but had never really examined or tested them in any systematic way. As we spoke, I could see that the job she was describing would require me to look at the world from a very different perspective.

"We're looking for the sort of people who sit down between flights in a crowded airport with a good book, and then never open it," she said, "because they're too engrossed in studying the people around them." A successful case officer, she said, has to have empathy for people and a restless curiosity about the world, a drive to understand how things work, to understand the causes behind events. He must be resourceful and flexible, to think well on his feet. He has to be able to write quickly, succinctly, and well. And he can't be in it just for himself, because he has to know, going in, that he will never get external recognition for what he does.

She went on to describe the various specializations in the Directorate of Operations, and a typical career progression, from street case officer or reports officer up through ascending layers of supervisory and then management responsibility. It was intriguing and intimidating. I had never particularly suffered from a lack of self-confidence, but I genuinely wasn't sure I could do this. I kept my doubts to myself.

"You have an impressive background," she said. "Your academics, your language ability, your time abroad all count in your favor. We can determine whether you have the psychological makeup we're looking for, and the writing and other skills we need. What you need to decide is whether you want to do this." My answers were equivocal.

"I'm going to suggest a book for you to read," she said. "*The Night Watch*, by David Atlee Phillips. That will give you a better idea of what this is all about. If you're interested, call me, and we'll start the process."

That night I called Paula from my motel room. I mentioned the appointment with CIA. "Oh?" she replied warily.

"You wouldn't believe what they want me to do," I said. We agreed we could never do anything like that.

"Just too weird," she concluded.

By the time I arrived home the next day, she had already retrieved *The Night Watch* from the library. Over the next two days, we both read it. Phillips had had an exciting career, encompassing both high achievement and abject disaster. Although heavily involved in the failed invasion of Cuba at the Bay of Pigs, he rose eventually to be chief of the CIA's Latin America Division. What most came through, though, was what a decent, humane fellow he was; he didn't fit at all the popular image of the cold, calculating, flint-hearted spy. As his life story unfolded, it was easy for us to identify with him and his clever, independent-minded wife. On the morning of the third day we looked at each other. "It *would* be a job," she said.

I've never been much good at long-range career planning. But I did at least have a marginal talent for recognizing an opportunity when I'd stumbled over it. The application and vetting process was long, extending over seven months. As I went through the stages of submitting a lengthy, 36-page personal history questionnaire and various writing samples, taking a battery of psychological and vocational tests, speaking with a psychiatrist and a senior officer of the Near East Division and, finally, passing a polygraph examination and undergoing a background investigation, it began to dawn on me that I had somehow found precisely what I had been looking for all along. Not for the first time in my life, I discovered that it was much more important to be lucky than good.

I entered on duty as a junior officer in the CIA's Directorate of Operations, the Clandestine Service, on January 14, 1979, the day Shah Mohammed Reza Pahlavi fled Iran. Less than two years later, after a year of rigorous training and some months devoted to brushing up my French and preparing on the desk, I found myself a member of the Near East Division, on my first assignment in North Africa. Over the eleven years that followed, essentially the decade of the eighties, we moved from one foreign assignment to another, six in all, in locations in the Near East and Western Europe. In all of them, I dealt almost exclusively with Middle Eastern issues. For most of that time I was under "official" cover, posing as a bureaucrat of one stripe or another, typically for a couple of years at a time. What I ostensibly did often bore little resemblance to my actual job. For two particularly exciting years, I traveled almost constantly through Europe, the Middle East, and the Far East, posing in a variety of guises, using aliases and false documents. The personalities I assumed in those days were usually much more interesting than me. It was like acting. I got to a point during that time where I could no longer sign my name without pausing for a split second to make sure I knew who I was supposed to be at the moment.

Wherever I was, my job in those years was to recruit foreigners as intelligence sources—"agents," or "assets" in CIA parlance—and to "handle" or "run" them as spies. That meant to meet or otherwise to communicate with them in secret, to provide them with direction, and to debrief them for intelligence. The technology involved in the clandestine tradecraft we employed grew steadily in sophistication in those early years of the digital revolution, but ours remained, as it had been from time immemorial, a "people" business, just as Dotty had told me at the outset. People are complicated, and spies perhaps more so than most. Finding the motivational key to persuade someone to betray his or her country or organization, often at great risk, is difficult, exacting, and soul-searching work. Moral ambiguity is the spy's constant companion. Once recruited, an asset must constantly be assessed and tested for changes in his motivation or his access to information. The price of failure can be high: agents can be discovered and "turned" to work against you, suborned by third parties to serve several masters or, in the case of a terrorist, lead you to your death. And yet, all the while navigating this mental and moral wilderness of mirrors, an officer must maintain a close and empathetic relationship with his or her source, lest the basis of the relationship be undermined. The case officer's workspace is the palette of human character. In embracing the mix of high-minded and base motives that characterize most sources, you learn similar lessons about yourself.

I found that being a CIA case officer was not a job at all: it was a way of life. There was not a part of my existence it didn't touch. Excursions with friends or school outings were engineered or manipulated to provide opportunities to meet and develop potential sources. A picnic in the countryside or a day at the beach provided cover to case a site for a subsequent clandestine meeting. I would excuse myself from a seemingly casual restaurant dinner with friends to walk out the back and make an untraceable call to a contact. Nothing in life was simple; everything had a dual purpose.

Although never directly affiliated with CIA in any way, Paula had in effect signed up for this with me, and she and our young family became an integral part of my dual life. I found she often had better, more instinctive insights into people's character than I did, and I learned to pay attention to them. Many nights she lay awake into the wee hours with instructions as to whom she should call if I failed to return from some late-night assignation.

On one occasion, disaster struck: A "principal agent" I was running, a known enemy of a rogue, terrorist-supporting state, whose job was to manage a network of subagents, was betrayed by one of them, a childhood friend, and slain by a hit team. Fearing I might be next, my superiors in Langley demanded first that we take a "vacation" in the mountains, and then that we leave the country, permanently. We had to say good-bye to our home and to our friends, on very short notice.

It was passionate, all-encompassing work. In the words of a female colleague, in CIA your job becomes your mistress. As such, it inevitably takes a toll over time on marriages and families, and at various points ours was not excepted. But life in those years was hardly grim; it was intoxicating. For every night Paula spent worrying as I stalked through some seaside slum, there were others spent at chic dinner parties or elegant receptions. She was able to find nursing work whenever she liked, in embassies, in private schools, for oil companies, for the Peace Corps. We made wonderful friends, of many nationalities and from many walks of life. Life in poor developing countries had a colonial feel, with large houses, servants, and leafy tennis clubs. Vacations took us from exotic medieval towns in Yemen, to Roman ruins in North Africa, to the teeming markets of Hong Kong, to the topless beaches of Antibes.

Among my relatives and friends, only my parents knew that I was working for CIA. My in-laws went to their graves not knowing what their son-in-law did for a living. My father, in particular, was skeptical of my chosen profession; for the first decade or so, he thought of it as a phase that I would eventually outgrow. My mother, though, was more curious. On one of her visits, we spoke alone in the garden, away from possible microphones. She asked me pointedly whether I liked what I was doing. "Mom," I said truthfully, "I love this so much it scares me."

As the years passed, my skills as an officer and my devotion to the organization developed easily, and in tandem. The autonomy, clarity, and personal discretion offered by fieldwork, I would learn, had no equivalent in the pestilence of Washington's bureaucratic politics, even for the most senior officials. My progress was recognized in steady promotions, and I was given two field commands of my own, first as a "base chief," subordinate to a chief of station located elsewhere in the same country, and then as a station chief in my own right.

To outsiders, however, my success was not apparent. Advancement in my "cover jobs" kept pace for a time with hidden reality, but then necessarily plateaued. Although no one said it, it soon appeared to friends and family that my career must have stalled. This was an inevitable part of the clandestine life, just as Dotty had warned. But I also recognized that the near-total reliance on the good opinion of those inside CIA had the effect of reinforcing a potentially dangerous arrogance and a suffocating insularity in an organization whose work already inclined it toward both. I enthusiastically shared that culture, but was wary of it.

For many of my colleagues, collecting human intelligence was an end in itself: for them, how others used the intelligence we gathered may have been a subject of interest, but it was someone else's worry. That was never the case for me. Our basic training in the Directorate of Operations (DO) had included a couple of weeks of familiarization in all-source analysis provided by the Directorate of Intelligence (the DI), the analytic wing of the CIA. My DI instructors offered me the opportunity to leave the DO for the analytic ranks. I didn't take them up on it—the lure of overseas adventure was too compelling—but I retained a strong interest in what they did.

Having worked hard and taken risks to gather human intelligence, I was keen to ensure that it was accurately reflected in the finished product that went to policymakers. In my intelligence reports, I frequently included comments to provide context and perspective. And when I felt the analysts were getting something wrong, I would sometimes write to complain. On occasion, field stations overseas were asked to comment, and to provide an on-the-ground perspective on major analytic pieces being prepared in Langley. More often than not, my chiefs would ask me to write such comments for them, and I was not shy about initiating field appraisals in response to major events.

But nothing attracted my interest like National Intelligence Estimates. Usually referred to as NIEs, these are the highest-level and most comprehensive pieces of analysis produced by the U.S. government, and are meant to represent the considered, bottom-line judgments of the entire intelligence community on the great analytic questions of the day. In the late 1980s, when I was dashing about the world in "non-official" cover, meeting with Iranian sources, the intelligence community prepared one of a series of major National Intelligence Estimates devoted to assessing the future of the Iranian revolution. The NIE's drafters sought the help of my station, and I was assigned to assist them. I became fascinated by the process, and particularly by the role of the national intelligence officers, or NIOs. Each specializing in a distinct geographic or functional area of responsibility, they were organized in a communitywide organization called the National Intelligence Council, the NIC. They were the senior representatives of the intelligence community to the policymakers and to Congress, and they had the ability to place their individual stamp on the community's views.

It was quite rare for a clandestine operator to become an NIO, but by no means unheard of, particularly for the Near East and South Asia. A number of legendary Near East case officers had become NIOs, and they were my role models from an early point. I became convinced that operators had a huge natural advantage over desk-bound, bookish analytic types, as there was simply no substitute for having a visceral, on-the-ground familiarity with the culture and the mind-set of a place. I felt that to be a first-rate operations officer, and to give Washington all it really needed, you had to be a skilled analyst as well. I didn't accept the usual categories and boundaries that existed in my profession, and when I took over my own station, I made it a point to become a thorough expert on all the relevant issues and to weigh in actively in the Washington-based analytic process, at least as far as distance would allow.

In the summer of 1991, Paula and I returned to Washington, our toddler son and his Filipina nanny in tow. Right away I tried to land a job on the National Intelligence Council, and sought the help of my deputy division chief, who had himself been an NIO in the past. "Not so fast," he said. "You've been out for eleven years, and you owe us time on the desk."

With the end of the First Gulf War, the U.S. government was trying to contain Saddam Hussein, and if possible to engineer his ouster. Within months, regime change in Baghdad was the stated policy of the U.S. administration, and CIA was expected to produce it. I became the first deputy chief of a new and very large headquarters unit in the Near East Division, the Iraq Operations Group. This was my first serious introduction to "covert action." The normal authorities of the CIA only permit it to gather intelligence around the world, not to try to influence or change the course of events. To do that requires specific authority from the president, contained in what is called a Presidential Finding.

The process of drafting such a finding, working it through the bureaucracy to the president for signature, briefing members of the Congressional Oversight committees, and gaining the necessary support from the Pentagon, the State Department, and others was new to me, and I threw myself into the task with great enthusiasm. I thought the George H. W. Bush administration had made a great mistake in allowing Saddam's military to violently suppress the post–Gulf War insurrections in Shiite-dominated southern Iraq and in Kurdistan, in the far north, and I was eager to do my part to set things right. Within a short time, I was traveling back out to the region to consult with our chiefs of station and to hold initial meetings with a prominent Iraqi would-be revolutionary.

Naive as I was, this provided an education for me in the politics of covert action. The Near East Division chief at the time was convinced by past history that nothing good would come to the agency from an involvement, yet again, in trying to mount a foreign coup. It was a common sentiment in an organization that had been burned frequently and badly in the past, taking the fall for bad decisions by presidents who wanted the CIA to provide magic solutions to intractable foreign problems. The chief could not refuse the White House outright, but he did not want his fingerprints on our activities either, and he essentially ignored us. His passive opposition did not make a whit of practical difference to me, but I carefully noted it. In my view, CIA should not get to pick and choose its missions. We were a tool of statecraft; so long as what we were asked to do was legal, I felt, we owed the president our best efforts.

We also had an obligation, I believed, to illuminate the potential downsides of what we were being asked to do, and to make the case for the overt policy enablers that would be necessary for a realistic possibility of success. The world had changed radically since 1953, when a CIA-sponsored coup in Tehran had restored the Shah of Iran to his throne with relative ease. At the very outset, I sent a memo to my seniors within the agency, providing a negative assessment of the chances for success in Iraq, stating that we would not simply walk into Baghdad and engineer Saddam's overthrow "like some latter-day Kermit Roosevelt overthrowing Mossadegh." With the support of CIA's deputy director for operations (the "DDO," now referred to as director of the National Clandestine Service, or D/NCS), and although still only a GS-14—the civilian equivalent of a lieutenant colonel—I paid individual calls on each of the members of the Deputies' Committee, the second-highest foreign policy-making body in government, to seek their support for overt actions, such as setting up humanitarian "safe zones" along Iraq's borders. In each instance, I was received politely, but left with expressions that said, "Don't let the door hit you on the way out." The only member of the Deputies' Committee at the time who seemed willing to entertain my ideas on Iraq was the then-under secretary of defense for policy. It was hard for me to gauge his seriousness as a thinker, but he was willing to explore unconventional ideas and seemed willing to take risks. I would come to know Paul Wolfowitz far better during the George W. Bush administration.

Less than a year after my return from overseas, an opening appeared at the National Intelligence Council for a deputy NIO for the Near East and South Asia. With the grudging acceptance of my division managers, I applied for it, and was selected. The following year opened up new worlds for me, as I was frequently the face of the intelligence community with senior administration officials and with Congress. The NIO, Ellen Laipson, and I made a good team, in part because our backgrounds were so different: I was the operator; she the scholar, from the Congressional Research Service of the Library of Congress. We produced a series of National Intelligence Estimates, including yet another on Iran. Life could not have been more stimulating. On any given morning, I could look at the papers to see what would be on the minds of policymakers and Congress, and immediately convene the best analysts in the community to produce an instant, ad hoc assessment for them. This was the sort of access and impact I had dreamed of.

My time on the NIC was not to last long. Only a year into the assignment, I was asked by the deputy director for operations, Tom Twetten, to be a candidate to serve on the staff of Peter Tarnoff, the under secretary of state for political affairs. Tarnoff, the third-ranking official at State, a member of the Deputies' Committee, and the day-to-day foreign policy manager for the department, was an old friend of Twetten's and was interested in broadening representation on his staff beyond the State Department. Tarnoff selected me from among the available candidates, and made me his senior staff advisor for the Near East, South Asia, and counterterrorism.

My year of direct involvement in the policy-making process provided stunning insights into the hidden realities of Washington politics. It was an intensely disillusioning experience. In that first year of the Clinton administration, it was obvious that the president was not particularly interested in foreign policy, and seemed only to get engaged when a developing problem turned into a crisis. At that point, the various cabinet secretaries and other senior officials would learn what the president wanted and fall into line. But in the meantime, left to their own devices with little policy direction from the White House, they and their respective departments and agencies fought one another like children in a sandbox. They seemed primarily interested in protecting their bureaucratic turf and their departmental prerogatives. No agency head wanted to be seen by those in his or her organization as failing to defend its interests; that would be a sign of weakness. Bureaucratic strength, I learned, was the coin of the realm. The national interest seemed incidental.

Similarly, within the Department of State the bureaucratic infighting was vicious, as the various bureaus contended with one another to press their settled positions on whatever issue was at hand. No one, it seemed, was willing to take an independent view, or to consider the relative merits of another bureau's argument. More often than not, even the most trivial issues would have to be taken to the secretary of state for decision.

And that was when things worked well. Just as frequently, department seniors behaved like schoolyard bullies. If someone seemed to have senior-level backing on an issue, regardless of its merits, others would be reluctant to offer a contrary view unless they, too, had the support of a department senior, and preferably someone who had the ear of the secretary, to back them up. If not, it was better to capitulate early and act as though you supported the prevailing idea all along: the last thing you would want was to appear to have been "rolled"—forced to back down. As a State Department friend pointed out, the natural posture of the Foreign Service officer was to have a finger in the air to determine which way the political wind was blowing. I often found myself at a disadvantage in this sort of infighting, as my "principal," the under secretary, generally did not engage on Middle East issues and would defer to others, such as Dennis Ross, the Special Middle East Coordinator in charge of the Arab-Israeli peace process, instead. In a typical exchange, I'd send Peter a carefully reasoned memo advising him to take a certain position on an issue. "Sounds good," he would scrawl in the margin. "Take it up with Dennis." That was a non-starter for someone inclined toward contrarian views. No one was going to be interested in what I thought unless I had the backing of someone who was feared.

The consensus view of me in the department, conveyed to me by a friend, was telling: "Smart guy, articulate, knows the issues; but strangely oblivious to political considerations." They had it partly right. I wasn't oblivious; just headstrong, and a tad self-righteous. If anything, though, a year in their building actually increased my respect for State Department officers, who were almost uniformly smart and dedicated; but I pitied them the corrosive, soul-destroying environment in which they worked, and wondered how they tolerated it.

It was with considerable relief that I recrossed the Potomac to return to Langley. For all that CIA could be arrogant, insular, and parochial, I found life among those whose profession demanded lying, cheating, and manipulation an oasis of decency compared with what I'd found in the policy community. That said, my year at State was invaluable, and I would not soon forget its lessons.

Back at CIA, I was given a management job that again threw me into controversy. The Counter-Proliferation Branch was the largest in the Near East and South Asia Division, and no wonder. With the exception of North Korea, all the primary countries of nuclear, chemical, biological, and missile weapons concern were in those two regions: Pakistan, Iran, Iraq, Syria, and Libya. Although we had clear direction from the White House to aggressively confront a growing problem of global proliferation, my immediate superior was no more inclined toward risky operations against proliferators than he was against Saddam Hussein. My predecessor as chief of the Counter-Proliferation Branch had catered to the division chief. Not wanting to be in the position of having to provide a report to the president as the last screw was being placed in some rogue state's nuclear device, I set out to encourage field stations to launch new reporting initiatives, and to assure them of technical and financial support when they did. My chief made his contrary views known to me but did nothing to stop me.

I quickly found that headquarters' support to counterproliferation operations in the field outside the Near East and South Asia was
a disorganized mess. Because it was a global problem, with technology transferred across continents, several of the geographic divisions
in addition to the Near East had set up branches to deal with their parts
of the problem. Coordinating my branch's actions with those of other
divisions across multiple lines of independent bureaucratic authority
was a nightmare. I showed up one day at the office of the deputy director for operations to brief a routine operation with nine other people,
representing seven other offices, in tow. The DDO was predictably appalled.

Asked to come up with a way to fix the problem, I and my people
drew up plans to create a new division, which would combine the various DO proliferation shops in one coherent organization capable of
coordinating activities on a global basis. To my amazement, the plan
was approved. As I was deemed too junior to receive a divisional command, Jim Pavitt, who would become a good friend and mentor, was
named chief of the new Counter-Proliferation Division; I was its first
chief of operations.

Not everyone was happy with this arrangement. The Near East Division, whose loyal officer I still remained, had just lost its largest unit,
and its leaders did not fail to notice that I was the culprit. No sooner
had I been assigned to the new division than I received a call from Near
East's deputy chief, who summoned me to his office for a little avuncular advice. "Keep in mind," he said, "that if this new division fails—*as it
might*—you will still need a place to come back to."

By this time, I had spent five years in Washington, and was more
than eager to return to the field. Although in a bit of a doghouse with
the Near East Division, I managed in the next few months to line up a
chief of station assignment with help from elsewhere in the Directorate.
Paula was at least as eager as I was to return to overseas living. In fact,
our plans were already quite advanced when I got an unexpected call.

Dave Cohen had recently been elevated to DDO. As a career analyst, he was an unusual selection, and in the insular and chauvinistic
Directorate of Operations, an unpopular one. A brash, outspoken Bos-

tonian from the tough Dorchester neighborhood, Cohen was not one to be intimidated, and seemed determined to leave his mark on the Clandestine Service.

This was a time of considerable ferment in the DO. The arrest of Aldrich Ames for treason two years before, the first known instance of a currently serving case officer being "doubled," had been an unprecedented shock. Many of us felt a deep sense of shame. The shame was compounded when it was revealed that Ames had clearly been a troubled and grossly inadequate performer for some time before his recruitment by the Soviets, but that his managers had consistently failed to address his shortcomings. There was much soul-searching over this, and it led to a number of reforms, including a new emphasis on training in leadership and management that the directorate had long lacked.

There were other changes afoot. Huge advances in technical collection and information technology were making it possible to provide much better guidance and support to operations. The support ranks were no longer solely the province of secretaries, clerks, and logisticians. Highly skilled technical and analytical professionals were gaining a place in the directorate, and case officers like me could feel their relative dominance in the organization starting to slip away. New categories of DO professionals, such as so-called "targeters," were being created. Case officers felt threatened by these changes and many lobbied against them, claiming that this was evidence that the Clandestine Service was becoming distracted from its core mission. Cohen organized a number of discussion groups, typically of mid-ranking officers, to talk through these issues and build consensus for reforms.

I had first come to Dave's attention through my work in counterproliferation, and he included me as a participant in these groups. I was quite vocal in these forums, telling my fellow case officer colleagues, in effect, that they should "get over it." As case officers who recruited and ran agents, they were going to remain the "jet jockeys" of the CIA. But if the Clandestine Service was to remain relevant and continue to improve, we were going to have to encourage more involvement by highly skilled technicians and analysts. That was going to mean providing both them and the often-overlooked reports officers, the substantive intelligence experts of the directorate, a far greater share of the credit for success, greater organizational prominence, and a share of management positions that had traditionally been the exclusive domain of the spymasters.

Dave was impressed by my progressive views, and he wanted me to help institutionalize them. He asked if I would take over as chief of training at the DO's famous school of espionage, "the Farm." This was completely unexpected, and a huge departure from normal practice. Typically, chiefs of training were very senior officers, for whom the appointment was a final "retirement tour," a mark of respect and a reward for years of service. In giving the position to a young up-and-comer, and one who had not yet even entered the "super-grade" ranks, Cohen was signaling change. Complaints were not long in coming; Dave ignored them. To one senior officer who pointed out that I was still several promotions shy of the requisite grade level, he replied: "Well, that's easy to fix."

Dave gave me the option of declining the position, but it was an easy decision for me to make. This was a huge honor, and a tremendous opportunity to effect change in the directorate. Not incidentally, it also carried the promise of promotion. Keeping our son, who had some special educational needs, in the United States for a bit longer would not be a bad idea either. Rather than the Middle East, we made plans to move to southern Virginia.

With typical good fortune, I was arriving at just the right time. The personnel cutbacks of the post–Cold War "peace dividend" years had largely run their course, and recruitment of new officers was again on the upswing. Blessed with a strong staff, many of whom had just returned from overseas, I was able to turn them loose to reform the training curriculum and make it reflect the current state of the art as cutting-edge espionage was being practiced in the field.

At what we affectionately called "Camp Swampy," I worked to make the training of the next generation of spies conform not to where our directorate was, but to where I thought it should be going. More and more I found that the key to implementing what I wanted at the Farm lay in changing what was being done with newly arriving officers elsewhere, both before they arrived in my charge, and after they left. I found myself spending an increasing amount of my time up north, in Washington. Some criticized me for it, but I had great people working for me, and I delegated freely.

It was passionate work. The basic operations course in CIA is a full-immersion, twenty-four-hour-a-day, life-changing experience. When I had completed my own training years before, I had sworn I'd never be back. But now, in preparing a new generation of spies, I felt tied to the organization and to its history as never before. Having a chance to step back and analyze what we did, I was taken anew with the uniqueness and the romance of our profession, and did all I could to convey that sense to our young officers. With characteristic immodesty, I sincerely felt I understood the essence of what we were about better than anyone else. Finding that we were teaching professional ethics without any central doctrine to work from, I wrote a formal professional code of ethics for the Clandestine Service, the first ever. Years later, it was formally adopted, not just as a training aide but as the code of professional conduct for the service. It was probably the most lasting contribution of my career, and in some ways the one of which I'm most proud.

Life among the forests, streams, and meadows of the sprawling compound was like a throwback to a simpler era. Socially dominated by residents of prime child-rearing age, the Farm away from the classrooms and firing ranges was very family-centered. Our son Doug learned to fish, to ride a bicycle, and to camp in the woods. Living among trusted colleagues behind high fences and security patrols, not only did we not lock our houses; most of us didn't know where the keys were. Grade school children would ride their bikes to the bus stop, leave them unlocked, and find them unmolested. The only reminder that we were not living in Mayberry circa 1955 was the distant sound of gunfire wafting from the ranges in the afternoon, and the occasional thumping of special-ops helicopters as they whooshed overhead at treetop level during the night.

In those years I developed a relationship with our new director.

George Tenet took an active interest in training, and insisted on regular briefings. He never missed a graduation exercise. While being driven back to the airstrip one night after listening to one of my graduation speeches, he asked of the DDO where I would be assigned next. Told it would be Islamabad, Pakistan, he demurred. "I think we need him in the Levant," he said. The CIA was being actively drawn in as an intermediary between the Israeli and the Palestinian intelligence and security forces, as the Clinton administration pressed for a comprehensive peace agreement between them. George was personally engaged in the effort, and wanted someone he knew and could trust to manage it.

Once again, the benign forces of fate intervened. Shortly thereafter, Tenet went on a long trip to the Middle East in the company of the new chief of the Near East and South Asia Division. It was rumored the division chief wanted the peace process job for himself. Whatever his motivation, he convinced George that I should be sent to the Punjab, after all. It was a close call. Rather than facing three years of growing frustration and helplessness as the Arab-Israeli peace process foundered on the shoals of the second intifada, Paula, Doug, and I boarded a plane for South Asia.

———

We are all the products of our experiences. In my case, as I look back, I can see now that nature and events had conspired to produce, by the age of forty-four, an individual with a highly idiosyncratic, perhaps even contradictory, set of attributes. While still at the Farm in the late 1990s, and influenced by the organizational fads of the time, I began to meet with a so-called "executive coach." My coach would not have been confused with Stephen Covey: she had the looks and manner of a Jewish grandmother. I loved her. "You know," she said to me one afternoon, "there is no one more loyal to this organization than you. And yet your relationship to it is essentially subversive."

I found the observation jarring at the time. But as I look back, she may have been right. Here was a highly idealistic and loyal member of an organization who never saw it quite for what it was, but rather for what he wanted it to be. His attitude toward authority was ambivalent. If he judged his leaders harshly, he could still empathize with their challenges and their foibles, and his judgments seldom carried over to the organization that recognized and empowered them. To him, organizations were not important in and of themselves—missions were. So long as the justifying mission was there, the organization existed to be reformed. It was no surprise that he had been subtly at war with every bureaucracy he had ever been a part of. Though understanding his place in the closed, insular world he occupied, he nonetheless was forever looking outside his own area of responsibility, and was constitutionally incapable of staying in his own lane.

Whether all that made me a subversive, as my coach alleged, I still don't know. An iconoclast? Perhaps. A contrarian? Definitely. For better or worse, this was the person whom the CIA assigned as its chief of station in Islamabad, Pakistan, in the summer of 1999.

Part Two

THE ROAD TO WAR: PAKISTAN, THE TALIBAN, AND AL-QA'IDA

Chapter 3

THE BEST OF TIMES

WITNESSES LATER SAID THAT there had been something very peculiar about that vehicle. For some reason, its driver appeared to be having no end of trouble parking. First he would move forward a few feet, and then he would reverse slightly; after a pause, he would advance, and then reverse again. He must have repeated the process a dozen times, each time just barely changing the vehicle's orientation. There appeared to be no reason for what he was doing. After all, he was in the middle of an empty lot, located 100 yards or so beyond the back perimeter wall of the American Embassy, several hundred yards distant from the official Chancery building, on whose top floor I sat at that moment. There were no vehicles or other obstacles around him. Why so fussy? Was he having problems with the transmission? Peculiar indeed.

I suddenly heard a dull *whump*, the sort of sound you feel in your gut. In a split second I was on the floor. Several colleagues who had been conducting a briefing just stared at me in wonder, unmoving. "Get *down*," I barked.

The first instinct of most people in such circumstances is to rush to the windows to see what's happening. That's what people had done the year before, in August 1998, when they heard shooting outside the American Embassy in Nairobi, Kenya. Many had been cut to pieces in a hail of shattered glass when the subsequent explosion went off. I ordered that we low-crawl into the central hallway, where we would be buffered by the offices on either side of the brick embassy building. For several long minutes the entire population of the embassy's top floor waited, hunkered down; when at length I peered cautiously around the doorway and through a window, I could see a burning white truck in the middle distance.

The attackers had been quite clever. Three ordinary SUVs had been rigged to fire a pair of 109-millimeter Chinese-made rockets each, through rear windows whose glass had been replaced with semi-opaque plastic sheeting. In addition to the embassy in Islamabad, the plotters had simultaneously fired by remote control from a vehicle in another parking lot across town at the American Embassy's Cultural Affairs building; the rear window of a third vehicle had been aimed at a tall downtown apartment building that housed several UN offices. Although the latter two buildings had been struck, no one was killed; a Pakistani guard at the U.S. Cultural Center was badly wounded by shrapnel. Subsequent forensic analysis would show that the two rockets fired at the Chancery had sailed in tandem over the building just above the second-story window where I'd been sitting, missing by a few feet. I and several of my colleagues had been saved by a slight miscalculation: although the rockets had been aimed at a proper degree of elevation to strike their target, the designers had failed to adjust for the vehicle's suspension. The recoil had caused the front springs to depress, raising the rockets' trajectory a few degrees. Had they been much closer, it wouldn't have mattered. It was my fourth month in country: Welcome to Pakistan.

For a professional intelligence officer, trouble is good, and in Pakistan, then as now, there was more than enough trouble to go around. A turbulent country of over 160 million, Pakistan in 1999 had been independent for fifty-two years, a product of the Partition of former British India in 1947. Since then, it had fought four wars with its much larger South Asian neighbor, the last of which, the so-called "Kargil War," ending just weeks before my arrival. Even to a foreigner living there, Pakistani hatred of India was palpable. Much, but by no means all of that animosity revolved around the status of the former princely state of Kashmir, in the far mountainous north. A majority Muslim region that Pakistan expected to receive at Partition, its princely ruler had decided otherwise. Now, most of it lay in Indian hands following the first Indo-Pakistani War of 1947; it remained divided along a highly militarized cease-fire line, the so-called "Line of Control." Lacking the conventional military means to seize the rest of Kashmir outright, Pakistan had long encouraged and supported violent subversion there against the occupying Indian Army, whose political repression and rampant abuses against the local population further exacerbated the situation, and provided yet more motivation for Pakistani skulduggery.

Pakistan's brief existence had largely coincided with the Cold War. The fact that India quickly aligned itself in the mid-1950s with the Soviet Union, and became a major recipient of Soviet military hardware, further encouraged anti-Communist Muslim Pakistan to align itself with America. When at about the same time the United States organized what later became known as the Central Treaty Organization (CENTO) to discourage Communist encroachment in the Middle East and Southwest Asia, Pakistan became an enthusiastic member. Collaboration against the Soviets, particularly in the intelligence sphere, between Pakistan and the United States may have been discreet, but it was both important and effective. It is largely forgotten now, but when Francis Gary Powers was shot down over the Soviet Union in a U-2 spy plane in 1960, precipitating a major diplomatic crisis, the airfield from which he took off was located in Peshawar, Pakistan.

Pakistani-American cooperation increased greatly after the 1979 Soviet invasion of Afghanistan, when Pakistan's intelligence service, a military organization known as the Inter-Services Intelligence Directorate, or ISI, acted as a conduit for CIA-supplied money and weapons—eventually to include U.S.-made Stinger antiaircraft missiles—to the Afghan *mujahideen*, or Islamic resistance fighters. The joint program of support to the *mujahideen* was a signal success, and by 1989 mounting military losses forced the Soviets to withdraw from Afghanistan. In those days, CIA officers referred to the Afghan war as the "anti-Soviet *jihad*." The term *jihad*, meaning "struggle," had not yet become a pejorative.

The decade of the 1980s marked the zenith of U.S.-Pakistani intelligence cooperation, and perhaps of U.S.-Pakistan relations more generally. Partly by way of compensation for the important risks and expenses borne by Pakistan during the anti-Soviet *jihad*, America provided considerable military and economic assistance, including F-16 fighters and generous development programs.

But right from the start, hidden within this general regime of bonhomie and close cooperation were tensions and contradictions, which regularly came to the surface. For the United States, Pakistan was an important but problematic ally. Its development as a democracy was anything but smooth, and its regular military coups were an embarrassment for its American patrons. Its wars and near wars with India, and its brutal repression in East Pakistan (now Bangladesh), were problematic, to say the least. More pointedly, as the *jihad* days of the 1980s gave way to the 1990s, Pakistan was seen increasingly by some to be working against broader American policy in the areas of counterproliferation and counterterrorism. That period also saw a growing tendency in Congress to try to legislate foreign policy, to make it more difficult for the executive branch to favor short-term, expedient goals over what Congress saw as more important, longer-range American interests. In most administrations, after all, there is a great temptation to focus on the most immediate and tangible challenges, rather than speculating over the potential long-term unintended consequences of present policy. And so the administrations of the eighties and early nineties sought to preserve as much flexibility as possible in dealing with a long-term problem case like Pakistan; Congress, from the late 1970s onward, sought assiduously to curtail that flexibility.

In 1985, the so-called "Pressler Amendment," introduced by Senator Larry Pressler of South Dakota, mandated that the administration must certify, on a yearly basis, that Pakistan did not possess nuclear weapons in order for it to remain eligible for U.S. assistance of any kind. Desperate to preserve Pakistan's help against the Soviets in Afghanistan, the Reagan and George H. W. Bush administrations certified Pakistan as a nuclear weapons–free state in the early years after the statute's passage, despite a growing body of evidence to the contrary; they probably violated U.S. law in the process. But when the Soviets evacuated Afghanistan in 1989, the administration's motivation to bend the law disappeared, and in 1990, Pakistan was sanctioned by the United States, losing virtually all of its U.S. military and economic assistance at a stroke.

The fact that the U.S. government had waited until Pakistan appeared no longer useful before deciding to enforce the Pressler Amendment was not lost on the Pakistanis. To them, the American measure was all the more galling because it was imposed selectively, at a time when they felt they had every legitimate right, and indeed a vital national security interest, in countering the perceived nuclear threat from India. New Delhi had tested a nuclear device as early as 1974. Pakistan, unlike India, was vulnerable to U.S. non-proliferation sanctions precisely because it had aligned itself with Washington; India had no corresponding fear of a Soviet version of the Pressler Amendment. For years, Washington and Islamabad had played a little diplomatic game: Islamabad would lie, denying its interest in developing nuclear weapons, while Washington would capitalize on the lie to maintain support for the Afghan *mujahideen* and bolster Pakistan as a regional ally. It all worked nicely, until Washington stopped playing.

Meanwhile, Pakistan's sponsorship of Islamic fighters, which had been useful to the United States when there were Soviet forces to be attacked in Afghanistan, began to seem much less so after the Soviet withdrawal. Pakistani patronage of the *mujahideen* had been part of a program pursued during the 1980s by Pakistan's military dictator, General Zia ul-Haq, to "Islamize" both foreign and domestic policy. General Zia died in a plane crash in 1988, but his policies survived him. Just as the Soviets were withdrawing from Afghanistan in 1989, Indian repression triggered a spontaneous popular uprising in Indian-held Kashmir. For the government of Pakistan, and particularly for the Pakistan Army, it was quite natural to encourage and support fundamentalist groups within Pakistan who had previously provided assistance to the Afghan *mujahideen,* and who now wished to infiltrate across the Line of Control to participate in the anti-Indian *jihad* in Kashmir. Within a few years, Pakistani militants, secretly supported by the Pakistan Army, had largely taken over the Kashmiri fight from the Kashmiris themselves. The fact that these militants frequently employed terrorist tactics did not much concern the Pakistanis, who considered them freedom fighters; but it threatened to put Pakistan on the U.S. State Sponsors of Terrorism List.

In yet another instance of congressional legislation of foreign policy, beginning in 1979 the secretary of state was mandated by statute every year to examine all available intelligence to determine which countries had provided material aid to terrorists. I commissioned the review on Pakistan in 1994, during the year I worked for the under secretary of state. For several years running during the nineties, Pakistan came very close to being placed on the State Sponsors List. Had that happened, Pakistan, a key U.S. ally just a few years before, would have been relegated to the status of a rogue state, joining the likes of Iran and North Korea. Fearing the long-term consequences of such a move, U.S. policymakers took refuge, barely, in the fact that the damning intelligence on Pakistan could not quite meet a legal standard.

In May 1998, India formally tested a series of nuclear warheads. Despite strenuous efforts by the United States, which offered a lifting of sanctions, access to weapons, and other blandishments, Pakistan followed suit within days, conducting five weapons tests of its own. Washington was deeply annoyed. In the summer of 1999, Pakistan brazenly infiltrated regular army troops across the Line of Control in the mountainous Kargil district of Kashmir, setting off a brief but sharp conflict with India. By the time I arrived in July 1999, U.S. relations with Pakistan were at an absolute low; it was hard to imagine how they could be worse. But within a few months, on October 12, General Pervaiz Musharraf, the chief of Army Staff, overthrew Nawaz Sharif, Pakistan's democratically elected prime minister, in a bloodless coup. Under Sharif, corruption had been so rampant, and his systematic abuse of democratic institutions so egregious, that the U.S. Embassy judged at the time that his overthrow in a military coup *enhanced* the chances for positive democratic change in the country. Nonetheless, for having toppled an elected government, U.S. law imposed yet further American sanctions on the military regime of General Musharraf.

None of this might have mattered very much to most Americans; after all, the United States had largely washed its hands of South-

Central Asia after the Soviet withdrawal from Afghanistan in 1989. When the formerly Soviet-supported Afghan Communist government of Mohammed Najibullah finally fell in 1992, the many Afghan warlords formerly supported by the United States and Pakistan fell to fighting among themselves. Afghanistan descended into political anarchy, and Kabul was laid waste in fratricidal warfare. Thirteen years of continuous conflict had weakened traditional tribal structures throughout the country; warlords and petty strongmen commanding armed militias, free of the constraints and responsibilities of traditional tribal leadership, terrorized much of the country.

In the southern Afghan city of Kandahar, the situation became particularly bad. By late autumn of 1994, the city was divided among rival warlords who ruled their fiefdoms with impunity. On the main highway passing through the area, drug-smoking criminal gangs set up roadblocks to extort travelers, sometimes seizing women from buses and raping them. A group of some thirty local clerics, all veterans of the *jihad*, and their students, or *talibs*, acting at the direction of an obscure former *mujahed* named Mullah Mohammed Omar whom they had sought out to lead them, openly declared themselves and ordered the criminal gangs to disperse. When they refused, Omar's men attacked one of the most notorious of the criminal checkposts, where a pair of women from Herat recently had been raped, tortured, and killed, and drove them off. This caught both the attention and the imagination of the citizens of Kandahar, tired as they were of lawlessness and victimization, and a surprising dynamic quickly took hold. Local merchants provided the *talibs*—who called themselves the Taliban—with money, vehicles, and weapons.

The Taliban had begun as one of many small, independent militias fighting against the Soviet occupiers around Kandahar during the *jihad* of the 1980s. What distinguished them from other groups was their overtly religious rather than tribal orientation. Their members were drawn from a generation of young refugees from the Soviet war, many of them orphans, who had grown up in camps inside neighboring Pakistan and been educated in *madrassas*, or Quranic schools. When they and others of their background returned permanently to

Afghanistan following the Soviet withdrawal, their estrangement from traditional Afghan life had left them with tenuous ties to tribe or place. Though many had fought against the Soviets or in the subsequent anarchy, they were of a younger generation than the discredited warlords. Following the mini-uprising against Kandahar's criminal highwaymen, they flocked in large numbers to Omar's movement. The Taliban quickly became a local political force to be reckoned with, and several of the principal warlords in the area joined, rather than fight them, setting a precedent for the future.

From its initial modest successes around Kandahar in 1994, the Taliban movement spread rapidly northward like a cleansing flame. The misogynistic, strictly fundamentalist brand of Islam absorbed by its members in the *madrassas* of Pakistan was intolerant and unforgiving, but it was seen by many Afghans, beset by crime, lawlessness, and anarchy, as precisely what the country needed. The Taliban may have been primitive, but they were righteous. Their string of military successes over the next two years was based not so much on their military prowess as on the political embrace of the Afghan Pashtun population, which in many places rose up against their warlord oppressors as the Taliban approached. Large areas came over to the movement without a fight. By the end of September 1996, Kabul had fallen to them.

But the Taliban's attraction for Afghanistan's Pashtun population did not extend to the other major ethnic groups, largely concentrated in the north of the country—the Tajiks, the Uzbeks, and the Hazaras. The Hazaras, religious Shiites, came in for especially brutal treatment at the hands of the Sunni Muslim Taliban. The ethnic minorities of the north banded together against the Taliban under the auspices of the United Islamic Front for the Salvation of Afghanistan (UIFSA)—popularly known as the Northern Alliance. By the time of my arrival, the Northern Alliance was locked in a bitter civil war with the Taliban and was being slowly pushed back into the far northern and northeastern reaches of the country.

It is often alleged that Pakistan's intelligence service, the ISI, created the Taliban. That is certainly untrue. But Islamabad was quick to embrace the student movement, and to provide it with support primarily through the ISI, seeing in it a means of unifying the fractious Afghans under the rule of Sunni Islamists with strong ties to Pakistan. The fact that the Taliban was willing to fight to the end against the Northern Alliance made it all the more worthy of support in Pakistani eyes, especially given the Alliance's close ties to both Russia and India. Since the dawn of its existence, Pakistan has lived in perpetual fear of being surrounded by hostile forces in thrall to India; in addition to its natural sympathy for their cause, Pakistan's support of the Taliban was an obvious means of pursuing its larger geopolitical interests.

Neither the continuing strife in Afghanistan nor Pakistan's support to the obscure Taliban movement would have been of much concern to the U.S. government, had it not been for yet another actor in this regional drama: Osama bin Laden. Son of a billionaire Saudi construction magnate, bin Laden had played a marginal role in the anti-Soviet *jihad*, bankrolling a modest number of Arab fighters who had come to help defend Afghan Muslims against the godless invading Soviets. Radicalized by his experience in the 1980s, bin Laden became more so in 1990 as a result of Saudi Arabia's willingness to host American troops sent to drive Iraq's Saddam Hussein from Kuwait in the First Gulf War. His vocal opposition to the U.S. troop presence in his native country soon came to the unfavorable attention of the Saudi government, and bin Laden was forced to seek refuge in Sudan, where his efforts to organize violent Islamic extremists into a new organization that he called *al-Qa'ida* or "the base" first brought him to the attention of CIA and the U.S. intelligence community. In response to persistent American complaints, Sudan eventually prevailed upon bin Laden to go elsewhere; and in 1996, just as the Taliban was consolidating its hold on Kabul, bin Laden and a small number of followers pitched up in Afghanistan.

The numbers of these followers, most of them Arabs, steadily grew. They were not monolithic. Many came simply to support the Taliban and fight against the Northern Alliance. Eventually, they formed a separate military unit, the Arab 555 Brigade. Others sought terrorist and paramilitary training in the string of camps set up by al-Qa'ida in Afghanistan. Of these, only a relative few were vetted sufficiently to be allowed to swear *bayat*, an oath of loyalty to bin Laden, and to become formal members of al-Qa'ida. But although it may have been difficult for outsiders to distinguish among them, as a group these international followers of bin Laden were referred to by the Afghans themselves as the "Afghan Arabs."

Bin Laden's "declaration of war" on the United States later that year of 1996 still did not attract much attention in the West, but the events in East Africa of August 1998 changed all that. The truck bombs that were set off nearly simultaneously at the U.S. embassies in Nairobi, Kenya, and Dar es-Salaam, Tanzania, were quickly traced to al-Qa'ida and bin Laden. Within weeks, the United States launched retaliatory cruise missile strikes against several of bin Laden's training camps in Afghanistan. These were largely symbolic—the U.S. government couldn't very well do *nothing* after the East Africa attack—and they predictably failed to hit their principal target; nonetheless, the Clinton administration was adamant thereafter that something be done about bin Laden. It demanded that Mullah Omar and the Taliban turn him over to American justice; when the Taliban refused, the United States imposed economic and diplomatic sanctions, and convinced the United Nations to do the same.

American ardor for justice in the case of bin Laden did not extend to taking many risks to see it come to pass. Sending in U.S. commandos to take out bin Laden was out of the question—never seriously considered—and would have been difficult in any case, as we lacked bases in the region from which to stage. More precisely targeted air or cruise missile strikes were a possibility, but dependent upon precise, real-time intelligence sufficient to avoid collateral casualties. That was difficult to come by in those pre–Predator drone days. On the few occasions when such intelligence was available, the administration decided that the risk of harming innocents was too high.

American reluctance to take risks in pursuit of bin Laden did not make us shy about browbeating the Pakistanis to do so. Pakistan was one of only three countries in the world to recognize the Taliban as the legitimate government of Afghanistan. The fact that it was willing to treat with, let alone support, the hosts of our terrorist nemesis added a marked note of anger and outrage to the usual stiff, pious tut-tutting of our official communications with the Pakistani government.

Under the circumstances, it was obvious that CIA was just going to have to come up with a way of dealing with bin Laden on its own. As I had seen so often in my career, faced with an intractable foreign policy problem and risky, unpalatable choices to deal with it, the default position of the U.S. government was to leave it to CIA to solve—preferably in a neat, tidy, and untraceable way. This, among many other things, would be my task in Islamabad: To arrest, or otherwise to neutralize, a man and an organization that Director of Central Intelligence George Tenet had described publicly as the greatest current threat to U.S. national security. I was to do it with little or no help from the rest of my government, in the most obscure, primitive, remote, and war-torn country in the world, and without breaking a federal law that barred CIA from engaging in assassination. And oh, by the way, the sole potential ally to whom I might plausibly turn for effective help in this endeavor had been thoroughly and systematically alienated by my government as well. Apart from all that, my job would be easy. All the same, I couldn't have been more pleased to take it. In the Clandestine Service, this is what we do. I had spent years preparing for a challenge such as this. For me, these were the best of times.

It is said that in a typical three-year tour of overseas duty, the best that can be hoped for is two years of effective work: the first six months are spent figuring out what you're supposed to be doing, and the last six months are spent seeking and then preparing for the next assignment. By December 1999, after I had been at post for six months, I could see that what we had been doing to date with regard to bin Laden and al-Qa'ida was not working, and was unlikely to. I would have to start thinking about the problem in a different way, and come up with a new way to solve it.

Chapter 4

WARNINGS AND FOREBODINGS

FEBRUARY 2000

A MBASSADOR BILL MILAM WAS on one of his rants. The complaint was a familiar one—his weight. "You're so damned abstemious," he complained. "I wish I could do that. I just can't stop eating. I ought to have my damned jaws wired shut." Cantankerousness was one of Milam's most notable traits, and for me, an endearing one. I couldn't help but like the man, though he did have a habit of trying to make my life harder than it should be just to show he could. He had his reasons for doing so.

Some weeks before, Milam had been at Sunday breakfast at a local sporting club with a colleague, an administrative officer who was a notorious gadfly. He looked around the dining room at the large number of unattached males having breakfast alone or in small groups. "Who the hell *are* all these people?" he grumbled. "I don't know any of them." His companion saw his opportunity, and seized it.

"They're all Grenier's people," he said. He paused for effect. "You know, he runs this place." The ambassador said nothing for some minutes, seemingly concentrating on his eggs. At length, he stood to leave.

"*I* run this place," he snapped.

I was in no doubt myself as to who ran the U.S. Embassy in Islamabad. As chief of station, I technically answered to the director of Central Intelligence; Milam, as the U.S. "Ambassador Extraordinary and Plenipotentiary," technically reported directly to the president. Our relative places in the federal pecking order were clear, and I was best advised to remember it. I depended on the ambassador's support, or at least on his forbearance. My push to increase our capabilities in Afghanistan was bringing an ever-growing stream of temporary staffers ("TDYers," as they were called) to town, and their mysterious activities were no doubt exciting considerable *sotto voce* commentary among my colleagues. I needed their silent cooperation to keep a low profile on the comings and goings of my people, and it just wouldn't do to alienate them. That was particularly true of the ambassador. I knew that if some of my station's activities were to come to the unfavorable attention of the Pakistani authorities, it was to the ambassador that I would have to turn for political support. "Remember," he told me shortly after my arrival, "if you want me with you at the crash landing, make sure I'm with you at the take-off." I took that to heart, and went out of my way to bring him as much into the picture as possible about what I was doing. Still, I had rather more independent authority than Milam was comfortable with, and he sometimes went out of his way to demonstrate who was in charge.

Now, as we hurtled southward through the night in the back of his BMW limousine, ambassadorial flags snapping, toward the nearby army town of Rawalpindi, I felt the need of his support acutely. I was hoping Milam would be able to get for me something I hadn't been able to get on my own: some level, at least, of consistent Pakistani support against al-Qa'ida.

A few weeks before, the security authorities in Jordan had uncovered the so-called "Millennium Plot." Al-Qa'ida-linked operatives had been caught secretly storing a huge quantity of explosives for use in a coordinated series of planned bombings of hotels and other tourist attractions frequented by foreigners along the Jordan River Valley. If there were any doubts regarding al-Qa'ida's intention to mount another terrorist strike on the scale of the East Africa embassy bombings of 1998, this had put such doubts to rest.

Among those implicated in the Jordan plot were a pair of expatriate Palestinians: One of them, Khalil Deek, a Palestinian-American resident in Peshawar, in Pakistan's far northwest, had recently been arrested by the Pakistani intelligence service and rendered to Jordan, his country of origin, via a special Jordanian military flight. He had fallen victim to a scenario in which the Pakistanis had both compelling evidence of his complicity in a foreign crime, and such precise information regarding his physical location that they could not have failed to take action without seeming complicit in his activities.

While this success was gratifying, it had involved a concurrence of events that would be extremely difficult to duplicate on a regular basis. If we were to have any realistic hope of capturing the second, and far more important, of the two Palestinians, we would need active Pakistani support in tracking him down.

Zayn al-Abidin Muhammad Husayn, better known as Abu Zubayda, had been on the CIA radar screen for many months. A senior logistician for al-Qa'ida, we knew he had been transiting regularly through Pakistan between Afghanistan and the wider world, facilitating the movement of Arab recruits to and from the training camps located in Taliban-controlled areas. The extent of his importance to al-Qa'ida had just been demonstrated in Jordan. He was the proximate reason why Milam and I were meeting this night with General Musharraf, the chief of Army Staff and, for four months now, Pakistan's military dictator.

Entering Army House, the traditional residence of Pakistan's military chiefs, was like stepping back in time. The architecture, the atmosphere of the place, was redolent of the British Raj. On the surface, the meeting seemed to go well. Musharraf received us cordially and informally. A soft-spoken and unprepossessing man of medium height, he carried himself with a quiet, earnest dignity. Though he may have seized power in a military coup, there was nothing of the bluster or bravado one might have associated with a former commando whose notable military career had been associated rather more with daring than with reflection. Musharraf listened intently to Milam's presentation. Pronouncing Zubayda's unfamiliar Arab name with care, the ambassador laid out the case. Here was a very dangerous man, a senior lieutenant of bin Laden's, who had been implicated by the judicial authorities of Jordan in a major terrorist operation. We knew that he was frequently transiting Pakistan, and we needed Pakistani help to apprehend him before he could strike again. All very straightforward. But the key to the ambassador's pitch was an implied threat, couched as a simple political reality: for if, God forbid, there were another major al-Qa'ida terrorist operation against the United States in which Abu Zubayda were implicated, and if Pakistan were seen to have been unwilling to bring his activities to an end despite the clear opportunity to do so, the implications for U.S.-Pakistan relations would be severe, if not catastrophic.

Looking at me, Musharraf asked whether information regarding Zubayda had been shared with General Mahmud Ahmed, director-general of the ISI—the infamous organization with which CIA had worked so effectively against the Soviets. I said it had. I pointed out that success against Abu Zubayda would require more of Pakistan than simply to take action based on U.S.-supplied information. We needed active, dynamic cooperation between our two countries, and specifically between our two intelligence services, if we were to generate the real-time, actionable intelligence necessary to find, fix, and apprehend this man. The general replied simply and straightforwardly: He would speak with General Mahmud. The United States could count on Pakistan's full cooperation against this terrorist threat.

The meeting ought to have buoyed my confidence, but it did not. I felt Musharraf had been sincere. He would no doubt have taken the action we requested if he had been in a position to do so himself. But he was not. As the four-star chief of Army Staff, he presided as a rough "first among equals" over the Pakistan Army's nine Corps commanders and the handful of other three-star generals, including General Mahmud of the ISI, who made up Pakistan's senior military leadership. All had considerable autonomy of action, and none more so than Mahmud, particularly given his history with Musharraf. When Musharraf deposed Nawaz Sharif, Pakistan's elected prime minister, the coup had actually been launched on the orders of the formidable Mahmud, whose troops controlled Islamabad at the time. It was Mahmud who had placed Sharif under arrest for trying to dismiss Musharraf. This was a debt of loyalty of which Musharraf had to be thoroughly mindful.

As for Mahmud himself, having been quickly named the new Director-General of the ISI after the October coup, he became thoroughly immersed in investigating the financial "crimes" of the Sharif family and their political cronies, and had not found time to meet with me until early December 1999. During that initial meeting, he had shown no great enthusiasm for intelligence cooperation with the CIA. I would immediately embark on a sustained effort to win Mahmud over, but that process had hardly begun when Milam and I ventured to Army House.

This did not mean that Musharraf was incapable of ordering Mahmud to take action. He could if he chose. But given the huge number of challenges with which the newly launched dictator had to deal in his effort to thoroughly reform the Pakistani political system and prepare it for "true democracy," it seemed clear to me that he would not undertake the sustained effort necessary to get Mahmud to take action against his will unless he perceived a compelling reason to do so. However potent Milam's implied threat had appeared to me, it was obvious from Musharraf's reaction that he did not perceive it that way. To him, a clash with the United States over al-Qa'ida was some vaguely hypothetical future possibility; hardly something to dwell upon when he had many more present and immediate crises to deal with. One could see that the warning from Milam hardly registered with the self-styled "Chief Executive" at all.

As we rode together back to Islamabad, I tried to be as upbeat as I could. It was becoming apparent to me, though, that if I wanted Mahmud's cooperation, winning it was going to require a great deal more effort from me.

Chapter 5

ROMANCING THE TALIBAN

I WAS WAITING IMPATIENTLY IN front of Ambassador Milam's residence, trying to suppress my natural urge to pace: it
looks undignified, and I wanted to make an appropriate impression on our arriving guest. Lowland Pakistani winters are mild by
most standards, but this night was cold and damp, and I hadn't bothered with a coat.

Arrangements for the visit had been made by an embassy contact,
a Houston-based Afghan-American by the name of "Akbar." Twenty
years in the intelligence business had taught me to be distrustful of
Akbar and his ilk; rogue regimes always attract opportunists, operators
looking to develop unsavory contacts with an eye for the main chance.
Still, whatever one might think of his character, Akbar had shown he
could deliver; and the package he was delivering that night was the
deputy foreign minister of the Taliban, Mullah Abdul Jalil Akhund—
known widely as "Mullah Jalil."

Akbar himself was something of a phenomenon. For all that he was
a Pashtun, he was the last person you would expect to have effective relations with the Taliban. He was a heavy drinker and a smoker, where
no real *talib* would tolerate either. In a country where beardless men
risked being arrested on sight, he remained defiantly smooth-cheeked.
True, he had the protection of both Mullah Jalil and his boss, Taliban
foreign minister Wakil Ahmed Muttawakil; but in a country run by
narrow-minded religious obscurantists and awash in religious police,
it was a marvel that he could operate the way he did. His audacity was

perhaps his greatest ally: anyone so willing to openly flout the rules must be powerful indeed.

His appeal was simple. He had apparently convinced Jalil and a handful of others that if ever international sanctions could be lifted, he would be the man to bring them the commercial rewards they sought. Thus he was desperate to find some way past the bin Laden roadblock, and he had curried multiple contacts within the U.S. government in hopes of brokering an understanding with the Taliban.

This could hardly be called a clandestine contact. It was being held, after all, in the ambassador's residence on the high-profile American Embassy compound in Islamabad, surrounded by high walls and guarded by Pakistanis. We had gone to some pains, however, to keep the meeting discreet: Akbar was conveying Mullah Jalil in his own vehicle, rather than an official Taliban car. Where the Taliban ambassador to Pakistan, Mullah Abdul Salam Zaeef, would normally have been expected to participate, he had pointedly not been informed of this meeting. And where all guests normally were screened at the gate, I had made special arrangements to ensure that the passenger in the backseat of Akbar's rented Toyota Land Cruiser would remain unmolested behind darkened windows. Milam had taken the further precaution of dismissing his staff early for the evening.

The man who emerged from the SUV was no more than five foot seven. He had a round, childlike face, notwithstanding the standard full, untrimmed beard. He was dressed conventionally for a *talib*, in a dark gray, winter-weight *shalwar khameez* and sleeveless black vest, which he wore over a thick nut brown woolen sweater. The uniform was completed by the usual rough brown woolen blanket, which he wrapped about him like a cape, and a black Kandahari *pugaree*, whose long loose end draped down in front of his left shoulder. He wore this turban pushed back on his head, revealing a close-cropped widow's peak.

A seeming majority of Afghan males of Jalil's age and background had been shot up in the previous two decades of war, and the deputy foreign minister was no exception: he walked with a pronounced limp, favoring his right leg. It was only after he took his place to the ambassador's left, with his crossed legs pulled up beneath him on the settee, and began slowly rubbing his aching right ankle, that I noticed two discordant details. On the floor beneath the couch were a pair of black Reeboks in place of the usual sandals, and tucked into his breast pocket was a very expensive Mont Blanc pen—both, no doubt, gifts from the redoubtable Akbar.

When State Department officers hold a ritual discussion with a foreign counterpart in which neither side departs from standard, previously reported positions, they will often describe the contact in shorthand, citing "an exchange along familiar lines." For the most part, the phrase would have applied here, if the meeting itself had not been so novel. Milam took the lead, laying out the U.S. demand that bin Laden be turned over to American justice. Jalil countered by inviting the U.S. government to present its evidence; if the Taliban found it compelling, he said, it could try bin Laden in its own Islamic courts. Milam explained, in turn, that the procedures in a Taliban court would not meet the requirements of U.S. or international justice. Round and round they went for some time. Akbar translated, though it was clear that Jalil's understanding of English was sufficient to require only occasional assistance. My presence at such an exchange was unusual, but Milam had felt that Jalil's willingness to meet outside the usual diplomatic channels suggested a flexibility that I would be in the best position to exploit.

Mullah Jalil, unlike most of the Taliban leadership, had been extensively educated outside of Quranic schools, and I had expected to see in him some signs of genuine sophistication. What I saw in his eyes was a sort of rude cunning. Although his words conformed to Taliban orthodoxy, one had the distinct impression, enhanced by Akbar's presence, that this was one *talib* with whom we might be able to deal.

We took a break from discussions, and I escorted both Akbar and Jalil to the front foyer. Akbar, craving a cigarette, dashed outside. As soon as the front door closed behind him, Jalil, who clearly knew my CIA affiliation, turned to me. "We must stay in touch," he said, inclining his head toward the front door, "but he must not know." I agreed that Akbar was not to be trusted. But how could we meet? Jalil said that he was staying with Zaeef, the Taliban ambassador in Islamabad, and that without Akbar's help, he could not escape his official entourage to meet alone. I knew he had no secure means to call me from Kandahar: there was no cellular system in Afghanistan, and the few available landlines were run through the Pakistani exchanges at Peshawar and Quetta, specifically designated for official Taliban government use. All, of course, were subject to official Pakistani monitoring.

"If you had a satellite phone," I asked, "could you call me without anyone knowing?" He could, he said, but it would be difficult and risky to hide the device. If he were seen to have acquired a sat phone solely for his own use, it would generate suspicion. "But if I will bring it for the others to use also, I can speak with you alone."

"So much the better," I thought. Yet how to get a sat phone to him in Afghanistan? Akbar represented the only readily apparent means available. But Jalil feared that his Afghan-American friend would avoid providing any means of independent contact that might diminish his own role as intermediary. "Leave that part to me," I told him, just as Akbar reentered the house.

When at length the evening's diplomatic discussion ended and the two were sent on their way, I was left to ponder what this unexpected opportunity with Jalil might represent. Depending on his motives, which did not seem entirely altruistic, it could mean an opportunity to recruit Mullah Jalil as a senior "penetration" of the Taliban, and the chance to use him to influence Taliban policy regarding bin Laden covertly; or it might all prove an elaborate effort on the cleric's part to manipulate me in pursuit of a combination of personal and Taliban ends—hardly inconsistent with Jalil's apparent character. Yet again, it might represent a combination of both. Whatever the case, this was precisely the sort of game I was eager to play. I was already hard at work trying to develop indirect means of forcing a change in Taliban policy toward bin Laden and the Afghan Arabs. Mullah Jalil might provide a far more direct means of doing so. Before the winter was out, the game would be on in earnest.

Chapter 6

THE WAR THAT NEVER WAS

T HE WINDOWLESS CONFERENCE ROOM was somber, its periphery bathed in shadows. Only the polished wood table that split its middle could be seen clearly. As I approached from my place at the back wall, I had a dramatic sense of emerging into the light. I instinctively decided to use my best rhetorical flourish first: I said nothing, and instead paused to survey the audience slowly. Seated on the far side of the table, in the middle, was the newly elected president, George W. Bush. On either side of him were members of the White House staff: to his right, national security advisor Condoleezza Rice and chief of staff Andrew Card; to his left, deputy national security advisor Stephen Hadley and the vice president's chief of staff, Lewis "Scooter" Libby. Far to the president's right sat George Tenet. On my side of the table, their backs to me, were the other assembled senior leaders of the Central Intelligence Agency.

The pause had its intended effect. All on the other side of the table looked up from their notepads. After several long seconds, I turned squarely toward the president. "Mr. President, as *your* station chief in Islamabad. . . ." I heavily emphasized *your*, which slightly startled him, and the president, whose manner had previously been jocular, suddenly turned serious. He looked at me intently. George Tenet, too, looked up quickly, and fixed me with a lingering stare. I couldn't tell if he liked the gambit—he no doubt considered me *his* station chief—but I definitely had his attention.

Though this visit was the president's first to CIA, it had the warm feel of a homecoming. The CIA Headquarters building, after all, had recently been named for Bush's father, the former president and former CIA director. It was obvious from the start of his administration that this president had been imbued, perhaps through paternal influence, with a fundamental respect and appreciation for the CIA, which we all felt had been lacking under Clinton, who had seldom met with his director of Central Intelligence. George Tenet, on the other hand, and at Bush's insistence, was providing the president's daily intelligence briefing in person and, despite originally having been a Democratic appointee, seemed likely to stay on for the long term. He had clearly struck up a warm personal relationship with the chief executive. I was one of three overseas station chiefs who had been included to add some operational color to our first formal headquarters briefing of the new president.

My approach was intimate. I wanted the president to feel that everything I and my station were doing, we were doing for *him*. My responsibilities, I said, included both Pakistan and all of Taliban-controlled Afghanistan—close to 90 percent of the country. I focused on Afghanistan. Since December 1999, I explained, we had departed from CIA's previously myopic focus on bin Laden himself, and taken account of the fact that his al-Qa'ida followers and the foreign *jihadists* associated with them, whom we referred to collectively as the "Afghan Arabs," had become a menacing force in their own right. They would pose a continuing terrorist threat to us and our allies, even if bin Laden were to die immediately of natural causes. And the key to their continued presence and growing power in Afghanistan, I stressed, was their sponsorship by the ruling Taliban.

Therefore, in addition to tracking bin Laden's daily movements about the country through tribal intelligence sources in hopes of effecting his capture, we had turned the full bore of our intelligence collection on the Taliban, with noteworthy success over the previous eighteen months. I listed in detail the key Taliban ministries, leadership structures, and al-Qa'ida training camps which had been penetrated. I explained our insights into intra-Taliban politics and intentions. Dr. Rice seemed particularly impressed. She nodded her head approvingly as she bent forward, taking notes.

I described the tribal reporting networks we had put together, blanketing much of the country. These were built around what we referred to in the business as "principal agents," or PAs, reporting sources who were tribal leaders or other socially prominent individuals, most of whom had been marginalized by the narrow, clerically dominated Taliban leadership. Trained and constantly vetted, they could report securely to us, usually via encrypted satellite communications. In turn, they maintained elaborate networks of informants, usually individuals bound to them through tribal or family loyalties. Through these networks, we could track the pulse of political, military, and social developments around the country, using the natural overlaps in coverage among them to confirm or deny information we were acquiring elsewhere, and to check on their reliability. Reports from these networks would trickle in to the principal agents, sometimes literally on camelback, and would be recorded, sorted, and amalgamated by the PAs for secure transmission to my station. Having filled the ten minutes I had been allotted, I wound up my segment of the briefing in time for the president and his team to file out for the next stop on their itinerary.

As significant as anything I had briefed, however, was what I had chosen *not* to brief. When I intentionally maligned our previously "myopic" focus on bin Laden, I was referring to a covert action campaign initiated during the previous administration and pursued vigorously during my watch, and which one might have expected to be the centerpiece of my presentation. My station had been given secret "lethal" authorities under a Presidential Finding signed by Bill Clinton to pursue bin Laden. But those authorities did not amount to a license to kill. For nearly my whole career, CIA had been strictly governed by Executive Order 12333. Signed by President Reagan and having the full impact of law, E.O. 12333 barred the CIA from engaging in assassination. Afghans in our employ could attempt to capture bin Laden, and could defend themselves if bin Laden and his security entourage violently resisted. If the Saudi terrorist mastermind was killed in the process of resisting capture, that would be fine; but neither we nor our confederates could take any action whose *intent* was to kill bin Laden.

Just a few months before my briefing of the president, a tribal network we had been using to monitor bin Laden had come to us with a proposal. They were familiar with the pattern of bin Laden's movements, and although they could not predict with any degree of certainty precisely when the Saudi would move from one place to another, they knew the key road junctions he would inevitably traverse when approaching or departing the various locations he routinely visited. They proposed to bury a huge quantity of explosives beneath one or more of these junctions, and to set them off when his motorcade passed over. We had to tell them immediately to stand down, and to threaten a complete cutoff of support if they even entertained such a notion. If we'd done otherwise, we would all have risked prison.

In effect, we were telling our tribals they could kill bin Laden if he resisted arrest, which he certainly would, but that nonetheless they could not set out to kill him. If that's a bit difficult for a Western-educated sophisticate to wrap his head around, one can image how it must have sounded to an Afghan tribal. Simply blowing up bin Laden would have enabled our Afghan confederates to get away cleanly, with minimal risk. A firefight would not just have cost them casualties but would have made it almost inevitable that their tribe's involvement would become known, inviting the full retribution of the Taliban and the Afghan Arabs on the heads of their families and clans. None of our Afghan friends engaged in monitoring bin Laden would tell us this, for fear of losing our support; but by March 2001 it was more than clear that while they were happy to track the Saudi terrorist, they would not take the risks that conformity with American law demanded to try to arrest him, no matter how much they protested to the contrary, and no matter what threats or inducements we employed. We had no choice but to continue trying, and I hoped to be proved wrong, but confidence was waning.

On almost any given day, our Afghan tribal "assets" could tell us what town bin Laden and his traveling entourage were staying in. But experience had told us that they were most unlikely to develop information precise enough—concerning not just what town bin Laden was staying in, but what house and even what room he occupied—to overcome the U.S. government's past objections to CIA-proposed cruise missile strikes.

Having concluded that the covert action campaign against bin Laden in which we were still actively engaged was most unlikely to succeed, there seemed little reason to spend precious presidential briefing time making false promises or lame excuses—especially as it was a legacy of the previous administration. Add to all that our growing conviction that bin Laden's entry into paradise would not solve our larger problem with al-Qa'ida, and one can understand why I chose to focus my remarks elsewhere.

But in explaining to the president and his national security team how we had successfully widened the aperture on our intelligence gathering in Afghanistan to include the Taliban, there was a far more significant point that I had declined to make to the president: I and my station were preparing a tribal war against the Taliban in the south. We couldn't launch it, of course, until we had presidential permission in the form of a new finding, but the fact was that we had taken our program against the Taliban of the past year and a half a big step further in the most recent six months.

We had begun to reach out, usually through trusted intermediaries, to a host of former Pashtun commanders who had been prominent during the anti-Soviet *jihad* of the 1980s. Almost none of these commanders had fared well since the rise of the Taliban. Although some were fighting now under the Taliban flag in the civil war against the Northern Alliance, they were clearly not trusted by their clerical masters. Most had been sidelined, disarmed by the Taliban, and left to sulk, either in their home tribal areas or in exile across the border in Pakistan.

Some of these commanders refused to meet with us. Some, currently cooperating with the Taliban, agreed to communicate only through trusted intermediaries, for fear their dalliance would be discovered and severely punished. A Pakistani-based warlord serving then as the Taliban minister for tribal affairs, Jalaluddin Haqqani, demanded we pay him the equivalent of $80,000 just for the privilege of meeting. (His financial demands went unmet.) Many others, however, were pleased to reestablish contact with CIA after a lapse of some ten years, even if a few were resentful at having been ignored by us for so long. For these individuals, we had high hopes.

Although some of the former commanders were potentially valuable in the short term as intelligence reporting sources, our main purpose in contacting them was, ultimately, to foment an armed rebellion against the Taliban. I could not mention any of this to the president because it would have appeared that I was attempting to bypass my chain of command to lobby for a change in U.S. policy—something CIA was never supposed to do. Findings were supposed to come from the president to the CIA, not the other way around. In practice, the process was much more fluid, but this did not seem like the time to be getting out ahead of my leadership—at least not in their full view. I was confident that if we could set the groundwork sufficiently to provide some promise of success, such a presidential directive would come to us eventually, but it wasn't going to be sought that day, and certainly not by me. In the meantime, though, I was determined to do everything possible to get internal CIA support for my ideas, and to be prepared for the day when the hoped-for presidential order might come.

JULY 2001

The cramped apartment was a mess of luggage and tired, jet-lagged bodies. Paula, Doug, and I had just arrived in Rosslyn, Virginia, from Pakistan on R&R leave when the phone rang. "Can't be for us," I thought. "No one knows we're here."

The woman's voice on the other end of the line was coolly efficient. "Mr. Grenier," she said. "Director Tenet would like to see you in his office tomorrow at 7:30 AM."

"Gosh, they're good," I thought.

As I strode the next morning into the director's office, a number of others were gathering as well: John Moseman, Tenet's chief of staff; Deputy Director John McLaughlin; Cofer Black, the director of the Counterterrorist Center, the famous CTC; and John Rizzo, the acting general counsel. George was fussing behind his desk, and looked up briefly to wave me over to the long conference table. As he took his place at its head, he dropped a large pile of papers in front of him.

I was thunderstruck. The stack comprised a long series of cables I had sent to headquarters, some dating back to the previous year; they traced the evolution of my thinking on how we could take the fight to the Taliban. Long passages had been highlighted and annotated in the margins in George's hand.

In these messages I had laid out the possibilities suggested by our intelligence. In fact, those opportunities had multiplied in the four months since my briefing of President Bush the previous March. Significant areas under Taliban control were starting to become restive, as patience with draconian clerical rule was wearing thin. Mullah Omar's enforcement of a ban on opium poppy cultivation had not helped him in this regard, denying thousands of Afghan farmers the ability to produce the most lucrative crop available to them.

In particular, there was growing dissatisfaction within the Taliban itself with bin Laden and his Arabs, who had become a veritable state within a state. They did as they liked, and went where they wished, never bothering to inform their hosts, let alone seek their permission. The Arab al-Qa'ida leadership did not trust the Taliban, whom they considered primitives, and made no pretense about it. As bin Laden constantly moved about the country, his bodyguards would never reveal his travel plans in advance to the Taliban security guards who accompanied them everywhere, keeping the Afghans always on the periphery, a mere outer layer of security.

While al-Qa'ida's financial subventions to the Taliban and the skilled fighters in the Arab 555 Brigade were valued, neither the Arabs themselves nor their money were seen as an unambiguous blessing. Arab fighters serving on the front lines of Afghanistan's civil war mirrored the arrogance and religious prejudices of bin Laden's immediate entourage, and the economic dislocations brought about by the Arabs' money, particularly in the Taliban heartland of Kandahar City, were creating serious problems for leading members of the movement. Senior Taliban officials were being priced out of the prime real estate being bought up by bin Laden's people. Even Mullah Omar himself was leery of the Saudi's transparent attempts to curry independent favor with governors, commanders, and other senior Taliban officials through his lavish gifts, and sternly warned bin Laden in a letter that all financial assistance to the Taliban should be channeled through him.

Omar, we knew, was not about to break with bin Laden: he shared the Saudi's messianic vision of global *jihad*. Mullah Omar's formal title was *Amir ul-Mumineen*, "Commander of the Faithful," and for him this was not just an honorific. Although bin Laden's relationship with Omar was complicated, he was adept at flattering his Afghan benefactor and playing on his pretensions as a world historical figure. The concerns of Omar's key lieutenants, however, were closer to home. Many would have been glad to see the Afghan Arabs go. In a Pashtun, a streak of extreme xenophobia is never far from the surface, and among many in the Taliban leadership, their Arab irritation had rubbed that vein raw. Akhtar Mohammed Osmani, "Mullah Osmani"—the Taliban's Southern Zone commander and the number two in the movement to Omar himself—was particularly opposed to bin Laden's presence, and had been vocal about it, as our agents were reporting.

My idea was that if we could capitalize, through liberal application of money, on the restiveness of a number of the significant Pashtun tribal leaders with whom my station was in touch, and if we could tie their limited armed insurrections to popular resentment of the Afghan Arabs, we would at least get the serious attention of the Taliban leadership, which might conclude that hosting the Arabs and bin Laden was more trouble than it was worth. I certainly did not think that my tribal rebellion—if we could pull it off—would ever succeed in actually toppling the Taliban outright. My hope was that genuine concern over the viability of their rule in the Pashtun homeland would exacerbate tensions among Omar's senior lieutenants over the Arab presence, and that this, in combination with certain positive inducements we could make, might just convince Mullah Omar to find a pretext to break with bin Laden and the rest of his problematic Arab guests.

As the Taliban, and particularly Mullah Jallil, had made clear to us, there were significant things they wanted: in particular, they craved international recognition as a legitimate government. They very much wanted to take over Afghanistan's empty seat at the United Nations. Having pacified most of Afghanistan, some, at least, in the leadership—witness Jalil's dalliance with Akbar—wanted to get out from under international sanctions to pursue business opportunities.

My thought was that if we could arrive at the right combination of pressures and inducements, we might create a situation where the Taliban *shura*, or leadership council, could persuade or compel Omar to break with bin Laden and force him and his al-Qa'ida followers to flee to locations where we and our allies could hunt them down more easily. That was the theory.

In the spring of 2001, shortly after the March presidential briefing at CIA Headquarters, I laid out my thinking for Ambassador Milam. We agreed that as I pursued the right to employ new sticks against the Taliban, he would take on the task of acquiring corresponding carrots. He paralleled the efforts I was making in CIA channels with an ultra-secret "Nodis"—for "No Dissemination"—cable of his own, alluding obliquely to what I was doing, and seeking support for rewards that could be offered to the Taliban in return for bin Laden's expulsion.

The ambassador's efforts were met with cold silence. No one in the State Department would say why in print, but we soon learned their reasoning through visiting officials. "Look," one said to me, displaying the exquisite if sometimes craven feel for political self-preservation that had so frustrated me during my year in their building, "anything even suggesting leniency toward the Taliban is a political loser." The Taliban had a rather serious PR problem in the United States, to say the least. Their vicious, bloody-minded repression of women, in particular, was winning them no friends in America. Mavis Leno, wife of the famous comic and talk-show host, was appearing on national television accompanied by women in *burqas*, the traditional head-to-toe covering imposed on women in Taliban-controlled areas, highlighting the injustices of clerical rule in Afghanistan. It was hard not to empathize with their cause, but we were putting ourselves in a situation with the Taliban where we could no longer take yes for an answer regarding bin Laden. In the meantime, televising *burqas* in the United States was not having much effect in Afghan villages.

As I laid all this out for the director in his office, he peppered me with questions and took notes. Much had changed since March at the Washington end, as well. Where new covert action against the Taliban had not even been on the agenda in the early spring, it was very much on the agenda now. A growing pattern of intelligence from around the world, both human and technical, had convinced Tenet and the CIA leadership that a major attack by al-Qa'ida was not only certain but imminent. In a series of meetings with Condoleezza Rice, Tenet and Cofer Black had convinced the administration that the United States should go on the attack. But there was no consensus as to how that should be done.

Deputy Director McLaughlin noted that there would be a Deputies' Committee meeting at the White House in a few days' time to discuss the issue. The Deputies' Committee was the second-highest body in the national security system; their job was to vet ideas and make proposals for consideration by the cabinet-level Principals' Committee. "Take Bob with you," George said. "He understands all this better than anyone."

Sending my vacationing family ahead without me, I put off my annual pilgrimage to Cape Cod so that I could try to influence the options that would be put in front of the deputies. What I found at the NSC was more than discouraging. Attempting to explain to a senior staffer with specific responsibility for South Asia the idea of driving a wedge between the Taliban and al-Qa'ida, he asked: "You mean there's a distinction between the two?"

Zalmay Khalilzad was the NSC's newly appointed senior director for Southwest Asia and the Middle East, and he would be leading the discussion of policy options. An old Afghanistan hand and a genuine regional expert, I had first met him in the early 1990s, when he worked for Paul Wolfowitz at Defense. I would later come to know and admire him. He listened attentively to what I had to say, but on July 13, as I sat in the back row in the White House Situation Room as McLaughlin's "second," I could see that Zal was just all over the map. Rather than advocating a systematic campaign to bring serious, sustained pressure to bear on the Taliban, as I had hoped, he presented a smorgasbord of disaggregated ideas. One proposal he particularly stressed was for creation of a "Radio Free Afghanistan." I inwardly sighed. Rather than fomenting rebellion against them, we were proposing to persuade the Taliban with words—and the words of foreigners, at that. It was a long, quiet ride with McLaughlin back to Langley.

If there was a lack of clarity and consensus in downtown Washington, the same was true within CIA itself. CTC's Cofer Black had had little to say at the morning meeting with Tenet, which after all had been my show, but I knew that thinking within the Counterterrorist Center was at cross-purposes with my own. I considered CTC an important institution in CIA, and a necessary one. It was the central institutional repository of knowledge concerning terrorist groups around the globe, and the only unit capable of efficiently coordinating and supporting their pursuit across the artificial lines by which the CIA's geographic divisions divide up the world. As station chief, I depended on the center to provide many of the people and all of the funds I needed to support my operations in Afghanistan. Much later, I would actually have the privilege of leading the organization as its director, after it had expanded to several times its pre-9/11 size. But while they may have known a lot about terrorists, those in CTC often exhibited little understanding of the cultures, institutions, and social and political dynamics of the regions where those terrorists operated.

The senior ranks of CTC, I noted, were disproportionately populated with Africanists, as Cofer himself. Officers who grew up and spent their early careers in the relatively benign operating environment of sub-Saharan Africa tended to develop quickly, and to rack up the agent recruitment records that drive early promotions. As a result, the Africa Division consistently created rather more senior officers than its tiny management ranks could absorb. The Counterterrorist Center was a natural place to which they could migrate. I found the center's lack of understanding of Afghanistan and Pakistan a trial, but a manageable one, at least for the moment.

Several of the senior CTC managers had become greatly enamored of the head of Afghanistan's Northern Alliance, the former *mujahideen* commander Ahmad Shah Masood. CTC had been sending senior emissaries to meet with him in his mountain redoubt of the Panjshir Valley, in Afghanistan's far northeast, for perhaps a year and a half. Their hope was to win his cooperation in finding and capturing bin Laden. It may have been worth a try, but I knew this was a desperate pipe dream; although much too adept a politician to say so, Masood was far too busy defending what little territory remained in his hands from the Taliban onslaught to do much against bin Laden, ensconced as the Saudi was in the heart of Taliban-controlled real estate. If we wanted to get bin Laden, I was convinced, we were going to have to do it through the Pashtuns.

I shared CTC's reverence for Masood, who was an accomplished military commander, a liberal-minded leader, and a true intellectual. For what it was worth, I supported the idea of maintaining close ties with him. But I was realistic about what he could actually do for us, which at that stage was little. I felt it was important for us to ensure, to the extent we could, that Masood and the Northern Alliance not be swept from the field, if for no other reason than to maintain them as a potential card to be played against the Taliban. But in addition to being in no position to capture bin Laden for us, they had neither the military absorptive capacity nor the tribal standing in the south and east of the country to be able to seriously pressure—let alone defeat—the Taliban. I favored giving them modest support; but too vigorous an effort would merely make the ongoing Afghan civil war more acute, further consolidate Pashtun support for the Taliban, and reinforce the latter's need to maintain ties with its benefactors in al-Qa'ida. Completely throwing in our lot with Masood would have the opposite of the intended effect. The Taliban was a southern problem; the solution lay in the south. Nonetheless, when asked how to ratchet up pressure on the Taliban, CTC's answer, again and again, was to reinforce the Northern Alliance.

Before leaving again for Islamabad in the waning days of July 2001, I had a lengthy meeting with the CTC leadership to try to bring them around to my views. I got nowhere: my friends in CTC found me, and my ideas, utterly unpersuasive.

Chapter 7

THE OUTLIER

JULY 29, 2001

T HE CABIN WAS DARK, the dishes had been cleared away, and there was little sound to compete with the low thrum of the aircraft engines. I was reclining in my seat, beginning to drop off to sleep, when I felt a subtle presence, like soft breathing, above my face. Thinking it was my imagination, I opened my eyes slightly, to find a dark-haired woman leaning over me.

"Are you awake?" she whispered. Slightly startled, I glanced around me. "Yes," I breathed.

"We must speak," she said. She inclined her head toward the forward end of the cabin. "Five minutes."

I had first met Ambassador Maleeha Lodhi almost two years before, while waiting in a salon at the official Pakistani prime minister's residence. General Musharraf's overthrow of Prime Minister Sharif had taken place just a few weeks earlier. With no one else to occupy it, the general was using the ornate, Moorish-style mansion as a venue to receive guests while in Islamabad, away from his official residence at Army House.

The room was flooded with bright sunlight, streaming in from floor-to-ceiling windows. A peacock strutted on the lawn outside. Sitting alone, I looked up to see a slight and strikingly beautiful woman as she approached from my right. I recognized her immediately. Dr. Maleeha Lodhi, from a leading Pakistani family, was a well-known and eminent scholar, the former editor of Pakistan's leading English-language newspaper, and a former diplomat, having previously represented the government of Benazir Bhutto as ambassador to Washington. Now she had been designated by Musharraf to serve again as Pakistan's envoy to the U.S. capital.

She took a place beside me. She glanced knowingly when I told her my position; she obviously recognized who I was. "Well," she said in a mellifluous voice, "*you* must be having an interesting time *here.*"

She was dressed in traditional *shalwar khameez*, in complementary shades of pastel green, with an offsetting silk *dupatta*, or shawl, draped over her chest and back over her shoulders. Perfectly groomed, she seemed much younger than her long résumé would imply, but it was impossible to say by how much. She exuded an aura of competence and command, combined with an almost girlish curiosity and, disarmingly, a hint of mischievous fun.

Suddenly she stopped. What was I doing here? I explained that Ambassador Milam and his political counselor, John Schmidt, were meeting with the Pakistani chief executive, and that I was cooling my heels in case I was called upon to address some issue or other. Her eyes widened in surprise for a moment, and then, as quickly, a veil of anger fell over them. We both realized at once that she was in an impossible position. She had been summoned to meet with General Musharraf immediately after his meeting with the American ambassador. She could not be included in the current meeting, as she had not presented her credentials in Washington, and so as yet had no official status. And yet here she was, sitting outside and therefore seeming pointedly excluded from the meeting. The exiting guests would understand the reasons for this, but still she would look slightly ridiculous, as though loitering outside a stage door she could not enter.

Just then, a pudgy brigadier from Army Protocol wandered into the room. She was on her feet and at him in a flash, in a salvo of elegant but acidic Urdu. A serious mistake had been made at her expense, and someone was going to pay. The hapless fellow fell back three steps, wincing, and then turned and scampered down the hallway like a scalded dog. Her fury momentarily slaked, Lodhi turned on her heel and marched across the room to a low settee. She whirled and flung herself on the middle cushion. There was a long pause. "Shit," she said.

Now, as we leaned in the shadows against the forward bulkhead, Ambassador Lodhi was equally direct: She wanted to know what was going on, and she insisted that I must tell her. We were on a British Airways flight from London to Islamabad. I was returning from my consultations in Washington; she was traveling to Pakistan in advance of an expected visit by Christina Rocca, the U.S. assistant secretary of state for South Asia.

The Pakistani foreign minister, Abdul Sattar, had recently visited Washington and had been "shellshocked," she said, by the vehemence of U.S. views regarding Pakistani support for the Taliban. "What do you think I've been trying to tell you for eighteen months?" Lodhi had told him. Senior officials in Pakistan didn't want to acknowledge the growing U.S. anger and apprehension. Her detractors, she charged, were quick to play the "gender card," suggesting that as a woman, she was panicking. Now that Sattar had gotten an earful for himself, perhaps they'd begin to understand what was at stake.

For months, in terms similar to those employed by Milam and me in our early 2000 conversation with President Musharraf, Lodhi had been warning Islamabad that the next attack by al-Qa'ida would generate a major response by the Americans, and that the consequences for Pakistan, as the most important defender and ally of the Taliban, would be severe. What, she wanted to know, was the chief of station telling General Mahmud, director-general of the ISI? So far as she could tell, Mahmud was "serene," stating that he had no problems with CIA, based on "decades of good relations" between Langley and the vaunted Pakistani intelligence service.

That last phrase, the one about "decades of good relations," stung me. In fact, at my instigation, we had tried a new tack with Mahmud and his service following my failed February 2000 meeting with Musharraf. Our charm offensive had been keyed to General Mahmud's visit to Washington a month later, and to George Tenet's subsequent visit to Pakistan in June of that year. I had lavished as much favorable attention on Mahmud as I could.

My idea, adopted readily by Director Tenet and Jim Pavitt, who had now risen to be the agency's deputy director for operations, was that during the reciprocal visits by the two intelligence chiefs, we should distance ourselves from the rest of the U.S. government, and appeal for ISI help based on the long cooperative relationship between our services, of which our spectacularly successful joint effort during the anti-Soviet *jihad* of the 1980s was the most prominent example. Our pitch was that effective intelligence cooperation against al-Qa'ida would get the favorable attention of the U.S. government, and perhaps lead to a wider thaw in relations. "Help us help you," we said.

During his March 2000 visit to Washington, in sharp counterpoint to his unpleasant contacts with the Department of State and the National Security Council, we treated Mahmud with warm respect and fêted him and his senior officers at clubby dinners in the countryside. Having learned that Mahmud had written a thesis at the Pakistan Army Command and Staff College on the battle of Gettysburg, I arranged a special tour and walked the entire battlefield with him and his staff, accompanied by an eminent Civil War historian from the U.S. Army War College.

It appeared for a time that the "good cop" approach might work: during Tenet's visit to Pakistan in June 2000, General Musharraf, in the presence of both Mahmud and myself, promised a vigorous program of counterterrorism cooperation, including establishment of a joint counterterrorism unit. But it was all for naught. As soon as Tenet's plane cleared Pakistani airspace, Mahmud began assiduously to avoid me. When at length he agreed to meet with me in September 2000, he finally responded to my repeated appeals for concrete follow-up by saying, "What's the next item on your agenda?"

Now it appeared to me that not only was General Mahmud not following through on the Pakistani chief executive's commitments, but that my moderate tone was perhaps leading him to believe—or at least to claim—that CIA's message was different from what Pakistan was getting elsewhere in the U.S. government. This was both embarrassing and galling.

Our message in Islamabad, I assured Lodhi, was the same as hers. General Mahmud wasn't hearing it, I said, "because we don't talk."

"That has to change," she asserted. The United States and Pakistan must cooperate on Afghanistan, and so must the intelligence services.

"Look," I said. "The reason we can't get there is that Pakistan won't engage on the issue. If your government would level with us, and explain the national interests being served by your support of the Taliban, we could work with you to find an alternative means of addressing your problems and pursuing your interests. Pakistan seems convinced that the United States has ulterior, unstated goals in Afghanistan, and we can't counter those concerns if they're never expressed."

Lodhi agreed. "We've got to do something before Pakistan is blamed for the next al-Qa'ida attack. And violence in Afghanistan is affecting Pakistan as well; it must be eliminated at the source."

Time is of the essence, I stressed. Al-Qa'ida, we knew, was planning to strike us again. "It's not a matter of if, but of when. Between us, we have to find a way to make them understand." The ambassador had the haunted look of someone who could see the future when no one else in her government could. Her agenda and mine were certainly not identical, but they overlapped. My goal was to neutralize bin Laden and deny a platform to al-Qa'ida before they could launch another strike against U.S. interests; her goal was to avoid having Pakistan take the blame if and when such a strike occurred. The key to realizing both our goals was Mahmud. If he could be induced to provide some effective cooperation against al-Qa'ida, whose operatives and facilitators were transiting Pakistan with impunity, it might help us disrupt the next attack, and it would change the prism through which Pakistan was seen in the U.S. government. Lodhi's was clearly the only compelling voice of reason in the Pakistani government, but she was an outlier, with little internal support; I did not envy her position.

"You must engage with Mahmud," she insisted again. "Besides," she added, with a sly smile, "he likes you."

Chapter 8

COUNTDOWN

MALEEHA LODHI HAD CLEARLY checked out. She was staring up at the ceiling, making little pretense of listening. Both she and I had heard this monologue many times before. In the West Wing of the White House, small increments of power and influence are measured in square feet of office space and proximity to the Oval Office. The space accorded Condoleezza Rice, the national security advisor, was relatively capacious, and included a small seating area and a conference table, set by a working fireplace. But her deputy Steve Hadley's office, where we were sitting, could have been mistaken for a broom closet. The Pakistani ambassador was forced to sit upright and primly, lest her right knee touch my left. Seemingly oblivious of the uncomfortable setting and the evident lack of interest from two thirds of his audience, Lieutenant General Mahmud Ahmed droned on with his usual precise diction, in a deep, sonorous voice. He was at his articulate but tiresomely pedantic best.

Maddening as he was, I had long found Mahmud to be a fascinating character. In an army formed on the British model, he was the prototype of the British-style officer. From the bristling mustaches, to the ascot, to the ramrod-straight posture, to the swagger stick tucked under his right arm, he might have stepped out of a picture book of the early twentieth-century British-Indian Army. A classicist and an intellectual, his discourse was strewn with references to Clausewitz, Bertrand Russell, and Aristotle. In his telling, the Amu Darya River, which set the northern border of present-day Afghanistan, was the ancient

Oxus; modern Istanbul was Constantinople, or Byzantium. And yet he startled me on one occasion by quoting, at length and by heart, the lyrics of a recent sentimental Western pop ballad.

Mahmud was said to have rediscovered religion as he entered middle age, and he clearly wore both his personal piety and his pro-Taliban sympathies on his sleeve. In neither respect was he unusual. But among many, to me overwrought, foreign observers he represented something more. He was darkly reputed to be among the "closet Islamists" in Pakistan's military leadership, holding religiously inspired political views and insidiously advocating a "jihadist" foreign policy.

In any event, for all that he was an unabashed apologist for the Taliban, it was hard to imagine such an urbane and sophisticated man having much personal sympathy for a group of primitive obscurantists who brutally repressed women and refused to see them educated. His strikingly pretty young wife, whom I had met, was highly literate, sharp-tongued and opinionated. Mahmud had told me with some pride that he and his daughter, with whom he was obviously close, were reading Stephen Hawking's *A Brief History of Time* so that they could discuss it together.

Given the strong ties between the Northern Alliance and India, Pakistan saw support for the Taliban as in its national interest, a view Mahmud clearly shared. But one could not reconcile the private man with his evident personal enthusiasm for the Taliban, which appeared to go well beyond considerations of Pakistani national interest, without assuming a large measure of social and cultural condescension toward Afghans, and what these benighted tribalists might legitimately aspire to. That, too, was consistent with his character.

Now, having regaled Hadley with graphic stories of the obscene depredations of the Afghan warlords whom the Taliban had deposed, he went on to describe the impossible challenges they would face in trying to track down bin Laden on our behalf—in the unlikely event they ever agreed to do so. "The peaks of the Hindu Kush," he intoned dramatically, "rise over 20,000 feet, and the valleys are so deep that the sun never penetrates." Allowing for some poetic license, most of what Mahmud had to tell the deputy national security advisor, along with other senior officials around town, was true enough; and all of it was irrelevant.

In a cable to headquarters in advance of Mahmud's September 2001 visit, I had warned my senior leadership that "his mission is not engagement, but pacification." At the time of my hushed late July conversation with Ambassador Lodhi on the flight to Islamabad, there had been yet a glimmer of hope. Now, a little more than a month later, I had concluded that so long as Mahmud was in place, there was no realistic prospect of gaining active Pakistani support either in attacking and disabling al-Qa'ida's infrastructure in Pakistan, or for a prospective effort to drive a wedge between the Taliban and bin Laden in Afghanistan. We would have to proceed on our own, I said, and hope the Pakistanis would turn a "blind eye" to our cross-border efforts in the likely event they discovered them. Pakistani interference with us would be more easily avoided if we could convince them that we did not seek the downfall of the Taliban per se, but only to drive al-Qa'ida from its safehaven.

Neither Mahmud nor anyone else in the Pakistani government seemed to have any brief for bin Laden or his Afghan Arabs. Logically speaking, and so long as it was kept quiet, there was no reason for them not to cooperate in a limited campaign against al-Qa'ida, and seemingly every reason to do so, if they hoped to rebuild their relations with the United States. In his final lunch at CIA Headquarters, Mahmud suggested that we bribe Afghan tribals to track down bin Laden. But he pointedly did not offer any assistance in the effort.

As we rode together in the back of a chauffeured car up the George Washington Parkway toward the CIA Headquarters building for a final, unpleasant meeting with Cofer Black and CTC, I put the question to Mahmud directly: Given that bin Laden's presence served no Pakistani national interest, why did he refuse to cooperate against the Saudi and his terrorist followers? There was a long silence. Was it because of the Pressler sanctions? I asked. Mahmud paused, and looked away. "Yes," he said quietly. It was something I already knew, but his admission was nonetheless significant. The ISI chief had no interest in rebuilding relations with America; he was too busy nursing resentments over the past.

Within Afghanistan, I wrote that August, our best intelligence indicated that ties between Mullah Omar and the Arabs were strengthening, while the animosity of Omar's senior lieutenants toward the outsiders was growing. These opposing trends had not yet created a fissure in the leadership, and it was not yet clear which side would predominate. On August 27, I sent another message to headquarters, pressing again for an integrated U.S. policy to produce and exploit such a break in Taliban unity. Once again, I argued that if we were permitted to foment a tribal uprising in protest of the Arab presence in Afghanistan, we might sufficiently empower the anti-Arab elements in the Taliban *Shura* to force Omar to expel bin Laden.

CIA, unable to reconcile the conflicting advice between CTC and myself, sent a draft covert action proposal to the NSC combining both our ideas: We should reinforce the Northern Alliance, it said, while simultaneously encouraging a tribal uprising in the south. The White House tabled the draft for further study.

Lacking the new authorities we sought, my officers and I pressed forward aggressively with what authorities we had. In the second half of August, our southern tribal contacts distributed hundreds of "night letters"—propaganda sheets slid under doors or tossed over compound walls in the dark of night—in and around Kandahar, decrying bin Laden and the pernicious presence of Arab foreigners. We hoped they would convey the impression of a groundswell of popular opposition to al-Qa'ida.

The September round of Washington meetings almost concluded, and just before departing once again for Pakistan, I met with Ambassador Lodhi over a private dinner in a restaurant overlooking the Potomac. Though neither of us said so, the sense of resignation was palpable. She could not move her government, and I could not move mine. In fact, there was little of substance for us to discuss.

Mahmud planned to stay on in Washington for several days after my September 7 departure, so that he could make a reciprocal meeting with the chairmen of the two congressional intelligence oversight committees, whom he had hosted at a lavish outdoor dinner in Pakistan a few days before, on August 29. Their meeting was scheduled for September 11. That morning, as the general and Ambassador Lodhi sat in the Capitol with Representative Porter Goss and Senator Bob Graham, the group was suddenly approached by an aide who reported stunning news from New York. A television set was turned on, and all watched the scene of smoke rising from the twin towers, until the order came to evacuate the building. I was watching the identical scene from my office in Islamabad.

As the two Pakistanis were driven west down Constitution Avenue, they suddenly saw a plume of smoke rise in the sky off to their left, in the direction of the Pentagon. Time was up. As some of us had feared, and to a greater extent than we could ever have imagined, life as we had known it was about to change.

Part Three

THE FIRST AMERICAN-AFGHAN WAR

Chapter 9

NON-NEGOTIABLE
DEMANDS

SEPTEMBER 15–16, 2001

I WAS LYING ON MY back, staring up at the ceiling. It was well past midnight, but sleep was impossible. A thousand jumbled thoughts were competing feverishly in my mind. Suddenly it occurred to me: directly across the hall, in a similarly spare hotel bedroom, lay a stone killer whom I'd been threatening for several hours, however politely, with annihilation. Given the animation of our previous discussion, he was surely as wide awake as I was. I couldn't be sure what sort of impulse control he possessed, but what I had seen from him so far was not reassuring. Outside, down the hall, I could hear the soft murmurings of a group of heavily armed Taliban guards keeping vigil. I was unarmed, and my only ally was an Iranian-American Dari translator in the next room, who might have weighed all of 120 pounds. The latch on the door was laughably flimsy. I got up from bed to push a heavy armchair up against it. That wouldn't slow down an intruder very much, but at least I'd be assured of being awakened. The drop from my second-story window, I noted with perhaps undue optimism, didn't look so bad.

Since our initial encounter at Milam's residence at the beginning of the year, Mullah Jalil and I had established a pattern of regular *Inmarsat* satellite phone calls. I would dial him up at prearranged times from the rooftop veranda of my home, which afforded an unimpeded view of the night sky. The deputy foreign minister was cagey and opaque,

and gave no sign of willingness to compromise himself in any mean-
ingful way; still, he was an intriguing contact, and our conversations
gave me some further insight into Taliban thinking. Our interactions
would not have been nearly as useful if it were not for the regular
flow of clandestine reporting we were receiving from recruited, vetted
agents concerning intra-Taliban dynamics. Their reports provided me
the context in which to interpret Jalil's delphic pronouncements.

I had reached Jalil within twenty-four hours of the 9/11 attacks, and
pressed him to meet with me. The response came quickly, and from a
familiar, if not entirely welcome quarter.

Akbar called to say that Mullah Jalil and Mullah Akhtar Mohammed
Osmani could travel from Kandahar to meet with me in Quetta; would
I be willing to meet with them? I didn't have to consider long. Mullah
Osmani was the Taliban's Southern Zone commander, in charge of all
Taliban forces in the movement's southern stronghold, and the de facto
deputy to Mullah Omar himself. Our reporting indicated that Osmani
was strongly and vociferously opposed to bin Laden. I could only speculate as to what he intended in coming to meet with me; but this might
be the opportunity we had been looking for to exploit the differences
between Omar and his senior lieutenants over their Arab guests. The
meeting was set for Saturday, September 15, at a quiet hotel in Quetta.

I wanted to keep this meeting as discreet as possible. My travel
via commercial air to the remote capital of Baluchistan Province, the
southern gateway to Afghanistan, mere days after the al-Qa'ida attacks
in the United States, would surely have been flagged to Pakistani officials. But as luck would have it, our defense attaché, who had control of
a small aircraft, was sending a team to Quetta to evacuate a U.S. Army
officer studying at the Pakistan Army's Command and General Staff
College. At my behest, they filed an official flight plan, but one that
failed to mention a couple of extra passengers: my Farsi/Dari translator
"Tom," and me.

I was glad to have Tom with me, though not everyone would have
felt the same. Tom had started out in CIA as a Farsi-language instruc-
tor, and a good one. But even in that limited role, he quickly developed a reputation as a rather difficult personality within the CIA's

Farsi-speaking subculture. Blessed, as many in the Clandestine Service, with a healthy ego, and aspiring, again like many on the periphery of espionage, to get directly involved in clandestine operations, he had managed to migrate into real-time operational translation—the task he would be performing for me. Like many translators, a certain amount of exposure to what case officers do had convinced Tom that he could do the same as they, and perhaps better: rather than merely translating others' words, he felt he ought to be running the operations himself. The insular CIA culture is highly disposed to promotion from within. Several of Tom's supervisors had accommodated him by arranging for him to be trained in operations, despite a certain lack of the requisite judgment and self-control—which he had demonstrated in his first operational assignments. The challenge then became to rein Tom back in. Given his raised expectations, that was far more easily said than done, and many shrank from the job.

Still, Tom was a damned good translator. I had found that if he respected you, if you treated his contribution with the importance it deserved, and if you were firm and prepared to watch him very closely, he could be a real asset. Besides, he was amusing company.

In informing my headquarters of what I was doing, I was careful to stress that my objective in holding this meeting was primarily operational, not diplomatic. Yes, I would press the Taliban leadership to accede to the U.S. demand to turn over bin Laden. But my primary purpose would be to make direct contact with Osmani to see if I could exploit his animus toward the Arabs.

Tom and I arrived at the hotel in the late morning, and made contact with Akbar, who had just traveled overland from Kandahar. The two Afghans, he said, would be following close behind. Tom and I sat and waited. The hours dragged past, excruciatingly. I had a sense that each passing minute was a lost opportunity. I knew there was little time before an American attack might commence, but there was yet no way for me to know just how little. Finally, as dusk fell, Akbar knocked on my door. Osmani and Jalil had arrived. Seized by my own nervous anticipation, I expected that they would sit down with us immediately. I had somehow forgotten who I was dealing with.

"No," said Akbar. "It has been a long journey, and the road is very bad. They will need time to pray, to eat, and then to rest. They will meet with us at nine."

"Of course," I thought, shaking my head.

When at length we sat down, it was at a large round table. Mullah Osmani sat opposite me, with Akbar to his left. Tom sat to my left, and to my right, Mullah Jalil hunched over a stack of blank white sheets of paper. Akbar translated Osmani's Pashtu into English; Tom translated my English into Dari, which all of the others understood, even if they were not all comfortable speaking it.

Jalil began. He and Osmani had met with Mullah Omar the day before, September 14. Omar had authorized them to meet with me to find a solution to the impasse between us. They had no authority to make any agreements, he said, but could work with me to make proposals to present to Omar for his approval. With that, Jalil bent over and began writing in a sweeping, florid script. He hardly said another word throughout the proceedings, deferring entirely to Osmani, who was much the senior. It soon became clear that the deputy foreign minister was only present as a witness and note-taker.

I carefully stated that I was in precisely the same position as they: I had no authority to reach binding agreements, and could only refer ideas for possible approval to Washington. That said, I went on, I was confident that there would have to be at least three elements in any proposals we might develop for there to be any hope of Washington's agreement: Osama bin Laden would have to be rendered to justice in the United States, or killed in the attempt; other al-Qa'ida fugitives on whom there were formal U.S. indictments would likewise have to be detained and turned over; and all of the foreign militants in the Arab camps would have to be expelled to their countries of origin, and the camps permanently closed.

Beyond the first demand, I knew, I was speculating on my own. Four days after 9/11, Washington had yet to formulate any detailed message to the Taliban beyond the long-standing demand to turn over bin Laden. I felt certain, though, that the United States would insist on justice for other known, senior al-Qa'ida members on whom there were outstanding warrants. I had scoured the files to develop a list of some fourteen individuals thought to be in Afghanistan, and on whom we held judicial warrants. If we were going to demand the arrest of the al-Qa'ida leadership in Afghanistan, the Taliban was likely to demand specific names, and we certainly couldn't trust their discretion as to which al-Qa'ida members to turn over, even in the unlikely event they agreed to it.

As for the simple fighters in the camps, I knew it was unlikely that the Taliban could capture many of them even if they wanted to; they would probably scatter as soon as it was clear what the Taliban was up to. Most were only "guilty" of fighting against the Northern Alliance at that point, and not directly involved in international terrorism. Surely the U.S. government was not about to take them into custody. CIA had long been in the business of working with sympathetic countries to render such militants to their places of origin; once they had been driven out of Afghanistan, and particularly in the context of a striking post-9/11 upswell in international support, there would be opportunities to do so again. The important thing, I knew, was for the Taliban to make clear to these foreigners that they were no longer welcome—to end the safehaven. I couldn't be sure what Washington might say later on, whether they might demand unrealistically that all the militants be rounded up and turned over to us, but left on my own I was not about to make the perfect the enemy of the good, not in a chaotic place like Afghanistan.

Osmani then launched into his own preamble. The situation was difficult, he said. Both the United States and the Afghans would have to take domestic opinion into account. That said, the Taliban would not risk the destruction of their nation for the sake of one man. Bin Laden and his followers were a common problem for both countries. Both would have to work together quietly—he stressed quietly—to solve it.

I was silently elated. This was precisely what I had hoped to hear; now we were getting somewhere. When I asked for his ideas as to how we could accomplish this, though, the *Maulavi* (senior mullah) had none. What could I propose?

I said there are any number of ways we could cooperate to do what is necessary, and we could work together to flesh out the details. But there are just a few broad approaches we could take. I listed them, as possible points of departure: Mullah Omar could publicly announce on his own that the attacks in the United States against civilian targets were contrary to Islam, and take action on his own against the perpetrators. As a slight permutation of that approach, he could state that he had demanded and received proof from the Americans of bin Laden's responsibility for the horrific attacks on their soil, and was taking the appropriate action on that basis. If, on the other hand, such a public approach was too difficult, the Taliban could move against both the individuals and the camps quietly, with no public announcements, and allow others in Afghanistan to speculate that foreign forces had done this without Taliban knowledge. If such direct but unattributed action were also too difficult, the Taliban could quickly and quietly facilitate our contact with willing commanders susceptible of being suborned with money, of which there were many, and allow them to render bin Laden and his lieutenants and to close down the camps at our direction. Finally, if all these approaches were unavailing, the Taliban could simply step aside and allow U.S. forces to take action unopposed, merely providing quiet guidance and intelligence.

Osmani paused, looking downward, and began to slowly shake his head. No, he said, none of these options would work. The Taliban could not take actions against al-Qa'ida without their becoming known. The people would never accept this: they would rise up. On the other hand, any direct U.S. actions in Afghanistan would also become known, and would be seen as an invasion. Afghans would reflexively resist, he said. Taliban units would not just stand aside for the Americans, even if ordered to do so.

With more than a little exasperation, I wound the conversation back to where we had started. "The Taliban will not sacrifice their country for the sake of one man," I quoted. If bin Laden were a common problem for us, and if my proposals were unworkable, what alternative could he suggest to save his country?

The conversation ebbed and flowed for hours, frequently generating eddies that threatened to spin the meeting out of control. Several times, Osmani began to launch into a rant. "If you attack us, we will defeat you, just as we defeated the Soviets!" Each time, I cut him off before he could elaborate.

"This is *haram* [religiously forbidden]," I said. "It is not the place of man to predict the future. Whether we are to be victorious or defeated will be in God's hands." Countering a bearded Islamic obscurantist, a senior mullah at that, on religious grounds, I found, was deeply satisfying. "The only thing we can safely predict," I continued, "is that if war comes, it will be a disaster for everyone, victor and vanquished alike, and it will destroy the Taliban movement. Your enemies—and they are many—will seize the opportunity, and will make no end of problems for you. We have a mutual interest in seeing that these things do not happen."

At one point I said, "Look, I have not come here just to threaten you." This elicited a chuckle from both Afghans. Jalil looked up from his paper.

"He knows us," he said, looking at Osmani. And then to me, with a smile: "Threats don't work very well with us." Pashtuns pride themselves on their defiance: If you have your foot on the neck of a Pashtun, it is said, he will use his last breath to curse you.

Time and again, I presented myself as the intermediary, who knows and respects both sides. I compared myself to a man sitting at the top of a high hill. On one side, I can see a train hurtling down a track. On the other side, I can see another train, moving at speed around the curve in the opposite direction. Only I can see that the two trains are on the same track, and that by the time they see each other, it will be too late to stop. It is my responsibility, I said, to try to avoid the crash.

In the end, after five hours of exhausting and mostly circular conversation, the only counterproposal I could coax from the Southern Zone commander was that the United States, on its own and without help from the Taliban, should recruit a small group of Afghans to attack bin Laden. Others, to include senior indicted members of al-Qa'ida, he said, should be left alone.

"I do not think any of your proposals will work," he reiterated, "but we will bring them to Mullah Omar, and he will decide." Even Akbar, sympathetic to the Taliban as he was, was disgusted.

"You've given him every opportunity," he said. "And he has given you nothing."

Minutes later, alone in my room as the clock struck two, I was obsessed with the need to speak alone with Osmani. The animus he expressed toward bin Laden, I felt, was genuine, and confirmed our reporting. Perhaps his refusal to engage with me was due to the fact that all details of the meeting were to be reported by Jalil to Omar; he would gain nothing by appearing to make concessions when in the end the decisions would be made by the Taliban chief alone.

Just before dawn, I had Tom place a call to Osmani's room. Another voice answered. "I must speak with Mullah Sa'eb," Tom said, using the commander's Taliban nickname.

"He is not here," came the response. Osmani had left.

SEPTEMBER 16, 2001

It was unusual to see General Mahmud with such an entourage. Normally, we met alone, or with one or two others at most. This time, he was flanked by a large number of his senior people. They would not have been there had he not wanted them; but they must have been expecting quite a show.

For me, the question had been whether I should conduct such a show at all. The instinct of an intelligence officer is always to be as discreet as possible, to reveal nothing, particularly to a foreign service, unless it is absolutely necessary. That would have been particularly true with the ISI.

But I resisted my instinct. President Musharraf had pledged his support to us, and Mahmud had indicated verbally, at least, that he was on board. The ISI chief would have every motive to avoid the coming conflict, and as a longtime Taliban supporter, his influence with them could prove useful. There was no question in his mind as to what we would do if we did not get satisfaction. He had seen with his own eyes Americans' frenzied reaction to the 9/11 attacks: "Like a wounded animal," he had said. His testimony regarding what he'd seen firsthand in Washington might prove persuasive to Mullah Omar. And it was most likely that he would come to know of my meeting with the two Afghan clerics in any case; there was little point in gratuitously alienating him by appearing to hold out. Better to bring him at least partially into confidence and encourage his cooperation, at least for the time being.

I gave them a lengthy, arm-waving, blow-by-blow account of the proceedings in Quetta. All sat in rapt, silent attention. At the end, Mahmud pronounced himself "amazed." I had seldom seen him so animated. "This is a huge breakthrough," he enthused. He was particularly seized with Osmani's "agreement in principle" to find a solution to the bin Laden problem. This was much further than he had ever gotten in his own past discussions with the Taliban. The fact that Osmani had failed in the end to come to closure on any of my proposed solutions was not a worry, he said, and merely reflected Osmani's lack of instructions from Omar. "These are exploitable concessions," he noted, which he would use in his meeting with Omar, scheduled for the following day. We arranged to meet as soon as he returned from Kandahar.

As a frequent visitor to ISI Headquarters, I was used to letting myself out. As I rose, however, a round-faced major from ISI protocol leapt to his feet to escort me. Once we had descended to the ground floor and stepped outside into the courtyard, he gave me a look of frank admiration. "You did everything you could, sir," he said, beaming. I did not take this necessarily as a good sign. If my efforts seemed so heroic to the ISI, I thought, I must have gone too far.

In my report to Langley that night, I confessed I found it hard to share the ISI chief's optimism. "It may be," I said, "that Mahmud has greater insight into Taliban character than I." But it was even more likely that he was hoping against hope to drag out some level of negotiations with the Taliban leadership as a means of forestalling American military action.

I would soon discover that my decision to meet with Mahmud had been the correct one. Osmani and Jalil, rather than returning straightaway to Kandahar, instead traveled to Islamabad to meet with Mahmud, to consult on their discussions with me and, presumably, to seek his help with the Americans. He received them later the same night he met with me. He had neglected to mention it.

SEPTEMBER 18, 2001

Everything, they say, is relative. Though someone else may think my current circumstances bad, to me they will seem very good if yesterday's situation was much worse. A bad situation will seem all the worse if my prior circumstances were particularly good. According to General Mahmud, this theory of existential relativity very much applied to the Kandahar of September 17, 2001.

News of the assassination of Ahmad Shah Masood on September 9, just two days before 9/11, had been received with elation among the Taliban leadership. The death of the illustrious leader of the Northern Alliance, they were sure, would bring them final victory in the civil war, and enable them to consolidate their hold over all of Afghanistan. When Mahmud and his delegation of Afghan specialists from the ISI and the Foreign Ministry arrived, though, they found their hosts in a very different mood, and one all the more gloomy for their recent euphoria.

Mullah Omar, in particular, seemed completely out of sorts. He put off afternoon prayers to meet with the Pakistanis—something unprecedented in Mahmud's long history with him. He was full of petulant, and sometimes irrational, questions: Why hadn't the Americans eliminated bin Laden before his arrival in Afghanistan? Now he was in the Taliban's lap, and what could they do about it? If the Americans had a problem with al-Qa'ida, why were they also pursuing the Taliban? Was it because the Taliban was Islamic? Besides, the 9/11 attacks had been far too sophisticated for al-Qa'ida; they couldn't possibly have done it. And irrespective of that, the Americans certainly had nothing to fear from bin Laden in future: he was "tethered to a nail," incapable of doing anything.

Mahmud, in his telling, had been brutally frank with the Taliban leader during their four-hour meeting. He described what he had seen of the Americans' furious reaction to the attacks in vivid terms. Their resolve to eliminate the threat from al-Qa'ida, once and for all, was absolute. Omar's pleas for bin Laden's innocence, he said, no longer mattered. The United States was committed to eliminating both bin Laden and the Afghan sanctuary; if the Taliban would not do so, the Americans would attempt to do so themselves. The Taliban, he said, would have to weigh the alternatives in the balance: one man versus 25 million Afghans.

In the end, the "Commander of the Faithful" had been ambivalent. On one hand, Omar was characteristically fatalistic, in the way fundamentalists are: "If war comes, it is the will of God." He agreed to send a trusted emissary to meet with bin Laden and to seek his voluntary departure, but did so without enthusiasm and with the caveat that bin Laden, now in hiding, would be difficult to find.

On the other hand, Mahmud found one great reason to be encouraged. Omar had decided to convene a consultative council of several hundred *Ulema*, or Islamic scholars, from throughout Afghanistan to advise him on the correct course to pursue toward bin Laden. Properly managed, this so-called "Supreme Council of the Islamic Clergy" could provide the Afghan leader the religious cover he needed to do what was politically necessary. They were expected to meet on September 19.

Finally, Mahmud wanted to create the opportunity, at least, for direct discussions between Omar and a U.S. emissary. Had the one-eyed cleric ever met with an infidel? Would he meet with such an emissary if offered the chance? The answer to both questions was yes, but Omar underscored that he would meet with an American only in secret, and only if given iron-clad assurances that no word of such a meeting would appear in the press.

Mullah Jalil, of course, had been included among the handful of participants in the meeting. As soon as it broke up and Omar went off to pray, he seized on the opportunity to help nudge events in the right direction: He brought Mahmud immediately to meet with Nur Muhammad Saqeb, chief justice of the Taliban Supreme Court, who would preside over the upcoming council of *Ulema*. He wanted to be sure Saqeb was aware of what was at stake.

Chapter 10

CHARTING THE COURSE

SEPTEMBER 24, 2001

T HE LARGE SCREEN CONTAINED two grainy, flickering boxes. I leaned forward on my threadbare office couch, squinting to make out the images in each. In one, I could see General Tommy Franks, the four-star combatant commander of the Central Command (CENTCOM), seated behind what appeared to be a long table of blond wood, flanked by two or three aides. In the other, a lone technician at CIA Headquarters stared mutely back at me.

I didn't know it yet, but the war plan which George Tenet had solicited from me the day before, and which I had submitted in such haste for his Sunday morning discussions at Camp David, had just been approved by the president and the War Cabinet that morning, a Monday. Now it was Monday afternoon on the east coast of the United States. No one had bothered to fill me in on much of what was happening back there. It was all moving too fast. All I knew was that I was to dial in for a SVTC (secure video teleconference) with Tenet, who was at CIA Headquarters, and with General Franks, at MacDill Air Force Base in Tampa.

The SVTC facility had been installed in Islamabad Station almost two years before, one of only a handful of overseas stations to have it at the time. Consisting simply of a large, wall-mounted screen, a remote-activated swiveling camera, and a separate audio link which, thankfully, could be muted, the system was far from perfect. The satellite-fed images were often grainy and indistinct, and the fact that both sound and video images had to be encrypted and then decrypted in each direction made for an unsettling transmission delay, often putting voices and pictures out of sync. Indeed, for much of the previous two years, the equipment had sat unused in my office. But during crisis situations—the Pakistani military coup of October 12, 1999, for example, or the multiple rocket attacks on U.S. and UN installations in Islamabad precisely a month later—the system had proved invaluable for what I liked to refer to as "feeding the Beast."

The Washington bureaucracy, whatever the agency or department, has its own structure and its own rhythm. These are fairly predictable. When a crisis occurs, however, the system and everyone in it seemingly goes crazy. I say "seemingly" because if you've lived in that world, as I have, you lose a normal layperson's perspective on what, by any objective standard, is irrational behavior. You understand why the bureaucracy behaves as it does and therefore, if you are clever, how to manipulate it.

Senior officials in Washington crave one thing: the illusion of control. Oh, yes, they get to issue policy pronouncements, and over time, they can nudge the ship of government roughly a few degrees in this direction or that. But for the most part, they are far removed from the actual work that is being done in their agencies, and they have little idea how it actually happens. Those at the tactical end must react to events on the ground and rapidly solve whatever problems come up, often with little or no time to seek guidance from higher-ups, and secure in the knowledge that whatever guidance they get is most likely to be useless anyway. Those in the upper reaches generally don't know the questions that have arisen, let alone the answers, and for the most part it doesn't matter: they attend their rounds of meetings and talk confidently to one another as though their actions had relevance. I know, because I've done the same.

Senior officials are not entirely stupid, however. They sense their impotence, and the way they compensate for it is by demanding information from those below them. It's rather like being a passenger in an airplane. You may be bouncing around violently in the clouds, ignorant of where you are in relation to the ground, and feeling distinctly nervous. Once you break through the cloud cover, however, and can see where you are, you feel much better: You feel suddenly in control of the situation. In fact, you have no more influence over your fate than you did before. What you do have is the illusion of control.

When a crisis hits, though, and events have been jolted out of their usual comforting rhythm, the inherent insecurity of the bureaucracy goes into overdrive. Those at the top demand to know what is happening and what is being done about it, and they turn to the midlevel bureaucrats for answers. The midlevel folks turn to the low-level folks, and if they don't know the answers, they blame the incompetence of the guys in the field. The hapless field types, meanwhile, who actually have to deal with the crisis and are completely preoccupied with the work at hand, often become even less communicative than usual, precisely when their input is demanded most. Their good work may eventually come to light, but by then it is likely to be too late, for all the elements that collectively make up the Beast, driven by a fear of looking incompetent themselves and forced to fill the void of their ignorance, will have permanently tarred the tactical people as ill-prepared idiots who have done little or nothing, and who have attempted to mask their incompetence with silence.

The experienced field person understands all this, and if wise, will turn the dynamic to his or her advantage. In those days, whenever a crisis event occurred, I always directed that a comprehensive Situation Report be issued immediately and followed up at regular intervals. That let people up the line know what was going on. As to what was being done about it, our job being intelligence collection, we would quickly issue an exhaustively detailed Collection Plan, informing headquarters of the posture of each of our sources, what tasking was being given to each one, when we expected them to report in, and the elements of the crisis they could be relied upon to cover.

This would overjoy the low-level people at the branch and group levels, because they could confidently brief their division chiefs as to what "we" were doing about the crisis. The division chiefs could then brief the deputy director for operations—the DDO—and his various acolytes, the associate deputy directors and other hangers-on, who could in turn brief the director and *his* deputy and other assorted satraps, all of whom could then pride themselves on how well this Swiss watch of an organization was operating under their tutelage. They, in turn, could preen, with seeming nonchalance, before their fellow agency heads and the White House about how they had everything in hand.

Of course, all this good feeling in Washington doesn't address the crisis; indeed, the effort expended by those in the field to feed the Beast has actually been a drag on their ability to do the real work. The entire exercise will have had the critical effect, however, of keeping the Beast happy, perhaps even motivating it to share some small credit with the lowly field hands, at least as an afterthought, and in any case permitting the latter to survive another day.

The usefulness of the video teleconference in this whole scheme was inestimable, particularly in an environment that demanded information on an ever more immediate basis. Cables, after all, took time to write. But by quickly gathering the right audience in Washington for an SVTC, and with a little drama and flair, you could answer all the immediate questions and gain some time to follow up with formal written reports.

Now, in the immediate aftermath of 9/11, when we were in a permanent crisis mode and the Beast was literally insatiable, the SVTC paid for itself almost daily.

As I mulled over all of this, I could see Director Tenet enter, and then just as quickly depart the headquarters screen. The director, the SVTC technician assured us, would be back with us presently. I had the distinct impression, however, that Tenet did not want to participate in this particular confab, and as General Franks grew restless, I could begin to see why. Speaking to no one in particular, the general launched off on a sort of monologue.

"Don't exactly know why I'm here," he began in a flat Texas drawl. "The Secretary said I should come up with a plan. I came *up* with a plan. Thought it was a pretty *good* plan. Briefed it to the President three days ago. The President *liked* it. Then this morning, the Chairman comes to me, and he says, 'Forget your plan. Right now the only plan is George Tenet's plan.' Says I have to see George Tenet to find out what the plan is."

This was my first real exposure to General Franks. He was tall and lanky, with a gray buzz cut, an angular face, and canny, intelligent eyes that crinkled at the corners. He was delivering this little speech in a wry, laconic tone. He didn't seem all that angry, but it didn't take a genius to see he was not pleased. This was clearly someone who liked to hide behind a folksy, self-deprecating manner—at least with people he couldn't control. Thankfully, I fell in that category. My initial impression, confirmed later on, was that while this might be someone who was easy to underestimate, underestimating him would be a big mistake.

"'Course, what do *I* know?" he continued. "It just seems to me like one of the things we learned in Vietnam was that if you have civilians micromanaging your bombing campaign, that's a big mistake. That's what we had in Vietnam. Didn't seem to me like it turned out too well." The general seemed to stop himself for a moment. I got the impression the phrase "civilian control of the military" might have popped into his head. "'Course," he added, "it's fine for them to set out the big picture, the big strategy. But when they start tellin' us, 'You gotta put a bomb on the corner of Doo-Wa-Diddy Street,' it just seems to me like that's goin' too far."

Suddenly, George appeared back in the conference room, where the general no doubt could see him on the screen. His voice trailed away: "'Course, what the hell did *I* know? I was just some dumb grunt standin' in a rice paddy somewhere."

Tenet started off in an energetic, upbeat manner. "General," he said. "I want to introduce you to my station chief in Islamabad." That formality out of the way, he continued, "As you know, we've had some discussions here at the Principals' level, and have agreed on a conceptual way forward in Afghanistan. At the suggestion of the Chairman and the Secretary, I wanted to walk you through our thinking, to ensure we're all working from the same sheet as you put together your battle plan. Bob was instrumental in putting these thoughts together, and so I think it would be best for him to lay it out for you."

General Franks generously allowed as that would be all right. Shortly after I started in, George excused himself, never to reappear. I'm sure he was busy, but his actions spoke volumes: as far as he was concerned, the decision regarding the plan had been made; he saw no reason to waste time convincing General Franks to follow the orders he had already received from Secretary of Defense Donald Rumsfeld and JCS chairman General Henry Shelton. Franks was doubtless going to be testy about receiving "guidance" from CIA, and I think George was just as happy to let me face the music on my own. I was faintly amused by all this; it was the boss's prerogative, after all, and I saw no problem in dealing with the general. I was not subject to his command, and that made all the difference.

In the event, our discussion went very well. General Franks strongly shared the view that Afghans should be in the lead in ground combat, with U.S. forces—especially air forces—in support. He felt that the target sequencing we laid out, focusing initially on "political" targets, also made perfect sense, and could be fully accommodated in the context of the forces and rules of engagement he was going to employ. I acknowledged that although we would want to hold off from immediately striking deployed Taliban units to the extent possible at the outset of hostilities, I also understood that it would be necessary under U.S. military doctrine to attack Taliban air defenses in the first wave, so as to eliminate threats to U.S. aircraft. I reassured the general that we were not recommending that even low-level elements in the Taliban get a pass for long. If we couldn't get traction, in George Tenet's phrase, in generating fissures within the Taliban leadership very quickly, indeed in a matter of days, U.S. forces would have carte blanche to hit any legitimate military targets that could be identified.

All in all, General Franks seemed pleased. We were providing him with the "what"—the intent—of the strategy, and leaving the "how" to him—with just one exception. We spent some time discussing the psychology of the Taliban, and I stressed the importance, particularly in the early stages of the air campaign, of striking our political targets with overwhelming force, as an object lesson to others not yet on the target list. However devastating our initial attacks, I said, they were unlikely to be as bad as the Taliban leadership imagined. I could see the general straighten up in apparent umbrage at that, but at first he said nothing. Briefly reviewing some of the high-profile political targets

we had recommended for strikes at the very outset of the campaign—
to include bin Laden's primary residence compound at the Tarnak
Qila, just southeast of Kandahar; the main al-Qa'ida training center at
Garmabak; and Mullah Omar's residential compound just to the west
of the Taliban capital—I underscored the importance of reinforcing,
not alleviating, the fear which currently was our greatest ally.

"If we give them reason to believe they can withstand the air campaign," I said, "they will quickly conclude that they can outlast, and ultimately defeat us, just like they did the Soviets." Any of the sequential
political targets we hit, I stressed, must be destroyed utterly—and that
went especially for Mullah Omar's compound.

This brought General Franks into full cry: "It'll be a smokin' hole!"
he howled.

Chapter 11

PERFIDIOUS ALBION

I AM AN ANGLOPHILE," my cable began. In fact, I had been an admirer of the British since boyhood, and my inclination in that direction had only been strengthened by my CIA experience. Winston Churchill once described the United States as "an imperial power—in the best sense of the word: That is, they define their interests broadly." At the time, he saw the United States as a junior partner in the business of global dominion. Now, clearly, the situation is reversed. Although their power and their place in the world have vastly shrunk, to me the British remain admirable in part because they continue to see their interests in broad, "imperial" terms. Practically alone among our allies, they are willing to take on responsibility in the world, and not merely to pursue their interests as narrowly defined. I believe it is this common view of our responsibilities, even more than our shared history and heritage, which stands at the center of the "special relationship," and which is responsible for the extraordinarily close ties between CIA and the British.

It was not an accident that the one foreign leader in attendance at President Bush's September 20 State of the Union speech was Prime Minister Tony Blair. Even before the speech, in the immediate aftermath of the catastrophe, a number of senior British intelligence officers, including Richard Dearlove, the head of MI6, traveled to CIA Headquarters to offer their support. I had no idea, of course, what our British friends might have raised in those discussions; but in the last week of September 2001, I began to get strange cables.

First I received a message from CTC/SO, the newly formed Special Operations Group of the Counterterrorist Center (CTC), now being given the primary role in providing headquarters support to CIA operations in Afghanistan. CTC/SO had been briefed concerning the alleged existence of a British-led militia force based in Quetta, which they were willing to place at CIA disposal. With an aggressiveness that foretold much about my future dealings with them, they asserted—asserted, mind you—that a number of paramilitary officers would be coming to my station in order to set up a base in the Baluch capital, from which they would begin to mount paramilitary operations into the south of Afghanistan employing our newly discovered militia allies.

This may sound anodyne to the casual observer, but it was not the CIA way. Headquarters could give the orders and set the objectives, but it was up to chiefs of station in the field to set the plan for how to achieve them. That's not to suggest that a station chief would have carte blanche; he or she would have to make the case for their proposed actions and seek headquarter's concurrence, but the process was always consultative, and the clear tendency was to defer to a COS's superior on-the-ground knowledge—particularly if the COS were a senior officer.

In any case, I had no idea what in blazes they were talking about. I had had a close relationship with a just-departed British diplomat, and I knew from him that the British government was involved in arming, training, and providing operational guidance to a Quetta-based unit of the Pakistani Anti-Narcotics Force (ANF) used to ambush drug-smuggling convoys in Baluchistan, but this didn't come anywhere close to the breathless description I had received from headquarters. The unit in question was not a militia, but part of Pakistani law enforcement. Unless the Paks were about to launch military operations into Afghanistan on our behalf, which they assuredly were not, this unit wasn't going anywhere outside Pakistan. For that matter, if the Paks wanted to invade Afghanistan, this would not be the unit they would send to do it. On the one occasion that the unit in question had crossed the border to attack drug-processing labs, it had been surrounded by a drug militia, captured, and its members sent back across the border minus their weapons and most of their clothing.

I paid a call on my British friend's newly arrived successor. The poor fellow was at a loss to explain these antics, and hardly knew what to say to me. He didn't want to directly contradict what we were being told from London, but in all honesty he couldn't confirm any of it. He admitted there was no independent militia. Not only were the two British advisors to the ANF not hijacking their drug-interdiction unit to lead cross-border operations into Afghanistan, but they had been confined for their own safety to their villa in the Pakistani military cantonment in Quetta, and were about to be withdrawn altogether.

It got worse. I received another cable conveying instructions from the deputy director for operations, my old friend and mentor Jim Pavitt. Following on his recent meetings with our allies, I was to provide all possible support to the British who, in addition to their "militia unit" in Quetta, had a number of impressive operational contacts that could prove of great value to our joint efforts. Details, he said, would be forwarded from London.

The details followed quickly enough. First, our friends claimed to be "in touch" with six named Afghan figures who could be instrumental in toppling the Taliban. Two we knew quite well, and didn't need British help in communicating with them. A third we also knew—and knew to avoid as a flagrant fabricator. As for the other three, we recognized the careful wording of the British claims to be a dead giveaway: it was clear that our British cousins were not actually in contact with any of them. Claiming the friend of a friend of a friend as your "contact" is one of the oldest tricks in the intelligence book, and one to which our British cousins often resorted when they wanted to stake a claim to a potential source and guard against CIA reaching him first. Now was hardly the time for this sleight-of-hand.

The cap to this whole sorry drama, however, was yet another claimed British contact, whom we'll call "Spectre." A senior, respected official, who will remain nameless for his own protection, had recently met for several hours with a wealthy and elderly expatriate Afghan businessman in the Persian Gulf. The old man had spun quite a tale, which the officer in question had apparently accepted uncritically. Glowingly described as a revered and prominent figure, with both religious and tribal authority, Spectre's followers, we were told, would gladly lay down their lives for him. Despite the fact that he had admittedly lived outside Afghanistan for decades, and had no means to communicate with any of his purported supporters—most of whom he had not yet identified to his British friend—he asserted that Kandahar was his for the taking. There were many more boasts along these lines; it was hard to decide which was most preposterous. There was a little wrinkle in Spectre's plans, however: the devotion of his followers notwithstanding, if he were to return on his own to Pakistan, he said, his life would be in mortal danger.

The senior British official was therefore demanding several things from us. He planned to travel to Pakistan on October 2, and wished to meet immediately upon his arrival with the director-general of the ISI. I was to set up that meeting, where I was also to make clear to the Pakistanis that they would be responsible to ensure Spectre's safety while he made contact with his people inside Afghanistan; the ISI's agreement in this regard would be a "test" of U.S.-Pakistani relations.

All this was breathtaking on several counts. Neither we nor anyone we knew in Afghanistan had ever heard of Spectre. The man was an obvious fraud. Many a naive, first-tour diplomat has been initially taken in by a story such as Spectre's, and later felt humiliated at the memory, but for a very senior, respected person to put forward such claptrap on the basis of a single meeting, with no attempt to vet any of the claims made, and then to demand, on top of it, that the United States make support for such an individual a "test" of a critically important foreign relationship—well, it was almost unimaginable. The whole thing would obviously fall of its own weight in due course, but I had no intention of wasting effort and valuable equities with the Pakistanis on it in the meantime. Unfortunately, the British sales job on the seventh floor of my own headquarters was going to make this whole thing extremely complicated and time-consuming to unwind.

All this could not have come at a worse moment. The demands on the station were almost overwhelming. We were thoroughly remaking our tribal reporting networks, taking organizations that had been built for peacetime intelligence reporting and adapting them to provide real-time support to the coming war effort: spotting military targets and making bomb-damage reports. Satellite communications and GPS devices were being pushed out as fast as we could get them to the far fringes of these networks, so that we wouldn't have to wait days and weeks for reports to filter up through the "principal agents" who led them. We had set up a war room, manned twenty-four hours, lined with campaign maps and shelves holding banks of satellite receivers, each of which bore a card identifying the source calling on it, his handler, the language the caller would require, and what response the caller should be given if his handler were not present. Newly trained officers, elderly contract annuitants, anyone Langley could find was being sent on temporary assignment to Islamabad. As non-essential staff were evacuated, carpenters were working far into the night subdividing their vacant offices to accommodate the new intelligence personnel flooding in. Meanwhile, we were feverishly trying to press reluctant Afghan tribal leaders forward to take the fight to the Taliban. Everyone was working punishing hours, seven days a week. I simply didn't have the time to waste on anything that didn't contribute to the effort.

I called the chief of the Near East Division (C/NE), on the secure line to headquarters, pleading with him to intercede with the senior leadership and make all this go away. He apparently had his head handed to him when he tried: his complaints regarding the British were dismissed as the sort of jealous rivalry we could not afford and that would not be tolerated at a time of crisis. In fairness, with U.S. officials caught up in the emotional wave created by these steadfast expressions of allied support, it must have been hard for them to imagine that the British would be handing up half-truths, exaggerations, and outright fabrications in their effort to gain a place at our side.

And so, on September 29, I began a secure video conference with my division chief by assuring him that I was a sincere friend of the British, and doing all I could to foster cooperation during the current crisis. I then went on to catalogue the fraudulent details of what we were being told by London regarding their Afghan capabilities.

That they should in fact lack the ability to do much inside Afghanistan, I said, was no surprise. I had been told some two years earlier that the UK had made a strategic decision to confine its Afghan-related intelligence gathering strictly to al-Qa'ida-related terrorist threats to the home island. In light of scarce resources, the British had had to make hard decisions as to what they would and would not try to cover; internal developments in Taliban-controlled Afghanistan, understandably, had fallen well shy of their threshold.

"Good," he said. "Write it up." When I protested, he cut me off. "Write it up," he said again, beginning with the phrase I had used to start the SVTC: "I am an anglophile." It was a tacit and embarrassing admission that he simply couldn't help me. I was going to have to get this turned off by myself.

But first, I was going to need some insurance. The British demand that we make Pakistani support for Spectre a test of U.S.-Pakistani relations sounded like diplomacy to me, and something far beyond my purview as an intelligence officer. I briefed Ambassador Wendy Chamberlin, who had replaced Bill Milam just a few weeks before, on what was going on. She got it immediately: "Tell them the American Ambassador forbids any involvement by this Mission in support of this British scheme." I thanked her warmly, and left: not a bad thing to have in my pocket, in case I needed it.

On September 30, taking some liberties with conventional format, I sent headquarters a cable entitled "Blood, Toil, Tears and Sweat: [Britain] and the War in Afghanistan." I laid it all out, trying with limited success to keep sarcasm in check. But at the outset, I was careful to detail the extraordinarily close relationship with our British counterparts which I had fostered over the previous two years, even sharing operational information with them. I was prepared, I stressed, to support any British activity that promised even a marginal contribution to the common effort—which pointedly did not include any of what was purportedly being offered to us by London.

The cable must have worked. Late that night of the 30th, I received a phone call from someone with a pronounced British accent indicating that the Spectre initiative was being suspended. There would be no senior British visitor on October 2. It was the last I heard of the whole sorry mess; the last, that is, until several months later, when the senior official involved with Spectre finally did make a visit to Islamabad. I wasn't about to raise any of it. I was embarrassed for him. To his credit, though, he apologized profusely.

I certainly was not a direct witness, and can only speculate as to what caused our British colleagues to temporarily take leave of their senses at a most inopportune time. But on reflection, one can readily see how it happened. Here was the British prime minister, standing shoulder-to-shoulder in solidarity with his friend the American president on the floor of the House chamber, offering any and all support in the aftermath of the greatest one-day calamity to befall the United States since Pearl Harbor. He then turns to his senior subordinates to ask what they can do to help. Putting myself in their place, "Nothing, sir," does not seem like an adequate response.

It is a tired axiom that war brings out the best and the worst in us. The extremes to which people can be driven by the pressures of a sustained national crisis take many forms, as I was beginning to see for myself. The disease was by no means confined to the British. Already, I was noting patterns of behavior in my own headquarters to suggest that my bureaucratic problems were just beginning.

Chapter 12

A DIP IN THE SHARK TANK

OCTOBER 1, 2001

I T WAS NEARLY MIDNIGHT. I was feeling bone-weary. We had already been at it for sixteen hours, and there was no end in sight; bad diet and too little sleep were beginning to take their toll. But as "Dave," my deputy, and I gazed up at the video screen, where images from the Pentagon were coming dimly into view, I could feel the familiar rush of adrenaline: "Showtime," I thought.

I was especially pleased to have Dave with me. In a departure from our routine, he had returned to the office after dinner specifically for this teleconference. Dave had been with me only a few months, assigned as my deputy in midsummer 2001. During the previous year, he had been the deputy chief of the South Asia Task Force in the Near East Division, charged with supporting us in the field. He knew all of our operations when he arrived, and had needed little time to be brought fully up to speed.

More important, Dave had knowledge and experience I lacked, which would be especially significant now. As a junior officer he had been directly involved in supporting the Afghan *jihad* of the 1980s, and had an encyclopedic knowledge of the old *jihad*-era commanders. Apart from those serving with the Northern Alliance, many of these men had since faded into obscurity. Our outreach campaign, begun in the latter half of 2000 in hopes of fomenting an insurgency against the Taliban, had brought us back into contact with a number of them, but they were unfamiliar to me. I knew a great deal about the Taliban and the power structure they had built up since 1994; but with the old commanders now coming into renewed prominence, Dave's first-hand knowledge of these reemerging personalities from the *jihad* days would prove, again and again, to be invaluable.

Dave complemented me in many other ways as well. His jocular, good-natured manner belied a hardheadedly realistic, often cynical view of others' motives. Where I was instinctively optimistic and willing to give others the benefit of the doubt, Dave was always there to point out the potential error of my ways, highlighting the consequences if my appraisals should prove wrong. He was always loyal in carrying out my directives, but for him it was a mark of loyalty to make sure I was looking at an issue from all sides before making a decision. We quickly developed a shorthand communication. He would look at me doubtfully when I would propose bringing someone into the fold and making him a party to one or another of our conspiracies, whether it was some other CIA element, the military, the FBI, the Drug Enforcement Agency, or a foreign intelligence service. "Big tent, Dave," I would say. Dave would shake his head. "My tent's not as big as yours."

He thought I was often ignoring his warnings, and indeed I usually ruled—contrary to prevailing CIA culture—in favor of sharing and inclusion, but his warnings were invaluable to me, and I often hedged my bets in response. A regular glance over the shoulder should be the natural instinct of the intelligence officer, and Dave was there to remind me.

Our differences also extended, fortunately, to our circadian rhythms. When 9/11 plunged us into permanent crisis, my work hours quickly shifted. I tended to be a night owl anyway, frequently returning to the office late in the evening after having dinner with the family and seeing my son off to bed. This tendency became more pronounced after families were evacuated, and particularly given the nine- or ten-hour time difference with Washington. Just as our day should have been winding down at 6:00 PM, Washington would be surging back to life at the start of their day, generating a new wave of immediate demands. I would remain to field them, taking dinner at my desk.

Dave would typically leave the office by 7:00 PM, much to my consternation at first. After a couple of days of this, I was about to bring him in for a closed-door session to sort things out, but just as quickly realized that Dave was absolutely right to do what he was doing. I was naturally staying at least until 2:00 AM, sometimes later, and not getting to bed until three or sometimes four. There was little point in Dave duplicating my efforts. When he left at 7:00 PM, he'd be back in the office at five or six in the morning, ready to review the overnight traffic and cull the most significant pieces requiring action and discussion. These I would find on my desk, neatly stacked and highlighted, when I returned to the office between 9:00 and 9:30 AM, and Dave would have me fully ready for the station ops meeting to make assignments and set the daily agenda at ten. The system worked brilliantly for us, and meant that the front office was typically covered for twenty-one out of twenty-four hours every day.

For me, though, perhaps the greatest blessing of our partnership was Dave's personality. He had a marvelous way with subordinates, able to provide them guidance and deliver sharp criticism when necessary, but always in a way that left them positive and well motivated. It was a rare gift. He was clever and funny, with a keen appreciation for the sheer absurdity we dealt with on a daily basis, whether it involved the quirks of the Afghan mind, the frequent mutual incomprehension of CIA and the military, or the outrages, intentional and otherwise, perpetrated by our own headquarters. Given the hours, the pressures, and the tensions we faced, I found that if we didn't laugh we'd go crazy, which was probably as good an explanation as any for the behavior of Washington, where manifestly no one was laughing.

Now, on the screen above us, I could see George Tenet leaning over to speak into Secretary Rumsfeld's ear, while gesturing in my direction. The participants on the other side were arrayed in tiers, in some sort of amphitheatre. In addition to Tenet and "Hank," the newly appointed head of CTC/SO, the headquarters support unit, I could make out Rumsfeld and, if I squinted, his deputy Paul Wolfowitz. Air Force general Richard Myers, chairman of the Joint Chiefs of Staff, was also present, but I didn't know it. I had no clue at the time what he looked like; in fact, it was his first day on the job. No one apparently felt the need to make introductions.

George invited me to walk the secretary through the war plan approved by the president and discussed with General Franks of CENTCOM a week before. I began by laying out the general concept of what we were trying to do, of employing military means as part of a broader political effort to remove the terrorist safehaven in Afghanistan. The Northern Alliance would necessarily be a part of the new political construct we hoped would follow, but we should be careful at the outset, I said, in providing them with bombing support. Too much progress too quickly in the north would cause the Pashtuns to re-coalesce around Mullah Omar. It was critical for the long term, I stressed, that we have Pashtun involvement in the effort to move Omar aside and change Afghan policy toward al-Qa'ida.

That support, I noted, was slow in coming. Most of the Pashtun tribal leaders and others with whom we were in contact were firmly on the fence, waiting to see if the Americans were serious, and wanting to know who was likely to prevail in a military confrontation before committing themselves. If U.S. airstrikes in the south were sequenced correctly, beginning with targets directly associated with Mullah Omar and al-Qa'ida, and executed with devastating force, it might change the psychology in the subordinate ranks of the Taliban leadership sufficiently to induce them to make a deal. Failing that, our early attacks could embolden independent tribal elements with whom we could treat much more easily, and perhaps induce them to seize the available opportunity to rise up against the Taliban.

Rumsfeld had sat through this exposition unmoved. I paused to get some sort of reaction, or to see if he had any questions. He was apparently unused to having briefers stop without being invited to do so.

"Well," he blurted with some irritation, "do you have anything else to say?" His hostility took me a bit by surprise. It wasn't until considerably later that I would see for myself, firsthand, just how terrified even senior Pentagon generals were of him.

"Well, sir," I replied tartly. "I've just laid out the conceptual outline of what we're trying to do. I could go on to walk you through each phase in chronological order, if that's what you'd like." I paused again. The secretary was apparently used to a bit more deference. He said nothing, evidently unwilling to give me the satisfaction of a response. I simply went on to describe the phases I'd proposed in my cable.

Paul Wolfowitz, deputy secretary of defense, interjected with a question. Was I proposing that we should withhold offensive military support from the Northern Alliance indefinitely? That, too, surprised me. In the plan, I had made an analogy between the current situation of the Northern Alliance and the position the Israelis found themselves in during the Gulf War of 1991. Although themselves the target of Iraqi missile attack, the Americans had impressed upon the Israelis that the most effective contribution they could make to the war effort was to stay out of it, lest their involvement break up the Arab coalition the United States had painstakingly cobbled together to confront Baghdad. Similarly, I said, we should try to keep the UIFSA commanders in the north from moving forward aggressively at the outset of the conflict, lest a U.S.-facilitated offensive from the north cause previously restive Pashtuns to fall in line solidly, once again, behind the Taliban. Knowing that this advice would run sharply against the grain within CTC, and perhaps elsewhere in the U.S. government as well, I had perhaps overstressed it in order to make the point. But I thought I had made it clear that we would know rather quickly whether our political strategy in the south was going to work or not. If not, indefinitely withholding military support from those in the north both capable of striking the Taliban and eager for our help, even if we had been spurned by potential allies in the south, would be more than stupid. At the end of the day, we would have to go with the allies we could get. Was his question a trap? It almost seemed that Wolfowitz was trying to set me up as a straw man, so that Defense could press an alternative approach. I could only guess at what was happening in the inter- and intra-agency shark tank back there.

"Not at all," I said. "As we go through the different phases of the plan, we will try to motivate first the Taliban, and then others in the south, to join the international coalition against al-Qa'ida. But if they fail to do so, and quickly, we will have to throw in with the Northern Alliance and take our chances."

Wolfowitz wouldn't let it go. "Oh?" he said, his voice trailing off. "That wasn't the way I read it."

Early years in the spy game. With Paula and our son Doug, then nine months old, in Nuremberg, Germany, November 1988.

Being inducted into the Senior Intelligence Service by CIA's then deputy director, George Tenet, in 1996.

Matchbook advertising a $5 million reward for Osama bin Laden for distribution in Afghanistan, in 1999. The small Arabic print at the bottom of the cover reads: "Danger—Close cover before starting fire."

Our residence in Islamabad, Pakistan, from 1999 to 2002. It provided a wonderful view of the Margalla Hills to the north of the city.

Pre-9/11 Pakistan. Hiking with Paula and Doug in the mountains of northern Pakistan near Chitral in the fall of 2000. The peaks of the Hindu Kush rise behind us.

Director Tenet meeting in his Langley office with Lt. Gen. Mahmud Ahmed, chief of Pakistan's storied—some would say infamous—intelligence service, the ISI, in March 2000. We would fail to gain his cooperation against bin Laden.

My half of two Pakistani rupee notes torn by Mullah Akhtar Mohammed Osmani, the number two figure in the Taliban, at our meeting in Quetta on October 2, 2001. His portions of the bills were to serve as bona fides for any emissaries he might send me. They were never used.

With Defense Secretary Donald Rumsfeld in my station office after our meeting on November 4, 2001. To the left are Under Secretary of Defense Doug Feith and Michele Sison, the deputy chief of mission in Islamabad.

With Hamid Karzai—third from the right—and five of the six tribal elders who were part of his initial guerrilla force. We met on November 5, 2001, a day after CIA arranged for their evacuation by U.S. military helicopter from Uruzgan Province, Afghanistan, to a Pakistani airbase in Jacobabad. Fourth from the left is "Jeff," my senior reports officer.

A portion of Afghan tribal leader Gul Agha Shirzai's anti-Taliban force immediately after crossing the Pakistan border into the Shin Naray Valley, Afghanistan, on November 14, 2001. Just over three weeks later, they would enter Kandahar City.

At the Peiwar Kotal Pass on the Pak-Afghan border on November 28, 2001. With me are Maj. Gen. "Jafar Amin" of the ISI, fifth from the right; his aide, second from the right; and an escort from the Kurram Militia. Behind us are the Safed Koh Mountains, through which we anticipated bin Laden and his followers would flee the American bombing of Tora Bora.

Fragment of a U.S. bomb which mistakenly fell on the Pakistani border post at Peiwar Kotal. It was given to me on November 28, 2001, as a souvenir by the *khassadar*—tribal policeman—who was nearly killed by it.

"Dave," my deputy, and me getting chummy with Senators John Warner and Carl Levin (on the phone), after providing a briefing on the progress of the war in December 2001. Moments later, Senator Levin would be complaining loudly after tearing his shirt on a weapons crate in the hallway.

View of Kandahar City from the roof of the Governor's Palace, early January 2002. Days before, CIA bomb experts had defused a parting gift from the fleeing Taliban, buried in that earthen roof: twenty land mines wired together and set to fire downward.

Another view from the Governor's Palace in Kandahar. The blue dome of the mausoleum of Ahmed Shah Durrani, father of modern Afghanistan, can be seen through the dust haze; next door is the shrine of Kerqa Sharif, where a cloak said to belong to the Prophet Muhammad (pbuh) is kept.

The outer wall of Mullah Omar's house, surprisingly intact after General Tommy Franks's promise to turn it into a "smoking hole." Second from right, facing the camera, is Haji Gulalai, Gul Agha's security chief, who would later become infamous for his harsh methods. At the far right is Ahmed Wali Karzai, Hamid Karzai's half brother, later to become the "strongman" of Kandahar; he would be assassinated in July 2011.

Sitting with Gul Agha Shirzai on Mullah Omar's bed, early January 2002.

Watching as the 15th Marine Expeditionary Unit is replaced by elements of the 101st Airborne Division at Kandahar Airport, early January 2002. Brig. Gen. James Mattis, the Marine commander, took me to observe the al-Qa'ida militants captured by the Pakistanis just south of Tora Bora, who were then being held at Kandahar.

19

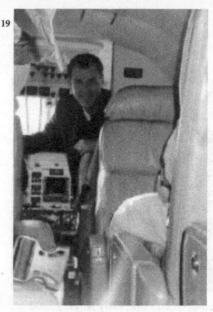

Looking back from the co-pilot's seat of the station aircraft on a stopover at Kabul, early January 2002.

20

Gen. Tommy Franks, Commander CENTCOM, during a briefing at ISI Headquarters, January 2002. In the right foreground is an appreciative Lt. Gen. Ehsan ul-Haq, director-general of the ISI. I'm dressed in mufti, about to depart for North Waziristan in the Tribal Areas.

With General "Jafar," far left, and the commander of the Tochi Scouts at the Ghulam Khan border observation post in North Waziristan, January 2002.

General "Jafar" and me with officers of the Thal Scouts in southern Kurram Agency, January 2002. Behind us is the Kurram River Valley.

The Safed Koh, or White Mountains, seen from Parachinar in northern Kurram, in January 2002. Al-Qa'ida militants, fleeing from Tora Bora, had come through the snowy passes a few weeks before. Some 130 of them were captured by Pakistani security forces.

A graveyard at Arawali, in northern Kurram Agency, where a number of escaped al-Qa'ida detainees were killed by Pakistani *lashgars*, or tribal militias. Women from the local tribes decorated their graves with prayer flags to honor them as *shouhada*—martyrs.

The British-era officers' guest quarters at Miram Shah Fort, home of the Tochi Scouts, in North Waziristan Agency, April 2002.

Inspecting the Saidgi border crossing in North Waziristan in April 2002. In the aftermath of U.S. Operation Anaconda at Shahi Kot, Afghanistan, American concern over al-Qa'ida fighters fleeing into Pakistan was at its height.

My Frontier Corps escort on a visit to the headquarters of the South Waziristan Scouts at Wana, South Waziristan Agency, in April 2002. I was responding to reports of "thousands" of al-Qa'ida militants in the area.

The defile at Shahur Tangi, South Waziristan, site of the famous ambush of a British-Indian Army convoy by the Mehsud Tribe, in 1937. Little has changed since.

A parting memento from our ISI colleagues at the "Clubhouse," presented to me in June 2002. ISI was responsible for apprehending many dozens of al-Qa'ida militants, and would capture many more—contributing a substantial part of the detainee population at Guantánamo.

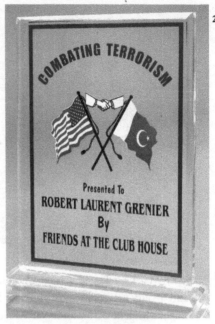

Front and back views of the medal I had struck to present to all visiting temporary staff who aided our efforts during my tenure in Pakistan. The medal was loosely modeled after the Afghanistan Campaign Medal of the Second Anglo-Afghan War of 1878–80.

31

With Maj. Gen. David Petraeus, commander of the 101st Airborne Division, and deputy national security advisor Robert Blackwill at a meeting with Petraeus's brigade commanders in Mosul, Iraq, late November 2003. Blackwill and I were assessing the rising insurgency, and what could be done about it.

32

A view of the Tigris River from Saddam Hussein's compound at Tikrit, his hometown. The compound was headquarters to the 4th Infantry Division, commanded by Gen. Raymond Odierno. Blackwill and I visited Odierno as part of our in-country assessment of the Iraq War in November 2003.

George jumped in. "We'll go through the phases quickly. If we don't get traction on one phase, we move to the next. We expect this to play out in a matter of days." George was always quick on the uptake. You could speak to him in shorthand, and he always understood exactly where you were going.

There was another point I wanted to stress. During the critical period after our air attacks began, Afghans would continue to behave like Afghans. They would operate on their own timetable and in their own way, not ours; and if we hoped to influence them, we would have to calibrate our timetable to suit. If senior elements in the Taliban were tempted to push Omar aside and to change policy on al-Qa'ida, they would have to meet and consult with one another; it would take time, and they couldn't meet in large groups if the leadership were under active air attack. As and when we had intelligence to indicate such a political dynamic was under way, we might want to pause our air operations selectively to give the process time to play out.

At that point, the screen went blank. We'd lost the satellite link. My senior communicator tried to reestablish it, to no avail. As no one called back, I could only assume they'd heard enough from me. But according to Bob Woodward's later account of the event, Secretary Rumsfeld had taken exception to my suggestion of a pause in our bombing operations. It had struck an old nerve with him, suggesting the unilateral bombing pauses staged to encourage negotiations with the North during the Vietnam War, which in the minds of many had made us appear like weak supplicants to Hanoi. There would be no bombing pauses, he said. The two contexts could not have seemed more different to me. I might have tried to explain, but of course I would never know of Rumsfeld's concerns. We are all products and, if we are not careful, victims of our experience. The secretary was famously experienced.

It was hard for me to tell whether this little exposition had gone well or not. The interpersonal dynamics viewed through the keyhole afforded by this teleconference suggested a lot of tension back there, but in the crush of events, no one, understandably, was briefing me on what was going on. I was generally left to guess what effect my input was having in the interdepartmental wrangle taking place as Washington prepared to go to war in Afghanistan.

Apart from Secretary Rumsfeld's curmudgeonly behavior, there had been another discordant note during the evening. At one point, Hank, the new head of CTC/SO, was explaining to the secretary about some of the Northern Alliance commanders, and mentioned that Isma'il Khan of Herat was a Tajik. Without thinking, I contradicted him, pointing out that although aligned with UIFSA and from an area with a substantial Tajik population, Isma'il Khan was himself a Pashtun. It was a blatantly stupid thing to do, publicly contradicting a colleague on a seemingly minor point in front of the most senior officials of the Defense Department. Extreme fatigue is my sole, inadequate defense. And my victim's reaction only underscored for me the idiocy of what I'd done.

"Oh," he said in a slow, deliberate drawl. "I hadn't realized that." It would have been bad enough if I'd been right; but I was wrong. God only knows where I had gotten the notion that Isma'il Khan was a Pashtun, but like so many *jihad*-era commanders, he had faded into insignificance and obscurity during the Taliban years, and was only now beginning to come back into the political conversation. It may seem like a relatively small thing, and for someone else it might have been. I will simply never know to what extent, if any, this little *faux pas* would contribute to our subsequent difficulties. But it certainly didn't help.

My past interactions with Hank had not been unpleasant, at least from my perspective. In fact, one might have thought he owed me a debt of gratitude. I had hosted him, as a mid-ranking CTC manager, during the previous year, and taken him on a tour of the Khyber Pass and some of the wilder spots in the North-West Frontier. Among these was Darra Adam Khel, an infamous village of expert gunsmiths who can produce counterfeit versions of virtually any firearm, from an AK-47 to a high-end Italian shotgun. While there, the ruling *malik*, or tribal elder, made a gift to both Hank and my son of innocent-looking fountain pens. When the nib of the pen was removed, however, it was revealed to be a firearm, from which a 22-caliber round could be fired at close range—the perfect assassination weapon.

As we attempted to board a return flight from Peshawar, Hank ill-advisedly placed the weapon in his carry-on luggage, perhaps thinking it was adequately disguised. It was immediately spotted by the young Pakistan Army trooper manning the X-ray machine, who demanded that Hank's backpack be opened for inspection. This threatened to get ugly: a U.S. counterterrorism official caught smuggling an assassination weapon aboard a commercial aircraft overseas. The fact that we were bloodying the Pakistanis over the laxness of their counterterrorism policies was probably not going to help. Seeing that the culprit was an American official, and not wanting to take the burden of the impending unpleasantness entirely upon himself, the *jawan* (soldier) made a move to summon his superior. This, I knew, could rapidly escalate out of control. Hank had no immunity from prosecution. Praising the young fellow for his perspicacity, I explained the situation, noting that the pen had been a gift from the local tribes, and claiming that its recipient had no idea of its true nature. By all means, I suggested, the offending item was dangerous and should be confiscated, but perhaps it would be best for all of us if we simply left it at that. The young soldier glanced again at Hank's official passport. After a moment's hesitation, he agreed, much to my relief. I would have occasion to wonder if I'd acted too hastily.

Chapter 13

VOX CLAMANTIS

OCTOBER 2, 2001

T HE CONTRAST BETWEEN THE two men could not have been greater. Mullah Osmani sat stolidly, his great bulk supported in an overstuffed chair to my left. In front of me, beaming and impish, sat little Mullah Jalil, perched on the edge of a high bed, his short legs dangling over the side. He was almost giddy with excitement, swinging his black Reeboks to and fro.

The diminutive deputy foreign minister had again been sent by Mullah Omar as an official note-taker for this, my second meeting with Osmani. By this time I was developing a genuine understanding of how Jalil operated. He had thrived in the Taliban system by making himself useful to as many people as possible, always managing to stay in the middle of the action, where he could manipulate the various players to his own ends. A meeting like this was what he lived for. Apart from serving as Mullah Omar's eyes and ears, it was impossible to know how many overlapping agendas Jalil might be trying to serve on this day. What was clear to me, though, was that for me to have any chance of success in this meeting, Mullah Abdul Jalil Akhund must not be a part of it.

Events were hurtling forward. On September 20, the same day that President Bush delivered his ultimatum to the Taliban in his State of the Union address, the Supreme Council of the Islamic Clergy, numbering 700 scholars, had issued its conclusions. It had partially—but only partially—opened the door to an acceptable settlement by recommending that the Taliban government should seek bin Laden's voluntary departure from the country. This was as far as they would go, but it provided an opportunity to the Taliban leader, should he choose to seize it. A day later, on the 21st, Mullah Omar promptly slammed the door shut, stating that he would neither turn over bin Laden nor ask him to leave. If there were any ambiguity on that score, that same day Mullah Abdul Salam Zaeef, the Taliban ambassador to Pakistan, held a press conference in Islamabad designed to remove it.

General Mahmud of the ISI, beginning to despair, made one final effort on September 28, leading a group of eight Pakistani *Ulema*, well-known religious extremists all, to meet with Omar in what Mahmud himself described as an attempt to induce the Taliban to do the minimum necessary "to get the gun to swing away from their heads." If there was nothing for the moment to be done about bin Laden, Mahmud suggested, perhaps the Taliban leader could agree to release the eight humanitarian workers from Shelter Now International, who had recently been arrested for Christian proselytizing; or perhaps he could hand over some of bin Laden's lieutenants; or at least he could allow Americans to inspect the al-Qa'ida camps, to demonstrate that their occupants had fled. All suggestions were in vain.

As the alternatives to all-out war against the Taliban were being systematically foreclosed, I could sense that attitudes in Washington were hardening in tandem. Even a few days before, the tone had been quite different, at least at the White House. The president, who had not yet delivered his public ultimatum of the 20th, had reacted to George Tenet's report of my September 15 meeting—and the implicit possibility of a shift in Taliban policy—with open interest.

"Fascinating," he had said.

Similarly, when my war plan was approved by the president on September 24, he and the cabinet principals still held out the possibility of a continued role for the Taliban, provided its leaders agreed to break with Omar and meet U.S. demands. All, including Condoleezza Rice and Vice President Dick Cheney, agreed that we should not hit the full Taliban leadership at the outset of our military operations, lest we discourage an intra-Taliban split.

Over a week later, though, in the face of Mullah Omar's recalcitrance, I could feel the political landscape shifting. Flying south from Islamabad on a 1980s-vintage twin-engine aircraft which General Mahmud had put at my disposal, peering through the early morning dust haze at the razor-edged mountain peaks of Baluchistan, the utter remoteness and desolation of the surroundings provided an apt metaphor for my situation. I was entering the wilderness. One could sense that in the past few days, as manifested in a dozen subtle ways, all American efforts were now vectoring inexorably toward war. You could see it in the attitudes on display during the teleconference with Secretary Rumsfeld the night before. It was no longer clear to me that Washington would accept any deal, even if an alternative Taliban leadership were prepared to offer one. Once the mental break is made, and war has been deemed inevitable, events take on their own momentum.

Someone with a greater sense of political self-preservation would have dropped this effort entirely. I had at least had sufficient good sense to get George Tenet's prior verbal permission for this meeting, conveyed to me by the chief of the Near East and South Asia Division. In the process I had stressed that my main goal was to induce Osmani to break with Mullah Omar. At a minimum, I hoped to sow serious divisions within the Taliban leadership. I could not rule out greater success, however, and had to contemplate the possibility that Mullah Osmani and the rest of the Taliban *Shura*, the leadership council, would reject Mullah Omar, accept U.S. demands, and find a way to turn bin Laden and his fourteen most senior al-Qa'ida lieutenants over to us in a bid to retain power. That might have been a welcome development ten days before, but I had the sense it might be unwelcome now.

I knew that this mission, no matter how carefully pursued, would carry with it the taint of *negotiation*, the very idea of which had become anathema, from what I could divine of the current climate in Washington. The president himself had said that there could be no ambiguity— you were either with us or with the terrorists—and that his demands of the Taliban were not up for negotiation or discussion. As a practical matter, however, even finding the modalities to meet U.S. demands would require discussion, if not negotiation, and a refusal of all discussions would scuttle any chance of non-military success. However remote the chance of a peaceful conclusion to the crisis, I felt, it should not be cast away lightly. I was haunted by the thought of the disasters that had befallen both the British and the Russians in Afghanistan, and I feared that a similar fate could befall us if we attempted to achieve a political objective using exclusively military means.

I was not concerned about exceeding my authority, per se; I essentially had none, and I knew it. I had no specific instructions, no approved talking points, little guidance other than what I might logically draw from the president's September 20 speech and from the war plan approved a few days later. I had no mandate whatever, beyond the strictly operational one given me by George Tenet. But I saw that lack of guidance as a blessing. At that stage in my career, I had had comparatively little direct exposure to group foreign policy deliberations at the cabinet and subcabinet level, but I had seen enough to have little faith in them, at least on this topic and under the current circumstances. In the prevailing climate, I feared, a request for guidance would have elicited a series of narrow, sterile, and pugnacious ultimatums, which would inevitably elicit a similarly knee-jerk response from the Taliban.

No, I thought: Better to go without talking points. If I could come up with some formula to meet Washington's demands in a way palatable to the Taliban, I could at least present Washington with a clear proposal to which they could respond as they chose. I would have done all I could. Nor was I concerned about reaching a political agreement I was not authorized to reach. I intended to make clear that I had no authority to agree to anything—only a willingness to try to find solutions, which competent authorities in Washington and Kandahar could then accept or reject.

However it might look, my country would lose nothing from what I might do. The worst that could happen would be that I would mislead Osmani and others in the Taliban leadership into thinking that if they broke with Omar and accepted American demands, the Americans would deal with them as a legitimate authority. If the Americans later refused to abide by such a tentative "agreement," the damage to the Taliban's leadership cohesion might already be irreversible, and we would gain great advantage as a result.

No, the United States was not going to lose anything by what I would do that day. The day's only likely casualties would be my reputation and my career, for having had the temerity to elaborate, however tentatively, on the president's stark ultimatum. No matter how remote the chances of success, though, I was not about to see America get bogged down in an endless and futile Afghan campaign, and then spend the rest of my life wondering whether, if only I had had sufficient moral courage, history might have been different. Against that dire possibility, the potential sacrifice of my career seemed a paltry price to pay.

The ISI had arranged for me and Tom to meet with the Afghans in a villa normally used as sleeping quarters by their own officers, located in the old British Cantonment area of Quetta. When we arrived, we could see that the villa was small and ill-suited to our needs. The only place where we could hold a meeting with even minimal privacy was in a bedroom. In the few minutes before Osmani's expected arrival, Tom and I shifted the furniture around to make a small seating area around a low wood table. I arranged to have Osmani to my left and Tom to my right; I had no intention of making room for Jalil.

The idea of keeping the proceedings secret from the Pakistanis might have seemed ludicrous. There had been no way to avoid their playing host to the meeting, and thus they had been able to choose the venue. Given that this was clearly not a normal meeting area, and given that most organizations do not spend money to plant permanent bugs in temporary quarters used by their own officers, it seemed likely to me that if they wanted to monitor our meeting, they would have to use what we referred to in the business as a "quick-plant" transmitter. Having placed one or two of these myself, I looked under every piece of furniture, searching for the telltale signs; I found none. The most obvious and simple candidate was a small handheld radio buzzer placed on a nightstand, used for summoning the tea-boy. I had seen such devices in ISI facilities any number of times. I had no way of knowing whether it had been tampered with, but in a surfeit of caution I disassembled it, removed the battery, and muffled it in a drawer in the bathroom.

When at last Osmani made his entrance, Jalil swept inside in his wake. Seeing no chair, he hopped up on the side of the bed, and waited expectantly.

"Haji Mullah," I began, using Jalil's Taliban nickname. "I am very sorry." I went on to explain, falsely, that I was under strict instructions from Washington to deliver my message directly to Mullah Osmani, and to no one else. As much as I would wish to include him in this meeting, I simply had no choice but to ask him to leave. Shocked and crestfallen, Jalil looked desperately to Osmani for support. Mullah Sa'eb looked on impassively: Jalil would get no help from that quarter. At length, the gnomish cleric hopped down from his perch. Head bowed, he limped slowly and petulantly from the room.

Meetings conducted with a translator usually fall into a formal, stately, almost Victorian rhythm, and this one was no exception. I would speak a paragraph at a time, and then wait as the translator conveyed what I'd said. If there is an advantage in that, it is that you have ample time to formulate arguments while your words are being conveyed. When receiving the response, you can devote full attention to the speaker's body language and expression, and wait for the words to arrive later. Such meetings thus often take on the deliberate cadence of a chess match.

This one started with a rapid exchange of moves. I began: "The *Ulema* have stated that bin Laden should leave Afghanistan, but Mullah Omar has rejected this. In effect, he has declared himself an enemy of America. Will the rest of the Taliban join him as declared enemies of America?"

Osmani saw where this was going, and jumped ahead: "You won't be able to replace the Taliban with oppositionists," he said.

"Look," I countered, "only Afghans can make a permanent solution for Afghanistan. The United States will be able to chase the terrorists away, but without a responsible Afghan government, they can come back. If the Taliban is willing to be that government, this will be acceptable to us; but if not, war will inevitably come, and Afghanistan will again experience the chaos of the early 1990s. Your enemies will return. No one knows how it will turn out. All that is sure is that it will be a disaster for Afghanistan, and the end of the Taliban."

Waving his hands for emphasis, the outsized mullah launched into a long string of excuses. "Bin Laden," he said, "has become synonymous in Afghanistan with Islam. The Taliban can't hand him over publicly any more than they can publicly reject Islam. Neither Omar nor the rest of the *Shura* like the Arabs; they want to cooperate with America, they do, but public threats from the United States have aroused the people and boxed the leadership in politically. Besides," he complained, "Omar has made a public commitment to bin Laden; he can't simply renounce it now. He would like to be rid of this man, but his hands are tied. In fact, Omar sent a messenger to bin Laden five days ago; he reminded Osama of the *Ulema*'s decision that he should leave the country. 'You must deal with them,' he said."

Osmani went on: "I can track Osama down and kill him if you like, but I can't use my own troops. That would be too public; my role would be known. For that, I have to find outside operatives. This will take time," he ended.

I shook my head. "Washington will see this as a delaying tactic," I said. "They might have listened to this months ago, before 9/11, but it's too late now. The United States is preparing for all-out war as we speak. If you want a risk-free solution, you won't find it. If you want to save the Taliban and your country, you're going to have to take risks."

Osmani's voice took on a desperate tone: "Your threats have created big problems for us. Afghans are reacting emotionally . . ." His voice trailed away.

I cut him off. "What's done is done. If threats have been made, they can't be unmade. There's no point in trying to change the past. The point is to find a way to save Afghanistan."

The big man paused, and slumped lower in his chair. He had been speaking rapidly and animatedly, but he suddenly looked very tired, played out. There was nothing left to say. He removed his turban, and put it aside. Looking down, he said: "Then you suggest a solution."

This was the opportunity I'd hoped for.

Years before, while planning a potential military coup in Baghdad, I had read *Coup d'État: A Practical Handbook*, by Edward Luttwak. In it, Luttwak lists the sequential steps that traditionally must occur for a coup to succeed. I could see them as a checklist in my mind as I spoke.

"Mullah Sa'eb," I began. "You are the second-ranking member of the Taliban. You are widely respected; you have great power and influence. You command the Taliban forces in and around Kandahar. Only you can save your country. Omar, by your own admission, is bound by his pledge to Osama. He will fall as a result, and he will take the Taliban with him. But you are not bound by such a pledge, nor are the other members of the *Shura*. *You* can take the actions necessary.

"First," I said, "you must rally your troops and seize control of all key government buildings in Kandahar, as well as the principal roads and intersections. Anyone in a position to resist you must be placed in detention. First among them must be Mullah Omar. No one is suggesting he should be harmed," I cautioned, "but he cannot be allowed to communicate with anyone. Your most important objective," I went on, "is to seize Radio Shariat, the voice of the Taliban, and to make an immediate announcement. You must tell all Afghans that you are acting at the direction of the *Ulema*. It was they, after all, who put Omar in power in the first place; he has refused their direction, and now you are forced to seize power to obey their dictates. You must declare that the Arabs are no longer welcome, and demand the departure of al-Qa'ida from Afghanistan.

"Immediately thereafter, you must move against bin Laden. He and those around him will resist violently, and will have to be killed. No one will have to know that you have done this; the Arabs have many enemies. The other Arab fighters, having heard your decree and learned that bin Laden is dead, will get the message: they will flee. As for the fourteen Arabs on the list I have given you, they must be captured and quietly given to us. Again, once they have turned up in American custody, no one need know how they got there. With so many Arabs fleeing, many will assume that they were captured in neighboring countries.

"I understand that this will carry risks for you. But you have already told me you don't care about your own life. This is your opportunity to save your country."

I added one final point: "You should know that we can give you anything you need to get this done." The implication, which the Mullah clearly understood, was that I was prepared to give him large sums of money. He would not rise to the bait.

"I won't need any assistance," he said.

The commander began to mull over what I'd said, reacting aloud. He had no problem taking the quiet actions we demanded against bin Laden and the fourteen others. But why did he have to make a public announcement expelling the Arabs?

I explained that the change in Taliban policy to deny safehaven to the Arabs would have to be announced publicly to be effective. Any specific actions they took to implement their policy and to meet our demands, however, could be kept secret, so long as we could see the results.

My promises of secrecy were not quite so ridiculous as they might appear now. Afghanistan at that point had no cell phone system, no international phone service of any kind outside of a handful of government-controlled lines into Pakistan, and no independent media. The country was nearly opaque to the outside world.

Ideally, I knew, Osmani should have moved against bin Laden and the other fourteen *before* publicly announcing the break with al-Qa'ida, which would only alert the Arabs. But this was Afghanistan. I knew that any attempt to arrest bin Laden and the Arabs, even if made in good faith, would not be efficient, quick, or clean. And word of Osmani's arrest of Mullah Omar and seizure of Radio Shariat would spread quickly among the senior Taliban commanders; it would have to be explained in the context of saving the country from the abuses of the Arab foreigners. Better to get the public announcement first. Once made, it couldn't be walked back; it would disrupt the Arabs; and it would probably create massive dissension and confusion within the Taliban, which would create opportunities for us, both political and military. Those would be the most achievable goals. If we got bin Laden and the others in the bargain, so much the better.

"All right," he said. "But if we change our policy on bin Laden and al-Qa'ida, why can we not let the other Arabs remain as refugees?"

I was becoming exasperated, and let it show. Pashtuns are supposed to be xenophobes, after all, and Osmani perhaps more so than most. "Why do you want to invite trouble from the whole world for the sake of a handful of Arabs?" I was waving my arms for emphasis. "Rather than worry about a few Arab refugees, why don't you concern yourself with the millions of Afghans who have been refugees for years?" The big man laughed, and shook his head slowly.

"You are right," he said.

I warmed to the subject. "Look," I said. "We realize we made a big mistake when we abandoned Afghanistan after the Soviets left. We will not make this mistake again. For a friendly Afghan government willing to oppose the terrorists, the United States will provide massive humanitarian relief. We will assist the Afghan refugees to return to their homes." I was not entirely making this up. A few days before, Condoleezza Rice had journeyed across the river for several hours of briefings on Afghanistan. She had described the post-Soviet abandonment as a mistake, and had asserted we would remain engaged in Afghanistan for the long term.

By now, Osmani was grinning and nodding. "This is very good," he said. He reiterated the one overt and the two covert elements of the plan. "I will bring your proposal to Omar."

I nearly fell out of my chair. This was not where I was going at all: the proposed actions had been for Osmani, not Omar. I hadn't seen this coming. Still, I thought, reflecting quickly, in the unlikely event Omar agreed and actually followed through, it would be all the same to us.

I summed up where we were: First, I stressed, however one might describe what we had done, this was not a negotiation. President Bush's demands remained as stated; what we had agreed was a possible way for the Taliban to meet those demands. Second, as neither of us had been empowered to reach a binding agreement, we would have to seek the approval of our respective masters. Third, we would need a dedicated means of secure communication—secure, at least, from the Taliban and the Pakistanis. Finally, and most important, I said, fixing my hulking friend with a stare, if Omar should refuse this proposal, as in all likelihood he would, it was up to Osmani to step in, seize power, and do it himself.

The Mullah looked at me with apparent resolve. "I will do it," he said.

In an instant, the tension of the previous three hours was cut. Osmani suddenly seemed buoyed and happy, as though a great weight had been lifted from his shoulders. He rose to his feet and folded me in a Pashtun man-hug, left arm over my right shoulder, right arm gripping me about the waist. Over the next several minutes, I gave him an Inmarsat, instructing him in its use, and we agreed on time windows when we would be available to speak. At his suggestion, we ripped a pair of Pakistani bank notes, each taking half: these would serve as bona fides if either of us were to send an emissary to the other. Afterwards, we fairly marched together out the door and down the hall, where we were joined by Jalil and "Brigadier Farid," our ISI host, who had arranged a huge lunch of mutton and rice.

Despite the volume of food, such lunches are usually quick affairs, with little conversation. I watched closely as Osmani ate happily, and with great gusto. When we had finished, he got to his feet. Abdul Salam Zaeef, the Taliban ambassador to Pakistan, would be flying down from Islamabad later that day. Osmani and Jalil would remain in Quetta to receive him, and the three would then travel by road to Kandahar the following morning, October 3. Again I pressed Osmani to respond to me quickly, on October 4 if at all possible. Again the burly man embraced me as though I were a long-lost brother, and turned to leave.

When we arrived at the Quetta airfield, I was informed that General Mahmud would arrive presently to accompany me on his aircraft. I had turned down his offer of the previous day to accompany him to Quetta, where he would be meeting with Taliban foreign minister Wakil Ahmed Muttawakil. He had offered to arrange a separate meeting for me with Mullah Jalil's boss, but I had had no interest. There was too much to do, and I could ill afford to waste a day. By all accounts, Muttawakil was a comparatively decent fellow, but it was my assessment, based on our intelligence, that he had no influence with Omar or the rest of the senior leadership. He was a mere factotum, given the thankless task of trying to present the Taliban to the West in the most favorable, or least negative, light possible. He had no independent political power base, and commanded no troops. He would be useless to me—though not to Mahmud, who shared the Taliban envoy's public relations goal of somehow deflecting the Americans from their current path.

As I surveyed the area, my attention was immediately drawn to the far side of the field, where a slim, distinguished-looking gentleman with a full beard was standing with a small group. He towered over the others, but what most drew my eye was the distinctive turban he wore. The headdress was highly unusual in this context, and yet seemed vaguely familiar. As he slowly ambled across the field, it occurred to me: despite his age, the gentleman was wearing a Quranic student's turban, of the sort frequently worn by bin Laden himself. Given the deference he was shown by others, I thought he must be some local notable.

By this time, Mahmud had arrived, and he joined me to wait as the technicians did their final checks on the aircraft. Looking up to see the tall gentleman's approach, he addressed me with a flair. "Bob," he said. "This . . ."—he paused for effect—"is Imam." The old man had the playful, avuncular face of a clever grandfather; his eyes registered satisfied amusement as a look of surprised recognition came over mine. Colonel Sultan Amir Tarar, the infamous "Colonel Imam," was a longtime operative of the ISI's Afghanistan section. He had distinguished himself by his service with the Afghan *mujahideen* during the anti-Soviet *jihad* of the 1980s, and had gone on to function as a liaison between the ISI and the Taliban during the latter's rise to power in Afghanistan. Most recently, he had been the Pakistani consul general in Herat, a suitable position through which to maintain links with Afghanistan's leaders and, presumably, keep a watchful eye on what the Iranians were doing in western Afghanistan. Now, with the apparent imminence of hostilities, Colonel Imam and his ISI colleagues were being withdrawn; he had just arrived in Quetta after having traveled overland from Herat and Kandahar.

Imam had long been distrusted by the Western powers generally. For him, work with the Taliban was not just a matter of statecraft but of personal passion: he had long shared the extremist Islamic ideology of his clients. For those claiming that the ISI could never be trusted and was in thrall to "rogue" elements, Colonel Imam was exhibit A. I could not have been more pleased to meet him.

Throughout the long ride to Islamabad on the prop-driven airplane, Imam and I bantered back and forth as he told stories of the *jihad* in excellent and colorful English, and I plied him with questions about the various *mujahideen* commanders. I found the old warrior marvelous company. When I called attention to the distinctive pin he wore on his waistcoat, he identified it as the insignia of the Special Services Group, the special forces of the Pakistan Army; he removed it and presented it to me with some ceremony. "But you must never wear it," he said with some misgiving. Well aware of the strict military admonition against wearing an award or designation one has not earned, I laughed and assured him that he had nothing to worry about.

The sun was setting as we rolled to a stop at Chaklala Airbase in Rawalpindi. Barely pausing for goodbyes, Imam rushed off the plane to join a ragged group of airport workers who had spread out in a field just off the tarmac for the *magreb* prayer. I would never see him again. Well understanding that the retired ISI annuitant could not be trusted under the circumstances, the ISI leadership sent him home for the duration of the First American-Afghan War. When, a number of years later, I learned that he had been called back to duty, it was clear to me what that meant for Pakistan's policy toward the Afghan Taliban.

Imam would meet his demise in January 2011, in a field in the South Waziristan tribal agency. His public execution was presided over by the head of the so-called "Pakistani Taliban," Hakimullah Mehsud, himself since killed, reportedly, in a U.S. drone strike. Having tried to mediate between the government of Pakistan and the religious fanatics who had turned against it, Imam was ironically taken hostage and eventually murdered by those whose extremist cause he had long championed. He stands as a symbol and a stark reminder of the fate that waits in store for all those who would use religious extremism as an instrument of policy. He may finally stand as a poetic symbol of the Pakistani state itself.

Chapter 14

A FALL FROM GRACE

H E WAS NOT THE prototype of your typical CIA officer. "James" wore his long hair tied back in a ponytail. I had known one or two young officers in the recent past whose dress and body ornamentation hinted at an extracurricular lifestyle confined to weekends and carefully shielded from colleagues, but James was quite unabashed. Had he been a case officer, his eccentricities would probably have been written off as a somewhat unusual manifestation of a common psychological profile among his peers: extreme independence, inner-directedness, and a confident self-regard bordering on narcissism. But James was a reports officer. Gentle and mild-mannered, one would hardly have branded him an egotist; still, an independent spirit and a benign indifference to social expectations were doubtless assets for a young, first-tour male breaking into a field long dominated by women.

I sank to one knee by his chair, so that we could speak without disturbing the others, clacking away at their keyboards in the reports officers' bullpen.

"I want you to take the lead on this debriefing. From now on, you're the SNI Referent. You're to follow all the traffic, and I'm going to direct anyone with information on the detainees to make sure it gets to you: maps, locations, diagrams, everything. This is yours." It was a heavy responsibility to place on the shoulders of a young man with a few months' experience. Lives, including those of two Americans, might depend on him as a result, but he was smart, thorough, and I knew I could rely on him. He had absorbed too much of the agency's understated professional ethos to show it, but I could tell he was pleased and excited.

In early August 2001, eight members of the German-based humanitarian NGO Shelter Now International (SNI) had been taken into custody by the Taliban in Kabul on suspicion of Christian proselytizing. Among them were two young American women in their twenties, Dayna Curry and Heather Mercer. There were very few Americans in Afghanistan, and the plight of these two, suddenly subject to the medieval brutality of the Taliban penal system, quickly gained the attention of high-level American officials in both Islamabad and Washington.

This was no ordinary consular case. Apostasy is considered a crime throughout the Muslim world, and for the Taliban, it was a crime punishable by death. Woe betide any Afghan even suspected of having been converted to Christianity. The likely sanction to be meted out to those non-Muslims alleged to be the agents of such waywardness was less clear, but certainly something one would wish to avoid.

At first, I strongly doubted their guilt. Given the obvious dangers involved in spreading Christian faith in Taliban-dominated Afghanistan, I thought it most unlikely that the SNI arrestees would have been so naive as to attempt it. Other religiously based NGOs active in the Muslim world are careful to confine their activities to humanitarian relief. No, it seemed to me far more likely that the arrests were the product of rumors, Taliban paranoia, and a general Afghan distrust of foreigners. Surely the charges against them would not withstand serious scrutiny.

David Donohue, the consul general in Islambad, was a tall, angular man in his forties, a mild-mannered and rather patrician New Englander. He and I had a constructive professional relationship, though our duties seldom brought us into contact. Paula and I got to know him and his wife socially through a local hiking club. Though he was always unfailingly friendly and polite, I still sensed a slight wariness in his dealings with me. I had the distinct impression that he was not entirely comfortable with the CIA. Imagined or otherwise, such diffidence on the part of State Department colleagues was neither uncommon nor, given our secretiveness, difficult to understand; I certainly didn't take it personally.

David moved quickly to engage Atif Ali Khan, a competent, Pashtu-speaking Pakistani lawyer with knowledge of *sharia*—Islamic law—and experience in Afganistan. Ali hadn't been on the case in Afghanistan very long before the evidence against his clients was revealed to him: to our chagrin, materials on the SNI detainees' computers made it clear that they were, indeed, seeking to convert Afghan Muslims to Christianity. This was going to make their situation infinitely more difficult. It is always easier to plead innocence of an alleged infraction than to contest the justness or validity of the law in question, and arguing for religious tolerance with the Taliban was a losing proposition. At that point, official efforts shifted further in favor of politically inspired pleas for clemency, rather than legal defense.

In August and early September, some form of clemency seemed a good bet. The Taliban were not entirely unmindful of their international reputation, even if they frequently acted as though they were. Already heavily sanctioned through the United Nations for harboring Osama bin Laden, their global stock had reached an all-time low as a result of their destruction of the so-called "Bamian Buddhas"—two monumental statues, the larger of which some 150 feet high, carved in the sixth century into a sheer rock cliff in the Bamian Valley, and officially listed as a World Heritage Site. The Taliban dynamited the statues as pagan idols in March 2001, claiming it a religious necessity to do so, despite protests from around the world and contrary religious rulings from some of the globe's most eminent Islamic scholars. A wave of international revulsion followed. If there were a time when the Taliban might be induced to make concessions to world opinion, this appeared to be it. As of September 4, our intelligence indicated that Mullah Omar was leaning in favor of trying the SNI detainees in court to establish their guilt (and thus justify their arrest), and then releasing them as a humanitarian gesture. On September 6, Francesc Vendrell, the UN secretary general's personal representative for Afghanistan, met with Mullah Jalil on the matter. Jalil gave clear indications that he was trying to work out some arrangement that would provide a public relations boost to the Taliban.

All that changed following the events of September 11. With the United States threatening to go to war, it was clear that U.S. policy regarding bin Laden and al-Qa'ida was not going to change in deference to the SNI detainees; and with the Americans set to attack no matter what the Taliban did about the detainees, it was unlikely the Taliban would release them. In his State of the Union speech of September 20, in an obvious reference to the detainees, President Bush included in his list of demands of the Taliban that they "Release all foreign nationals, including American citizens you have unjustly imprisoned. . . ." But that exaction would not come into play unless and until the Taliban first turned over bin Laden and the rest of the al-Qa'ida leadership. When General Mahmud's September 28 plea to Omar for the detainees' release elicited no response, the ISI chief held a separate meeting with Mullah Jalil to press for action. Jalil gave his best spin, suggesting there would soon be a two- or three-day trial, followed by the detainees' expulsion. His optimism was unconvincing. By the time the American bombing started, it was clear to us that the only way the detainees were going to be freed was if someone bought them out—or forcibly took them.

The eight—four Germans (three women and a man) and two Australians (one woman, one man), in addition to the two American women—began their incarceration at the Dar ul Tudib Reform School, but by late September they were moved to a prison controlled by the Taliban's General Intelligence Directorate located near the Iranian Embassy and the office of the UN High Commission for Refugees. We hoped against hope that they would stay in one location long enough for us to gather the intelligence necessary to support a rescue effort.

In early October, we got two big breaks. First, one of my case officers made a terrific recruitment of an Afghan source with regular access to the General Intelligence prison. Thanks to "Isfandiar," now we could be sure of the detainees' location and monitor their condition, while incrementally building a detailed picture of the facility where they were being kept. The second break came from an unexpected quarter. A friend at the British High Commission called to say that one of their nationals, a female journalist, had recently been incarcerated and then quickly freed by the Taliban, and was available at the British High Commission in Islamabad. She had had direct contact with the female detainees, and had briefly shared their spaces at the General Intelligence prison. This was the opportunity for which I mobilized James, telling him to work in tandem with "Marco," the senior JSOC liaison officer assigned to work with us. Marco understood precisely what a hostage rescue team would need to know, and so could guide our intelligence-gathering efforts.

We would soon learn just how exacting JSOC's planning process was. If a target facility has a staircase from the ground to the second floor, JSOC will want to know how wide the opening is, and whether a trooper with full gear will fit through. They will want to know how many stairs there are, and the height of the risers, so they will know how many stairs to take at a stride as they enter. If there is a door at the top, they will want to know whether it opens to the left or to the right, the position of the latch, and whether it is likely to be locked.

Marco and James found the British journalist to be quite remarkable: She had an absolutely photographic memory. By the time they finished, they had extraordinary detail on the entire facility, including the physical layout, the external security posture and procedures, the numbers of guards posted during the day and at night, where they stood, where they slept, and where they kept their weapons. Everything that we could corroborate with satellite photography and through Isfandiar checked out. Marco came to me.

"When we train, we never give ourselves this much information," he said. "This is more than we would ever have a right to expect." Now JSOC could begin to put together a serious rescue plan. A mock-up of the prison would soon be constructed in North Carolina, and a commando team designated to train on it.

Chapter 15

THE WAGES OF SIN

S HE WOULDN'T SAY MUCH, and she didn't have to. Her tone of voice said everything. Nearly twenty-four hours had passed since I'd reported on my second meeting with Osmani, and I'd made a secure call to the front office of the Near East Division to get a read on the reaction from the seventh floor. It was obvious that the deputy division chief didn't want to talk to me.

"You'd better talk to [the Chief]," she said. I knew the drill. She wasn't going to take the responsibility to pass the bad news to someone more senior than she. Still, I wanted to get a better idea what was coming.

"Look," I said. "Surely they don't think I've somehow abused my authority." She wouldn't take the bait.

"You'd better talk to the Chief," she repeated.

The night before, immediately after my late return from Quetta, I'd sat before my computer with an important decision to make. "Officers," it is said, "seldom suffer in their own dispatches." I feared that this dispatch might prove the exception. There were two paths I could take: One would be to provide a minimalist account of my conversation with Osmani, focusing on my attempt to induce him to launch a coup against Omar. That way, if he came back later with an offer to implement a deal, either on his own behalf or Omar's, I could simply present the offer to Washington without a lot of unhelpful detail about who had initially proposed what. On reflection, though, this path, in addition to being disingenuous, was fraught with peril. Depending upon future developments, it would invite detailed questions later about what Osmani and I had actually discussed. My failure to report fully at the outset might bring no end of recrimination. No. It would be better to lay it all out, in full detail. Some at headquarters might not like it, but at least it would answer all their questions preemptively. And in any case, I was absolutely convinced I had done the right thing.

The finished product came to over ten pages. In my comments at the end, I made a number of predictions. First, I said, there was little doubt that Omar would reject the offer being conveyed by Osmani. As for the chance that Osmani would lead a coup, his apparent resolve at the end of our discussions and my own high hopes notwithstanding, it was unlikely he'd do it. The problem, I opined, was not a lack of toughness or decisiveness; he had both. Nor did I think his devotion to Mullah Omar was completely unqualified. But after eight hours of conversation, I felt I had some insight into the man. The problem with Osmani, I concluded, was that he simply lacked imagination. In the cold light of day, and without external encouragement, I didn't think he could see himself playing a larger role than the one he currently occupied.

Still, I went on, we had to be prepared for unexpected success, which would carry problems of its own. The demanded public announcement of a break with al-Qa'ida would be straightforward: either Osmani would do it, or he would not. The attack on bin Laden and the arrest of the others, though, would not be so easy, even if attempted in unambiguously good faith, which was highly unlikely. Bin Laden had been making himself scarce, and might take time to track down. Many of the fourteen al-Qa'ida members we had under indictment were actually rather obscure, might not be well known to the Taliban as they tended to remain segregated, and might be difficult to find. We would have to be prepared to set deadlines, and hope that our arbitrariness was not working against us. Our Taliban interlocutors would doubtless seek more time to delay a military strike. Nonetheless a coup against Omar would probably create fissures within the Taliban that would cripple their ability to defend against the hoped-for U.S.-Afghan coalition against them.

In any case, I concluded, even if he did not move against Omar, the link with Osmani could prove useful to us in the early stages of a military campaign. He was primed for our planned message that we were attacking al-Qa'ida and its known supporters, not the Afghan nation. Even if he wouldn't take action beforehand, the outbreak of hostilities might yet spur Osmani to take the steps we wanted, particularly if Omar were killed early on. In those circumstances, he would be far more open to our influence than he was presently.

When he called me back, the Near East Division chief wasted no time in letting me have it. "Do you know what the Director said when he read that cable?" he fumed. "He said he wished he hadn't read it. . . . That should have been a two-page cable; instead, you've sent ten. . . . There may be some things you say to get someone to cooperate, but you shouldn't have put it in cable traffic." I found that last bit particularly offensive.

"So now we have to be politically correct in our internal operational traffic?" I thought. "Was I sounding too sympathetic to the Taliban for them?" If that's where we were going as an organization, I wanted no part of it. I was already seeing growing evidence that they were losing all professional objectivity back there, getting swept up in the emotional tide, and it wasn't pretty.

"Listen," the chief went on. "You're a very good chief of station. You need to get out of the policy business, and get back to your job." There was more than a little irony in this. Years before, during the First Gulf War in 1991, the chief had dealt with a senior Iraqi official, and had had a similar opportunity to sow dissension among the enemy. The official had asked the chief's guidance; lacking policy direction, he had declined to provide it, demanding instead to know what the official intended to do on his own. Ultimately, the Iraqi had concluded that he was being entrapped, induced to make statements opposed to Saddam's regime so that he could be blackmailed. He had stalked off. Some would have said that the chief's cautious approach was the correct one; but this story had stuck with me over the years as a prime example of the cost of timidity. The chief was a good guy, a highly respected senior officer, one who had been something of a mentor and model to me in my junior days. In this instance, though, I had no intention of following his example.

"They're trying to figure out how to respond upstairs," he went on. "You'll get a cable tomorrow." I had been running on adrenaline for days, and now I suddenly felt exhausted, almost beyond caring. There was little point in arguing; I wasn't going to overcome a lifetime of professional caution with a few one-liners. And besides, he wasn't the one I needed to convince; it was the seniors upstairs.

"And for God's sake, get some sleep," he concluded.

"What a good idea," I said.

OCTOBER 4, 2001

"Ref[erenced] cable received a mixed reception at Headquarters," the response began. That was rather more positive than I had been led to expect. It went on to state that if the Taliban leadership responded positively to my overtures, headquarters would be prepared to put their proposal on the table for policy consideration. A decision, it cautioned, might be days in coming. The tone of the message made it clear that headquarters did not relish the potential opportunity to make such a proposal, and that no one in the policy world would welcome having to decide how to respond in such ambiguous circumstances.

More than thirteen years later, having incurred nearly 15,000 casualties and having spent hundreds of billions of dollars, with the United States heading for the exit after a textbook exercise in imperial overreach, it is a little hard to sympathize with those concerns.

Later that morning, I pulled Dave, my deputy, aside. "There's no way my career will survive this war," I said.

"You're wrong," he said. "You're just overreacting."

"Oh, this latest dustup might not do it," I said. "But I'm not going to change the approach I'm taking, and there's no way I'll survive when this is over. It will come down on my head; no one else's. But just remember you heard it here first." It was actually a liberating feeling, to know that you were finished. If I'd had any inclination to pull my punches before, I had no such inclination now.

Later that day, I briefed Wendy Chamberlin on what I was up to, and made the same point.

"Hah," she snorted. "The people at your headquarters are just jealous. I've been jealous of you myself. Just ignore them." I could have hugged her.

OCTOBER 8, 2001

I looked up to see Tom leaning breathlessly through the doorway. "He's on the line!" he said. I didn't have to ask who.

Following our meeting in Quetta on the 2nd, Mullah Osmani had called me on October 6. As translated by Tom, he told me he'd met with Mullah Omar, who had a message to convey. According to Omar, the emotions of the Afghans were running very high. "That again," I thought. Nonetheless, Omar would make some announcements soon. Of course, he could not make the announcement we had demanded of him right away, as he would have to calm the Afghan people first, due to the American threats . . .

"Mullah Sa'eb," I began. "There is no time for this. Omar will not carry out the demands; Afghanistan will be destroyed. It's up to you to seize power, as we discussed."

There was a long pause.

"I'll think about it," he said. Would he consult first with potential supporters? "No," he replied. He would consider what to do on his own. After some back-and-forth, he agreed to call me by noon the following day—October 7.

That was the day, I knew, when the first American strikes would be launched. Mullah Omar's compound was at the top of the target list. The day passed without the promised call; late that night, Afghan time, the first aircraft and cruise missiles struck their targets in and around Kandahar and Kabul. Our tribal networks had been working overtime to provide precise geocoordinates for the bombs.

Even before Tom's announcement of the Southern Zone commander's 10:00 AM call on the 8th, we had already received initial reports from our best source in Kandahar. Omar's compound had been struck by several cruise missiles. Guards and several people in the one-eyed leader's household, including his uncle, had been killed, but Omar himself was narrowly missed. He had left the compound just thirty minutes before.

Not long into the conversation, I pointed out that I had warned this would happen. Osmani began shouting and Tom, without a glance at me, began shouting back. "You see? It's just like we told you! You will not even see them!" This was getting completely out of hand. I grabbed Tom's arm, causing him to look up, startled, as though I'd shaken him awake.

"Calm down," I said evenly. Tom returned to translating. I asked Osmani if he'd given more thought to my advice.

"I can't speak now," he said; "I'm very busy." He hung up. I knew precisely what occupied him. We had just received another report indicating that the Taliban *Shura* had concluded that the Americans would invade Afghanistan by sending an army westward to attack Kandahar along the main road from Quetta. Osmani, as the Southern Zone commander, had been charged with constructing defensive positions east of the city.

Later that evening, I received yet another call, this time from Jalil. "Everyone is in an uproar," he said. It was obvious to Jalil that the initial attacks from an unseen enemy had left senior Taliban officials "quite afraid," as he put it, but no one would admit it. And although most of the senior Taliban leadership had been quietly hoping that Omar would take the decision of the *Ulema* as an excuse to expel bin Laden, they were not admitting that now, either. At this point, in the face of foreign attack, he said, the Taliban leadership could only back down through the intercession of some third party, like the Organization of the Islamic Conference. In any case, the leadership had scattered to separate locations; no one wanted to meet as a group for fear of attracting an airstrike. They could communicate by "wireless," of course, but to actually reach a consensus within the *Shura* on a new course of action they would have to meet together to confer face-to-face, and at length: "You know how we are."

I did indeed. I wrote up the conversation as a formal intelligence report, making clear that the source, whom I could not identify by name, was both uncontrolled and hostile, and that his comments were meant as much to influence as to inform. Nonetheless, much of what he had to say rang true to me. In a separate comment in the report, I noted that while the source's remarks were clearly self-serving and that he hoped to see a halt to the airstrikes, the scenario he described, of Taliban officials being culturally incapable of making group decisions unless able to meet face-to-face, contained a large measure of truth.

But none of that mattered. The time for diplomacy was over. Now the logic of war would have to run its course. The political structure of Afghanistan, such as it was, was about to be smashed. The ultimate success of our venture would depend upon creating a new one, and neither I nor anyone else had the slightest idea what it would look like.

Chapter 16

SON OF KINGS

THERE WAS ANOTHER OBSERVER of the initial American airstrikes in and around Kandahar, a surreptitious one. Hamid Karzai, having arrived in Kandahar Province by motorcycle with two companions just the day before, was keeping a low profile. His discovery by the Taliban would have meant a swift and violent death.

Months before, in the spring of 2001, as we were laying the foundations for what we hoped would be a tribal uprising, a small number of my officers had been charged with meeting multiple Pashtun tribal leaders known to oppose the Taliban. We wanted to assess their ability and their willingness to actively undermine the mullahs in Kandahar, in the event we received a presidential order to try. Particularly as these were Afghans, we'd paid little attention to their claims—which invariably exaggerated their influence and the numbers of loyal fighters they could put in the field—and had focused instead on what they could demonstrate on the ground. Though we lacked the authorities necessary to take military action against the Taliban, at that stage we didn't need them. If a contact claimed large numbers of followers in various locations willing to do his bidding, we wanted to see that demonstrated through verifiable intelligence gathering and dissemination of propaganda, before we ever had to consider whether to turn these people loose to generate armed mayhem.

Hamid Karzai had been but one of these tribal leaders, and by no means the most promising at the time. Educated and urbane, fluent in many languages, Karzai was a prominent member of the so-called "Rome Group," which had formed around Muhammad Zahir Shah, the former Afghan king, driven into exile in 1973. Hamid was a well-known proponent of religious tolerance and multiethnic unity among Afghans. As such, he played well in the diplomatic salons of both Europe and South Asia. There also was no denying his family and tribal pedigree: grandson of a respected Afghan politician and son of a notable tribal leader, he was now the preeminent elder of the Popalzai, a prominent tribe of the Durrani Pashtun tribal confederation. Durranis had been kings of Afghanistan since the mid-eighteenth century.

Still, I had my doubts about him. He had been a Pakistan-based fund-raiser and administrator during the anti-Soviet *jihad*, with few if any credentials on the battlefield. Whatever his political attractions and abilities, he certainly didn't seem like a warrior. What did most distinguish him was his burning desire to drive the Taliban from power. The Taliban had killed his father, gunning him down on a street in Quetta on July 14, 1999, just after my arrival in Pakistan. A month later a massive truck bomb exploded just outside the outer wall of Mullah Omar's compound in Kandahar, killing several members of his household. There was never any evidence connecting Karzai to that attack, but the Taliban were convinced he was behind it. They had even tried to have him extradited from Pakistan shortly before 9/11, and had plotted to murder him in the event they were refused. "By their enemies," it says in Christian scripture, "ye shall know them."

Once in direct contact with him, we quickly came to realize that beneath the Pashtun's smooth, regal manner lurked a considerable amount of anger and resentment—and not just toward the Taliban. Hamid deeply resented the fact that the United States had abandoned Afghanistan after the Soviet withdrawal, and had apparently been content to see it fall under the sway of Taliban brutality. "Where have you been all this time?" he demanded. Make no mistake: this was not a man who would ever be a "controlled" source of the CIA. But to achieve his political goals in Afghanistan, he would need American help; and we would need his, or that of others like him, if we were to achieve ours.

Serendipity and luck play far larger roles in our lives than many of us are prepared to admit. Having established preliminary contact with a large number of Afghan commanders, it was necessary to spread out responsibility for vetting them among a larger number of officers. Given his isolation from the main body of the station, I was keen to have "Greg," one of my dispersed "base chiefs," the head of a small unit subordinate to me as station chief, thoroughly integrated into this effort. My assignment of Greg as Hamid Karzai's contact was arbitrary. I'm sure I had good reasons for making this particular decision at the time: I just can't remember what they were. In any case, fate would reveal it to have been an inspired choice, and no less so, I would contend, for having been inadvertent.

On the surface, they made a very odd pair. As smooth and polished as Hamid was, Greg was blunt and profane. A tough, wiry paramilitary specialist with an outrageous Fu Manchu and an even more outrageously ironic sense of humor, he did his best to hide an incisive intelligence beneath multiple layers of self-deprecation. Also hidden beneath that flinty exterior, though, was a rather thin skin, and a sensitive soul.

Paramilitary specialists in the Clandestine Service are a wary and misunderstood breed. Chosen for their military knowledge and abilities, they live within an organization in which people are generally valued for an entirely different set of traits. Most receive a measure of espionage training, but for them it is almost always an underdeveloped, secondary skill. They consider themselves warriors, but are not allowed to be real soldiers. Normally called upon to provide training and guidance to irregular, indigenous forces, or to serve as a liaison between U.S. Special Forces and CIA spies, they have a foot in both camps, but are generally not fully accepted in either.

Greg was among the relative few in his tribe who excelled in both intelligence and paramilitary operations; but the same could not be said for all those paramilitary specialists who clambered to join his team after I'd approved his nomination as base chief. He took strong exception when I tartly pointed out that I was looking for intelligence officers and not gunslingers to join him, and so I went out of my way when he arrived in the field to cultivate him. It was time well and amusingly

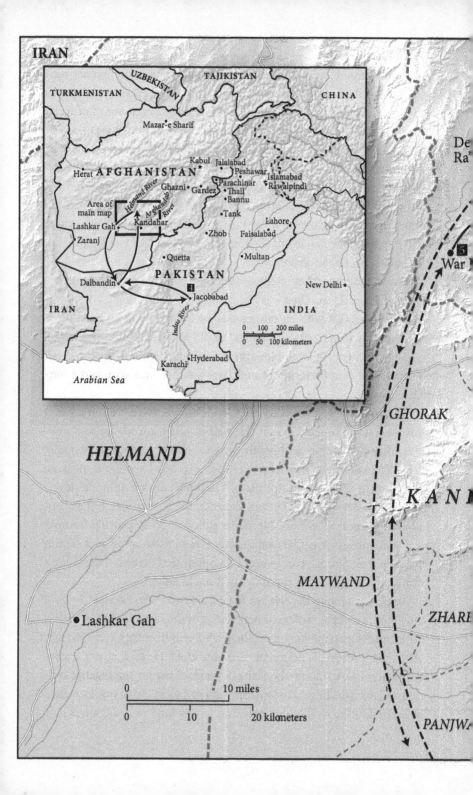

IRAN

UZBEKISTAN TAJIKISTAN

TURKMENISTAN CHINA

Mazar-e Sharif

De
Ra

Kabul
Herat **AFGHANISTAN** Jalalabad
Peshawar
Ghazni Gardez Parachinar Islamabad
Thall Rawalpindi
Bannu
Area of
main map
Lashkar Gah Kandahar Tank
Zaranj Lahore
Zhob Faisalabad
Quetta Multan

PAKISTAN
Dalbandin New Delhi
Jacobabad
INDIA

0   100   200 miles
0 50 100 kilometers

IRAN

Karachi
Arabian Sea Hyderabad

War

GHORAK

HELMAND

KAN

MAYWAND

•Lashkar Gah ZHARI

0   10 miles

0   10   20 kilometers

PANJWA

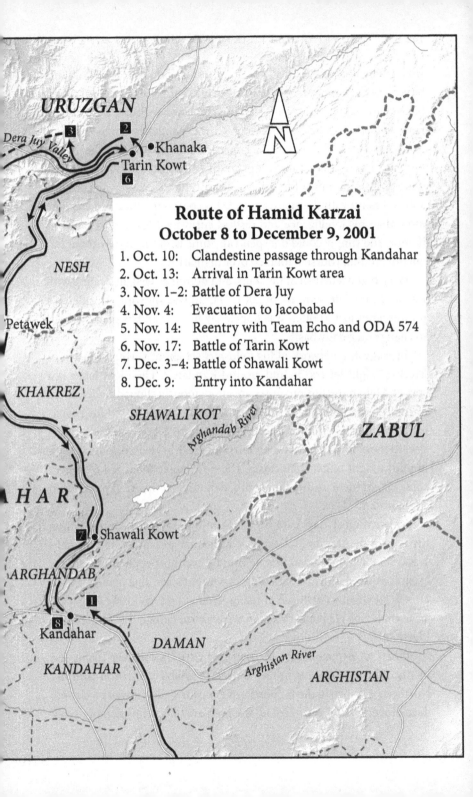

URUZGAN

Dera Juy Valley

3

2

● Khanaka

Tarin Kowt

6

N

NESH

Petawek

Route of Hamid Karzai
October 8 to December 9, 2001

1. Oct. 10: Clandestine passage through Kandahar
2. Oct. 13: Arrival in Tarin Kowt area
3. Nov. 1–2: Battle of Dera Juy
4. Nov. 4: Evacuation to Jacobabad
5. Nov. 14: Reentry with Team Echo and ODA 574
6. Nov. 17: Battle of Tarin Kowt
7. Dec. 3–4: Battle of Shawali Kowt
8. Dec. 9: Entry into Kandahar

KHAKREZ

SHAWALI KOT

Arghandab River

ZABUL

H A R

7 ● Shawali Kowt

ARGHANDAB

1

8

Kandahar

DAMAN

Arghistan River

KANDAHAR

ARGHISTAN

spent. Greg and I developed a bond traipsing about the gun shops and bazaars of old Peshawar, and hoisting drinks late into the night at the fabled Khyber Club. Socializing with our spouses, we found wry camaraderie as the husbands of sharp-tongued, independent women who were distinctly underwhelmed by the supposed brilliance of their husbands. I found in Greg an avid student of South Asian history, and a gifted linguist. Within months of his arrival at post, he was bantering comfortably in Pashtu with the guards outside his compound. But perhaps even more than his intelligence and restless curiosity, I learned to value his humor. You simply could not spend any time with the man without frequently finding yourself doubled over in hilarity.

Greg had needed all of his skills, and humor as well, in dealing with Karzai. In the late summer of 2001, Hamid was showing considerable promise, but just as often was hopelessly mercurial. His plans seemed to change on a daily basis.

In August, a network of his followers set about surreptitiously delivering "night letters" in and around Kandahar. The night letter is a sort of Afghan institution: notes are anonymously slipped under doors or tossed over compound walls in the dark of night. Used for propaganda or intimidation, its effects are insidious. It conveys the impression to those in power that their enemies are everywhere, moving with impunity right under their noses. Hamid's people managed to deliver some 800 of them during the month, denouncing the Arab presence in Afghanistan.

By late August, days before 9/11, Hamid was already contemplating his return, perhaps to Helmand or Kandahar provinces, the primary seats of Taliban power, so that he could direct his people more closely. Greg counseled him against doing so without a sensible plan, but even after 9/11, when Greg began pressing Karzai to return inside as quickly as possible, the elements of a plan were excruciatingly slow in coming together.

When on September 26 the ten-man CIA "Jawbreaker" team, led by my old friend Gary Schroen, arrived to establish a liaison with the Northern Alliance in the far northern Panjshir Valley, it was a welcome development, but it ratcheted up the pressure on us considerably. Gary was making a start at reinforcing the capabilities of the Taliban's fierce ethnic rivals in the north; that meant all the more that we needed to get something going in the south, although that would be a far greater challenge. Beset though they might have been, the Northern Alliance had large, established, relatively conventional armies equipped with tanks and heavy weapons; they still controlled substantial amounts of territory in the north. Gary and his team faced considerable hardships and dangers, certainly, but nonetheless were able to operate in relative security behind friendly lines. In the south, it would be completely different. Any teams we contemplated inserting there would be behind *enemy* lines, operating as guerrillas in an insurgency mode.

Having had responsibility for the past two years for all of Taliban-controlled Afghanistan, the task in the south naturally fell to me. CTC, though a headquarters support organization, had jealously retained control of our contacts with the Northern Alliance in past years, and now insisted that Jawbreaker, and any other teams in the north, would report directly to it. This was an anomaly: normally, one would have expected our contacts with the Northern Alliance to have been maintained by an overseas CIA outpost—perhaps in Central Asia. But there was no such outpost there on a par, in terms of influence or bureaucratic heft, with Islamabad. The normally desk-bound headquarters case officers in CTC were able to assert primacy in the north in a way they never could in the south. Thus, the CTC-vs-Islamabad, Northern Alliance-vs-southern strategy dynamic, which had arisen in the spring of 2001 through differences of opinion as to how best to exert pressure on the Taliban, was now being further reinforced.

Before 9/11, we had hoped for a Presidential Finding that would permit us to encourage, fund, and support a Pashtun insurgency against the Taliban; the finding never materialized. Now, within days of the attacks in New York, Pennsylvania, and Virginia, we had all the authorities we could possibly want or even imagine; and an administration that previously would not be railroaded into fomenting armed action on the part of anti-Taliban Afghans was pressing us breathlessly to do just that, as quickly as possible.

Night after night, in the days and weeks after 9/11, my officers had been meeting with tribal leaders, former Pashtun warlords from the *jihad* era, and representatives of some currently serving Taliban commanders. Each morning they briefed me on the myriad excuses they had received for inaction. Even after the U.S. air campaign started on October 7, the bottom line was that most of these self-regarding warriors were not about to declare themselves against the Taliban, and take the risk of attempting to rally their respective tribes, until they had a better idea of how this fight would turn out. In a land where internecine warfare was endemic, you learned to pick your fights carefully, and generally entered only the ones you were relatively assured of winning.

The Taliban commander of a base which housed a training camp for al-Qa'ida fighters actually had the temerity to send word via a courier that he had defected "secretly," and was "with us in his heart." We sent back word that until he did better than that, he would be considered an enemy subject to attack. Another encounter, between a Dari-speaking officer and a very well known but now aging senior commander who had distinguished himself against the Soviets, particularly sticks in my mind. The officer was young, slender, soft-spoken, almost effeminate in manner. After an hour or so of polite conversation, during which he heard and diplomatically rejected a long list of excuses, the officer finally lost his temper. Rising to his feet, he stood over the grizzled old warrior.

"You call yourself commander? You're no commander—you are a coward. You are not even a man; you are a woman! You are a disgrace to your tribe!"

He went on in this vein for some time, and these were the more polite words he used. In fact, the impact of what he said actually suffers in translation from the Dari. I winced as he recounted it. To any self-respecting Pashtun, these were fighting words, cause for an all-out blood feud. But the old commander had just sat there, head down, and taken it. He simply did not want to risk ending up like Najibullah, the former Communist president of Afghanistan, who had been castrated, dragged behind a vehicle, and hanged in public when captured by the Taliban.

Given our lack of progress with others, Greg had been under all the more pressure to get Hamid back inside Afghanistan. Still, plans kept changing. On September 30, Karzai told Greg he had hit on a plan to go to Ghor Province in the west. There he could receive assistance from Isma'il Khan, the Northern Alliance commander whose base of strength was in Herat. He would then make his way east and south to his tribal area. This plan, too, fell through.

Sometime during this period I had received a direct call from Hank. He underscored the importance of getting CIA teams formed on the Jawbreaker model matched up with cooperating Afghans in the south. I told him I couldn't agree more, that he could see from the cable traffic we were pressing every likely candidate we could find. We had particularly high hopes for Karzai, I said, but in the end, as stipulated in the war plan, success would depend on the willingness of Afghans to confront the Taliban. I was confident that southern anti-Taliban leaders would emerge, but in the meantime I would not make promises I didn't know I could keep. To that point, neither of us had told the other anything he didn't already know.

Then Hank suddenly went off in a new direction. Did I think Karzai would be willing to work closely with Isma'il Khan if the latter were able to move forces down from Herat? This was entirely speculative, as the old Herati commander had not yet returned to his base of support. I replied blandly that Khan would not be able to operate very effectively outside his traditional tribal area, but that certainly he and Karzai got on well; Hamid had even briefly considered trying to stage from Khan's area. Hank was noodling something, but I had no idea what— that would become clearer later on.

On October 1, looking ahead to what we hoped would be the imminent arrival of Karzai in Afghanistan, we had sent a cable providing our initial thoughts on when and how an American team should be dispatched to join him. Although CIA had taken the lead in the north with Jawbreaker and only been joined by Special Forces later, we believed that we should have Special Forces with us at the outset in the south, where we would be operating behind enemy lines. The ability of professional military operators to provide laser guidance to aircraft flying in close combat support would be critical, as would our ability to extract a team that suddenly found itself *in extremis*. We should only contemplate bringing Americans in to join Karzai, we said, when he had rallied a sufficient number of fighters to hold territory and defend a landing zone. Our thinking was very much influenced by Greg, but the truth was we were all making it up as we went along.

Now that Karzai had at last returned to his homeland, we would have to see what he could do, before doing very much ourselves. That was the plan I had advocated initially, and I saw no reason to change it. The American war against the Taliban, I remained convinced, would have to be an Afghan war, albeit American-supported, if the Americans were to have a hope of ultimate success.

Chapter 17

NO RETURN

I CALLED JALIL AT 10:00 AM. "Where is the Commander?" I asked.

"Mullah Sa'eb will call you in one hour," he replied. In the two days since the start of our air attacks, the Taliban gadfly had been doing what he did best. As the leadership could not convene as a group, he was visiting them individually, trying to see if there were any common sentiments he could exploit. In addition to Osmani, he had called on Mullah Akhtar Muhammad Mansur, the influential minister of aviation, and the governors of Kandahar and Herat. It seemed that he was probably trying to put together a coalition to convince Omar to change course. "If I can sit with my friends . . . We can consult . . . Maybe they will decide something," he said. He didn't sound hopeful.

At eleven fifteen, Osmani called. "Our situation is very good," he said. "The people are standing against your bombing. But the people of America will also be hurt."

"We are avoiding innocent people," I said. "We are only harming those who harm us, and those who protect them."

"No, innocent people have been martyred. You are responsible."

Several times, I tried to raise our past conversations, to discuss what we might do together to change the situation. Each time he rebuffed me.

"You are not going to get anything by force," he said. "We can't do anything while your attacks continue. If they stop, then we will talk. I am very busy. In two days we will talk again."

It was the last time we spoke.

Chapter 18

SON OF THE LION

T HE FIRST THINGS YOU noticed were the feet. They were gigantic. From my current posture, sprawled on a stone floor, Haji Gul Agha Shirzai's feet dominated my field of view as he paced maniacally across the wide sitting room in a billowing white *shalwar khameez*. Next to me, sitting cross-legged, was Gul Agha's American-educated uncle, Engineer Pashtun. Perched close by on the divan and leaning forward intently were "Mark," whom I had assigned as Gul Agha's CIA contact, and "Greg R," a young Special Forces Army captain, who had been sent to aid us with our military planning. A large map of southeastern Afghanistan was spread before us, on which the Engineer was making very precise markings.

Pashtun had prepared carefully for this briefing. He set forth his campaign plan in crisp military fashion, describing complicated feints, lines of attack, and blocking actions. According to Pashtun, their fellow Barakzai tribesmen across the line in Afghanistan had provided them with considerable intelligence concerning fixed Taliban positions, troop strengths, and armament throughout the area extending from Spin Boldak on the main Quetta-to-Kandahar highway, north for 100 miles or so along the Afghanistan-Pakistan frontier, and west to Kandahar City.

War, I knew, had been the family business for many years. Gul Agha's father, Haji Abdul Latif, though a humble teashop owner in his late sixties at the outset of the Soviet occupation, had taken up arms against the foreigners and fought them throughout the decade of the

1980s. He was by far the most successful and revered commander in the southern region, popularly referred to as the "Lion of Kandahar." Gul Agha, his eldest son, had been his principal subcommander. When Abdul Latif died in August 1989—thought to have been poisoned by his enemies—his son took the honorific "*Shirzai*—Son of the Lion." It was how he preferred to be addressed, and how he referred to himself. No sooner had he greeted me in his home than Shirzai pulled out a large pile of photographs. With Engineer Pashtun translating, he provided me with a sort of rough photo journal of the war against the Soviets in the south. Many of the pictures were of a broadly smiling Gul Agha, surrounded by his brothers and his clansmen, posed in front of various pieces of wrecked or captured Soviet equipment.

After the collapse of the Communist government in 1991, Gul Agha rose to become Governor of Kandahar from 1992 to 1994. He had the dubious distinction of being the first provincial governor ousted by the Taliban. Fleeing to Pakistan with his closest kinsmen, he had quietly nursed his grudges in Quetta, waiting for the opportunity to return. Now, it seemed, his moment had come.

As Pashtun continued with his briefing, he indicated where Shirzai's main force proposed to cross the Afghan frontier. From there, he said, Shirzai would immediately divide his force, sending one unit south to block any Taliban advance from Spin Boldak. The remaining fighters he would subdivide again, independently striking fixed Taliban positions farther north before reunifying them for a direct assault on Kandahar. It struck me as a plan worthy of Stonewall Jackson or George S. Patton, but it hardly conformed to my notion of Afghan warfare, or of the likely capabilities of Gul Agha's fighters. Pointing to a large Taliban unit equipped with tanks which appeared to have been left intact to his rear, I inquired how Shirzai would propose to deal with it.

Pashtun responded without a moment's hesitation. "Oh, your air force will take care of those." I glanced up at Greg and Mark.

"If you are expecting help from the U.S. Air Force, I would suggest you coordinate with these young men very carefully."

Throughout the Engineer's exposition, Gul Agha was hardly even an observer. He would try to sit quietly as Pashtun explained the plan in

English, which he could follow only with difficulty. Every few seconds, he would leap to his feet, and recommence his rapid pacing. He would pull at his hair, cover his head with his hands, and cry out in Pashtu.

"Oh, oh! I can't stand it! I can't eat! I can't sleep!"

Engineer Pashtun looked at me. "He's been like this ever since the bombing started. He's been waiting for this for many years." As the Engineer went on to explain, Shirzai was determined that this opportunity would not pass him by. In the preceding weeks, he had been gathering together trucks, tents, and medical supplies, staging them in different compounds around the Quetta area so as not to attract too much local attention. Weapons were more difficult to come by in bulk, but he had assigned various family members to make limited purchases around the area, again so as not to invite undue scrutiny. Couriers had been sent to various Barakzai clans across the border to begin mobilizing their support. It was obvious to me that these were people who understood the process and logistics of a military campaign.

I also knew Langley would not be enthusiastic about Gul Agha. His time as governor in Kandahar had not exactly left him covered in glory. While there was little direct evidence of serious personal misdeeds, he had clearly been unable, or perhaps unwilling, to control the excesses of others. But there were few good alternatives. As the American bombing campaign moved forward, and as pressure increased on CIA to come up with a revolt in the south, Pashtun warlords and tribal leaders were not lining up to declare war on the Taliban. Here was a man, whatever his limitations, who had the political standing, the tribal pedigree, and the military experience to lead an uprising in the Taliban homeland. Unlike Hamid Karzai, he had been a successful field commander during the anti-Soviet *jihad*. And if there were any questions about his motivation, they had been erased, at least in my mind, that night. The only question was: Did he have the capability to follow through? There was only one way to find out, and no alternative but to try.

Chapter 19

"AS FLIES TO WANTON BOYS . . ."

WITHIN A COUPLE OF weeks of the twin intelligence breakthroughs on the Shelter Now International detainees and the General Intelligence prison where they were being held, Marco reported that JSOC was well along in its planning to take down the site and secure the prisoners. Once there, I had no doubt that JSOC could successfully assault the facility and rescue the detainees. That left serious questions about how they would get to and from the place. Attacking the prison by helicopter was out of the question, they decided: it would make too much noise in a dense urban area and provide too much advance warning of their approach. Instead, they would land an aircraft in a stretch of desert, disgorge vehicles, and drive into the city to approach the prison on the ground. Once secured, they would then drive the detainees to an assembly point in a field just outside of town where helos could briefly touch down. The JSOC operators wanted to leave as little to chance as possible: Concerned about minefields and Taliban checkpoints, they wanted moving imagery of every foot of the driving route. We arranged to procure a nondescript vehicle so that JSOC could outfit it with videocameras which could operate through the headlights, and came up with a pretext for a source to drive the intended route at night, unaware that he was on a filming expedition. By late October, we were getting close. We might have a realistic opportunity, we thought, in a matter of days.

The two Americans' parents—Dayna Curry's mother and Heather Mercer's mom and dad—had arrived in Islamabad to be close by, and to do what they could to support diplomatic and legal efforts to free their daughters and to provide them whatever moral and physical comfort the Taliban would allow. Ambassador Chamberlin hosted them at the residence.

To our great surprise, we were informed by headquarters that Heather's father, John Mercer, was a former CIA case officer who had retired under cover. This, of course, was an extremely sensitive piece of information, which might have complicated the detainees' situation to no end if it were revealed to the Taliban. It was not feasible for us to tell the parents about the clandestine efforts under way. John was a possible exception, and although I wondered slightly at the propriety of providing him with information which would be denied to others, it seemed to me a positive thing for us at least to provide some comfort to the one person we could. With headquarters' blessing, we made discreet arrangements to get John into our station spaces in mid-October. I spent the better part of an hour with him, and briefed him in general terms, at least, on the efforts we were making, and our growing confidence that we would be able to mount a rescue effort in the coming days.

I did not mention to him two other potential rescue efforts in which I had little confidence. The first involved the ongoing efforts dating from Gary Schroen's arrival in the Panjshir to arrange a ransom or bribery deal through Northern Alliance intelligence chief Engineer Aref. Aref worked on a number of such initiatives, perhaps the most promising of which was through the Taliban's deputy interior minister, Mullah Mohammed Khaksar. Khaksar appeared to be particularly well placed to work a deal for the surreptitious release of prisoners held by the Intelligence Directorate, which he had previously led. I was highly skeptical, though. The SNI detainees had gained a great deal of notoriety; arranging their "quiet" release did not seem likely, particularly as there would inevitably be a dauntingly large number of people who would have to be party to the conspiracy—any one of whom could sabotage the arrangements. Even if they were successfully freed, exfiltrating the detainees from a prison in Kabul across an active fighting front to the Northern Alliance side was going to be dangerous, and could easily have gotten the detainees killed. Nor did I think the connection between Aref and Khaksar particularly significant: Afghans were infamous for talking while fighting—it's the Afghan way, not unlike what Mullah Jalil was doing with me. We monitored developments closely, ready to intervene if we thought Jawbreaker might be about to allow Northern Alliance intelligence to take what we considered unwarranted risks with the detainees' lives, but said nothing in the meantime. Negative kibitzing on our part would have been seen as parochial-minded advocacy of our own efforts, and we didn't want to squander our credibility unnecessarily.

Far more troubling was a message we received from Berlin. The Germans, we were told, were making arrangements with some cooperating Afghans in Kabul to attempt to free the detainees, and wanted to coordinate with us. A group of what they described as "Pashtun clan members" working at a Kabul hospital had hatched a plan to bribe the guards and free the prisoners. We sent the Germans a series of questions: What was the hospital workers' tribe? What were their links, tribal or otherwise, with the guards? How many guards were involved? What was the status of their negotiations, and what specific arrangements had been made for a transfer? Once they acquired them, how would they spirit the detainees out of Kabul, and where would they go? The answers were not reassuring. First, much of what the Germans' Afghan contacts had reported about the prison we knew to be inaccurate. As for the identities and affiliations of the Pashtun hospital workers involved, the Germans only knew that they were from the same clan— did it matter which one? And as for the plan, the clan members, they said, were prepared to free the detainees "in an Afghan way." That's precisely what we were afraid of.

We shot back immediately: The Germans should be reminded that there were two American lives at stake here, and strongly discouraged from taking any action without consulting fully with us in Islamabad. We had our own intelligence initiatives under way, and needed to be sure we were not working at cross-purposes. We would be pleased to meet with their local representatives or anyone else, but we absolutely had to confer face-to-face with those responsible for this operation.

A few days later, Dave and I found ourselves looking at a very young visitor from Berlin. Accompanying him was a rather wild-looking middle-aged German. I had heard of this fellow, but had never met him. From the way the young man introduced him, it was unclear whether he was a government employee or some sort of co-optee; I suspected the latter. It would be fair to say that his comments and demeanor did not suggest a high degree of professionalism.

The young fellow, at least, seemed sensible enough, but was obviously in way over his head. He was dealing with his Afghan contacts at long distance—he did not specify the means of communication—and he obviously knew little about Afghanistan or its culture. The clan members' plan, such as it was, was to drive a van to the front gate of the Intelligence Directorate at night and attempt to reach a financial deal with the guards for the detainees' freedom. They would need a significant amount of cash for the purpose. If their attempt at bribery failed, they would simply shoot their way inside, grab the eight detainees, and make good their escape. They would then drive out of the city, avoiding roadblocks and firing on anyone who attempted to stop them.

It did not take any particular genius to suggest ways in which this plan might go badly wrong. I simply could not believe that sensible people would actually propose such a scheme. Dave and I left our guests in no doubt as to what we thought of the plan, and made clear we could not support it in its current form. We suggested some tangible steps they could take to begin to vet the identities and capabilities of their contacts. They accepted the advice quite meekly.

I followed up with an immediate message to headquarters, urging them to approach the German government at whatever level they thought appropriate to make clear that we opposed what they were proposing to do, and that we would hold them responsible for any harm that might come to Americans if they were to take action on this basis. It was the last we ever heard of it.

With all the progress we were making, and all our good fortune to date, I was beginning to allow myself some measure of optimism.

But late October brought devastating news: after weeks of effort and planning, and on the verge of mounting a rescue mission, we learned from our source Isfandiar that all eight detainees had been moved to another prison. A few days later he was able to clarify that they were in fact being shuttled back and forth between the Intelligence Directorate facility and the new prison, frequently but not always spending the night at the new location, and then returning during the day to the Intelligence Directorate. All our planning was predicated on a nighttime raid, and we could not be sure in advance where the detainees would be on any given night. Beyond its location, we knew next to nothing about the new prison. We were practically back at square one, starting over. It was a crushing disappointment.

Shakespeare's *King Lear* contains a lament at man's impotence in the face of unknown forces that control his fate: "As flies to wanton boys," he says, "are we to the gods. They kill us for their sport." The detainees themselves, being devout fundamentalist Christians, doubtless had a much more benign notion of the forces controlling their fate than did I. But whatever one's notions of the Deity, fate held many more surprises in store for the detainees, and for us.

Chapter 20

THE AMBUSH

OCTOBER 27, 2001

I COULD SEE THAT this would be no easy meeting. "General Jafar Amin," counterterrorism "Czar" of the ISI, sat glowering on a couch at the far end of the long, narrow salon, a grim-faced "Brigadier Adnan" by his side.

The story, by now, was well known. A few days before, on October 23, Abdul Haq, a famous *mujahideen* commander from the anti-soviet *jihad* of the 1980s, had left Peshawar and crossed into Afghanistan in an attempt to organize a tribal rebellion against the Taliban. According to press reports, he had entered with fewer than twenty followers, hoping to garner support among his fellow Ahmedzai tribesmen in the Azra district of Logar Province. There he had a mixed reception, and had continued onward with few, if any, additional fighters. On the night of the 25th, his small band was trapped in the narrow Alikhel Gorge in his native Nangahar Province, hemmed in by Taliban units both in front and behind. Deprived of an escape route as Taliban reinforcements poured in, he called for help via sat phone to his nephew in Peshawar. The nephew, in turn, contacted James Ritchie, one of a pair of wealthy, eccentric American brothers from whom Abdul Haq had reportedly been receiving financial support, and who was standing by in Peshawar to monitor the Afghan dissident's progress. Ritchie then contacted his associate, Robert "Bud" McFarlane, the former national security advisor to Ronald Reagan, who suffered disgrace over his involvement in the Iran-Contra affair. McFarlane rang up CTC's Global Response Center, the GRC, to pass on word of Abdul Haq's plight and his location. CTC diverted a missile-armed Predator drone to go to his assistance. Later that night, the drone operators located Haq, whose group by this time was locked in a vicious and hopeless firefight with the Taliban. Having only one missile, the Predator operators employed it to blow up a Taliban pickup truck. It wasn't nearly enough; there was nothing to do from there but watch helplessly as Abdul Haq was captured. By midday on October 26 he was dead, strung up in public by the Taliban.

That evening, the international press was awash in stories variously sourced to Haq's embittered Pakistan-based relatives and associates, to McFarlane himself, and to the Taliban. As underscored by virtually everyone, it looked like a colossal American failure to support an uprising by a genuine anti-Taliban Pashtun leader; as such, it could not have come at a worse time, precisely as we were trying to induce other Pashtuns to take similar risks, and to assure them of American support if they did so. It may not have mattered, but in fact, the appearances were quite deceiving.

I had had little contact with General Jafar before 9/11. We had met often enough, though, for me to get an inkling that there might be some surprises lurking behind the dour, bluff exterior of this short, square-jawed, heavyset man with the deep, rumbling voice.

For one thing, there were the occasional flashes of sardonic humor. But my first memorable impression of Jafar came in a pub in Gettysburg, Pennsylvania, during the CIA's early 2000 "charm offensive" aimed at General Mahmud. Our mixed CIA-ISI delegation stopped for lunch, just after General Mahmud's "staff ride" of the Civil War battlefield. As would befit representatives of an Islamic Republic, each of the Pakistanis ordered juice or tea as the waiter made his rounds. One would not have expected otherwise, particularly under the intimidating gaze of General Mahmud. When the waiter came to General Jafar, though, he didn't hesitate. There was more than a hint of defiance in his voice as he ordered a beer. It may seem a small thing, and I suppose it was. But I could see then that this was a proud and confident man, independent-minded and contrarian, who was not about to kowtow to anyone.

On September 16, 2001, a clear, sunny Sunday, Ambassador Chamberlin and I had had our first post-9/11 meeting with General Mahmud, who had returned to Pakistan from the United States the day before as the sole passenger on a CIA aircraft, one of the first to enter American skies after the disaster. At that meeting, Mahmud proudly presented General Jafar as the ISI's newly anointed counterterrorism "Czar," promising that he would have full authority to do everything necessary to demonstrate Pakistan's firm solidarity with the United States in the just declared "War on Terror." As Mahmud waxed enthusiastically, Jafar inclined his head toward me. "Czar?" he said, *sotto voce.* "More like a Rasputin."

I'm sure that Mahmud had his own reasons for selecting General Jafar for what would now be ISI's most important task. But there was another factor at work, of which Mahmud was probably quite unaware: for Jafar, this fight was personal. I had met with him several times at ISI Headquarters during the days following 9/11, during the interim when the ban on international flights made Mahmud's quick return impossible. He told me about a brother-in-law, to whom he was quite close, who lived in Manhattan. Jafar and his wife were trying to reach her brother by phone, to no avail. After two days, fearing the worst, Jafar was distraught and angry. Even after the brother-in-law and his family later proved to be fine, the general fairly seethed as he spoke of the ordeal, and of who had been responsible for it. His banked fury rivaled that of any American I'd met. No one who sat with him in those days, as I had, could doubt where he would stand in the coming struggle.

It may simply have been our good fortune that this former tank commander occupying this largely thankless job in ISI was a tough, hard-driving taskmaster who had no patience with religious extremism, and who could be counted upon to demonstrate the unambiguous seriousness of purpose on terrorism which Mahmud himself could never muster. But if it seemed obvious to me, and to others in CIA who had dealt with Mahmud, that his heart would never be in the counterterrorism fight, we apparently were not the only ones to have reached that conclusion. On October 8, President Musharraf announced a series of promotions, elevating General Muhammad Aziz Khan—a key Corps commander and one of those, along with General Mahmud, thought to be most sympathetic to religious fundamentalism—to the largely ceremonial four-star post of chairman of the Joint Chiefs of Staff Committee. Though they both wore three stars at that point, Aziz Khan had less seniority than Mahmud; in the Pakistani military system, that meant that Mahmud must retire. In one clever stroke, Musharraf had kicked one problematic senior officer upstairs and out of the chain of command, and in the process removed another from a post where he otherwise stood to do considerable harm.

The Pakistani president never confided his thinking to me, nor to Ambassador Chamberlin so far as I know, but he must have known he would never get more than grudging compliance from the headstrong Mahmud in carrying out a policy designed to confront the religious extremism which officers of Mahmud's persuasion had long done so much to promote as an instrument of state power. In appointing Lieutenant General Ehsan ul-Haq in Mahmud's place, he could at least be assured that his policies would be carried forward vigorously. For us, thankfully, it also meant that Jafar would now be unchained. All this stood behind the anger on such vivid display now.

"If you were going to send this man across the border, why the hell didn't you tell us? We could have helped you." Now we had an unmitigated and embarrassing disaster on our hands, he said, and it had all been avoidable.

The fact was that my station's involvement in Abdul Haq's ill-fated mission had been marginal, to say the least, and even that was against our will. As my officers had assessed the relative capabilities of the various anti-Taliban Pashtun commanders, Abdul Haq had always failed to measure up. Yes, he had been a respected *muj* warrior against the Soviets and the Afghan Communists, one who had inflicted heavy losses on his enemies, and been seriously wounded in the process. He had also established a reputation within the Rome Group around Muhammad Zahir Shah, the last king of Afghanistan, as a broad-minded and idealistic statesman of sorts, a Pashtun like Hamid Karzai who was willing to reach across ethnic and sectarian lines to make common cause with the Tajiks, the Uzbeks, the Hazaras, and others. As such, again like Hamid Karzai, he played very well to foreign audiences, and was a regular fixture in international salons. David Katz, the longtime

U.S. consul general in Peshawar and a respected Afghan hand, held the former commander in high esteem. By all accounts, he was charming and charismatic, even if the unflattering sobriquet "Hollywood Haq," with which CIA had tagged him years before and which had stuck to him since, suggested a preoccupation with image over substance.

As chief of station, I had kept an advisedly low social profile during the previous two years, and thus was not directly exposed to Haq's siren song. In the meantime, what my officers turned up on him was not encouraging. We knew that broad appeals to nationalist sentiment would only prove useful if they could motivate those inside Afghanistan to take an armed stand against the Taliban. The Taliban may have claimed a mandate from God, but at the end of the day they ruled through the barrel of a gun, and only resort to arms would unseat them. We were looking for commanders who could generate that type of support within Afghanistan, and from all accounts, Abdul Haq was not among them. The fact that he was suggesting to others that he had CIA support likewise made us extremely wary: someone confident of his ability to command guns inside Afghanistan would not have felt the need to misrepresent himself.

None of this is to suggest that we had any animus toward the former Ahmedzai warrior. We just didn't see any military capability there, whatever Haq's political appeal. We felt it would be irresponsible to sponsor or to encourage him, and said so in formal communications with headquarters.

We were therefore surprised to see a cable in late September instructing Greg, my up-country base chief and Hamid Karzai's contact, to meet with Abdul Haq and offer him support. Bud McFarlane, who apparently maintained one or two high-level contacts at CIA Headquarters, appears to have been the prime driver behind this idea, but precisely who he spoke to and how the order was then generated within CTC remains obscure. No one seemed to want to claim ownership of the idea after the fact.

Greg arranged through David Katz to meet with Abdul Haq, as ordered. Told that the former commander planned to enter Afghanistan imminently and failing to persuade him to wait until he had clearer indications of armed support, Greg did manage to coax him into accepting a satellite phone so that we could at least remain in touch and report on his progress. Haq promised to send a runner to the consulate the following morning to pick it up. The runner never materialized. Haq entered Afghanistan the same day.

It was obvious that Jafar was completely unpersuaded by my story. I was asking him to believe that CIA had had no role in encouraging Abdul Haq to cross the border; that we had had no established means to communicate with him; that we had only been made aware of his ambush by the Taliban through an improbable series of last-minute phone calls for which a now obscure and largely discredited former government official was the critical linchpin; and that nonetheless a CIA-controlled drone had just happened to be loitering on-station at the critical moment and in the right place to come to his assistance when attacked. I could hardly blame Jafar. In his place, I wouldn't have believed me, either—not for a second. It all just happened to be true.

The meeting ended uncomfortably: me sticking firmly to my story, and Jafar just as firmly unconvinced. I'm sure, though, that when we parted that morning, Jafar felt he'd underscored for me a valuable lesson. Indeed he had. I could see that he was at least as concerned over the fallout from the Abdul Haq disaster as I; and that whatever ambiguities might exist in the Pakistani attitude toward the Taliban, I could count on Jafar's support if and whenever I needed it.

Apparently feeling they hadn't done enough, CTC/SO sent us a cable later on October 27, demanding to know who had provided McFarlane with the phone number of the Global Response Center. In addition to being an outrageous accusation, there was more than a little irony in this, as McFarlane reportedly had been in direct touch with headquarters before Haq's entry into Afghanistan, and it was they who had demanded that the station offer him support. Dave and I were still shaking our heads over this one as Greg, believing he was the primary suspect, fired off a blistering message denying any involvement in the debacle other than what our supportive headquarters colleagues had mandated. If we had needed any confirmation, this was it: Langley was definitely in unfriendly hands.

Chapter 21

DRESS REHEARSAL

OCTOBER 29, 2001

LL THE WHILE HE listened, General Franks kept looking at me out of the corner of his eye. His gaze conveyed what I considered to be the proper mix of keen interest and wary skepticism. I had developed the clear sense during our first videoconference in September that the general from Midland, Texas, was an extremely canny fellow; his interactions now with our two Afghan guests were greatly reinforcing that impression.

The general was leaning forward in an overstuffed chair. Spread out on the low coffee table before him were stacks of photographs and a now familiar campaign map festooned with carefully drawn arrows, all converging on Kandahar. Now, however, the arrows emerged from a long, narrow valley on the Pak-Afghan border whose name had only recently entered our lexicon: Shin Naray.

Sunlight streamed into the room from a huge picture window. One could see dense thickets of olea, acacia, and tecomella extending gently upward for several kilometers, to a point where the Margalla Hills rose almost vertically from the streambeds below, eventually disappearing, ridge upon ridge, into the bluish haze of the northern Pakistani sky. I had always thought the view from the U.S. ambassador's office was the most spectacular in Islamabad. The scene inspired a sense of infinite possibility, which is precisely what Engineer Pashtun was now trying to convey.

General Franks had sent word before this, his first post-9/11 visit to Pakistan, that he wished CIA to introduce him to some Afghan

162

tribal leaders. Already concerned by CTC's clear lack of enthusiasm for Shirzai, I seized on this as a potential opportunity to develop General Franks's independent support for him. I had given Mark, Shirzai's contact, strict guidance as to how I wanted these two Barakzai to look and act: Franks wanted to meet with Afghan tribals, and by God I wanted him to know he was getting the genuine article. Engineer Pashtun, I knew, was given to Western dress, and I could see from my own first meeting with him that years in exile had caused Shirzai to adopt the outward appearance of a Pakistani feudal lord, rather than that of the Kandahari tribal leader he was. "Turbans," I had said. "Make damned sure they're wearing turbans."

Also before the meeting with Franks, Mark and his Special Forces partner had impressed upon our friends that if they expected to have U.S. air support, they were going to have to undertake their assault on Kandahar in stages. Their willingness and ability to take the war to the Taliban capital was going to have to be demonstrated before American support would come, and so Engineer Pashtun adapted his plan accordingly. As he laid it out for Franks, Shirzai and a small band of armed, truck-mounted followers would cross the border and enter the Shin Naray Valley at its far eastern end. They would immediately move a small blocking force to the narrow western entrance to control access to the valley from the Afghan side. The valley could then serve as a secure rallying point for Shirzai's tribal followers from the Afghan side of the border, easily defended from high ridges to the north and south— provided the fighters materialized, I thought, and provided they did not kill the ex-governor when they did. Once he controlled this territory, we could provide Shirzai with a drop of weapons and ammunition for those who would join; and once he had successfully engaged hostile Taliban forces, we could provide him, in principle, with a CIA–Special Forces team. If Langley should prove unwilling, my hope was that pressure from General Franks would force the issue. This was where the general's patronage might prove useful later on, although I was not prepared to say so just yet.

There were other little wrinkles in the plan with which we did not burden the general. As Shirzai would be entering Afghanistan by road,

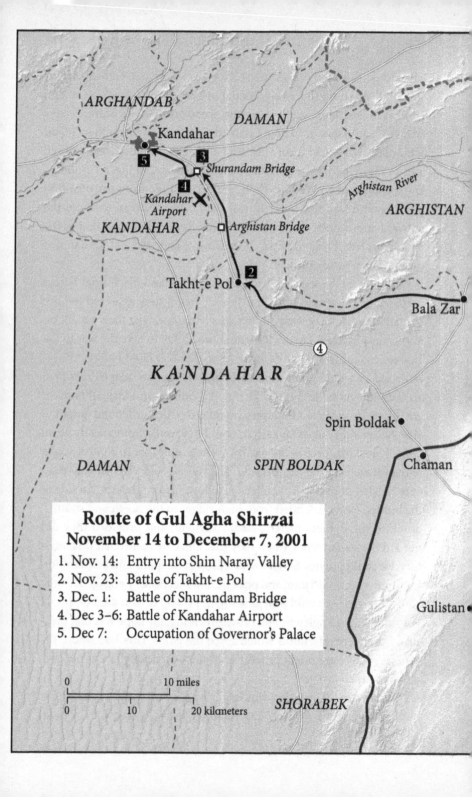

ARGHANDAB

DAMAN

Kandahar

3
□ *Shurandam Bridge*

4
Kandahar Airport ✕

Arghistan River

ARGHISTAN

□ *Arghistan Bridge*

5

KANDAHAR

Takht-e Pol •
2

Bala Zar •

④

K A N D A H A R

Spin Boldak •

DAMAN

SPIN BOLDAK

Chaman •

Route of Gul Agha Shirzai
November 14 to December 7, 2001

1. Nov. 14: Entry into Shin Naray Valley
2. Nov. 23: Battle of Takht-e Pol
3. Dec. 1: Battle of Shurandam Bridge
4. Dec 3–6: Battle of Kandahar Airport
5. Dec. 7: Occupation of Governor's Palace

Gulistan •

0		10 miles

0	10	20 kilometers

SHORABEK

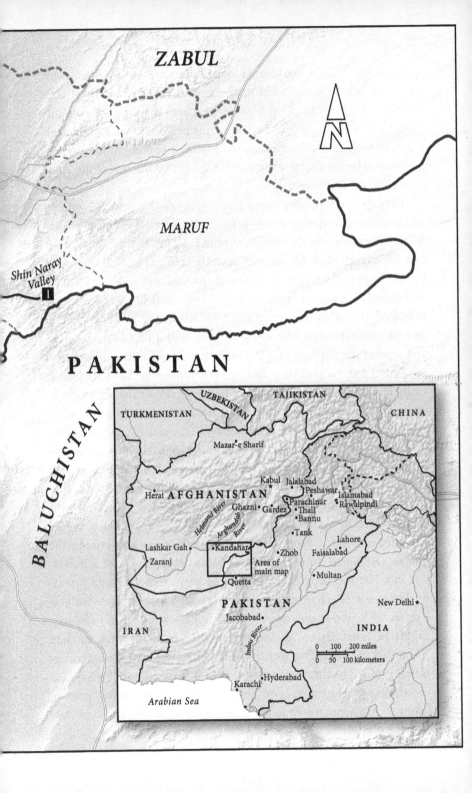

and in armed force, I would need to make advance arrangements with the ISI to ensure there would not be any armed confrontations with Pakistani troops at any of the border checkposts. Given the possibility that advance warning of Shirzai's plans could find its way through the Pakistanis to the Taliban, I would have to seek my headquarters' permission before doing so; and with CTC's rabid distrust of the Pakistanis, I knew, this would be hard to obtain.

There was yet another cloud forming on the horizon. As with so many of these recurring issues, Dave had a clever, if obscure, phrase for it. "The game's on the radio," he would say. "Everyone wants to get into the game." With Afghanistan and Pakistan suddenly at the top of the U.S. national security agenda, everyone wanted a piece of it. Unsurprisingly, perhaps, a number of CIA domestic field offices suddenly managed to find an immigrant pizza deliveryman who could claim a second cousin/brother who was an Afghan warlord ready to lead a revolt against the Taliban, or a Pakistani tribal *malik* who knew where bin Laden was. Most of these stories were transparent fabrications and easily brushed aside, even if they required precious time and effort to do so. One of them, though, seemed to hold at least marginal promise.

The chief of one of our domestic offices, a capable and respected officer whom we'll call "Mark C," had made indirect contact, through a tortuous line of intermediaries, with an infamous Afghan heroin smuggler known as Haji Juma Khan Baluch. A native of remote Nimruz Province, in the far southwest of Afghanistan near Iran, Haji Juma Khan offered to put us in touch with Abdul Karim Brahvi, a former governor of Nimruz Province who had been driven into exile by the Taliban. Although some might have balked at dealing with a notorious international drug dealer, it seemed to me that we could not afford to be too selective in choosing whom we might associate with, so long as we kept our eyes open and did not allow ourselves to be manipulated. Juma Khan was clearly attempting to do just that, and had the advantage of dealing with stateside American contacts whose ignorance of Afghanistan made them ripe for exploitation. Perhaps his most outrageous gambit, breathlessly reported to us, was his offer to "permit" American forces to use a desert airstrip in the Registan Desert, some 100 miles southwest of Kandahar. Juma Khan's permission wasn't terribly valuable, as he didn't control the strip or any territory remotely close to it; in fact, he had nothing to do with it. The landing field and an associated compound had been built by royal princes from the United Arab Emirates for their use, for a few weeks each year, in hunting the migrating houbara bustard through the trackless desert south of Kandahar. We encouraged Mark's pursuit of the lead, making clear that under no circumstances should any long-term commitments be made to Juma Khan; any assistance provided to him should be calibrated, we said, solely for the limited purpose of making contact with Brahvi, and encouraging his return to Nimruz.

Dave and I were suspicious, to say the least, of the response from CTC/SO. Guarded as they were about Gul Agha, they could hardly have been more enthusiastic about Karim Brahvi, though his tribal base in the far southwest would make him a minor irritant to the Taliban, at best. We could only guess at the combination of factors behind their eagerness. The Clandestine Service greatly values loyalty: like many closed societies, at its best it is a band of brothers and sisters; but at its worst it is a scrum of competing mafias. I had no idea what links existed between Mark C and the leaders of CTC/SO, but suspected they were significant. I supported the effort to encourage and empower Brahvi: it would do no harm, I reasoned, and might do some good. But I was wary.

Now, having sat patiently through Gul Agha's enthusiastic exposition on the past military triumphs of his family and his tribe, as well as his expressions of gratitude for American assistance against the Communists, and having made a show of solemn respect for Engineer Pashtun's prowess as a military tactician, General Franks smiled, and thanked them for their excellent briefing. With a nod to Mark and me, he said he was sure they would continue their preparations in close coordination with us, and he looked forward to further word on their progress. As he stood to leave, I could almost see him wink.

In the month since our first videoconference and well before his meeting with Shirzai, General Franks and I had begun to develop an odd sort of indirect relationship. Shortly after hostilities commenced on October 7, the CIA representative to CENTCOM, Pat Hailey, forwarded to me a series of questions, for my eyes only, from the general soliciting my analysis of the progress of the campaign. I was happy to provide it, but this put me in a potentially awkward spot. I certainly didn't want anyone at headquarters interfering in any way with the analysis I provided to the CENTCOM commander. On the other hand, if they were to find out about this channel from anyone other than me, it would look as though I were bypassing my own organization and chain of command to provide uncoordinated advice to a senior intelligence customer—which, of course, was precisely what I wanted to do. My excuse, valid as it went, was that this was what General Franks had requested, and I was responding in good faith. I therefore informed headquarters of the request, including the general's desire that neither the questions nor the responses be disseminated, and nonchalantly told them I would fulfill it. Fortunately, no one raised an objection.

This was but the first of a series of inquiries I received from the general throughout the war, to which I did my best to respond. I would send my analyses off to Pat to be conveyed to Franks, and wouldn't hear another thing until eventually I received another set of questions.

It wasn't until months later that I learned directly from Pat about the typical sequence of events surrounding these exchanges. General Franks, apparently, was quite mercurial and exceedingly demanding of his staff, with various subordinates regularly coming into, or falling out of, his favor. According to Pat, one of the best ways to chart who was in and who out was to examine the list of authorized recipients of my bits of wisdom. The chosen would meet with the general in a closed-door session to review my recommendations and discuss the progress of the campaign. As my comments usually contained at least some implied criticism of whatever it was the military was doing at the time, General Franks would typically react badly to my pieces: He would fulminate aloud, asking what the hell I knew about thus-and-such, and questioning why he'd asked me in the first place. The first couple of times, Pat concluded that my advice was being dismissed out of hand. But then he would notice various things being tweaked in apparent response to my observations, and in a couple of weeks or so, another set of questions would emanate from the general's staff for passage on to me.

On only one occasion did I try to provide unsolicited advice. Catching wind that CENTCOM intended to launch an airborne Special Forces raid on Mullah Omar's compound west of Kandahar City on October 19, I was incredulous. I phoned Pat.

"Why are we doing this? Don't they know no one's there?" I asked. Omar's compound had of course been struck with cruise missiles, at my suggestion, on the first night of the air campaign. Omar had not been back there since, and we knew from our sources in Kandahar that no one else was there, either.

Pat cut in before I could go any further. He wanted to save me the trouble. "Bob," he said. "God himself could not turn this off." Let us say I got the clear impression from Pat that there was considerably more of intra-DoD politics than military necessity in this operation, and that the desire of the Rangers and of Delta Force to demonstrate the relevance of their airborne capabilities in what was shaping up to be a CIA/ Green Beret fight might have had a great deal to do with it. It may also have been that General Franks and the Pentagon were eager to demonstrate visibly to the American public that action was in fact being taken against the Taliban on the ground, as well as from the air. Whatever the case, Mullah Omar's compound was indeed empty when the special operators arrived. While extracting, they came under heavy fire from a Taliban force which rushed to the scene, and one American was wounded. Worse, a helicopter staged at Dalbandin in Pakistan as part of a Quick Reaction Force associated with the operation rolled over in a "brownout" while attempting to land. Two Rangers were killed. It was cold comfort that we were not the only ones having to suffer politically inspired meddling from stateside; at least for us, the consequences thus far had not been lethal.

In the valley of the blind, it is said, the one-eyed man is king. There are advantages to knowing a bit about an esoteric topic that is suddenly deemed important, and about which almost no one else knows anything. Although I was almost completely oblivious of it, I had gained some notoriety during this period at CENTCOM and in the West

Wing of the White House, and a nickname to go with it. Just after General Franks's arrival in Islamabad, I journeyed to the suite of offices commandeered by his staff to pay a call on General Jeff Kimmons, the CENTCOM "J-2," or intelligence chief, with whom I had been regularly conferring on the secure phone from Tampa. Informed that he was not there, I began to spell my name for the enlisted clerk. A look of recognition immediately came over his face.

"Are you 'Islamabad Bob'?" he asked. "Oh, sir! You're famous!"

Chapter 22

NUCLEAR NIGHTMARES

T ODAY'S BRIEFING WAS GOING to be different. You could tell immediately from the body language and the expressions on their faces. But no one let on. There was a protocol to be followed.

As was the custom after every interrogation of Dr. Bashir, the lead interrogator reported to my office in the early evening, as soon as he had returned from the "Clubhouse," a joint facility we had established with the ISI. We had observed this exercise off and on since October 27, when the station and ISI had begun joint interrogations of Dr. Bashir-ud-Din Mahmud, the president of Ummah Tameer-e Nau (UTN).

UTN was founded in March 2000 as a non-governmental organization, devoted to providing humanitarian services in Afghanistan. It was one of many trying to provide relief and comfort to Afghans— including a number of Islamic NGOs of an extremist orientation, some of which were known or strongly suspected of providing financial support to terrorists. What distinguished UTN from all other NGOs active in Afghanistan was both the composition and orientation of its membership. Most of the nine leading members of the group were retired nuclear scientists or military officers; all were religious fundamentalists and devoted supporters of the Taliban. Their non-member "patron" and sponsor was none other than the infamous Hamid Gul, a retired lieutenant general of the Pakistan Army and former director-general of the ISI, who had become highly visible as a rhetorical promoter of global *jihad* and an outspoken advocate for the Taliban.

Sultan Bashir-ud-Din Mahmud, UTN's president, was the former director-general for nuclear power of the Pakistan Atomic Energy Commission (PAEC). During the early part of his career, he had been at least indirectly involved in Pakistan's atomic weapons program, and for a while was project manager for Kushab, a heavy-water nuclear reactor designed to produce plutonium for weapons. It was perhaps not incidental that after Pakistan's first nuclear weapons tests in 1998, Dr. Bashir was honored with a significant civilian award, the *Sitara-e-Intiaz*, by Prime Minister Nawaz Sharif. What most attracted scrutiny to Dr. Bashir, though, was not his scientific background but his radical political orientation and bizarre pseudoscientific theories. He espoused the view that Pakistan's nuclear weapon should be the common property of the entire *Ummah*, the global Islamic community. He wrote extensively about the impact of sunspots on human affairs, and made predictions about the role of terrorism and nuclear weapons in precipitating doomsday. In his later years at PAEC, some of his colleagues actually had doubts about his sanity.

The fact that an Islamic extremist with crackpot ideas about the end of the world, substantial knowledge of nuclear weapons–related technology, and a belief that such knowledge should be spread widely was now actively engaged in Afghanistan and therefore in at least close physical proximity to al-Qa'ida was enough to give some pause. On that basis, it was natural that UTN would attract at least a certain amount of low-level suspicion in the West. The fact that it didn't seem terribly active in Afghanistan—its overt activities appeared mostly limited to operation of a flour mill in Kandahar—gave rise to speculation as to what the organization might actually be up to. Beyond suspicion, though, there was little to go on. I made my first, low-level request of the ISI for information about UTN in January 2001, though I can no longer remember what triggered it.

After 9/11, the context in which the Islamic NGO was viewed changed radically. With al-Qa'ida having graphically demonstrated its ability to strike a staggering blow against the United States, the fear was that this might only be a precursor, and that more devastating means might be employed against us at any time. Within weeks, we began receiving sketchy reports from two of our European allies concerning past activities of UTN, alleging that they may have been involved in passing nuclear-related information to rogue states—information which the Europeans had not shared with us previously. What they were now sharing was unspecific and provided neither corroborating details nor any clue as to how it was acquired, without which there was no way to judge its credibility. Intelligence services are loath to share anything that might point to the identity or nature of their sources, but what they had given us was almost useless; it seemed a combination of rumor and innuendo: "These people appear to be up to no good; we recommend you find out what they're doing." They refused to allow us to share even this sketchy information with anyone else.

By October 1, with several such reports in hand, I decided I had seen enough. We needed to take action. CIA had long been in the business of collecting information on nuclear and other WMD proliferation, particularly where there was a threat of proliferation to terrorist groups. I had played a central role in setting up the Counter-Proliferation Division. Now CTC was setting up a separate office, CTC/WMD, to pull together all information and leads pertaining to al-Qa'ida's efforts to develop nuclear and other mass destructive capabilities. I proposed to them that we approach the Pakistanis for help in investigating UTN.

This was hardly my default position. After all, CIA is in the business of collecting intelligence, and whenever possible would prefer to do so on its own. But now time was of the essence. I was not so much concerned about what UTN might do in future. With open hostilities about to start, it was unlikely that the NGO would be able to maintain its previous pattern of travel and involvement in Afghanistan, and if it had al-Qa'ida clients, those individuals were unlikely to be available while ducking U.S. bombs. Opportunities to collect information on UTN activities going forward would probably be sparse. What we really needed to know was what capabilities it might have shared with al-Qa'ida in the past. For that, Dr. Bashir and company would need to be interrogated, and we could do that only with Pakistani assistance.

At length, headquarters relented, and provided me with so-called "tear line" information: approved text, which could be cut out along a tear line from a cable and presented to a cooperating service. What I received was disappointing. It was essentially a number of vague and unsubstantiated assertions about Dr. Bashir's involvement in sharing nuclear information with unauthorized parties, and reasons to suspect UTN might be doing the same with al-Qa'ida. When I presented it to General Jafar on October 10, he was unimpressed.

"This is all circumstantial," he said. Bashir was a national hero. Bringing him in for questioning was likely to create a political firestorm, particularly if it was done in response to foreign pressure. Jafar was going to need more than this.

Two days later, thoroughly frustrated, I sent another message. By now those of us in Islamabad knew that one of our European partners did indeed have substantial information which could be used to convince the Pakistanis that Bashir posed a potentially significant threat, both to their interests and ours. The Europeans had come clean with us, but still insisted that we could not use their information with the Pakistanis. To me this was completely unsatisfactory, given the potential threat, but headquarters insisted that we had given the Pakistanis enough: hadn't we told them Bashir was a dangerous man? In exasperation, I cabled: "There is an important distinction between evidence and assertion, and unfortunately the Pakistanis are aware of it." I proposed that George Tenet weigh in directly with the head of our sister service. With their information in hand, the U.S. government—probably Secretary of State Colin Powell—could approach President Musharraf. As Pakistan had cut its ties with the Taliban and was currently providing the United States with a platform from which to make war on both the Taliban and al-Qa'ida, the Paks had to realize that they were nearly as liable to retaliation as the Americans, and far easier to reach. Any credible indication that Bashir and UTN had shared dangerous technology with al-Qa'ida would have to be seen as a potential threat to them as well. The problem was that no Pakistani official was willing to concede that a revered scientist would do such a thing, absent compelling evidence.

Our allies again would not accede to our wishes, and there was no high-level approach to Musharraf. As a result of my badgering, though, Jafar did consent to allow joint CIA/ISI interrogations of Bashir and his colleagues, including use of the polygraph.

One of CIA's most accomplished interrogators, Barry McManus, happened to be with us at that moment to advise on another issue. He agreed to stay, and he was introduced to Dr. Bashir on October 27. Playing on his North African appearance, McManus presented himself as a Moroccan journalist: "Dr. Abraham." He could help Bashir to clear his name, he said, but only if the Pakistani scientist were willing to accept his methods of assuring the veracity of his sources. "Do you want all the world to see you as a terrorist?"

Bashir quickly saw through the ruse, and the countermanipulation began. Identifying McManus as an African-American, he recounted the history of the American civil rights movement in impressive detail. "Shame on you, Dr. Abraham," he said. How could someone of his background assist in oppressing an innocent man? Over three hours of contentious conversation, they nonetheless established a certain rapport.

"You need help," McManus reminded him. "Would you rather speak with me, or with *them*?" *They* remained unidentified; Bashir agreed to be polygraphed.

The questioning continued for two more days, interspersed with repeated polygraph examinations, but the environment was not at all what we wanted. Bashir was being handled very deferentially by the Pakistanis, and was allowed to return home at night. Unsurprisingly, he was not making any damaging admissions: he had met Mullah Omar, as expected, but denied ever having met bin Laden. Though both the polygraph and McManus's experience told us Bashir was withholding information, we had nothing concrete to confront him with, and no idea what he might be hiding. The interrogations were going in circles. The Pakistanis' patience was wearing thin.

Then, while being questioned on October 30, Dr. Bashir had a sudden cardiac episode and collapsed in a heap. The Pakistanis summoned a doctor, who administered nitroglycerine and committed Bashir to a hospital for observation. The scientist seemed enfeebled. For the Pakistanis, that was the last straw. They were ready to call a halt to the proceedings, though I was insistent that the questioning continue. Assuming from my obduracy that I must have information I was not revealing, Jafar confronted me.

"If you've got evidence, you need to show it."

Again, I sent a message to our European friends. Their suggestion was that we wait until Bashir's release from temporary ISI custody, which seemed imminent, and approach him on our own with what we knew, threatening that we would reveal his past activities to Pakistani authorities unless he came clean on what he was withholding. This struck me as naive. Why would the UTN chief ever trust us not to take what we knew to the Pakistani authorities, and why, if confronted with past misdeeds, would he give us more damaging testimony to use against him—if indeed there was any? We would need to leverage the Pakistanis; this was where Bashir lived, and they were the only ones who could pose a credible threat to him.

On the night of October 30, our sister station in the concerned capital set up a video teleconference with the counterpart service, so that I could explore an alternative approach. I suggested that we present their service's information to the Pakistanis as though it were our own. And rather than cite the real method employed in collecting it, which had been devious, we would state that it had been acquired through a CIA bugging operation outside Pakistan. In short, I proposed to provide the Pakistanis with the truth by wrapping it in a bouquet of lies. Finally, the Europeans agreed.

On November 1, I met with Jafar with a "white paper" in hand, and briefed him in detail on its contents. A few years previously, Bashir had met for two days in a Persian Gulf city with a mixed group of Arabs. He had provided them with a preliminary design for a dual power/desalination nuclear plant, as well as details on plutonium production at Pakistan's Kushab reactor. A few months later, he met with them again, this time elsewhere in the Gulf. In the course of these discussions it became clear that UTN members had had similar talks with the government of Libyan leader Muammar Qadhafi. Bashir was clearly interested in doing nuclear-related business, but for some reason there had been no follow-up meetings.

Jafar's reaction was immediate. If what I had briefed was true, Dr. Bashir had grossly violated the oath taken at the time of his retirement not to reveal details of his nuclear-related work. The general was embarrassed and angry. Jafar would be a full ally in getting to the bottom of this now, for reasons of his own.

Beginning on November 3, after his release from the hospital, Dr. Bashir's questioning was more focused, and less friendly. Confronted with precise and detailed information on his past dealings with the Arabs, he quickly acknowledged the Gulf meetings, and provided further details. He had no problems passing a polygraph examination concerning the completeness of his testimony. The nuclear-related meetings with the Middle Easterners had apparently gone nowhere. But on questions regarding his activities in Afghanistan, Bashir was still coming up "deception indicated," in the polygraphers' parlance.

Rather than sending Bashir home that night, the Pakistanis permitted the questioning to continue. McManus, joined now by a colleague from Washington, was able to set up a tag team, and so maintain a constant, focused interrogation for forty-eight hours straight. This is what had set the stage for the pivotal November 4 briefing in my office.

The two interrogators took their places on the couch, with Dave and me sitting across from them. As always, I closed the door.

"Okay," I said. "Let's have it."

It had been an eventful day. A series of failed polygraph exams had made it apparent to Dr. Bashir that there was no easy way out. The unauthorized meetings in the Gulf had turned his Pakistani government hosts against him. No longer could he depend on the benefit of the doubt, or a presumption of innocence; now the presumption was one of guilt. He would have to tell more of the truth if he hoped to satisfy us.

He had met Osama bin Laden in Kandahar, at a large dinner with many guests, in the spring of 2000. Introduced to the great man as an eminent nuclear scientist, Bashir had immediately been engaged by him in an intense conversation. The tall Saudi was very curious. Bashir explained to him the two paths to acquiring fissile nuclear materials—by enriching uranium, or by reprocessing spent nuclear fuel to isolate plutonium. They discussed how difficult it might be to build a nuclear bomb. Bashir referred to the first successful American effort of the 1940s—which he mistakenly termed "Fat Boy." Bin Laden was also curious about chemical and biological weapons: How difficult were they to build? How effective were they?

With bin Laden that evening was another Arab, whom we'll call "Abu Zaydan." Abu Zaydan didn't say very much, but he visited Dr. Bashir the following morning. With him he brought a crude metal vessel, about the size of a birdcage. There was a view-port on one side, covered by a metal slide. In the bottom of the container was what appeared to be a small nugget of metal. Abu Zaydan indicated that the nugget was supposed to be radioactive; he believed it was uranium 235. Could Dr. Bashir identify what it was? The Pakistani scientist could not, but he doubted that it was fissile material. It seemed to Bashir that his Arab friends had probably been victims of some sort of nuclear scam, and that the nugget was a gamma ray source, of the sort used for medical imaging. He could provide no compelling reasons for his conclusion. Abu Zaydan told him nothing about where the nugget had come from. In response to Zaydan's questions, Bashir hand-sketched a design for a crude nuclear device.

Dr. Bashir met again with Abu Zaydan later that year, in the fall. They had further discussions. Beyond that, Dr. Bashir was vague. The Americans wanted to question him more, but the doctor was exhausted after two straight days. The Pakistani participants insisted that the session come to a close.

Dave and I sat calmly throughout the exposition. We posed a few questions.

"Write it up," I said. I would want to see the distribution—the list of recipients—before the cable went out. We couldn't know yet what these preliminary revelations might mean: perhaps a great deal, perhaps very little. Perhaps the contact with bin Laden and Abu Zaydan had amounted to talk, and little more. Perhaps today's admissions were but a first installment in a nightmarish serial. In any case, there was likely to be considerably more to the story, and excruciating pressure on all of us to ferret it out. Just one thing was certain: This cable, when it hit Washington, would go off like a high-yield nuclear device.

Chapter 23

THE PRODIGAL

NOVEMBER 5, 2001

A S THE SMALL PLANE made its long, shallow approach, I looked down warily at the flat roofs of the densely packed houses. They ended abruptly at a high brick wall; just beyond, one could see the end of the runway. I had heard the stories of potshots being taken at U.S. planes on the glide path into Jacobabad Airbase. Given the base's proximity to a well-armed local citizenry, I was happy to be aboard a Pakistani, and not an American, military aircraft.

The ISI pilot taxied to a remote end of the base. We stepped out, and my logistics guys began wrestling heavy boxes to the tarmac. Not at all sure of the plan, I stood in the dusty breeze and waited.

Presently, I saw a small car bouncing down the dirt road leading toward us, official flags fluttering from both fenders. The base commander got out and walked toward me stiffly, a swagger stick tucked under his right arm. I had been prepared for this. General Ehsan had offered to make the necessary discreet arrangements for us while telling the base commander as little as possible. The commander would not be pleased, he said, and would insist upon meeting me as a minimum indication of deference to his authority. After a rather formal welcome, the commander indicated that he had placed an empty building at the disposal of my team, as requested by General Ehsan. He then paused, as though waiting for some elaboration. I couldn't be sure precisely what Ehsan had told him, but we had what we wanted, and the commander certainly wasn't going to get anything further from me. I thanked him for his assistance and watched as he departed.

I was surprised to find that our Afghan friends had been housed in a one-story abandoned school building. Blackboards lined the walls. Hamid Karzai was padding about in a *shalwar khameez* and running shoes. His six commanders lounged on cots. Several were eating tinned American beef stew, cold from the can. All stood and squinted curiously as Karzai rushed up to greet me and "Jeff," my senior reports officer. Although we had figured prominently in one another's lives in recent weeks, this was the first time the diminutive Pashtun leader and I had met.

During the few days following his motorcycle-borne reentry of Afghanistan on October 8, we were provided only brief snapshots of the Popalzai chieftain's progress, as he made sporadic sat phone calls to Greg. After the October 9 call, when he reported from eastern Kandahar Province that he could see and hear airstrikes during the night, we again heard from him on the 10th, this time from within Kandahar City itself: more airstrikes; still had not encountered any Taliban.

The same day we received a curious cable from CTC/SO, lobbying for the quick introduction of a "foreign intelligence/unconventional warfare" team to join Karzai, though he was still moving essentially as a fugitive. Greg responded. "Hold that thought," he said, in effect. Karzai had still not demonstrated that he could survive in Afghanistan, let alone control a defendable area or provide armed protection for an American team.

Just a day later, Hamid had called Greg to say that he had been able to move a substantial distance northward, and was now in Tarin Kowt, the capital of his native Uruzgan Province. He indicated excitedly that he had about 400 fighters with him, and would need food and ammunition for them, urgently. Greg's response was measured: To receive airdrops, Hamid would need to locate and mark a suitable area with fires at night. This would require close and detailed coordination with us; brief, staccato phone calls would not do. Hamid should send clear textual messages using the covert satellite communications gear we had provided him.

On October 13, another excited message from Karzai: Now, he and 350 men had seized control of Tarin Kowt. They urgently needed a drop of weapons and ammunition in order to hold and defend it. This was unbelievably good news, but was accompanied by troubling reports from Kandahar. According to an excellent source, the Taliban were aware of Karzai's presence in Uruzgan, and were dispatching a substantial force northward to attack him. I sent a strongly worded message to CTC/SO, pleading for them to arrange a military drop to resupply Hamid's force before Taliban reinforcements arrived.

Airdrops were already a huge source of frustration. At the start of the American bombing campaign, at the president's behest, the U.S. military combined its initial strikes on al-Qa'ida and Taliban targets with drops of humanitarian aid to civilians. Out of fear of antiaircraft missiles—which, for all anyone knew, could include old U.S.-supplied Stingers provided years before to the mujahideen—American C-130s made these drops at night, and exclusively from high altitude. Drop packages blew far from the intended landing areas and broke up on impact, scattering supplies over a wide area and making them hard to recover. This obviously would not do for drops of weapons into small landing zones.

I consulted with "Jim M," a highly experienced paramilitary specialist who had worked for me at the Farm. I had brought him to Islamabad immediately after 9/11 to provide advice and serve as a liaison to the military. He explained to me that the U.S. Air Force riggers forward-deployed to Karshi Khanabad ("K2") Airbase in Uzbekistan, from where these supply flights were being staged, had lost a lot of institutional expertise in making halo (high-altitude, low-opening) drops, and were unfamiliar with the latest technology and techniques, some of which had been developed by CIA. I was incredulous. Jim was no CIA chauvinist: he had excellent relations with Special Forces, understood and respected their capabilities, and only wanted to see the mission get done. If he said there was a problem, there was a problem.

"Well, then, why can't we send our specialists up to Khanabad and share with them what we know?" Jim's eyes widened at that. Not possible; there was no way military riggers, who considered this their job and themselves the experts in it, would agree to have CIA come to instruct them.

"Okay, well, let's not say why they're going. Why not send them there, let them rub shoulders with their military counterparts, and let nature take its course?"

Jim shook his head. Wasn't going to happen. I held my head in my hands. We risked losing an irreplaceable tribal ally due to our inability to make secure airdrops, and all because of bloody-minded interagency politics.

I needn't have worried: we didn't have the materials in place to drop anyway.

"What the hell?" I said to Dave. "Here these geniuses at Headquarters are pressing us for weeks to get southern tribals fighting the Taliban, and now that we have some, they can't support them."

Headquarters responded to our October 13 plea, stating that materials earmarked for a "lethal drop" to Karzai would be moving from a stateside staging area in the southwestern United States to a European airbase on October 14 or 15. They would be ready to drop, they promised, by the 17th or 18th—provided, of course, that Karzai could survive that long.

In the meantime, CTC/SO had other preoccupations. On October 13, they disseminated a formal intelligence report to the entire Washington policy community stating that UIFSA—the Northern Alliance—had captured Tarin Kowt. I was incredulous. Karzai was not a member of UIFSA and had received no support or direction from the Northern Alliance, which was in no position to help him anyway.

Dave looked at me. "You don't get it," he said. "This isn't about the facts. It's about control. They control the relationship with the Northern Alliance. If they can pretend that Hamid is a member of UIFSA, they can use it to control this operation."

He was right, of course. So that's why Hank was so interested in linking Karzai with Isma'il Khan, the UIFSA-connected warlord.

"That's crazy. It will be political anathema in the south if Karzai is seen as a member of the Northern Alliance. And beyond that, we've been working the south for two years. We know the terrain and the players. Greg has the relationship with Karzai. Those idiots can't possibly micromanage this thing from thousands of miles away. We're the only ones who can do this."

"That's another thing," Dave said. "You know Hank has been talking to Greg on the STU-III [secure phone]. I don't like it. It's sneaky."

"Don't worry about Greg," I said. "He gets it. He knows exactly how this needs to work. He'll tell them exactly what he thinks, whether they want to hear it or not."

By then, Greg and I had fallen into a pattern of late-night phone calls and e-mail exchanges, frequently laughing and commiserating about the aggressive philistinism of CTC. In one memorable exchange, after a particularly foolish directive, he'd sent me a frustrated e-mail at one in the morning, threatening to light himself on fire in the middle of the Jamrud Road.

"Anyway, do you think I'm going to tell Greg he can't speak to Headquarters except through me? That's ridiculous. That's what they'd do. Let Hank talk to Greg. If he thinks Greg is responsive to him, maybe he'll give Karzai some support."

We sent a cable to Langley, giving it wide dissemination, formally pointing out that CTC/SO's report was factually inaccurate and should be recalled. I was sure they'd appreciate the help and advice.

Within days, the Taliban were pouring into Tarin Kowt and placing direct pressure on Karzai, as we had feared. It was increasingly difficult to track what was happening to him, as the frequency of his communications dropped off precipitately. The weapons package intended for him finally left the United States on October 16, well behind schedule; on the 19th, not having received any word on a drop zone, headquarters informed us it was diverting Hamid's weapons for another recipient—CIA's Team Alpha, accompanying Abdur-Rashid Dostum of the Northern Alliance, up in Mazar-e Sharif. Though headquarters was arguably responsible for Hamid's current distress, I couldn't blame them for the diversion; Karzai hadn't been able to designate a drop zone while on the run. But God only knew when another weapons package would be available.

Hamid finally contacted Greg on the 20th. He admitted that he and his fighters had never actually seized Tarin Kowt; they had only planned to do so. Now, with significant Taliban forces investing the area, he had been forced to change location three times in the previous five days. Worse, he frequently lacked facilities to recharge his sat phone, threatening his one lifeline to us.

Fortunately, the concentration of Taliban fighters in Tarin Kowt became sufficiently large to attract the attention of the U.S. Air Force. On October 22, Hamid reported that the previous day's air bombardment had been very successful. The Taliban headquarters in Tarin Kowt had been destroyed, along with a significant number of vehicles. Hamid had set up what he regarded as a fairly secure base of operations in the mountains just north of town. His previous force of 350, he said, had now increased to between 500 and 1,000. The wide disparity in numbers no doubt reflected the habit of Afghan fighters to wander back and forth from their farms and villages as need and inclination dictated, as well as what we had charitably come to regard as Hamid's bullish optimism.

Best of all, Hamid had finally set up a drop zone, and promised to have it properly marked with signal fires for a low-altitude nighttime drop, provided he was given forty-eight hours' notice. He asserted, improbably, that he could bring up to 3,000 tribal fighters into his ranks if he could seize Tarin Kowt, which had been abandoned by the Taliban in favor of scattering its forces into local villages to avoid further air attack. But again, he would need better weapons: his fighters were saddled with antiquated firearms, he said, and lacked anything heavier than assault rifles. They could attack isolated Taliban positions, but could not sustain a major battle. His entreaties were accompanied by an aggressive wish list, including PKM machine guns, RPG-7 rocket launchers, recoilless rifles, and ICOM radios.

With characteristic tough love, and still smarting over Hamid's exaggerated "conquest" of Tarin Kowt, Greg pointed out that to earn a weapons delivery, he was going to have to show more progress. Reliable, real-time reporting on Taliban positions in support of American airstrikes would be a good start, he said.

In the meantime, we were lobbying as hard as we could from Islamabad to get weapons to the Pashtun leader and his band of fighters. Finally, on October 24, an Air Force C-130 cargo plane made the first CIA weapons drop of the war—to General Dostum of the Northern Alliance.

Over the next few days, Karzai's tactical position deteriorated rapidly. Taliban movements forced him to change his location on the 26th, but he still was able to maintain the same drop zone, hoping against hope that the promised weapons would fall from the sky. On the 27th, he reported that he would have to move again the following day, and requested that CIA arrange tactical air (tac-air) cover to strike any Taliban units that pursued him. International radio broadcasts were now trumpeting the demise of Abdul Haq, and Hamid was sure the Taliban would redouble their efforts to track him down.

Tac-air was also becoming a sore point with me. As early as October 19, I had sent a message to headquarters proposing that we should have a dedicated air platform, either a missile-armed Predator or a C-130 gunship, constantly on station in the Kandahar area to strike Taliban leadership targets as and when they were revealed to us. The U.S. military was simply not moving nimbly enough to take advantage of opportunities that were being reported to us in near-real time. For example, on October 16, our best human source in Kandahar saw Mullah Omar driving out of town in a low-profile two-car convoy. The source immediately provided us with a full description of the vehicles, the precise time and location of their last sighting, and the direction of their travel. We put the target information out within minutes of our receiving it, only to get no response. The final straw came three days later: the same source provided detailed information on a Taliban convoy transporting Mullah Osmani and Kandahar governor Hassan Rahmani northward from Kandahar toward Tarin Kowt. Again, no military response.

I pointed out to headquarters that this was simply unacceptable. We might never have opportunities like this again, and could not afford to throw them away. If this had been garden-variety rumor from an untested source, it would be one thing. But this was our best source, thoroughly vetted, and someone who knew the Taliban leadership intimately.

Traditionally, the "source descriptions" provided in CIA reports are not very helpful to their readers, designed much more to protect the source's identity than to give the recipient a clear idea of the report's reliability. The credibility to be assigned even to a "highly reliable" source might vary greatly, depending upon the topic and how he acquired the information. A source might be reporting with full accuracy what he had heard, but might be unsure of the reliability of the person from whom he'd heard it. We in operations would know that, but our customers would not. An intelligence consumer would often be hard-pressed to distinguish the wheat from the chaff. Suddenly finding ourselves in a situation where our reports could mean the difference between life and death, my station cast off precedent and took the initiative to provide far more sourcing information to our military customers. Jeff, my chief of reports, took the lead and almost overnight fixed a problem I had long regarded as a scandal. I explained all this to CIA's military targeters in Langley, expressing the hope that by providing the military much more insight into the relative reliability of our reports, they would be able to reason with the Air Force and work out a new system for hitting so-called "fleeting targets."

I got a quick response. In a tone commonly used when speaking with a rather dim child, the headquarters targeting unit explained that while it might be possible to put dedicated air assets on station to strike "fleeting" Taliban leadership targets, the system in place for target discrimination still would not permit the type of strikes I was seeking. They provided a full description of the military's decidedly inflexible rules of engagement, as though quoting holy writ. The bottom line was that the military would not act unless there were "U.S. eyes-on" to confirm the targets they were given.

It was hard to imagine how U.S. eyes were going to confirm the presence of Mullah Omar in the backseat of a beat-up Suzuki. In frustration, I threw the problem back on them. It was all very good that they had such a brilliant and exacting system for vetting targets, but if it were going to result in our permitting senior Taliban leaders to travel unmolested despite our having reliably identified their locations, headquarters should take the initiative to fix this with the military, or else CIA should employ a Predator to strike the targets itself.

Trying to put the problem in a little more strategic context, I sent a long message to Washington on October 25, providing my view of the evolution of the war, and the actions that might affect its outcome—

with heavy emphasis on the need to make better, targeted use of our uncontested airpower. With a nod to W. B. Yeats, I entitled it "Slouching toward Kandahar: A Window of Opportunity to Crush the Taliban Leadership." The fact that the Taliban lines opposite UIFSA in the far north were so far holding up against U.S. bombardment did carry a silver lining, I noted. With the vast majority of Taliban forces still tied down far from the Taliban capital, we had a window of opportunity— perhaps a brief one—in the south.

We could see growing indications of Pashtun tribal restiveness around the country. In addition to Abdul Haq and Karzai, Haji Zaman Ghamsharik, a warlord from Nangahar, had also returned to his home area and was organizing armed followers. There were other indications of rebellion in Nimruz in the far southwest, in Kunar in the northeast, and among the Alizai tribe in Helmand. Enough tribal elders among the Gilzai Pashtuns in the east—in Khost, Paktia, and Paktika— were speaking openly about throwing out the Taliban that Jalaluddin Haqqani, the Taliban minister of tribal affairs whom we had tried without success to suborn months earlier, had been dispatched to appease them. Several of these elders from the eastern provinces were reaching out for assistance from Gul Agha Shirzai, the former governor of Kandahar. Shirzai himself, we knew, was also preparing to reenter the south from Pakistan—preferably with our support.

Our intelligence was giving us an excellent picture of the reaction in Kandahar to these developments. Mullahs Muhammad Fazl and Abdul Ghani Baradar, both senior commanders on the northern front, had been recalled to help plan the defense of the Taliban homeland. Mullah Osmani, who had overall command there, was beginning to arm the same local tribes which the Taliban had forcibly disarmed years before—a clear sign of distress, if not panic. Omar, Osmani, Fazl, Baradar, Interior Minister Abdul Razzak, and intelligence chief Hafiz Majid were all moving about Kandahar and southern Uruzgan provinces, constantly changing locations and refusing to meet together for fear of air attack.

This underscored, I said, our need to focus on striking the Taliban in Kandahar decisively before the window closed. But to do that we must focus on two things: making our targeted air attacks in the south more effective against the Taliban leadership; and, even more important, moving quickly to support those few southern tribals willing and able to effectively confront the Taliban, even at the relative expense of Northern Alliance commanders whom we had been disproportionately favoring.

The reassignment of Fazl and Baradar, I said, could presage an attempt by Mullah Omar to shift their troops southward as well. Fazl would later return north, but the larger point remained. "Even if Taliban defenses in the north should be broken, enough of their scattered fighters could make their way south to reconstitute a Taliban army . . . too strong for [our] lightly-armed tribals to match, and much too far away for Northern Alliance forces to reach. A defiant Taliban surrounded by significant numbers of loyal fighters in the remote south, supplemented by the Arabs and by Taliban guerilla fighters in the mountains of eastern Afghanistan (supported there by sympathetic tribals in the [contiguous] Pak tribal areas) would not be a welcome scenario. We recommend that we should strike quickly, using the capabilities at hand, while the southern advantage remains with us."

The same day, Greg chimed in from his base to underscore the point. "We understand competing requirements, and applaud the efforts of others," he said, "but [Karzai] is the only effective opposition force in the South, and [he] needs our support."

The response from headquarters was contradictory. On the one hand, to my surprise, CTC/SO had high praise for my cable, asserting that it had been "received exceptionally well," and reaffirming that we saw the situation in the south in the same way. A near-simultaneous message stated incongruously that Washington was interested in dispatching CIA teams to accompany two separate, completely unvetted Pashtun tribal leaders, with whom CIA had had only indirect contact to date, as they infiltrated back into Afghanistan. One, whom we knew to be a notorious fabricator, claimed to be returning to Kunar in the far northeast. Heavily engaged as we were with the Northern Alliance, a foothold there would have been less than useless to us at that stage, even if this fellow were serious—which we strongly doubted. The other candidate was a small-caliber figure whose home area was similarly far removed from the "Pashtun Belt." We had stressed the need to quickly pursue the Taliban where they lived, and neither of the candidates headquarters had identified would get us close.

On the other hand, CTC/SO strongly asserted that they "might well elect to defer" sending a team to join Gul Agha Shirzai, with whom Islamabad was now in touch, "until he has assembled a large group of fighters and shown an ability to engage the enemy in the field." That was sensible enough, as far as it went, but headquarters apparently saw no need to hold other candidates to such a standard. We feared that if Langley elected to assign CIA teams prematurely to unvetted and marginal figures, not only might these scarce teams be overrun by the Taliban and lost unnecessarily, but we would quickly become overstretched and incapable of supporting more substantial figures, such as Shirzai, whose base of support was in the Taliban heartland. We had reported a week earlier that we would soon know what he was capable of, and whether it would make sense to invest scarce CIA and Special Forces resources in him. Nonetheless, headquarters remained clearly and, to us at least, inexplicably hostile to this line of thinking.

Meanwhile, Hamid Karzai's position was growing increasingly tenuous. He reported to Greg on October 28 that Taliban forces were moving into Deh Ra'ud, a significant town west of Tarin Kowt, threatening to arrest tribal leaders deemed loyal to him. The elders there, he said, had held a *jirga*, or consultation, in his presence to discuss declaring open hostilities against the Taliban. We were encouraged that he was developing such a following, but thought it unlikely they could sustain a fight without significant new weapons. Hamid once again moved his drop zone to what he hoped would be a safer location. This time he pleaded for a weapons delivery on the 29th. We had been at this for sixteen excruciating days. Greg had to inform him the following day that the latest requested drop was being postponed, yet again, to the 30th.

"That is unfortunate," Karzai responded, as the Taliban had moved back into Tarin Kowt with 1,500 fighters. They were systematically arresting tribal elders suspected of loyalty to him, just as they were doing in Deh Ra'ud. Ominously, he added another item to his long wish list: a small, portable diesel generator and fuel, so that he could recharge his phone batteries while fleeing from the Taliban. Again, Greg weighed in to Washington with a plea not to miss the promised scheduled drop.

Otherwise, he said, "Base does not look forward to the next sat-com transmission with Karzai."

By now, the delay in supplying Karzai was beyond scandal, and approaching the criminal: heated messages were flying back and forth between headquarters and multiple field locations. The senior CIA representative at the "Joint Special Operations Task Force—North (JSOTF-N)," otherwise known as "Task Force Dagger," located at the same Karshi Khanabad ("K2") Airbase in Uzbekistan whence the aerial support flights emanated, suddenly weighed in for the first time. "Colonel Pete," as he was affectionately known, was a tall, gray-haired Army Reserve officer with a bluff, friendly manner and an outsize personality. He had entered the Clandestine Service relatively late in life, but had brought with him considerable knowledge of the military. Usefully, he had also been Greg's predecessor as my base chief.

Task Force Dagger had originally been set up to provide helicopter-borne "CSAR"—combat search and rescue—for downed U.S. aircrews in Afghanistan, but had quickly transitioned to provide a staging area for aerial delivery and for insertion of "Operational Detachments Alpha," or "ODA"s, of the Fifth Special Forces Group as well. These were the multiskilled, twelve-man "A-teams" being inserted with CIA to support the indigenous militias of the Northern Alliance.

In his message, Colonel Pete described an aerial delivery logistics train that was essentially broken. Too many items, he said, from too many places were being packaged, shipped, broken down, and then repacked at too many stops along the way to Afghanistan. This was creating the interminable delays that threatened to undo us in the south. Instead, he advised, items should be sent in bulk to a single forward staging area at an airbase utilized by the U.S. military much closer to the theater of operations. There, weapons and supplies could be packaged once in the correct combinations for the various receiving teams, rigged for aerial deployment, and forwarded on to K2 for final delivery.

Revealingly, he noted that Task Force Dagger had only just been informed of a potential requirement for aerial supply of Karzai in the south, and that no provision had been made for deployment of an ODA in his support. Pete pointedly contrasted this with the elaborate plans being formulated to field ODAs with a series of second-tier commanders in the north. Given the critical importance and tenuous status of Karzai in the south, he argued, Task Force Dagger should be slightly delaying a planned drop to Commander Muhammad Atta of the Northern Alliance, and diverting that package to the beleaguered Pashtun in Uruzgan Province. We could do this, he said, and still be able to make the drop to Atta in time to support his combined move with General Dostum toward Mazar-e Sharif.

Apparently sensing through Colonel Pete that CTC/SO's attitude was putting them at a distinct disadvantage in terms of planning for insertions in the south, Task Force Dagger sent word on October 28 that they were deploying, on their own initiative, a four-man "planning cell" to work with us in Islamabad. The planners were due to arrive on October 31. We were very pleased to receive them. I reported this development to Langley, and noted that it would be even more helpful if we and Fifth Group could plan in concert with headquarters.

While the bureaucratic wars raged, Hamid Karzai continued a more elemental struggle on the ground. On October 30, we received a report from the Predator operators: they had detected activity at Karzai's reported location, but could not find the pursuing Taliban. The Predator was just not useful as a broad search tool. Looking through the camera lens of a Predator was like looking through a keyhole. In order to follow the Taliban, they would need to have a precise location from which to start.

Later the same day, we finally got the much-anticipated word from Colonel Pete: Two C-130s had made a precision drop of nineteen bundles of up to 1,200 pounds each to Karzai's location. This was quickly followed by an excited call from Hamid.

"We've got it!" he said. "Some has gone astray, my men are gathering it . . . I'm a little busy now . . . I will call you tomorrow."

That night, Hamid contacted various international media outlets via his sat phone to announce his insurgent campaign against the Taliban. He had been wanting to do so for some time, but had been cautioned by Greg, who counseled him to wait until he had gathered more strength before waving a red flag in front of the mullahs.

Now, having met our own declared threshold, Greg came in with a formal request for an A-team to join Karzai, including specialists to guide tactical close-air support, supplemented with a couple of CIA "Ground Branch" paramilitary officers. It would be necessary to have substantial military presence right from the start, he wrote, as this would be a "UW" (unconventional warfare) campaign, quite unlike those under way in the north. This was his professional recommendation, he said, although deferring "to others more skilled and talented in this arena." That last bit was vintage Greg.

The response from headquarters was soon in coming. Citing the direct interest and involvement of DCI Tenet, they offered to provide a second drop to Karzai's forces within seventy-two hours. They would not yet approve introduction of a CIA/SF team, though, until Karzai could demonstrate his ability to seize and maintain a defensible perimeter. Otherwise, the threat of capture would be too high. It was gratifying to have headquarters quoting back to us the criteria we had advocated all along for infiltration of a team, but in this case we felt they were being too literal. This was doubly unfortunate because firm U.S. rules of engagement demanded that any close-air targets be designated by Americans, and attempts thus far to do so with a Predator had failed. Without Americans on the ground with Karzai, U.S. aircraft could not provide him effective protection.

Tenet, we were told, would be raising the issue of mandatory U.S. "eyes-on" with the Principals' Committee—the War Cabinet—in hopes of getting a change in policy. As soon as the intrepid Pushtun chieftain could demonstrate he would not be overrun, we were assured, we would get our team. To us, this was cold comfort. We doubted there would be a change in military doctrine, and without Americans on the ground with him to direct air support, we thought it unlikely Karzai's forces could defend a perimeter under determined Taliban attack.

Hamid responded enthusiastically to the idea of a second drop. Having all the weapons and ammunition he needed for the moment, he said he now would welcome food, warm sleeping bags, and proper foot gear for his fighters. Once again, his force estimate was very squishy. He had 100 fighters physically with him, but the rest of his force, he said, was split up into two additional groups. Altogether, he thought, his force might number anywhere between 300 and 500 men.

The next four days were an emotional roller coaster. On November 1, Taliban forces mounted in pickups and open-backed trucks rushed out from both Tarin Kowt and Deh Ra'ud, attacking Hamid and forcing his men to fall back. CENTCOM immediately vectored attack aircraft into the area, but had difficulty identifying targets. At various points, CENTCOM air controllers were speaking directly to Greg, as he attempted to relay targeting information from Hamid via sat phone. Nothing seemed to work very well. Karzai would excitedly relay what he was hearing from his men, trying to pinpoint targets he could not see himself. In frustration, he requested a helicopter, so that his men could pick out targets from above and report them directly.

Late in the day, Hamid reported that the Taliban had broken contact. The U.S. strikes, he said, had sent a clear message. His forces were taking advantage of the lull to change their position. He promised to send coordinates for a new drop zone as soon as possible; Greg had earlier relayed a request for a one-pallet drop of additional weapons, but nothing could be delivered in the short time available.

Late that night, as I paced the floor, we received another immediate message from headquarters. Intercepted Taliban communications indicated that Karzai's forces had been ambushed; could we contact Hamid to determine his status? Greg set about feverishly to do that. About 11:00 PM, unable to tolerate the suspense any longer, I called Greg on the secure phone for an update.

"I don't know what's happening, Chief. Hamid was supposed to have called over an hour ago." I feared the worst, but wouldn't say so. We chatted nervously for a while; the tension made me all the more susceptible to Greg's offbeat humor.

Suddenly: "It's Hamid, Chief. I'll call you right back." Initially overjoyed that Karzai was still alive, my relief was short-lived. I could vividly imagine the scene as the faltering insurgent pleaded for help from Greg while Taliban fighters closed in on him from all sides. A few interminable minutes later, and Greg was back on the line, repeating Karzai's halting transmissions, and mimicking their style.

"There is firing again . . . We must move . . . My batteries are failing . . . You must send me a generator . . . I will call you when we arrive at our new location." *Click.*

On and on it went through the night, through several more such staccato interactions, each raising many more questions than it answered, as the running fight between Hamid's tribals and the Taliban continued well into the morning of November 2.

Later that day, Hamid was able at last to send a textual transmission.

"We beat them like hell," it began. Hamid and his men had encountered a large Taliban force, including both Arabs and Pakistanis, as they were attempting to change their location the night of November 1. The Taliban immediately tried to surround them. After a lengthy, confused fight, Hamid's men had beaten them off. His force had again been divided into three: one group near Deh Ra'ud, and a second toward Tarin Kowt; he and his remaining fighters manned a command post, but without radios it was very difficult to coordinate with his other two units.

Greg sent a response: "Everyone in the U.S. government supports you. All we ask is that you maintain a continuous heartbeat. . . ."

Later on the 2nd, concerned that Taliban forces remained in the area and could attack again at any time, headquarters proposed that Karzai be supported with a BLU-82 strike. We appreciated the sentiment, but it was a terrible idea. A 15,000-pound "daisy-cutter" would have devastated a wide area. Our enemies would not be the only ones to suffer. After checking with Hamid, Greg immediately requested that they stand down: "Karzai depends on local support," he pointed out.

On November 3, unsure that he could maintain his position much longer, Karzai sent Greg a long message. He requested a helicopter exfiltration for himself and twelve of his senior commanders. He needed to confer face-to-face with us, he said. He could not sustain effective communications with us using the current system, and lacked the means to communicate with his own men over any distance. If we could retrieve him, he could quickly reinsert with his commanders and an American support team within seventy-two hours. In the meantime, the rest of his fighters would melt into the countryside, return to their villages, and await his return.

In the previous forty-eight hours, Hamid Karzai's tiny and almost hopelessly tenuous insurgency had suddenly entered the national consciousness. On November 2, *The Washington Post* ran a front-page story: "Pashtun Uprising Reported in Afghanistan," it read. With the death of Abdul Haq only days before, Hamid was seen as the last great hope for Pashtun opposition to the Taliban. Hamid's regular phone calls to international media outlets, "from deep inside Taliban-controlled Afghanistan," had no doubt helped to raise his profile.

In response to our request, and probably encouraged by Hamid's sudden prominence, General Franks immediately charged the Joint Special Operations Command to plan and execute his extraction. They agreed that someone who knew and could coordinate with Karzai should be on board. I wanted Greg on that helicopter. "Jimmy Flanagan," a cheery, highly skilled former Delta operator from CIA's paramilitary Special Activities Division who had only just arrived with us, would accompany him. Both flew immediately to Jacobabad, where they linked up with the JSOC shooters and the aircrews aboard a pair of CH-47 "Chinook" helicopters.

This extraction, I knew, would be a white-knuckle affair. JSOC operators live on precise advance planning, and are used to being masters of their own fate. This time they would be anything but. They would be flying at night into an unsurveyed and poorly marked landing zone that they had had little chance to study. For all they knew, the location to which they were vectoring might have been overrun by the Taliban before they got there. In their usual operational scenarios armed fighters closing on them are enemies, and treated accordingly. The instinct of Hamid's undisciplined militia fighters, no doubt, would be to rush toward the landing helicopter, carrying their weapons with them; that could well lead to a spontaneous firefight, and disaster for all concerned.

Greg gave Hamid clear, stern instructions: No one was to approach the helicopter; all weapons were to be kept out of sight. Greg alone would dismount from the helo and meet with Karzai on the periphery of the landing zone, where he should have his party—which had since been reduced to seven—organized and ready to leave immediately. Greg would then escort them, unarmed, to the helo.

Miraculously, it all came off smoothly. After picking up the Afghans, the helicopters touched down briefly at Dalbandin, in southern Baluchistan, and then swung northward to Jacobabad. Karzai was safely in our hands. I couldn't believe our good fortune. It was well before dawn on the morning of November 4, 2001.

I wanted to rush down to meet our guests immediately, but was delayed by another task. Secretary Rumsfeld was making his first, whirlwind overseas trip since 9/11. He would fly into Pakistan that afternoon of the 4th, and stop briefly at the embassy before continuing on to a meeting and dinner hosted by President Musharraf, departing Pakistan that same night.

The trip planners in the Office of the Secretary of Defense indicated that the secretary would have only an hour or so in Islamabad before meeting with Musharraf. He wished to meet with the chief of station, they said. The embassy responded immediately that of course Rumsfeld could meet the COS, who could be included as a participant in a briefing by the "Country Team." Rumsfeld's office fired back. No, they said, perhaps we have not made ourselves clear: the secretary has little time, and wishes to meet only with the chief of station.

This was all very flattering, and the secretary would probably not have cared, but he wasn't doing me any favors. Word that he would only consent to meet with me, and not even the ambassador, spread quickly among the embassy staff. I made a great show of concern and dismay over this. Ambassador Chamberlin, as it happened, would be out of town in any case, but I pleaded with the deputy chief of mission, Michele Sison, to "save" me from having to meet alone with the fearsome Rumsfeld.

Any chief of station depends greatly upon the support of others, and is well advised not to forget it. I had wonderful relationships with all the key section chiefs, as well as with Ambassador Chamberlin, whose independence of thought and bureaucratic courage I particularly admired, and I needed to maintain those relationships intact. Chamberlin, in particular, had the ability to make life hard for me, and sometimes exercised it. I could well understand the reasons why. The mission was in drawdown mode, with all dependents and non-essential staff sent away from post. She was under tremendous pressure from the State Department to keep the number of official Americans in-country to an absolute minimum, and was even forced to provide a daily headcount. I, of course, was working at cross-purposes, with new people pouring in almost every day. We clashed over it repeatedly.

"These people are on the gravy train," she told me one day.

"Look," I retorted. "All these people have jobs, and could easily be doing them safely behind a desk in northern Virginia. They're not out here for their health. It takes people to support a war effort, and we need them here." I took her on an unscripted walkabout of our spaces. As we randomly approached people crammed cheek-by-jowl at long tables—many didn't even have proper desks—I invited them to tell the ambassador precisely what they were doing.

She stopped me partway through the second room. "Okay. I take your point," she said. I didn't need to give her, or anyone else in the mission, an excuse to make things harder for me still. I had to show I was a team player.

When Secretary Rumsfeld arrived at my door, I was pleased to find him escorted by Michele Sison. Tall, vivacious, strikingly pretty, and—in view of her senior position—surprisingly young, she had cheerily greeted Rumsfeld on his arrival and simply refused to leave his side. The secretary, for his part, seemed very jocular.

"What do you know that I don't know?" he demanded of me, as soon as we were settled.

"Very little, I hope." We were sharing everything we knew with his department, I said.

"Tell me about Hamid Karzai."

I was careful at the outset to state that while of course some of my people knew him very well, I had not yet met the man.

"Oh, I have!" Michele said. She proceeded to provide the secretary impressions from her encounters with Karzai on the diplomatic circuit. We carried on in a relaxed fashion, the secretary posing questions and listening intently. After a few minutes, a doughy, bookish-looking fellow opened the door and walked in as if he owned the place. I would later come to know Doug Feith, the under secretary of defense for policy, much better, in the context of a very different war.

I talked about prospects for a broader insurgency in the south, and the difficulties we were encountering in getting Pashtun leaders to get off the fence and to commit themselves. The secretary glared. "And what are you doing about it?" he demanded in mock exasperation.

"Now you see what we live with," Feith muttered wanly.

It didn't seem that Rumsfeld had any particular agenda for the meeting. I think having heard my ideas about the conduct of the war, he just wanted to take my measure a bit. He would seek out my views again in future.

What I neglected to explain to him was that Karzai's exfiltration should be kept secret. It simply never occurred to me that I would have to. I thought it obvious that with Karzai having publicly announced his leadership of a genuine, independent, indigenously based insurgency in the heartland of Afghanistan, the last thing we would want to do was advertise that the U.S. military had been forced to fly in to save him from the Taliban. The secretary and I were operating on very different assumptions. I would soon regret the oversight.

Late that night, I met with General Ehsan, the new ISI chief, just as he was returning from dinner with Rumsfeld at the presidency. I briefed him on our surreptitious exfiltration of Hamid Karzai, requesting that he keep this information close-hold, and stressing that it would only be a brief period before Karzai would leave Pakistan to return to the fight. No one must know that he'd left. The general agreed, stressing that we needed to make quicker progress against the Taliban, and also offered me exclusive use of his personal aircraft for three days, so that we could ferry necessary supplies and equipment down to Jacobabad.

It was not until the following morning that I found myself in the abandoned schoolhouse that was now Hamid Karzai's home. After we had conferred quietly for a while, we joined his tribal colleagues in a circle. Hamid introduced his six commanders, extolling each in turn for his loyalty and bravery in confronting the Taliban. I asked a number of questions about their plans and the steps they would take upon their return, with Hamid patiently translating both questions and answers.

We spoke of our common interest in driving foreign terrorists out of Afghanistan, and the terrorists' Taliban protectors from power. I spoke of the assistance they could expect from America. The discussion was all very warm and bracing, but it hadn't yet told me what I really wanted to know. Finally, I put to them what was to me the obvious question:

"What you are setting out to do will be very difficult," I said. "You are taking great risks for yourselves, your families and your clans." I paused, looking briefly at each of them in turn. "Why are you doing this?"

"Muhammad Shahzad," a heavyset man whose body seemed to radiate energy and strength, had made a particular impression on me. He had piercing light green eyes, and bore himself with considerable dignity. Karzai had earlier told me privately of his loyalty. He had insisted on remaining next to Hamid at all times; at the points of greatest danger in the mountains, he had remained awake while Hamid slept, and had covered his leader with his own blanket to protect him from the wind. To that point, he had not said a word, but now he spoke for everyone. His answer was simple and direct:

"We're tired of those bastards from Kandahar telling us what to do in our own area." That I could understand; it worked for me.

Hamid, Jeff (the senior reports officer), and I then excused ourselves and stepped out to a separate room. I felt I had died a thousand deaths following Karzai's progress over the past few weeks through brief, often panic-stricken snippets, related secondhand. Now, at last, I had the opportunity to hear the complete tale, calmly, from the man himself, as Jeff took notes and asked questions.

As we knew, on October 8, Hamid and three companions had crossed into Afghanistan on Highway 4, the main southern route from Quetta, riding two motorcycles all the way to Kandahar. They spent the night with a trusted friend, from whose home they could see the booming flashes of a U.S. air raid. The following day they drove northward in a taxi until they encountered a Taliban checkpoint at the crossing into Uruzgan Province. The guard, a taciturn young man barely able to support a beard, was suspicious of the large bag in the back of their car, the one with the satellite phone secreted within it, and wished to inspect it. The taxi's occupants demurred, and two of their number went inside to speak with the officer in charge. Karzai and his remaining companion whispered together in the car. Their quest might end right then and there, they agreed, but they would not be arrested that day. They prepared their weapons. Their two friends emerged from the guardhouse. The senior officer, apparently, had not been interested—either in them or their bag. Leaving the border post behind, they continued onward without a stop until they reached Tarin Kowt, the provincial seat of Uruzgan. Hamid Karzai, the son of Abdul Ahad, grandson of the great Khair Muhammad Khan, and scion of the proud Durrani Popalzai, was finally home among his people.

The Pashtuns of Afghanistan are divided into two broad tribal confederations, the Durrani and the Gilzai. The former are concentrated in the central and southern regions of the country, the latter in the east. Tarin Kowt itself was comprised of perhaps 60 percent Durrani, with a plurality of those drawn from Hamid's Popalzai. As soon as he arrived in the area, Hamid traveled to Kotwan village to meet with the highly respected Amin Zadeh. Amin drew together key notables from both Durrani- and Gilzai-affiliated tribes, including representatives of all the local Popalzai. Together they pledged Hamid their support, but stressed to him that they had few weapons, and not enough ammunition even for those. In subsequent days, Hamid met local chieftains in Khanaka, and later in Ghojurak, canvassing tribal groups in virtually all the villages surrounding Tarin Kowt over the following two weeks. In one excursion in the Dera Juy Valley, his borrowed car got stuck in mud; he and his companions walked onward three hours up the valley to meet with seventy tribals.

Hamid conducted these meetings entirely in the open. He knew from listening to internal Taliban radio broadcasts that the authorities in Kandahar had become aware of his presence within three days of his arrival in Uruzgan, but they could do nothing about it at first. In fact, the deputy chief of the Uruzgan Provincial Council, a Taliban member, met with Karzai and offered to turn Tarin Kowt over to him. Hamid declined, saying he would only take the town when he could defend it. A couple of days later the same official reported that Mullah Omar had complained to the governor about Karzai, citing reports that the opposition leader was circulating freely. The governor explained that he lacked the forces to arrest the man, and feared the reaction of the local tribes if he should attempt it.

In late October, word came that a large Taliban force—the same one reported by our sources—was moving northward from Kandahar to find Karzai and arrest him. In Pashtun culture, failure to defend a guest is deemed a shameful breach of honor. Fearing that they could not protect him, the local elders asked that Karzai move to a more defensible area, promising to provide him with an armed escort. Hamid's core group of fifteen armed supporters was soon joined by perhaps thirty-five others; they walked eight hours up into the mountains. The newest volunteers had not been aware of the plan, and had left their homes without food, sleeping gear, or proper clothing.

They camped on a high plateau north of Dera Juy, flanked on the western and eastern sides by ridges that dropped off into steep, rocky, easily defensible slopes. Local farmers provided them with food. Another thirty volunteers arrived the following day. When the first weapons drop came on October 30, Hamid had about 120 fighters—considerably fewer, Jeff and I noted, than he had advertised to us at the time. The weapons, he said, were first-rate, fully assembled and ready for use. In addition to the light arms, he handed out ten PKM light machine guns and eight RPG launchers.

In addition to comestibles, local villagers were regularly providing Karzai's band with news about developments and Taliban movements in the area. On November 1, they reported that 200 "strangers" were making their way up the valley. Karzai had his men set up a checkpost on the main road below them, where they soon captured two Taliban fighters from Helmand. The two told them that a considerable force of Pakistanis and ragtag Afghans had parked their trucks farther down the valley, and were making their way on foot up the steep terrain from several different directions toward Karzai's position.

Hamid rushed to set up a defensive perimeter near his main camp along the western ridge, but before he could do so began taking fire, forcing him and his men to withdraw to a separate area where they had additional ammunition stores. Fortunately, they had managed to bring several of the PKMs with them as they fled. From the new position, they could both defend themselves and supply the fighters who remained along the western ridge. The latter were under sharp attack, particularly at the far northern and southern ends of their defensive position. "Mohamed Alwahhab," one of Karzai's commanders whom he did not know, kept up a tenacious defense at the northern end, but Karzai's men were driven back from the south. These joined Karzai, and the combined force abandoned the ammunition storage area, regrouped on higher ground, and then counterattacked, driving the Taliban back.

Hamid could listen to the Taliban communications on a captured radio. One of their commanders was trapped behind a large boulder as he took concentrated PKM fire from above. Someone ordered him to renew the attack, saying they were under direct orders from Mullah Omar.

"I don't care if the orders come from my father," the man had shouted back. "If I try to move, they will shoot my head off!"

The fighting continued until 2:00 PM on November 2, when the Taliban and Pakistanis broke contact and moved off. The PKMs, he said, had been decisive. Without them, they would surely have been overrun. The Pakistanis were particularly good fighters, and cruel: they had badly abused one of Karzai's wounded.

Hamid and most of his men had survived, but had no more water, and were very unsure of their position. They could not communicate with the men defending the eastern ridge, which was some way off. Hamid could see armed men through his binoculars, but could not be sure if they were his. If not, he would be in an untenable position. They held a *jirga* to decide what they should do; the consensus was that Hamid should arrange for himself and his senior commanders to be evacuated by the Americans, and then return with greater assistance, while the rest of the force dispersed for the time being.

As it turned out, Karzai's men on the eastern ridge had held their positions; there had been no immediate need to evacuate. It was an inestimable blessing, though, that they had.

Jeff and I said our goodbyes to Karzai and his elders, and I made my way off for a briefing by Captain Jason Amerine, commander to the ODA that had come down from K2 to accompany Karzai on his return to Uruzgan. He and his people had been studying maps of the Tarin Kowt area, and had come up with what struck me as a rather overcomplicated insertion plan. I wasn't about to try to tell this young man his business. The military part of this was his responsibility. I figured that so long as the Special Forces could move Karzai and his elders into a defensible position, U.S. airpower would protect them until they could assemble what we all hoped would be a larger fighting force.

I also took the opportunity to tour the bivouac area where our CIA people would be staged before inserting inside. Spotting Tom, my translator, who was slated to accompany the team, I pulled him aside.

"Can't you do something about the food?" I asked. I was mortified that we were providing the elders nothing better than cold beef stew, much as they seemed to relish it. Unsurprisingly, Tom had already established contacts at a decent restaurant in town; proper mutton and rice would soon be delivered to the gate. As we spoke, Tom was putting the finishing touches on some "field-expedient" clothing: he had taken a light military jacket, festooned with multiple mesh pockets but several sizes too large for him, and cut off the sleeves to make a vest. Just then, the bearded, hulking Special Forces trooper occupying the cot closest to Tom's was inquiring loudly as to the whereabouts of his jacket. We both looked at Tom's vest. The trooper burst out in incredulous laughter, amused at Tom's sheer audacity. I could only wonder at the reasons for Tom's apparent kleptomania. Perhaps he reasoned that as all the goods surrounding them were government-issue, they should properly be the property of all. Perhaps he was a just a romantic Trotskyite at heart. Whatever the case, he would not always find such tolerance in future.

Before leaving, I had a long chat with Greg and Jimmy. They would be responsible for the Afghan end of this venture, and had little idea what sort of tribal force Karzai would be able to organize when they went inside. We fully expected at that point that Hamid and his American team would be reinserting within three days. We were soon to be disabused. Once out, I didn't realize how difficult it would be to get Karzai back in.

Chapter 24

ENEMIES WITHOUT, ENEMIES WITHIN

NOVEMBER 13, 2001

A S THE TELEVIDEO FLICKERED to life, I could see the accustomed players. At the head of the table, facing directly toward us, was George Tenet. Next to him was Jim Pavitt, the DDO. Down the left side of the table, as we viewed it, were the usual suspects from CTC, including Hank. On the right, opposite them, were my colleagues from the Near East Division, looking sullen and cowed. Among them was Gary Spitzel, the highly capable chief of the South Asia Task Force, whose role in Afghanistan had been thoroughly eclipsed by CTC/SO.

This conversation promised to be an important one, as Gul Agha's preparations to reenter Afghanistan were approaching fruition and the conflict between Islamabad Station and CTC/SO was coming to a head. It was considered bad form to raise operational disagreements in front of the director; such issues were expected to be worked out at a lower level. With no checks and balances in the system, however, I was prepared to appeal directly to Tenet for decisions, without mentioning that these issues were in dispute. If CTC wanted to raise objections at the table, they would be free to do so.

Traditionally, the geographic divisions, and particularly the Near East and South Asia division, had controlled the bits of turf around the globe in which CTC sought to press its operations. The division's field officers were the ones conducting these operations, after all, and division management was able to provide guidance and a useful, moderating check on CTC's at times myopic zeal. In the aftermath of 9/11, those breaks were swept away. The effort to drive al-Qa'ida out of Afghanistan was the preeminent national security challenge before the U.S. government, and Director Tenet was the leader of that effort. He wanted a centralized, streamlined headquarters mechanism to deal with the war, and it was natural that he should find it in the Counterterrorist Center.

In order to give it greater independence, and in virtue of the fact that it combined elements of both the Directorate of Operations and the Directorate of Intelligence (Analysis), CTC had from its founding in 1986 been designated as the DCI Counterterrorist Center, placing it under the authority of the director. As a practical matter, though, CTC had always been subordinate to the DDO, the head of the Clandestine Service. But with George Tenet leading the war effort, CTC suddenly became his, in fact as well as in theory. George was too well attuned to what was happening around him not to have at least some idea of the controversies being generated, but he had neither the time nor the inclination to sort out disputes within the Clandestine Service. He just wanted to see things done.

Weeks before, on October 18, headquarters had evinced scant enthusiasm when we first broached the idea that Gul Agha would enter Afghanistan via the Shin Naray Valley. If there had been any doubts along those lines, they were dispelled by CTC/SO's cable of October 26, the one which had reviewed potential tribal candidates for direct CIA support, favoring several whose willingness and ability to confront the Taliban we knew to be highly suspect, and pointedly expressing reservations regarding Shirzai. Nonetheless, when I proposed on November 1 that we finance Gul Agha's purchase of enough additional weapons to equip an entry force of 150 to 200 men, headquarters agreed. They also agreed the same day, reluctantly, to my proposal to seek the ISI's help in facilitating the movement of an anti-Taliban tribal force across the border. This I had broached, in principle only, with General Ehsan on the night of November 4, the same night I briefed him on our extraction of Karzai. Ehsan was agreeable and did not press for any details of personalities or places, which I had no intention of providing him at that stage in any case. I knew that I could trust Ehsan and General Jafar, but I also knew that the actual facilitation on the ground would inevitably involve lower-ranking members of their organization, any one or combination of whom could well be Taliban sympathizers. I did not want to give the pro-Taliban types the opportunity to sabotage our plans by telling them too much, too far in advance.

Convinced by our difficulty in arranging arms drops to Karzai that we should avoid reliance on air supply to the extent possible, I had also arranged with General Jafar to procure weapons—a mixture of AKs and RPG-7s—from Pakistan Army stocks, sufficient for 500 fighters whom we hoped would join the initial cross-border party. The weapons were on standby; I intended to use this meeting to get approval to pay for and deliver them.

Colonel Pete in Karshi Khanabad had continued to play a useful intermediary role for us with the Fifth Special Forces Group. The Special Forces, concerned lest they be caught unawares and then whipsawed by changes in plan as they had been with Karzai, had asked Pete for full background information on Gul Agha, which we were happy to provide. It was becoming obvious to me that the Special Forces were chafing to get more ODAs into the south, and growing frustrated with what they perceived as high-handedness and arbitrariness on the part of CIA Headquarters. Kept informed by "Captain Greg" and a wizened, canny, tobacco-chewing Special Forces enlisted man of almost legendary experience, Chief Warrant Officer (CW3) Poteet, who had also been assigned to our station team, Fifth Group was keen to get into the fight with Shirzai.

Although General Franks's formal campaign plan specified at this stage that Special Forces could only operate in Afghanistan on a CIA lead—thus giving the agency effective veto power over whom the Special Forces could join up with in Afghanistan and when—I was pleased to forge independent links with the Green Berets, and to develop them as allies. The wisdom in doing so was reinforced two days later, on November 12, just before the video teleconference, when we received a treacly cable from CTC/SO, earnestly professing their interest in supporting Gul Agha with a CIA/SF team, but making what I regarded as a series of suspicious excuses as to why this might prove difficult in the end. The reasons would shortly become clear.

Now, however, Tenet opened the videoconference by asking me for an overview of the situation. I began by noting the recent successes of the Northern Alliance, which had taken Mazar-e Sharif and was launching a major attack toward Kabul. I confined my assessment of these events to their likely impact on Taliban strategy and morale, leaving aside the wider political implications. I had long been concerned about the impact among the Pashtuns of a Northern Alliance seizure of Kabul. I feared they would see it as a U.S.-facilitated power grab, which would undermine their support for the anti-Taliban uprising, such as it was, in the south.

Weeks earlier, almost immediately after Gary Schroen's arrival in the Panjshir Valley at the head of the "Jawbreaker" team, he and I had begun sparring in cable traffic over how to manage our support for the northerners and the ends to which that support should aim. Having compared the situation of the Northern Alliance to that of the Israelis during the First Gulf War of 1990, I felt strongly that a seizure of Kabul by the Tajiks and Uzbeks would make an eventual political settlement with the Pashtuns far more difficult. I had long had great respect for Schroen, an older, Farsi-speaking Near-East Division officer under whom I had previously served, and one with deep knowledge of Afghanistan. Although we disagreed on this and other issues, I fully understood and empathized with his position. With Ahmad Shah Mahsood assassinated, he had to forge a relationship of trust with General Fahim, the new commander of the Northern Alliance, and his key subordinate commanders, and to demonstrate that our professed support for them was genuine. Armies are blunt instruments at best, and Afghan armies perhaps especially so. With the failure of our efforts to overthrow Mullah Omar from within, we would need the Northern Alliance to fix the Taliban forces in place in the north while we organized a revolt against their southern capital, lest those forces re-coalesce in the south. To expect that we could successfully induce the leaders of the Northern Alliance to calibrate their efforts so as to achieve our objectives without achieving theirs was just unrealistic, and an unfair burden to place on Gary. I came to understand that; and in any case, by November 13, this had become a policy issue for Washington to deal with, not us, and a point of contention between Tommy Franks and General Fahim. There was nothing more I could contribute on that score.

Continuing my briefing for Tenet, I shifted attention to the southwest, where Karim Brahvi had returned to Nimruz. I spoke carefully, knowing that CTC/SO would seize on this development in hopes of reinforcing Brahvi's Lilliputian efforts at the expense of others. I noted that the ex-governor's armed return to Zaranj, the capital of Nimruz, had precipitated the flight of the local Taliban—"all half-dozen of them," I said. I could see Spitzel, the South Asia Task Force chief, burst out in a loud guffaw before he brought a hand to his mouth to suppress it. Tenet and the others continued to gaze ahead, stony-faced.

I downplayed any predictions of success for Gul Agha, whose forces were already moving, and whose entry into Afghanistan was set for dawn of the following day. We would soon see whether his predictions of support inside were accurate, I said. But if even remotely accurate, we should be prepared immediately to reinforce success. I mentioned the plan under way to provide truckloads of Pakistani weapons to Shirzai's fighters.

"Good idea," said George.

I added that once those fighters had demonstrated willingness to employ their weapons against the Taliban, we should quickly dispatch a joint CIA-SF team to join them, rather than diverting such scarce resources to the distant wasteland of Nimruz. Again, the director agreed. I thought I could detect a bit of fidgeting on the CTC side of the table; but no one raised an objection. I was prepared to take yes for an answer.

Chapter 25

SALVATION

THE LONG, RECTANGULAR ROOM was somber. Its occupants clung to the periphery, leaving an open space in the middle. All eyes were focused on a tall, rangy, dark-haired young man. "Jim," Isfandiar's case officer, sat next to a credenza along the far wall, on top of which a half-dozen sat phones were spaced at regular intervals. The only sound was Jim's shallow breathing. He had just been speaking urgently in Dari with a minor warlord, a street thug really, in Gardez, the seat of Paktia Province, 60 miles south of Kabul.

Our fears over the fate of the eight Shelter Now prisoners had grown steadily over the previous two weeks since the Taliban had abruptly changed their conditions of detention, virtually on the eve of a planned JSOC rescue attempt. Those fears greatly increased as the Northern Alliance finally broke through Taliban lines on the Shomali Plains and made a pell-mell advance on Kabul. We had had a good window on the status of the SNI eight during most of their confinement; but as the Taliban evacuated Kabul in panic, they were suddenly, and entirely, lost to our view. Now, just as suddenly, they had reappeared.

The warlord had told Jim he would be willing, for a consideration, to allow his eight guests to travel to the local airfield, as requested. But it would take time. There were at least two other tribal leaders who controlled territory between his area and the airport. They would have to be negotiated with. It would take time, he repeated. The conversation ended abruptly.

For Jim, JSOC liason officer Marco, and David Donohue, the consul-

209

general, it had already been a long day. Early that morning, David received a call from the office of the International Committee of the Red Cross (ICRC) in Islamabad. Afghan colleagues in Ghazni, they said, had called to tell them that Georg Taubman, leader of the eight SNI employees, was with them at the Red Cross office there. David had rushed to report the exciting news to Jim and Marco. After quickly consulting with the JSOC forward control base in Oman, Marco thought they could get rescue helicopters in to Ghazni that night, after dark. They settled on 11:30 PM as the target for a pickup.

David hurried to ICRC to speak on a sat phone with Georg, who in turn summoned the two American women, Dayna and Heather. He told them to be prepared to link up with their rescuers at eleven thirty; further instructions would follow.

Meanwhile, Jim got in touch with Isfandiar. When the Afghan source had learned on November 13 that the SNI detainees had been gathered up by their captors the night before to join the Taliban's southward exodus from Kabul, the loyal agent had set off in his car in hopes of somehow locating them. He found the Kabul-Kandahar highway choked with vehicles and armed men fleeing the Northern Alliance's advance on the capital. When Jim reached him early on the morning of the 14th, Isfandiar was sitting forlornly in Wardak, having spent the night by the side of the road. A group of fighters had stopped him and stolen his car; thankfully, he had somehow managed to keep his sat phone hidden.

"Get to the ICRC office in Ghazni right away!" Jim commanded, sending his agent off again to the south, this time hitchhiking. When several hours later Jim again heard Isfandiar's voice, the young man sounded scared.

"I am in the ICRC office with Georg and the local commander." There had been a general uprising in Ghazni on the 13th, forcing the Taliban to flee. Now the town was chaotic, alternating between joyful euphoria and armed tension. Various small-caliber warlords were staking out their turf in the absence of any clear authority. "The men here are very suspicious of me," Isfandiar continued, a slight quaver in his voice. "They want to know where I got the satellite phone."

"Isfandiar," Jim replied. "Listen to me. Give the sat phone to Georg. Be sure to give him the charger as well, and get out of there. Leave right away." He was happy to comply.

Over the next several hours, Jim held a series of conversations in Dari with the commander. Alternately ingratiating and truculent, the strongman kept changing his story as to what he could or would be willing to do with the foreigners on his hands. He seemed to recognize that his guests represented a financial opportunity, but the political situation on the ground was changing rapidly, almost hour by hour, and he had to accommodate for it. It seemed everyone in Ghazni was aware of the ex-captives' presence. Those whose cooperation was necessary to move them would want their cut.

The minutes ticked past 9:00 PM, and then nine thirty. It had been hours since Jim last spoke with the commander. Marco reported that the helicopters were in the air; their estimated time of arrival was about midnight Islamabad time, 11:30 PM Afghan time. I left the room, with orders to come get me if anything happened.

It must have been nearly ten thirty at night Afghan time when the phone rang again. Everyone leaned forward.

"Georg! Georg, where are you?" The SNI chief reported that the commander with whom Jim had been speaking earlier had agreed to allow the detainees to remain overnight with a local family, provided they promised not to leave the area. "Georg," Jim pleaded. "Do you know where the airport is? You've got to go to the airport."

"No. We cannot." The German was adamant. "This family have been good to us. If we leave, they will be in serious trouble." Jim was trying everything he could think of to get Georg to change his mind.

"Georg, listen to me. You have a responsibility to the others. The family will be all right."

"No. We will stay here tonight. I will hang up now." The line cut off. A collective groan went up from the group.

Sitting on the floor a few feet away, his back against the wall, Marco was staring intently at a laptop perched atop his knees. He was wearing earphones; a long black wire trailed from him to the window, where it joined a bundle of similar wires running upward to a series of satellite antennas on the roof. The two rescue helicopters continued churning through the night. They had a full complement of specialists aboard, from shooters to medics. There was even a hostage rescue psychologist with them. These guys never ceased to amaze. If we could somehow get our lost sheep to the retrieval point, the helos would be there to pick them up.

Marco was speaking quietly with the JSOC controllers in Oman via his encrypted Irridium phone. They, in turn, could relay his information to the helicopter pilots, and convey their responses. On the laptop Marco could see the map grid of the Ghazni airfield and the surrounding area. He had arbitrarily selected a grid point at the field, to which the helo pilots were now vectoring. JSOC had its grid point, but the detainees had no grid. Marco was filling his JSOC colleagues in on the latest developments.

Despite our best efforts, it appeared nothing else would happen until morning. Some drifted out of the room. David Donohue appeared stoic as usual, but his face was ashen. He had done everything he could to free the detainees since their arrest by the Taliban in August. He felt the tension more than anyone.

About thirty minutes later, the phone rang again. Georg seemed slightly out of breath, as though walking rapidly.

"We are on our way to the airport." A surge of energy coursed through the room. Jim relayed Marco's instructions: When they arrived at the airfield, they were to go to the most remote part, away from any people, and try to stay out of sight. They were to find a barrel, or anything that would contain a fire, and gather as much flammable material as possible. If there were any Afghans with them, the locals should stay back when the helicopters approached. They must not display any weapons. Anyone with a weapon was liable to be shot. They were to call as soon as they were ready.

It seemed like an eternity as the JSOC helos continued their approach from the southwest. Word spread; soon the operations war room was packed, despite the hour. The aircrew reported they were five minutes out.

"Georg, do you have everything you need?"

"Yes. Yes. But we haven't much wood."

"Start the fire. Make sure it's visible. Make sure you keep it going!"

Use of a fire to mark their location was less than ideal. The flames might "whiteout" the helo pilots, equipped with night-vision goggles. But there was no alternative. With Marco relaying word of their progress, the helos made their approach, low and fast, toward the airfield. There was no fire in sight. They circled once, and then again. At length, they spotted a fire, off in an isolated corner of the field, and made for it. The lead helo went into a hover and quickly landed, blades still spinning rapidly. Several of the crew made a few tentative steps forward, peering toward the fire barrel. Out of the shadows came a handful of bearded, turbaned men, carrying weapons.

As Marco relayed, secondhand from the Oman control station, what the crew was seeing on the ground, Jim was nearly shouting at Georg.

"Where are you? Why aren't you showing yourselves?"

My heart sank. Had they been taken hostage again? JSOC operators were trained for rapid, lethal missions. Dealing sensitively with armed and undisciplined militiamen was not part of their normal repertoire. One menacing move from the Afghans, and a firefight would surely break out. We didn't even know where the detainees were at this point. It had seemed that we were so close. Now the situation was turning into a disaster.

Jim relayed word from Georg. The detainees could hear a helicopter, but they were at a different part of the field. The helo had approached the wrong fire. The pilot revved his rotors, rose, and banked sharply away from the Afghans. Meanwhile, Georg reported that their fire was going out.

"Are the women wearing head scarves?" Jim asked. They were. "Well then, tell them to throw them on the fire!" Georg's sat phone, whose signal had been steadily weakening, cut out. Communication with the detainees was lost.

The helo swung toward the opposite side of the field. The pilot could see a small glimmer of flickering light. There were minutes of complete, seemingly interminable silence as Marco hunched forward, listening intently to the feed from Oman. Suddenly, he looked up.

"They're on board," he said.

Chapter 26

ENTERING THE RAPIDS

T HE VOICE ON THE other end of the line sounded unbelievably, almost maddeningly young. It was always like that with
the Predator operators. I suppose it was the combination of extreme youth and cocky self-assurance which always got under my skin.
"Do you have an update on the convoy?" I demanded.

"No, sir. The Predator has dropped off."

"What? Dropped off? What do you mean, it's 'dropped off'?"

"Too much time on station, sir. Had to return to base for refueling."
Always the clipped, pseudomilitary manner. It would have been nice if
the idiot had let me know before now.

"Well, when can you get another one on station?"

"About an hour, sir. Maybe a little more."

"The convoy will be long gone by then! How will you ever find it?"

"We know their average speed, where they're reported to be going,
and the likely route they'll take. We should be able to pick them up
again."

I was not reassured. Earlier on that November 14, we had received
a highly reliable report from one of our human sources in Kandahar
that the Taliban had dispatched a force of between 150 and 200 fighters, mounted in some twenty trucks, to attack Gul Agha in Shin Naray.
A few hours later, a Predator was able to confirm the movement of a
large convoy matching that description, moving eastward on the highway from the Taliban capital. And now we'd lost it.

Mark, Shirzai's contact, had immediately sent an encrypted message to the chieftain to warn him of the potential danger. We were able to source the information to aerial reconnaissance—we would never have intimated the existence of a human source for fear of compromising him—but there had been no confirmation from Shirzai's people that the warning had been received. This was shaping up to be a disaster. Shirzai had reported having 350 men under arms in Shin Naray, but we could hardly be sure of that figure, especially given the Afghan penchant for exaggeration. And even if the Taliban were attacking with an inferior force, they would have the potential advantages of surprise and the ability to concentrate their forces at one or two points of attack, while Shirzai's men were spread out in defensive positions all along the ridges flanking the valley. The Taliban were experienced fighters; we had absolutely no knowledge of the experience or martial qualities of the mob Shirzai had assembled. Why the hell hadn't we heard back from them?

I spent the next ninety minutes pacing up and down the hallway, bursting into the operations war room at what must have appeared to them like thirty-second intervals, asking whether we'd heard anything from Shirzai. Dave, who had stayed late for yet another video conference with headquarters and had noticed the long absence from my office, came looking for me as I wandered aimlessly, hunched over in frowning concentration.

"You've got to calm down," he said.

"How the hell can you be so calm?" I shot back. "The Taliban are about to attack Shirzai, and they don't even know what's coming!"

Dave smiled. "They'll be fine," he said. He had followed Gul Agha and his father closely during the *jihad*. "These guys know how to defend themselves."

Earlier that day, Gul Agha entered Shin Naray on schedule, just before dawn, with the Afghans' claimed 350 armed fighters and 23 vehicles. As promised, ISI arranged their unmolested passage past the Pakistani military checkposts along the Afghan border. An additional 300 fighters, lacking weapons and so useless for the moment, remained back in Quetta.

Many who have never dealt with them believe that the ISI is essentially a rogue organization, a sort of state within a state, pursuing its own independent policies and subverting the authority of the Pakistani government it nominally serves—particularly where Afghanistan and Kashmir are concerned. That view is far too simple, and fundamentally incorrect. In my experience, the ISI is a disciplined military organization that follows the orders of the chief of Army Staff, even if individual officers, and particularly those with years of experience implementing state policy in Afghanistan and Kashmir, have clear sympathies that they are not above promoting when the occasion presents. Their dealings with Gul Agha on this occasion were a case in point.

When Shirzai's people met with the ISI man in Quetta to arrange for road escort and for the eventual delivery of several truckloads of Pak military weapons, the officer carried out his orders to the letter; but during their meeting, when alone behind closed doors, he pointedly suggested to his Afghan friends that they were making a serious mistake in trying to overthrow the Taliban, one which they would regret, and one which they should seriously reconsider. The two faces of ISI at work.

No sooner had Gul Agha's fighters entered the valley and secured it than they raced into the villages of Arghistan district immediately to the west, where they surrounded a force of sixteen Taliban. Forty-five other Taliban fighters scattered through the area could also sense the shift in local attitudes, and surrendered their weapons. Gul Agha had not intimated to anyone on either side of the border, outside of his closest associates, precisely where he was going, lest the Taliban be waiting for him when he got there. Now safely ensconced, he immediately sent commanders north into Maruf and south into Spin Boldak to rally tribesmen to his cause, and ordered the 300 fighters left behind to join him. En route from Quetta that afternoon, though, they found the road blocked by pro-Taliban students from a Pakistani *madrassa* in Gulistan. Gul Agha ordered his men via radio to turn back for the time being rather than risk a violent confrontation. That same evening, the Taliban *Shura* in Kandahar lost no time in reacting, apparently intending to strike a crippling blow against the Barakzai chieftain before he could attract more disgruntled tribesmen to his cause.

Once again, as the minutes ticked past 1:00 AM, I phoned CTC's Global Response Center. "Have you located that Taliban convoy yet?"

"No, sir. We can't find it."

I was frustrated beyond belief. "How can we lose an entire convoy?" The watch officer explained that the Taliban was becoming clever at hiding from our overhead reconnaissance.

"They've probably hidden the trucks in a brush thicket somewhere, and placed dirt and branches over them." At least by now we'd received acknowledgment from Gul Agha that they were aware of the threat. But there was still a substantial Taliban force, unmolested and presumably lying in wait, somewhere in the vicinity of Shin Naray.

I was sufficiently convinced of Gul Agha's ability to survive the night, at least, to be able to return home for a few hours' sleep, but I felt on the verge of nervous exhaustion. The mood around the station had been considerably lighter just a few hours before, as Dave and I sat around in my office laughing and joking with a handful of other senior lieutenants, waiting for the second video conference in as many nights with headquarters to start. Everything had seemed to be going well since our long-distance discussion just twenty-four hours earlier. The Northern Alliance offensive had broken through Taliban lines on the Shomali Plains just north of Kabul far more quickly than anyone could have anticipated, causing a rout, and General Fahim's forces had already entered the Afghan capital. In addition to Gul Agha having just crossed the border, it appeared that Hamid Karzai's reentry into Uruzgan was imminent.

As loose as we felt, the contrast with our headquarters colleagues when they came on the screen could not have been greater. Unlike the night before, this time the room at the headquarters end was packed, the walls lined with straphangers. The DCI had called for the conference specifically to get my take on the day's events. From the grim expressions around the room, you would have thought we were *losing* the war. I looked at Dave. These guys were definitely not having fun.

I reviewed the latest developments from a Taliban perspective. The rapidity of the Taliban collapse had been predicted for me by the ISI's foremost expert on the Taliban, a distinguished-looking officer given to ascots and blazers who had spent years living in Afghanistan among the ISI's Taliban clients. His name was "Brigadier Suhail Majid"; I had known him for many months, but now that he had been given permission by his leadership to meet frequently with me, and to share with me what he knew, we had developed a genuine bond. Suhail had no idea when the Taliban lines might be breached—the American bombing of the World War I–style Taliban entrenchments across the Shomali Plains had been disappointingly ineffectual until shortly before November 14—but he predicted that once they were, the Taliban position would crumble quickly. The undisciplined Taliban forces were mortally afraid of being outflanked, he said; as soon as they saw units on either side breaking under attack, they would flee in panic. This is precisely what happened.

Once they found their lines broken, one might have expected the Taliban leadership to try to regroup their forces in Kabul to mount a defense of the city, but Mullah Omar had decided instead to abandon the northern capital and order the withdrawal of his forces. I was convinced that this was a mark of his ability as a strategic thinker—perhaps not all that impressive in its own right, but head and shoulders above the ability of anyone around him. He, perhaps alone, recognized that the rout of his army in Shomali had left the Taliban position in the north untenable. Rather than waste his forces in a hopeless rearguard action in Kabul, it would be better to try to effect an orderly withdrawal and regroup in the south. The problem for him was that while he could conceive of such a plan, his troops and subordinate unit commanders were incapable of effecting it. Rather than an orderly strategic withdrawal, he was now confronted with the dissolution of his forces in the north. The situation probably had not been helped by his previous decision to recall some of his most capable senior commanders to aid in the defense of Kandahar.

Still, it was quite possible that not all of the fighters now fleeing south would return to their villages; some might well fall back to Kandahar and Helmand provinces, where they could again be reconstituted in units and contribute to the fight. This argued, I said, for our rapid advance on Kandahar. The battle for the southern Taliban capital would constitute the second phase of the war. The third and tertiary phase, and perhaps the most difficult, would likely take place in the mountains of the east, I said, where al-Qa'ida and Taliban elements could find refuge among the fierce Gilzai Pashtuns and gain support from the even more radical religious extremists across the border in Pakistan. Routing them out from there would be the most difficult challenge we would face.

Right now, I said, the Taliban leadership is in shock. They will soon realize, though, that their situation is not so dire as they feared. "This fight is far from over," I concluded. I had no idea just how prescient those words were.

This was apparently too much for one of my listeners, a senior South Asia analyst from the Directorate of Intelligence, now seconded to CTC. He had been standing against the back wall of the conference room, looking increasingly agitated as I went on, but now he stepped forward to challenge me. "What do you mean, the situation is not as bad as they think?" he demanded. "The Taliban's forces have been heavily concentrated in the north, and now they've been thoroughly defeated. They're fleeing in disorder. Just how could their situation be any worse?" He appeared to be on the verge of a stroke.

I shot a glance at Dave. "These guys are out of control," I thought.

"Well," I said evenly, in my best therapeutic voice, "as you know, our intelligence in Kandahar is pretty good. We understand that the rumor rapidly circulating tonight among the Taliban leadership is that American commandos have landed at Kandahar Airport. To my knowledge, that is not true; the Taliban will awake tomorrow to find that the Americans are not yet on their doorstep, that all is not yet completely lost, and that they can fight on. But I certainly did not mean to suggest that they are in a good position." We all obviously needed some sleep. The video conference wound up shortly thereafter with George asking me to sum up in writing my thoughts on the progress of the war.

The events of November 14 had changed the complexion of the war, even if the struggle was far from over. Likewise, recent events had suddenly given me a decided advantage in my parallel bureaucratic struggle with CTC.

Hank's deputy, John Massie, had been scheduled to retire on September 11. He was said to have heard of the events in New York on the radio while driving out of the Langley headquarters for what he thought would be the final time. He made a U-turn and went back to offer his continued services. I didn't know him, and had never even spoken with him; he was reputed to be a decent fellow.

Shortly before the start of the November 14 video conference, he had called me on the phone with a singular proposal: "We'd like to send a team in with Brahvi," the ex-governor of Nimruz Province. "We can use the same team to support both him and Gul Agha. We'd like to have your support."

I was incredulous. It seemed obvious to me that abandoning Gul Agha in deference to Brahvi was an aggressively stupid idea, diverting scarce resources to a nearly useless sideshow. Now they were making the preposterous suggestion that one could effectively guide close-air support for Shirzai using a team located hundreds of miles away. Given the comments of the DCI the night before, CTC was aware that it could not divert a team to Brahvi unless I agreed to it. That was the only reason for Massie's call—otherwise, we weren't having this conversation. Surely he didn't think I was stupid enough to accept this? I almost felt embarrassed for John; this was the sort of fool's errand typically delegated to deputies.

"If you will consult a map," I began, uncharitably, "you will discover that Nimruz is in the far west, along the Iranian border. It has virtually no population, and no tribal affiliations of any use whatsoever around Kandahar." I paused. "This makes absolutely no sense. If you try to do this, you need to know that I will formally oppose it."

I had an uncomfortable feeling after I rang off. Could there be something happening back there that I was not aware of? The mere fact that CTC had the temerity to try to make such a proposal was alarming. I dashed off an immediate cable to headquarters. Entitled "Misplaced Priorities," it argued against sending a headquarters-proposed priority airdrop to Brahvi if that would mean a delay in providing support to Karzai and to Gul Agha in the coming days. It excoriated the hare-brained idea of diverting a Special Forces team from Gul Agha to

Brahvi in contravention of the stated wishes of the DCI. Rather than trying to make of Brahvi something he was not, I suggested, it would be far better to provide him with weapons and support for a task he might actually be able to perform: interdicting escape routes from Afghanistan into Iran which fleeing al-Qa'ida fighters might try to employ as they were driven out of the country. The main road from southern Afghanistan into Iran ran through Nimruz.

For good measure, I also argued against another idea being touted by some elements within CTC—reaching out for support from Haji Bashir Noorzai, yet another infamous opium smuggler, this time from Helmand Province, who had made indirect overtures to the Americans. He did have some tribal standing among the Noorzai, I averred, but controlled no guns, and thus would be of limited utility. And support to him would surely draw the outraged opposition of the British, who saw Afghan heroin as a direct threat to their population. Far more than we, they had been extremely active for years in attempting to interdict it.

The following morning, the 15th, I walked into my office to find that Dave, as usual, had lined up the most important cables from the overnight traffic on my desk. I looked at the one from headquarters on top. It stated that with five teams already having been sent to the Northern Alliance, and a sixth CIA/SF team, Team Echo, having accompanied Karzai on his reinsertion into Uruzgan, a seventh such team, Team Foxtrot, would join with Gul Agha. We were finally in the clear—or so we thought.

Chapter 27

CATARACT

NOVEMBER 17, 2001

A SMALL GROUP OF battered vehicles, packed with frightened Afghans and a handful of angry Americans, came roaring into town, pulling to an abrupt stop in front of the Americans' compound and spilling the occupants into the dusty street. Greg, fuming mad, trailed in their wake. Quickly spotting Karzai, he immediately accosted him.

"God damn it, Hamid. We're willing to fight with you. We're willing to die, if that's what it takes. But I'll be God-damned if we're going to do it alone. If you don't get some people over here willing to fight with us right now, we're leaving. I'm calling in the helicopters."

Since Hamid's extraction from a high plateau in Uruzgan on November 4, nothing had gone according to plan. Now, although he was finally back in Afghanistan, his unlikely mission was on the verge of unraveling altogether.

Less than two weeks earlier, I had only just returned to Islamabad from my November 5 visit with Karzai at Jacobabad when we received the first in a series of unwelcome surprises. Within hours of his meeting with me, Secretary Rumsfeld had revealed during a press conference that the U.S. military had temporarily extracted Hamid Karzai by helicopter from Afghanistan for "consultations" in Pakistan. We were mortified. As far as anyone was supposed to know, Hamid was in Afghanistan, leading a popular Pashtun rebellion against Taliban oppressors. Now the U.S. secretary of defense had given the lie to the whole thing. This infuriated Hamid, who was forced to make telephoned denials of dubious credibility to the press. It also precipitated some confusing and contradictory half-denials from the Pentagon as well. We could only hope the whole thing would go away once Karzai had been quickly reinserted.

The following day, November 7, I received a call from Greg.

"Chief, I think you'd better speak with Hamid." Apparently convinced that Rumsfeld's revelation had obviated the need to maintain the fiction that he was still in Afghanistan, Karzai was insisting that he should travel to Islamabad for meetings with officials and the press. Like Greg, I was aghast. When I got Karzai on the line, I wasn't sure where to begin, so I decided to engage him in a little Socratic dialogue.

"Hamid, Greg tells me that you're interested in coming to Islamabad."

"Yes. I thought it would be useful to meet with President Musharraf, and some ambassadors also."

"Well, haven't you been telling everyone up to now that you're in Afghanistan?"

"Oh, yes."

"And don't you think it's very important that you are seen as an independent leader, leading a popular uprising against the Taliban?"

"Oh, yes. That is very important. I must be independent."

"Well, if you were to suddenly appear in Islamabad, and it were obvious that you had been brought there by the Americans and the Pakistanis, wouldn't that make you seem much less independent?"

"Yes," he said thoughtfully. "I suppose that is true." There was a long pause. "So you think it is better if I don't go to Islamabad?"

I wasn't sure which was more disturbing: that Karzai would seriously entertain going on a media tour of the Pakistani capital, or that I could so easily talk him out of it.

In the meantime, Hamid remained in touch with his friends inside Afghanistan via the sat phone he had left with them. Their reports were not encouraging. The problem was circular: without Hamid there to rally them, it was difficult to raise enough armed men to assure his protection on his return. This required a change in plan. On November 9, Greg and Jimmy mounted up again for a return helo trip to Uruzgan, but rather than reinserting with Karzai, they dropped off the six elders. The Afghans would return to their villages to assemble a proper army for their chief. Greg and the ODA calculated that Hamid should have at least 500 men under arms to recommence his insurgency.

As the days ticked past, the wait became increasingly intolerable, particularly as the Northern Alliance gained greater military traction in the north. On November 13, with Mazar-e-Sharif having fallen and General Fahim about to launch his offensive toward Kabul, we sent out a cable to Langley advocating Karzai's early reinsertion. It was clear, we said, that his lieutenants would not be able to recruit 500 armed men in time; we would have to go with what we had. Meanwhile, we learned from Pat Hailey, the CIA representative to Central Command, that General Franks was growing increasingly impatient, fulminating that he would "order" Karzai back inside, perhaps compensating for the dearth of Afghans under arms with an increase in the number of Special Forces troops assigned to him.

Fortunately, we were not the only ones with deep misgivings about the future. Also on the night of the 13th, as Kabul was coming under Northern Alliance assault, Karzai received a call from Tayyib Agha, the head of Mullah Omar's personal office. The *talib* stated that the Popalzai chief was respected; but what, he wanted to know, was Karzai's program? What were his intentions? In light of the imminent collapse of the Taliban's position in the north, it seemed perhaps that they might be interested in exploring a potential peace option through Karzai, who was at least a Pashtun—but Mullah Omar's office director would not, and probably could not, say so. Without making any other commitments, Hamid indicated willingness to provide "safe passage," presumably to their villages, for any *talib* willing to lay down his arms. He would be seeing Mullah Omar the following day, Tayyib Agha replied; he would recontact Karzai thereafter.

Finally, on November 14, Greg and the Echo Team, including two JSOC operators, joined with part of Captain Amerine's eleven-man ODA 574, and loaded onto five helicopters for the nighttime journey to Uruzgan. The ODA had been "split" by Colonel John Mulholland, the commander of Fifth Group, who was too concerned about the dearth of loyal Afghans ready to receive Karzai to commit the full eleven-man force. The delay at Jacobabad had at least provided an opportunity for headquarters to send us several more CIA paramilitary specialists, augmenting the CIA presence on the team from two to five. But our luck did not improve. The insertion into a mountainous area near the village of War Jan, 35 miles or so west of Tarin Kowt, was a near disaster. As so often happened during helo landings in Afghanistan, thick dust on the ground was fanned by the rotor blades into a blinding "brownout," causing one helo to make a hard landing, breaking its nose gear. The landing zone was poorly situated, marked by three bonfires in a ravine; as two more helos came in to touch down, their rotors made rock strikes against the steep slopes on either side. A fourth craft, seeing this, peeled off and diverted to an alternate site, a couple of kilometers away.

Rocket-propelled grenades whizzed briefly overhead as the helos disgorged their passengers; the RPG-7s were suppressed with automatic weapons fire from the small Afghan reception team. Karzai, concerned that the diverted helicopter had gone toward a village controlled by Taliban sympathizers, and quite oblivious of any danger to himself, took off after it at a run in his white sneakers. Greg, Jimmy, and one member of the Afghan reception team ran in pursuit, catching him with difficulty at the top of a steep hill. It took two hours for the entire entry team to regroup in the darkness, and another three hours for them to make the dangerous climb down a cliffside to a mud-walled compound held by a local notable loyal to Karzai. One of the CIA paramilitary specialists had badly injured his ankle in the crash landing. An inauspicious start.

The following morning, Echo Team received its first airdrop of weapons, with Karzai overseeing their distribution to various small groups of followers who bounced seemingly randomly into the camp. Most took their weapons and returned to their villages; it was not at all clear how many of them Karzai would be able to rally to his cause when he needed them. To Echo, the whole exercise thus far was one of faith.

Reports filtering in from Tarin Kowt, though, were encouraging. The Taliban defeats in the north and rumors of Karzai's return were apparently feeding political restiveness in the provincial capital. That night, the Taliban deputy governor who had been so cooperative with Karzai, along with three of his colleagues, were beaten and killed, strung up in the street by an anti-Taliban mob.

With Hamid optimistically predicting that 2,000 supporters would be awaiting his arrival in Tarin Kowt, Greg agreed that they should move immediately to the governor's house. He made a priority request for an airdrop of food for a hoped-for 1,000 fighters: best to plan for success.

On the 16th, they began their tactical move toward Tarin Kowt. In his report that day, Greg compared the operation unfavorably with the Oklahoma land rush: A small band of armed farmers piled into whatever vehicles were available, and raced pell-mell to the east, with Echo trying to preserve as much order as it could. They arrived after nightfall, only to be informed by local leaders that a large number of Taliban were moving north to retake the town. Unsure how large a force they might face or when it might arrive, the ODA, now at full strength, moved out before dawn to set up an observation post on a ridge commanding the southern approaches to the area.

On the morning of November 17, the lead elements of a large Taliban force mounted in perhaps eighty vehicles, led by an old Soviet "BMP" armored personnel carrier, came into view. The Taliban split into three motorized columns, rushing forward across the broad, sandy valley below. With the first American attack aircraft coming on station, it was a perfect opportunity to catch them in the open. But as the Air Force combat controller began guiding the initial strikes, the rest of the Special Forces troopers turned to see their Afghan security contingent piling in panic into their trucks, about to flee. Faced with abandonment, having no vehicles of their own, and not enough guns to protect themselves from the onrushing Taliban, they had little choice but to jump into the vehicles themselves before they raced off. The little convoy's chaotic arrival back in Tarin Kowt was what prompted Greg's verbal assault on Karzai.

The Popalzai elder had been distracted as usual, speaking on a sat phone with the media, as was his wont, but the sight of Greg, fairly spitting with fury and threatening to leave, concentrated his mind. He immediately rushed off to find his most capable commander, ordering him to gather some men and return to the fight with Echo and the ODA. By now, the Taliban had long bypassed the ODA's initial observation post and the three columns were closing in fast on the town. Rushing to the closest high spot they could find, the Special Forces air controllers returned to providing guidance to the fighter-bombers high above. If the Taliban could make it into the town, both the Americans and the Afghans would be surrounded, and airstrikes would be useless. They were minutes from annihilation.

In Islamabad, CW3 Poteet, the redoubtable Special Forces veteran, burst into my office.

"My God," he said. "This is turning into a turkey shoot." Alerted that a major Taliban attack was under way with Americans in direct danger, fighter aircraft had been scrambled from carriers in the Arabian Sea and were being diverted from seemingly everywhere in theater. Poteet was listening in on the chatter as pilots requested clearance to make bombing runs on the Taliban columns, which continued to press relentlessly forward. There were so many aircraft, he said, they were being stacked in holding patterns to wait their turn.

"Everyone wants in on this!" It sounded like an easy victory in the making. We had no idea just how close the southern campaign was, even then, to catastrophe.

By the end of the day, of the approximately eighty Taliban vehicles involved in the attack, some forty-five had been destroyed, with the rest finally breaking off and fleeing in disorder. Many scores of Taliban were killed—most buried too quickly by local villagers to get any sort of accurate post-battle count. It was another huge setback for the Taliban, following on the heels of the fall of Kabul and the other disasters that had recently befallen them in the north, but this time in a Pashtun area close to Kandahar, which they had dominated almost since their founding and which was home to some of their most senior leaders.

Still, it had been a very close thing: even with the enormous weight of uncontested American airpower on their side, Karzai and his adherents in Tarin Kowt had nearly been overrun. Tactical stupidity—

rushing forward headlong in vehicles over open ground in spite of sustained air attack—had been at least as much a factor in the Taliban defeat as had U.S. air superiority. Had Karzai perished, as well he might, it would have left the Taliban free to concentrate their reserves on Gul Agha, and would doubtless have convinced the southern Pashtuns of the futility of resistance to the Taliban. It would certainly have changed the whole complexion of the struggle in the south, and might have forced us to "Americanize" the war and abandon altogether our strategy of assisting the Pashtuns in their own liberation.

As it was, Pashtun elders in Uruzgan who had been chafing under the Taliban but who had been unwilling to declare themselves without indications of imminent Taliban defeat were now coming forward in growing numbers to declare fealty to Karzai, their native son. They sought his patronage and promised fighters to his cause.

By any objective measure, neither Karzai nor Gul Agha, at this or any other stage, posed much of a military threat to the Taliban, per se. In those days I thought of them primarily as mobile lightning rods, able to attract attacks by Taliban forces who had no tactical answer for the problem of air-delivered smartbombs. With the relative immunity afforded them by American airpower, the threat they posed to the Taliban was primarily political, not military. It is worth remembering that many of the major victories won by the Taliban during their northward march in the first years of their existence were not won through force of arms. Instead, whole populations, tired of the depredations of feral local warlords, had risen up to embrace the pious rectitude which the Taliban represented, driving off their oppressors in the process and sending their sons to join its army. Now, the process was working in reverse. Our own understanding of this broad sociopolitical shift was hazy at best. The Taliban were far more capable of understanding what was happening to them.

Chapter 28

A WILDERNESS OF MIRRORS

H EY, CHIEF." THE COPS (Chief of Operations) was leaning through my doorway. "Jalil's on the line. He sounds pretty excited."

I hadn't been sure if I'd ever hear from Mullah Jalil again. But given that he was calling me, I was not at all surprised that he was upset. I crossed the hall and took a moment to collect my thoughts before picking up the sat phone receiver.

"Haji Mullah, how are you?" I said breezily.

"They tried to kill me!" he wailed. "They bombed my house!"

I feigned shock and surprise. "What? Haji Mullah, this is terrible! This was not supposed to happen! Are you all right?" The bombs had fallen the night before, destroying the Foreign Office Guesthouse where Jalil made his residence, at a time when he would normally have been present. He had left home just two hours before the attack; when he returned in the early morning, he found the place in ruins.

The start of hostilities on October 7 had done nothing to discourage Mullah Jalil from continuing to speak with me. On the contrary, it gave him all the more reason to stay in touch, and to try to manipulate me or to seek my assistance in pursuit of his many schemes. If there were a common denominator in the little cleric's constant machinations, it was that he hoped to find a way to end the war. To the extent that could be done on terms maximally favorable to the Taliban, so much the better; but he clearly wanted to find a solution to the conflict before it wrecked the movement. Within that overall framework,

229

though, there was no telling how many different conspiracies he might be pursuing at any given time, or how far he might go in his pursuit of each. For my part, I was looking for instances where our tactical interests might overlap, or where gambits he was pursuing to his own ends might be twisted or exploited in ways the mullah did not intend.

To say that Jalil was highly conspiratorial was not to say that he was particularly schooled in deception; his motives were generally easy to trace. You could never trust what he said, of course, but there were many instances when it was to his advantage to tell the truth, and in any case it was always useful to measure what he was saying against what we knew from other, more reliable sources. My contact with him also provided me a means to pass useful messages to the Taliban leadership.

In one of our conversations near the outset of the war, Haji Mullah suggested to me what he hoped I would see as a useful operational ploy. If I were to send a doctor in my employ to Kandahar, he suggested, say from another Muslim country, senior Taliban leaders would bring their families to him for treatment, thus providing the physician—and therefore me—with a wonderful means of eliciting information. Jalil would gladly facilitate the process, and help install the doctor. There were times when his manipulations were so childishly transparent they were almost endearing.

On October 18, Jalil suggested something more interesting. He hoped to arrange meetings between me and "some Taliban leaders and commanders." Some of the Taliban leadership would be aware of what he was doing, he said elliptically, and some would not; Mullah Omar, he said, would be in the latter category. As a test, and partly out of concern for some sort of ambush, I asked whether he would object to having these meetings set up with ISI assistance. He warily replied that that would very much depend on who in the ISI was involved. He readily agreed to my suggestion of Brigadier Suhail, the nattily attired Taliban expert and my good friend, but volunteered that under no circumstances should "Major Hadad," a radical supporter of the Taliban in the mold of Colonel Imam, be made aware of what was happening. In seeking General Jafar's agreement to employ Suhail in the effort, I underscored my concerns about Hadad and others of his ilk. Jafar fully understood: Imam, he said, had been sent back into retirement for just that reason.

The meeting took place in Karachi on October 24. The experienced officer I sent in my stead met with Abdul Qadir, the Taliban military attaché in Pakistan, who was acting as a personal emissary for Mullah Abdul Ghani Baradar, a co-founder, with Mullah Omar, of the Taliban, and now the Taliban's deputy chief of Army Staff. Baradar was a respected commander from the *jihad* era and, like Hamid Karzai, a Durrani Popalzai from Deh Ra'ud, in Uruzgan. Speaking through his emissary, Baradar promised to give us "five [senior] Arabs," presumably including bin Laden, but said there could be no change in overall Taliban policy concerning al-Qa'ida. That was unacceptable, of course, but an interesting beginning. We passed the emissary a satellite phone for Baradar's use, with an invitation to contact me directly.

On November 8, Jalil passed on a more interesting message still. Baradar, he said, wanted to join the opposition with 700 or 800 fighters from his home area of Deh Ra'ud. But first, the commander wanted to know two things: Would we support him? And second, were there any other Afghans who would fight? These were not unreasonable questions. If he were to break militarily with the Taliban with only a small force, Baradar would need our assistance to survive more than a few days, and unless other Pashtuns were willing to oppose the Taliban, he would be condemned to ultimate failure. Neither Abdul Haq nor Karzai had received effective assistance from us up to that stage; the former was dead, and the latter had barely escaped Afghanistan with his life a few days before. It was not at all clear whether any other Pashtuns would take similar risks.

But still, this didn't smell right. It sounded as though Baradar—or perhaps Jalil—hoped to lure Americans into an ambush, or to sniff out whether there were other Pashtuns who were preparing to take up arms against the Taliban. And even if Baradar were sincere, why would Jalil help him? Jalil had never given any indication that he would turn against Omar, or otherwise help us to eliminate other senior Taliban whose recalcitrance was standing in the way of a settlement. I responded that we would be willing to provide assistance to Baradar, or anyone else who took up arms against the Taliban for that matter, but that we would only do so if Baradar publicly broke with the organization and inflicted casualties on their forces. And as for others, Jalil should know that there were many Pashtuns who opposed the Taliban. The wily cleric indicated that he understood; he would convey our message to the deputy chief of staff. Days later, there was still no response from the senior Taliban commander. Jalil told me on November 10 and 11 that he had discussed the situation with both Baradar and Mullah Akhtar Muhammad Mansur, the minister of civil aviation. Neither, he said, could decide what to do.

It was around this time that Dave approached me. With all of us working eighteen-hour days, none of us could afford to expend unnecessary effort. Why was I wasting my time with Jalil? I took some umbrage at that, but it was a reasonable question, and it caused me to reflect. Sure, the chances of our getting anything really useful from this contact were undoubtedly remote. But in my estimation, the potential long odds opportunity to sow dissension among the Taliban leadership, unique as it was, made it worth the investment in time. And in all honesty, there was something else, too: I was drawn to this sort of contact like a moth to a flame. In the Clandestine Service, closing with the enemy—talking to terrorists, if you like—is what we do. I'm not sure I could have passed up the chance to spar with Mullah Jalil, even if, on some level, I'd wanted to.

And there was yet another reason to maintain contact with Jalil, one more devious. In mid-October, Jalil asked if I could ensure that his ministry's guesthouse located on the eastern outskirts of Kandahar along the Kandahar-Kabul highway would not be bombed. With that assurance, he would be able to stay there, and use the location as a safe place to meet with his Taliban colleagues, and thus develop information that would benefit us both. I readily agreed, and informed headquarters that this location should be carefully watched via aerial reconnaissance. If, as I suspected, Jalil eventually took advantage of this "no-fire" zone to host a significant meeting, it might provide us with an excellent opportunity to kill multiple members of the Taliban leadership at a stroke.

On November 16, with the Taliban in the throes of near panic over the recent fall of Kabul, Jalil reported that some of the senior leaders were discussing the possibility of surrender. That evening, we received a highly reliable report from a vetted source that Omar and other members of the *Shura* were meeting at the Foreign Office Guesthouse. This was what we'd been waiting for. The report had come to us late, though—well after the scheduled start of the meeting. We reported it immediately, in hopes there would still be time to strike. The presence or absence of vehicles in the area would tell us whether the opportunity were still live. Hours passed, with no indication of a reaction from the military. Once again, a rare chance had been missed.

I was awakened in my bedroom about two o'clock in the morning by a call from an old friend. "Dan," an experienced ops officer, was now the senior military targeting officer for CTC. It seemed that half the agency was being drawn into CTC one way or another.

"The Air Force wants to bomb the Foreign Office Guesthouse." Referring to Jalil by his code name, he inquired whether we considered him an asset. An "asset," in CIA parlance, is a recruited source, someone to whom we owe loyalty and protection. Mullah Jalil was certainly not that.

"Why do they want to bomb it now?" I asked. "It's too late. The meeting's over. [Jalil] is no asset, and I have no problem bombing his location, provided there's a target there. But killing [Jalil] by himself makes no sense: he's not a commander, he doesn't control any guns, and he's no threat to us. Since now the Taliban has used the place successfully for a high-level meeting, they're likely to use it again. We should wait, and bomb it then."

After we rang off, I had the suspicion that Dan had only heard a small part of what I'd said. He'd called with a simple question from the Air Force—"Was this a no-strike location?"—and I had given him his answer: "No." I had a sinking feeling I'd just signed the mullah's death warrant. I shook my head at the stupidity of it all.

As the next morning's phone call made clear, I had in fact done almost exactly what I'd feared. After Jalil calmed down a bit, we spoke about the situation, and whether the collapse of their position in the north might induce the Taliban leadership to explore terms of surrender. As we prepared to ring off, I again expressed concern about his plight, and the loss of his house.

"Where will you go?" I asked. The words were hardly out of my mouth when I realized my mistake: at this point, I was the last person in the world to whom he would reveal his whereabouts, ever. There was a long pause, followed by a dry, mirthless laugh. He hung up without another word. Dave must have noticed something odd about my expression as I walked through the outer office. He looked up at me quizzically from behind his desk.

"I'm becoming a very bad man," I said.

Mullah Jalil called me again on November 18. The leaders in Kandahar were discussing whether they should explore possible peace terms, and were seeking to establish channels to Karzai through Haji Bashir Noorzai, the drug lord, and Mullah Naqib, yet another *jihad*-era commander who was the master of Arghandab, just north of Kandahar. They didn't feel they could reach any decisions, though, until they could consult with some of the senior Taliban commanders fleeing from the north. Even if the commanders couldn't reach Kandahar, he said, Omar might be able to consult with some of them via radio if they could get as far south as Zabol Province. Apparently becoming impatient with his colleagues' reflexive indirection, Jalil himself was trying to get in touch with Karzai, he said. Two days later, he would succeed.

Chapter 29

REDEMPTION AND VINDICATION

NOVEMBER 19, 2001

T HE HELICOPTER SWOOPED IN low, dipping quickly between the high ridges on either side of the valley. No sooner had it landed than Gul Agha broke for it at a dead run. His speed was surprising for such a big man. His family members and senior commanders, who had been standing with him as they tracked the helo's progress, trailed after him as best they could in the darkness. Suddenly, he pitched forward, face-first, and fell heavily to the ground, as though poleaxed. The others coming up from behind stopped well short of him, appalled, and busied themselves in embarassed silence, studying the ground or the sky as their chieftain gathered himself, grunting, and slapped the dust from his clothes. As soon as he was upright and reoriented, Gul Agha resumed his sprint, this time not stopping until he had wrapped Mark in a smothering embrace.

The reasons for Gul Agha's enthusiasm were not entirely sentimental. Three days before, on November 16, one of his reconnoitering patrols came across the Taliban "lost convoy" we had been tracking the night of the 14th, now dug in a short distance from the western entry to the Shin Naray Valley. Quick requests for an airstrike made from Islamabad were denied, for the familiar reason: no U.S. eyes-on to verify the target. With a Special Forces ODA present, including a forward air controller, the Taliban vehicles might have been attacked from the sky in a matter of minutes. Instead, they remained at large, liable to strike

235

at any moment. From what we knew, it appeared Gul Agha had done all we could expect, but had received little support in return. We were tempting fate; we needed to get a team in with him as soon as possible.

"Duane," a paramilitary specialist sent forward by CTC, had joined the station a few days before. He'd been told by CTC/SO that once an initial team had deployed with Karzai, he would lead the next one dispatched in the south. That wasn't going to happen: Dave pulled him into his office for a private chat. Mark was a veteran station officer, Duane was told, and a highly competent one; he had deep knowledge of Afghanistan and of Afghan politics; and most important, he had established an excellent relationship with Gul Agha. Mark would be the one to lead the team.

"I don't trust this guy," Dave muttered to me after he and Duane emerged.

"Duane will be fine," I said. "He can't help what he was told. He doesn't care who's in charge; he just wants to get into the fight." I was right. Duane did an excellent job for us, and never caused a bit of trouble.

We sent out an immediate cable, proposing that Mark and Duane link up with ODA 583, which had been designated by Fifth Group to join Gul Agha and was assembling at Jacobabad. Two other specially trained enlisted men from the military's "Gray Fox" program were also available at Jacobabad to add to the team. I had worked with operators like them before. In addition to their military skills and specialized intelligence training, and their access to military communications, they had the benefit of being formally under our control, and so could be assigned as we saw fit, without Pentagon permission.

The following day brought good news. Several truckloads of Pak Army weapons arranged by General Jafar and turned over to Gul Agha's men at Quetta rolled into Shin Naray; these were augmented later the same day by several more weapons bundles, courtesy of the U.S. Air Force.

The morning of the 18th brought less welcome news. Gul Agha's people reported that while the Pak-supplied RPG-7s were fine, the AK-47s were old and heavily used, and many were essentially unserviceable. When I relayed this to Jafar at an emergency meeting at ISI Headquarters, the general didn't want to believe it.

"Afghans are reporting this to you?" When the word "Afghan" crossed the lips of this Punjabi tank commander, it sounded like a curse. I wouldn't be able to verify the report until my officers were on the ground and, given the number and varied provenance of Gul Agha's weapons, probably not completely even then, but I asked that Jafar look into what might have happened in the meantime anyway.

Shortly after I returned, Dave walked into my office. I could always tell from his expression when he was bearing bad news. We had developed a sort of joking protocol for such times. "Wait," I'd say, raising my hand. Walking out from behind my desk, I would lie down on the couch, staring up at the ceiling as though in a psychiatrist's office. "Okay. Let me have it."

But I could see that this was no time for jokes. The cable he handed me stated that the ODA at Jacobabad could *not* deploy to Afghanistan. Instead, a "pilot team" comprised of two CIA case officers—Mark and Duane—along with the two Gray Fox operators should join Gul Agha in Shin Naray alone. The military members of the team should remain at Jacobabad and would only be allowed to deploy if reporting from the CIA-only advance force justified the additional personnel. I was incredulous.

I was nearly as disbelieving when Hank himself picked up immediately on the other end of the secure line to headquarters. After the briefest of greetings, I got straight to the point.

"Hank, we've received a headquarters cable stating that only CIA personnel can deploy with Gul Agha, and that the ODA has to remain behind."

"That's right."

"Look, the Taliban has forces in the area, and they could attack Gul Agha's people at any time. We don't know for sure how many fighters he has, and we don't know whether they'll stand and fight. We need to have the military with us."

"Our people will be armed. They can defend themselves."

"No, if we're going to have to rely on ourselves, we need to have a minimum number of guns to maintain a defensive position until the team can be extracted. Besides, the most important thing for us is to be able to direct CAS [close-air support]. We need the ODA for that."

"The Gray Fox operators have been trained to direct CAS."

"Fine if they've had some training, but we need people who do this for a living."

"Well, it may sound harsh," he said mildly, as if in sorrow, "but if people are going to die, it's better we limit the number of casualties."

This was insane. The full team we proposed to send was already extremely small—sixteen people, at a maximum. If we sent in a much smaller number, with no organic link to the military and without any adequate means to defend themselves, then all surely *would* die if anything went wrong. As I began to protest yet again, Hank raised his voice in anger.

"Look, CIA has always gone in first. That's the model we've used all over the country."

Ah, so that was it: one-upping the military. In fact, what he was saying was not true. CIA officers may have deployed in advance of the military in the north, but it was different in the south, where we were operating behind enemy lines, and he knew it. When Team Echo had deployed with Karzai just three days before, CIA and the military had gone in together. But Hank had moved on. ". . . And another thing. What were you doing discussing a joint interrogation center with the Pakistanis? You had no authorization. . . ."

A few days before, in anticipation that the Pakistanis would soon be capturing Arab fighters and members of al-Qa'ida escaping across the Afghan border, I had raised with General Jafar the idea of establishing a joint interrogation center under U.S. supervision, in which we could invite friendly Arab intelligence services to participate as well. The idea would be to leverage our extensive intelligence and the Arabs' local knowledge and linguistic capability in one location, where information could be instantly shared among all of us, and where there would be continual CIA monitoring to ensure that no human rights abuses occurred. Jafar had responded enthusiastically, and was willing to take the idea to President Musharraf, but when I raised it formally with headquarters, CTC had quashed it.

Once again, I was being slow on the uptake. Here I'd thought this was a discussion. It was nothing of the sort. Hank might have been speaking still, but I could no longer hear him; his voice had been drowned out by a roaring sound in my ears. There was no point in continuing.

"Nice speaking with you, as always," I said. I held the receiver over the cradle for a moment, and then dropped it.

I sent an immediate message to Mark in Jacobabad, explaining the situation. We both knew that he had the option to back out, given the unnecessary risks he and the others were suddenly being asked to assume. I didn't mention it, though, and neither did he: it was his duty to go forward, and we both knew that, too. This was his operation, and he was the case officer for it. Mark was the doting father of five children.

Among the many dozens of officers rotating on temporary assignment into and out of the station during that time were a large number of annuitants, some long retired and quite senior in their day, including five former deputy chiefs of the Near East Division—three of whom were present at that moment. That night, the unofficial doyen among the annuitants, Dan Webster, wrote a long e-mail to Hank's deputy John Massie, with whom he had worked in the past. He recounted the history of CTC's "obstructionism," of which the current withholding of the ODA was but the most recent, and most egregious, example.

"Together," he said, "my retired colleagues and I represent over 300 years of operational experience. We all agree that in that time we have never, ever, seen such poor Headquarters support to the field. Please help us." I only heard about it later, but given the number of headquarters components living under the CTC boot in those days, it was probably inevitable that the e-mail would get out, and that it would go viral when it did. It apparently created a huge stir in the building. Someone even printed out a copy and passed it to Director Tenet, as he would tell me later.

The Special Forces were at least as outraged by this development as we were, but there was nothing they could do. We were still only in Phase Two of General Franks's four-phase campaign plan, which meant that military units could only enter Afghanistan to team with indigenous forces if they had CIA agreement; for the moment, as least, CTC would not agree. But when Mark and his colleagues boarded two helos at Jacobabad for the flight into Shin Naray the following night of the 19th, the young Special Forces captain commanding ODA 583, to his everlasting credit, insisted on accompanying them, and brought two of his troopers along, despite the lack of authorization. When I heard of it, I very much feared for this young officer's career. I was much relieved to learn later on that his superiors, apparently sharing his sentiments, had elected to ignore the episode.

The Special Forces, it seems, have formulas for just about everything. One such formula they use to estimate the number of fighters in an area involves counting the number of campfires they produce at night. CW3 Poteet was listening in on the cockpit communications as the SF helicopter pilots circled Shin Naray, marveling at the number of fires they could see on the surrounding valley ridges. They estimated that Gul Agha had some 1,500 fighters. The following day, the Foxtrot "pilot team" made a ground assessment and determined that Gul Agha's forces indeed numbered over 1,000 fighters. This was duly reported, accompanied by a request from the ODA commander to allow the remainder of his small force to join them. I don't recall a specific response from Langley, but within twenty-four hours of the commander's arrival in Shin Naray, his ODA was whole again.

NOVEMBER 23, 2001

"Abdullah! Abdullah! Is there anyone in that house?" Mark was shouting to be heard over the din of gunfire. Long bursts from AK-47s were being loosed right in front of them, while salvos of RPG-7 rounds were roaring overhead, fired from positions just behind. Hostile fire was emanating from a ridge and from a small mud-walled compound a short distance away. A strike on the compound might well destroy the house as well. Were there any civilians left inside?

"No, no! They have all run away!"

"Abdullah, are you sure? Are you sure?"

As soon as the bomb struck, the firing from the compound ceased. Minutes later, with smoke still hanging in the air, they entered the house adjoining it, only to find a woman, dead, inside. Next to her lay her eleven-year-old daughter, dazed by the concussion. Her left cheek had been flayed open, cut to the bone. They were just east of Takht-e Pol, located on Highway 4, a third of the way from the border post at Spin Boldak to the Taliban capital, on the sole east-west highway from Pakistan to Kandahar City.

Two days before, on November 21, with Gul Agha's force still in Shin Naray, it had appeared fleetingly that his advance might be far less contested. The Taliban commander in Arghistan offered to meet with Gul Agha's representatives just after dusk to negotiate a potential surrender. They apparently hadn't anticipated the Americans' ability to watch, through night-vision goggles, as they moved a large number of armed men to covered ambush positions surrounding the proposed meeting site shortly before the appointed hour. Rather than a negotiating party, the Taliban representatives attracted a hail of gunfire from Gul Agha's men, precipitating a short, sharp exchange. The same day, as Mullah Omar's office chief and Taliban spokesman Tayyib Agha made a two-hour visit to Spin Boldak on the Pakistan border, pledging before the media that the Taliban would fight to the death and prevail in the south, other Afghans claiming to represent Mullah Osmani and the Taliban finance minister, Abdul Wasi Agha Jan Mohtasim, contacted Shirzai's relatives in Quetta seeking negotiations. They were told they should look for Shirzai in Kandahar.

At dawn the following morning, Shirzai's force began to move out of the valley, swinging toward the southwest in the direction of Highway 4. Mark stood at the western entrance, counting men and vehicles as they filed past. The forty-two machines in the convoy included a wide assortment of pickups, elaborately decorated British Bedford "jinga" trucks (so-called because of the sound made by the metal pendants that typically hung by chains from the undercarriage of these garishly appointed vehicles), and even farm tractors pulling flatbed trailers. The start was not encouraging. No sooner had the column begun to exit the valley than one of the larger trucks broke down with a faulty transmission. Several men crawled underneath, and after a lengthy effort, it lurched forward once more, the rest of the file moving slowly behind it, until it broke down again less than a kilometer down the dirt track. Mark was beginning to wonder whether they would ever get out of Arghistan district, let alone reach Kandahar City. This time Gul Agha himself crawled under the truck and lay on his back, wrestling for forty minutes with the balky driveshaft. Once again, the truck was fired up and lurched forward. It would not break down again.

Apart from occasional sniping, the first day's march was largely unopposed. As with most such rump militia forces, it displayed an appalling lack of fire discipline. The sound of a gunshot from a far distance would usually be answered with a salvo of rocket-propelled grenades, fired at nothing and no one in particular. Word of Shirzai's advance was spreading widely through the area. That same day, in Spin Boldak, elders of the Achakzai tribe, apparently unimpressed by Tayyib Agha's boasts, approached local Taliban officials and asked them to leave.

The moving column's first night was spent at a little village called Bala Zar, about halfway between Shin Naray and Highway 4. From the villagers Shirzai was able to purchase enough bread and mutton for the entire force. The following morning, he held a *jirga* with the elders and senior commanders to determine where they should go. As a disproportionate number of the elders were from Arghandab, a lush agricultural area just to the north of Kandahar City, they lobbied heavily to liberate their home district first. The fact that Arghandab was administered by Mullah Naqib, Gul Agha's old rival and adversary, may have made him susceptible to their arguments. After some discussion, a consensus was reached: They would break off to the north and west, and go to Arghandab.

As the proceedings broke up, Mark, who had been listening with growing alarm, quickly pulled Gul Agha aside.

"Shirzai, what are you doing? What do you want with Arghandab? When Hamid Karzai arrives in Kandahar, is that where you want to be?" That stopped the Barakzai chieftain in his tracks. He looked back for a moment as the elders were beginning to shuffle off, and then leapt to his feet to get their attention.

"On to Kandahar!" he shouted.

The *jirga* is a peculiarly Afghan institution. Although held ostensibly to reach a consensus decision on some matter of public importance, it is often more about showing respect and giving prominent members of the community an opportunity to have their say, rather than achieving a particular outcome. Here the group had reached a firm consensus in favor of investing Arghandab and wresting it from the Taliban, only to have its leader arbitrarily overturn the decision immediately thereafter. The elders stopped and looked at one another. No one seemed particularly upset. They gave a sort of collective shrug, and remounted their vehicles: Kandahar it would be.

In typical CIA fashion, Mark was acting under the loosest of operating directives. He was to work closely with Gul Agha, leveraging the support of the military, and somehow seize Kandahar. There was no firm plan for how he would do this, apart from supporting Shirzai, and it would never have occurred to me to provide him with one. The situation was too fluid, and there were too many variables. He could only improvise as he went along. I and the station were there to provide support and assistance, and whatever guidance they might seek, but Mark and Duane were the case officers on this operation. It would be up to them to do as they saw fit.

CTC, seeing an opportunity to duplicate in the south the degree of direct control it nominally enjoyed in the north, insisted immediately after its arrival in Afghanistan that Team Foxtrot would operate as an independent entity, rather than as a sort of "mobile base" of Islamabad Station, as we had conceived of them. As soon as Mark and Duane crossed the Afghan border, we were told, they would no longer be formally subject to my command. Given the loose and informal way we normally operated, this was an amusing conceit, made all the more so when the crude satellite communications apparatus which headquarters had supplied for Foxtrot's use could not be made to work. The only remaining secure, dedicated CIA communications link available to Mark and Duane was an encrypted satellite commo package of the sort we normally supplied to our principal Afghan sources. Thus, their only two-way communications were point-to-point with the station. To communicate with their masters at headquarters, Foxtrot would have to do it through us. CTC/SO sternly admonished us that we were not to edit or otherwise interfere with Foxtrot's communications in any way; their missives were to be transcribed as received into cable format and forwarded on to headquarters. We all found this wryly entertaining—as if Mark and his colleagues would have somehow suffered amnesia, and now place their trust in the people who had tried to deny them military support not twenty-four hours before.

All day on November 23, the column made its slow way south and west, with Mark providing updates when he could. As night fell, they were approaching Takht-e Pol; they intended to stop as soon as they reached the highway. Mark reported some firing on their perimeter from straight ahead; elements of the ODA, he said, were going forward to investigate. Soon they were in a general firefight, with the ODA calling in airstrikes on Taliban positions. Just before midnight, they decided to break contact, withdrawing under fire after inflicting heavy losses in men and equipment, and having taken some sixty Taliban prisoners, including the famous "Commander Lalo." The following morning, they pushed forward again, only to find that the Taliban had largely abandoned the town. As of November 24, the main avenue of communication between Kandahar and Pakistan had been cut. It was a major turning point in the southern campaign. Gul Agha now had a straight path before him, down Highway 4, to Kandahar.

With Gul Agha's campaign well under way and vectored toward Kandahar, and with Hamid Karzai having survived the Taliban onslaught at Tarin Kowt and preparing to move south, we learned that yet more help might be arriving on the scene—but not in a good way. The U.S. Marines, we were told, were planning to seize the royal Emerati hunting camp and air strip in the Registan Desert 100 miles southwest of Kandahar—the one so disingenuously offered to us by Haji Juma Khan Baluch, the drug-runner—which they dubbed "Rhino." "Bill," an old friend, had been assigned as the CIA liaison to the invading Marines. As they marshaled their forces in southern Pakistan, he stopped in Islamabad to brief us before moving out. Bill had no idea what the strategic intent of this Marine Expeditionary Force might be, beyond investing Camp Rhino, but promised to keep us informed. On November 25, the first helicopter-borne units of what would eventually become a 1,100-man force began landing in the remote southern desert.

Dave shook his head. "I've got a bad feeling about this. Marines are so damned aggressive." If a large U.S. force were to move north and start destroying things, we knew, it would very likely have a negative effect on a political environment which was just beginning to turn in our favor. And with allied Afghan forces beginning to close in on Kandahar, we were concerned about the Marines' ability to distinguish friend from foe. There had been almost no advance warning of this development, and no way of telling whose idea it was, but it smelled to us like interservice politics and a ploy to get the Marines into the fight. This would bear close watching.

Shirzai's initial successes were nothing short of thrilling, and a vindication of the strategy we had long advocated against steadfast resistance from headquarters. Meanwhile, and perhaps not incidentally, I found myself embroiled in yet more difficulties with CTC/SO. When Mark had first arrived in Shin Naray, he had immediately verified the initial reports concerning the substandard Pakistani weapons. Everyone with whom he spoke had the same story, and he was shown a significant number of badly worn AK-47s. One was so old as to qualify as a genuine antique; he'd love to keep it as a souvenir, he said, but believed it would be suicidal to fire. I actually cut out the paragraph from Mark's message and showed it to Jafar.

The terrorism "Czar," for his part, was in a difficult position. The ISI does not have its own weapons stocks; he had arranged the delivery from the Pak Army Supply Corps, and now they wanted to be reimbursed, to the tune of a substantial sum. Jafar had gone out of his way to help me, and now he was on the hook. In response to his inquiries, the supply people had said that while the weapons provided may not have been new, they were perfectly serviceable and had come from standard Pak Army stocks. Without hard evidence to the contrary, there wasn't much he could say, and I could tell he still half-suspected that he was being framed by Gul Agha's people. It's possible that we had fallen victim to some surreptitious Pak Army conspiracy to undermine the anti-Taliban war effort, but I think it far more likely that some enterprising Pakistani supply officer had seen the opportunity to dispose of a lot of old weaponry cluttering his warehouse and get generously reimbursed for it.

The problem was entirely my fault. I could and should have had the weapons inspected on delivery, and did not; I was moving too fast, and operating on too many assumptions. It was a foolish mistake, perhaps decreasing the effectiveness of Gul Agha's force, and at the same time gratuitously handing CTC another stick with which to beat me.

Not satisfied with that degree of trouble, I went on to invite more. No sooner had the first weapons convoy made it to Shin Naray than I began to worry about resupply, particularly of ammunition. When Gul Agha and Foxtrot decided to move south to Highway 4, it occurred to me that this might give us an alternative means of resupply in the event the aerial route proved inadequate, which I fully expected. If Gul Agha were able to secure the road running east to the border from Takht-e Pol, perhaps we could resupply him by road from Quetta.

Again, I had no alternative but to turn to the Pak Army. Pakistan was awash in guns, but we lacked the time or resources to canvass the countryside to make purchases of a half-dozen automatic rifles at a time, to say nothing about quality control. This time I specified to Jafar that the weapons should be brand-new, and in their original packing crates. Jafar himself joined Captain Greg and Jim M., my senior paramilitary officer, to thoroughly inspect everything on delivery. It was pristine. Jafar had the weapons and ammunition loaded on three outsize "jinga" trucks, and prepositioned them, at my request, in Quetta.

Of course, I had no authorization for any of this, and I knew I'd never get it until the need was manifest, by which time it might be too late. I figured that if we turned out not to need these supplies, I could always return the shipment to Jafar, and would only have to worry about the cost of fuel and drivers. Even then, I was clearly out on a limb, but I thought about how I'd feel if Foxtrot were sitting on Highway 4, under attack from the west, unable to get adequate resupply from the air, and I were unable to do anything about it. The decision was an easy one.

With Shirzai's forces about to take Takht-e Pol, I requested authorization to reimburse the Paks for the first shipment, and permission to go ahead with purchase and road delivery of the second. I was told that under no circumstances was I to proceed with the second purchase; Gul Agha would be resupplied from the air. And as for the first deliv-

ery, I was treated to a prim lecture on prevailing prices for reconditioned weapons in the gray arms market. I was reminded that the Pak
weapons—as we had duly reported—were "substandard," and told that
I should negotiate a lower price. I was also pointedly told that while I
may have based my decision to make the first purchase on verbal approvals from the DCI and DDO at the November 13 video conference,
I should *not* have taken this as formal authorization, which can only
come in cable traffic. They were outdoing themselves. It was a response
worthy of Captain Queeg.

It wasn't until weeks later that Mark related to me the story of the
house-bombing at Takht-e Pol. The father of the injured girl had wept
openly and unashamedly after rushing to the scene. Although Afghan
tradition called for compensation for his loss, he refused it. He hated
the Taliban, he said. If the sacrifice of his wife was the price to be paid
for liberation, he would accept it. The Special Forces medic stitched up
his daughter and treated her as best he could.

I don't know exactly why I was so seized by the thought of this girl.
Perhaps it was Mark's vivid description that distinguished the scene in
my mind. There has been so much carnage, before and since. In the
many years of America's engagement in Afghanistan, how many civilian casualties have there been? But to me, this was singular. These were
my officers; this was our battle. This girl, somehow, was ours. When I
asked weeks later, Mark thought Gul Agha's people would be able to locate the girl's family. I spoke to a senior colleague in the Near East Division about setting up a fund to help her. But those initial sentiments
were soon obscured and then overwhelmed in an unending welter of
eighteen-hour days. There was still a war to be fought.

So many years later, there are times, alone in the dark of night,
when I still think about that girl. I wonder what became of her, and
how the scars we inflicted might have affected her prospects for marriage. I never saw her myself, never even knew her name. After a long
career, after involvement, direct and indirect, in so many wars, named
and unnamed, I have so few regrets. But if there were one thing I could
do over, it would be this: I wish I had done something to help that girl.

Chapter 30

SERENDIPITY TO INEVITABILITY

NOVEMBER 22, 2001

AN ODD FEELING SWEPT over me as my turn came to speak. It was one of those all-too-rare moments of clarity, when a million jumbled, contradictory sentiments suddenly fuse into a single, crystalline, articulable thought. I spoke of the horrors of 9/11, of events whose meaning and emotional impact many of us had hardly begun to absorb, pressed as we had been into immediate, incessant action. We would never have wished such horror and sadness to be visited on our country, I said, nor would we have wished for the present war. And yet, we should give thanks. For if these events had to come, thank God they came on our watch, since unlike nearly everyone else, it was in our capacity to do something about them. I raised a glass: "Let us give thanks," I said, "for the opportunity to serve."

It was Thanksgiving Day in Islamabad, and Wendy Chamberlin had generously thrown open her doors to the entire community, swollen as it was with visiting military personnel, itinerant CIA operators and analysts, and any number of outsiders from an alphabet soup of government agencies, to say nothing of what remained of our original, close-knit group. The sole price of admission: public words of thanks. It was a touching event, with many remembrances of those who had been uprooted from their homes and could not be with us. And yet, as it turned out, I spoke for many for whom our present efforts were a welcome outlet for unspoken grief, anger, and a sense of violation.

The following day, Greg called. During his extended stay in Tarin Kowt, he had had time to make regular secure sat phone contact with us in Islamabad to consult and provide updates. During that period I frequently would enter the station in the morning to find Dave in his office, talking and laughing uproariously on the phone. There could only be one explanation.

"You're talking to that damned Greg again, aren't you?" I'd call out, intending to be heard at the other end of the line, before picking it up myself.

On this post-Thanksgiving afternoon, I passed on holiday greetings, and asked how their day had been. He didn't have to tell me, actually. I had a clear mental image of what it was like: meager, monotonous, badly prepared food; scarce clean water; Spartan accommodations in cold mud huts where thick dust constantly hung in the air.

"Oh, Chief," he began, with apparently earnest enthusiasm. "You wouldn't believe it. Best Thanksgiving ever! They've got the biggest turkeys here you ever saw; ate so much we couldn't move. Just stuffed ourselves. Then, after we laid around awhile, we rolled on down to the ball field to watch Tarin Kowt take on Deh Ra'ud High. . . ." Before long, he had me laughing helplessly.

There were limits, though, to the extent to which good humor could compensate for the deprivations of the field. To those living in such conditions, the few small physical comforts that remain to them can take on immense importance. For one of the Special Forces communicators there with Team Echo, it was his morning cup of coffee. Each day, he would prepare it with infinite care, employing precise amounts of sugar and powdered creamer, scarce commodities that he carefully husbanded. On one such morning, just after completing his ritual preparations, his radio went off unexpectedly. Before running off to answer it, he solemnly balanced his cup on a rock, where it unfortunately fell under the gaze of Tom, the CIA Dari translator, whose light-fingered proclivities have been noted earlier.

According to contemporaneous accounts, it took three strapping Special Forces operators to pull the communicator off poor Tom. There might have been serious legal repercussions had they failed. But there was no question of Tom's staying: for his own safety, Greg placed him on the next available helicopter.

The shock of their defeat at Tarin Kowt had brought a welter of tentative probes from various prominent Taliban figures. On November 18, Karzai was contacted by an intermediary for Taliban minister of defense Obeidullah. Two days later, Mullah Jalil called him, as he had indicated to me he would, and was told by Hamid that if he surrendered, he would be treated well. As Jalil explained to me, the Taliban leadership was still frozen in indecision, waiting for commanders Dadullah-Lang and Muhammad Fazl to return from Kunduz. The Taliban commanders were trying to negotiate free passage for their men with General Dostum in return for the surrender of their weapons and foreign fighters. On the 23rd, the Taliban leadership was still waiting, and feared the negotiations with Dostum had broken down.

According to Jalil, the Taliban were continuing their talks, both with the drug-running Haji Bashir Noorzai—whom they had put out of business a year before, but who appeared to have somehow convinced them he could play an intermediary role—and with Karzai. Omar, he said, was constantly moving his location; he demurred when I asked precisely where. The cleric claimed that he was trying to persuade the others in the leadership to accept a face-saving way out; he hoped that they might do so if Karzai and Gul Agha would employ trusted mullahs to broker the negotiations. It was becoming obvious to me, though, that Brigadier Suhail's assessment of intra-Taliban dynamics was absolutely correct. The Taliban were incapable of making a group decision without Mullah Omar's involvement and support; and despite all the maneuvering around him, the Taliban chief still showed no sign of backing down.

On the 25th, Mullah Nooruddin Turabi, the justice minister, offered to surrender to Hamid, and was given a slightly different message. The fate of senior Taliban officials would be determined by international bodies, he was told, but they could count on Karzai's protection in the meantime. The offer, Karzai said, would be good for forty-eight hours only. It was perhaps not an accident that Hamid had spoken just minutes before on a sat phone call set up by Greg with Ambassador James

Dobbins, who was to be the senior U.S. representative to the Bonn Conference, arranged under UN auspices to determine the future of Afghanistan—and set to begin in two days' time.

As the political environment in the south rapidly shifted, Karzai was clearly making things up as he went along, as we all were. His instincts were generous, and he appeared inclined toward reconciliation, but he remained highly suspicious of the Taliban. He feared that Obeidullah might be trying to use negotiations with him as a stalling tactic in hopes that he could eventually consolidate the Taliban forces then besieged in Konduz, whose amnesty was being negotiated, into his planned defense of the south. But as these various bargaining initiatives gained momentum, Hamid expressed particular faith in Mullah Naqib of Arghandab, just north of Kandahar City. Naqib was clearly tolerated by the Taliban, who had allowed him to retain authority in his own area, but Karzai did not consider him aligned with them. He insisted to Greg that Naqib should be involved in any surrender negotiations with the Taliban.

In Islamabad, we had a less sanguine view of the former *jihad*-era commander and former Kandahar governor. We disseminated a warning, drawing on information from multiple sources, suggesting that Naqib was acting as a front for Taliban interests. They had not ceded any real power to him, we pointed out, and the twin facts that he was willing to play the intermediary and that he had the apparent trust of the Taliban leadership did nothing to ease our concerns. Naqib's warning to Karzai that the Taliban could not turn over their capital to him because the Arabs wouldn't allow it sounded like a lame excuse to our ears, and an effort to buy time. In fact, subsequent events would demonstrate that we were judging Naqib too harshly, but our attitude was a prudent reaction to the multiple intrigues around us.

Although clearly willing to treat with the Taliban to a degree which left us uncomfortable in Islamabad, to say nothing of Washington (to the extent Washington had any real inkling as to what was going on), Karzai was not about to risk international, and particularly American support by appearing in any way tolerant of al-Qa'ida or terrorism. Throughout this period there was no one close to him, the redoubtable

Greg notwithstanding, to whom he could turn for a definitive readout on American policy, as indeed no clear policy existed. To the extent he could intuit U.S. attitudes, they were reflexively hostile toward anyone associated with the Taliban. All political momentum was behind the upcoming Bonn Conference, scheduled to start on November 27, and the Taliban would play no role in it. Hamid's political room for maneuver in dealing with the clerical regime was thus extremely limited. He found himself in a position where he could provide politically expedient assurances to Taliban leaders, but with absolutely no guarantee in his own mind that he could make good on them. This would cost him—and Afghanistan—dearly in the future.

In the meantime, there were more mundane issues at hand. In the aftermath of Tarin Kowt, Greg estimated there were perhaps 500 Taliban survivors who might still be in the area. Concerned lest they come under renewed attack, the Americans organized the limited number of Karzai's fighters who could be fed and supported by such a small burg to man dug-in defensive positions to the east and south of the town. As of November 20, Greg was still describing Echo's position as "tenuous." They would need more weapons for the 700 or so fighters they believed they could currently call upon from villages in the area—given the fluid movement and uncertain loyalties of tribal fighters who came and went, one could never be sure—and estimated they would need between 1,000 and 1,500 fighters before they would feel confident in moving south toward Kandahar. Greg reckoned that it would take another ten days to marshal the required forces. One hundred forty AK-47s, along with thirty heavier weapons, dropped from the sky on the 25th, but more would be needed—or so they hoped.

Also in the immediate aftermath of Tarin Kowt, the ODA was informed of plans to add a fifteen-man SF battalion headquarters to their tiny eleven-man unit. This was an unprecedented departure from normal Special Forces doctrine, and certainly not welcomed by the ODA. It appeared the ultimate impetus for it came from Secretary Rumsfeld, who had been questioning for some time the prudence of leaving Special Forces units, which were being called upon to deal with cunning warlords in the field, under the command of mere captains. Greg strongly advised against this change in CIA channels, indicating that a substantial increase in American personnel was neither logistically nor politically wise, given Karzai's need to present a small but effective U.S. presence to his local constituency. Anything which suggested that the Afghans were an appendage to an American invasion force would entirely change the local psychology. Greg's objections, when conveyed to the military via headquarters, apparently carried some weight: the fifteen-man contingent was reduced to three, led by one Lieutenant Colonel Fox, an SF battalion commander. He took over the role of "senior military advisor" to Karzai on the 26th. Greg, of course, would continue to handle intelligence and politics.

November 28 brought another round of telephonic political discussions between Hamid and the Taliban. Mullah Abdul Salam Zaeef, the Taliban ambassador to Pakistan, known to be very close to Mullah Omar, called first. Would amnesty for his one-eyed leader be a possibility? Karzai replied that it might be, but that before any such action could be considered, Omar must first publicly break with the Arabs and turn over all foreign terrorists to the international community. This was strikingly close to the deal I had suggested to Mullah Osmani before the start of the war. Zaeef listened closely, and promised to convey the message to Omar.

In fact, the next call was from Osmani. The burly commander requested a cease-fire with both Karzai and Gul Agha, as well as a halt to the bombing of Kandahar. If the Northern Alliance would turn Kabul over to Karzai, he said, the Taliban would be willing to turn Kandahar over to him. This was an interesting gambit, particularly in light of our long-standing fears concerning the Pashtun reaction to the Northern Alliance's seizure of the national capital. Karzai again indicated that he would consider amnesty for senior Taliban—though this time, showing his characteristic volubility, he declined to include Mullah Omar in the offer—provided they publicly broke with bin Laden's Arabs. Once again, Osmani stated that he would convey the offer to his leader.

I had long marveled at the seemingly mystical hold which Mullah Omar seemed to exert over his followers, and which I had seen myself in the case of Osmani. From our intelligence, I knew it and could describe it; but until recently I had never really understood it. Once again, it was Brigadier Suhail who enlightened me. Omar, he said, was a very singular Afghan. He had a strategic vision which those around him simply lacked. Through his piety and the sheer force of his will, he was able to command their respect. But far more than that, he was a master of psychological manipulation, at least in the context of Pashtun culture: he was able to sow a healthy measure of rivalry and distrust among his senior acolytes, while forging strong bonds of loyalty with each. He was the hub of the wheel. Key governors, military commanders, ministers, and members of the *Shura* all maintained their connection to the organization primarily through him, while frequently distrusting those around them. Here we were seeing it play out again. Key members of the Taliban leadership would reach out singly to Karzai, almost never acting in concert; they seemed incapable of reaching a group decision without reference to Omar.

On November 30, Karzai's army began moving south in a thirty-five-vehicle convoy toward Khakrez. Late that night, after they had difficulty clearing a series of steep passes and one of their trucks had broken down, they decided to spend the night at the village of Petawek. They had finally passed into Kandahar Province. By any objective measure, theirs remained an almost laughably quixotic enterprise. Rather than the 1,500 militiamen Greg had projected they would need, they commanded at most 300, though these at least represented the best of those available. "Best" was a relative term; as Greg and Jimmy assessed the available forces, they concluded they could really count on just forty or so to stand and fight if they were to come under sustained attack by a large force. Together with Gul Agha's band of perhaps 1,500, well to the south and east, they were preparing to converge on the capital of a still dangerous foe that greatly outnumbered them. And yet everything had changed. Somehow, improbably, they were riding a tide of history which would raise them up, while engulfing their enemies.

Chapter 31

EARTHLY REWARDS

I WAS SITTING ALONE in my office, glancing up occasionally at the television in the corner, monitoring the ceremony taking place in the White House Rose Garden. I could see Dayna Curry and Heather Mercer standing by the podium. President Bush had just extolled the two women for their courage, faith, and perseverance, and now they were about to take turns to speak. My mind wandered off a bit. It must have been a day or so after the rescue that David Donohue had pulled me aside. "I want to tell you how impressed I am by your people. No one else could have done what Jim did." It was high praise, particularly coming from David.

I looked up again at the screen. I can't remember which of the two it was, but it seemed that in her enthusiasm one of the young evangelicals was going off script, and well over time. Never again, presumably, would she have such a platform to give witness to her faith. But one could see that there was little of calculation in what she was doing. Her demeanor bespoke the earnest naïveté which characterizes the saintly. Given the setting, it made for an interesting clash of cultures. Maybe it was my imagination, but the president was beginning to look a bit nervous, and there seemed to be an uncomfortable stirring among his aides on the periphery of the screen. I had had a bit of experience with presidential visits, and knew the extent to which the U.S. chief executive's every waking minute was carefully choreographed. It was clearly time for this press event to be over, and for the president to be moving on to the next thing. But until this young woman decided to finish speaking, no one was going anywhere. She literally held them captive before the cameras. I smiled. This was ending perfectly.

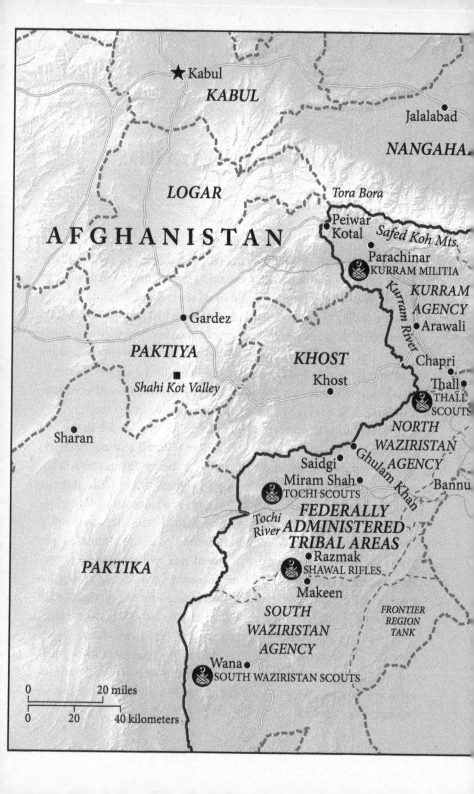

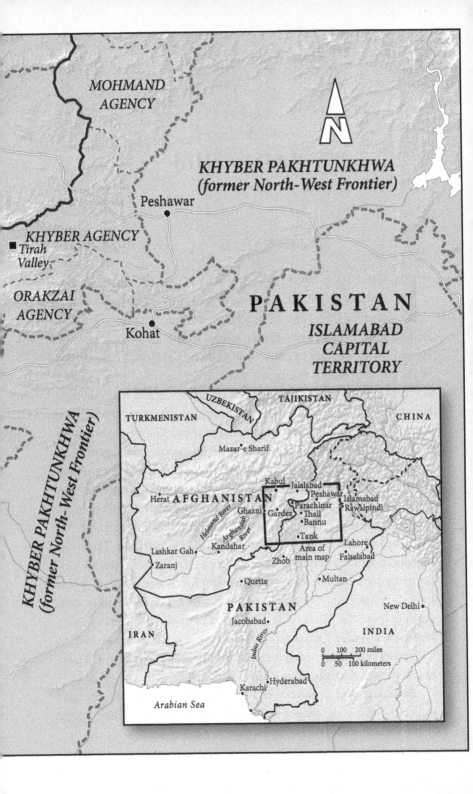

Chapter 32

BADLANDS

THE THIN WHITE CONTRAILS of an American B-52 bomber might otherwise have looked reassuring, arching in stark relief against an impossibly blue sky and tracing a path, no doubt, to Taliban or al-Qaeda targets to the north and west. But viewed where we were at the Peiwar Kotal border post, in the shadow of the Safed Koh Mountains just south of Osama bin Laden's sanctuary at Tora Bora, those contrails seemed menacing and unpredictable. We were standing before a half-demolished rough stone building with a mixed group of Frontier Corpsmen and tribal *Khassadars*, local police working under the authority of the Pakistani political agent. They pointed toward a pile of rocks and rubble several hundred meters up the road which had been the Taliban border post just seventy-two hours before. When the first American bombs started falling in the middle of the night, they said, no one had been much concerned: they had heard about the amazing accuracy of the U.S. airstrikes. The building where we were standing, one of three at the Pakistani post, would normally have housed a squad of sleeping *Khassadars*; as luck would have it, it was empty when the errant bomb struck. They were quite amiable about the whole thing. "No harm, no foul," they seemed to say. Just then, an older *Khassadar* with a deeply lined face approached me with a shy smile. He meekly handed me a large, jagged piece of shrapnel, as though returning something I had misplaced.

By the last week in November, I was seeing reports from Afghanistan indicating that a significant number of bin Laden's Arabs had sought

refuge on the high slopes of the Spin Ghar, or White Mountains—what
the Pakistanis called the Safed Koh—just south of Jalalabad, in eastern
Afghanistan. The sharp peaks of the Safed Koh run along a straight
east-west axis, defining a portion of the Durand Line, the frontier between Afghanistan and Pakistan. The region of steep mountainsides
and deep, plunging ravines on the northern, Afghan side of the peaks
is called Tora Bora. It should not have been at all surprising that bin
Laden and his men would seek refuge there: he was intimately familiar
with the area, having operated from that place during the days of the
anti-Soviet *jihad*. Comprising some of the most difficult terrain in all
of Afghanistan, riddled with caves and tunnels where men and supplies can easily be hidden, it is one of the most ideal places imaginable
for a beleaguered force to defend itself from ground attack.

It was also clear that if al-Qa'ida fighters were trapped and pursued
in that area, their most likely avenues of escape would run southward,
through the high passes of the Safed Koh, into the Pakistani Tribal
Areas just beyond. I met with General Jafar on November 23 to inquire
what could be done to interdict them if they tried. The tribal regions,
formally called the Federally Administered Tribal Areas, or FATA,
had been established during the 19th century as a buffer zone along
the wild, hostile northwestern frontier of what was then British India.
Divided administratively into tribal agencies, each was presided over
by an appointed "Political Agent" who combined executive, legislative,
and judicial responsibilities in one person, but who exercised his authorities strictly in accordance with local tribal norms and customs, referred to collectively as *Pushtunwali*. The provincial laws of the "settled
areas" did not apply in these frontier badlands. After the creation of an
independent Pakistan in 1947, the Pakistanis had maintained the same
system virtually without change.

Security in the Tribal Areas was maintained by organized paramilitary units raised from the local tribes, but led by officers of the regular Pakistan Army. The most famous such unit was and is the Khyber
Rifles. These units are referred to collectively as the Frontier Corps.
The role of the Frontier Corps is to maintain rough order, mediating
disputes among the tribes, and upholding the carefully exercised au-

thority of the political agents. The tribes are highly suspicious of the federal government, and jealously guard their independence. For the political agents, manipulation of tribal rivalries is at least as important as the threat of armed force in maintaining order and a rough equilibrium. In effect, the tribal agencies exist in a permanent state of armed truce, with the federal government of Pakistan treading carefully lest the tribes of a given area unite against it, forcing them to intervene with conventional forces in a fight in which fierce local militias hold important advantages. In many of the tribal agencies, virtually every boy above the age of twelve carries a rifle.

Aware of the tenuous state of security in the Tribal Areas and the limitations of the Frontier Corps, I was very concerned about what might happen if significant numbers of heavily armed Arabs came tumbling down from the high passes of the Safed Koh into Pakistan's remote Kurram Agency, particularly as they were likely to find considerable sympathy among the local population. In these circumstances, it seemed to me, the best we could expect from the Frontier Corps was some sort of trip wire, and I had no idea whether they were postured even to do that. Would it be possible, I asked Jafar, to organize some sort of rapid-reaction border control force to deal with what threatened to become a serious emergency?

Jafar shared my concern at the prospect of seeing hundreds of Arabs, possibly including bin Laden himself, successfully escape into Pakistan. Under his leadership, ISI had been working with us hand-in-glove for two months to dismantle systematically the extensive support infrastructure that al-Qa'ida had built up in the settled areas. Sensitive about his country's reputation, he was very much alive to the negative PR consequences for Pakistan if al-Qa'ida were to elude justice by gaining sanctuary there.

"Let's make an inspection," he suggested, "and see what can be done." I didn't need any coaxing. It was the one way we could see for ourselves the state of Pakistani border controls south of Tora Bora and make specific recommendations to strengthen them.

We set out early on November 28 in a Pak Army four-wheel-drive vehicle, with a driver and an orderly, soon joined by an armed escort. Jafar insisted that I travel in Pakistani dress, so as to keep a low profile.

Normally when Westerners are called upon to don ill-fitting folkloric clothing, they come away looking ridiculous, like Halloween refugees from a yard sale. I was having none of that. The best rule, it is said, is never—ever—to wear native dress. But if I were going to break that rule, I was at least going to be respectably kitted out, with a properly fitted *shalwar khameez* and a high-necked waistcoat. The one thing I neglected to bring was a proper winter-weight coat. Fortunately, Jafar anticipated the need, and covered for my oversight with a heavy parka.

We raced westward along the flat tableland of the Potwar Plateau, then plunged downward into the Indus River Valley. We crossed by the ancient bridge just below the brooding Attock Fort, where Alexander the Great had forded the Indus to mount his invasion of India. From there the landscape became much more variable, as we cut through narrow passes in a series of sharp ridges interspersed between broad dry watercourses. We stopped briefly at Kohat, an army town and home to Pakistan's Ninth Division. From there, we continued onward through Hangu, marveling at the narrow-gauge railway constructed by the British to carry supplies through the difficult terrain to their distant outpost at Thall, located at the eastern edge of the border between the Kurram Agency to the north and the North Waziristan Agency to the south. There we paid a short call on the commander of the Thall detachment of the Frontier Force Regiment, the only unit of the regular Pak Army in the area. I listened very closely to his briefing on available forces, anticipating that if we were to get agreement on a Pak Army deployment to interdict the southern passes leading from Tora Bora, the troops might well have to come from here.

Rushing onward, we were met by a small detachment of the Thall Scouts, the Frontier Corps unit charged with security in southern Kurram, who escorted us to their headquarters and another briefing by their commander. All this gave us some context on overall security conditions and the state of Pakistani forces in the wider area. But it was only an introduction to what we really needed to see: the status and deployment of forces in the so-called "Parrot's Beak," the wild salient of northern Kurram which made a sharp, narrow, westward triangular bulge in the Pakistan-Afghanistan frontier, and where it seemed bin Laden and his followers might emerge as they fled their U.S. and Afghan pursuers.

We continued north along the Kurram River, now escorted by two truckloads of scouts from the Kurram Militia, through the Chapri Post, past which no foreigners were allowed to venture without official permission into the dangerous areas beyond. The waning afternoon light gave the landscape—carved by millennia of floods—a timeless, ethereal quality as the road climbed up the flanking escarpment and then plunged back down, again and again, to the ever-shifting gravel bed of the valley floor below, crossing and recrossing the rushing torrent. Jafar was highly nostalgic about the area. Here he had served during the 1980s as the commander of a tank squadron charged with blocking a possible Soviet advance across the Afghan border and down the Kurram River Valley. The expectation was that if the Soviets sought to punish Pakistan for its support of the *mujahideen*, this would have been one of their prime axes of attack. As a young captain, he had had few illusions about how long he could resist the superior armor of the Soviet Army; his plan, once the last of his tanks had been destroyed, was to escape with his wife by disguising themselves as shepherds and driving a small flock of goats along a track to the east. In places where the river spread out in dozens of small watercourses across the broad rock and gravel expanse of the valley bottom, we splashed through shallow spillways flanked incongruously by weathered concrete "dragon's teeth" tank barriers.

We arrived just at sunset in the small garrison town of Parachinar, located on a flat, treed expanse defining the far northern edge of the Kurram Valley, flanked on the north by the towering peaks of the Safed Koh, and on the west by the northern end of the Sulaiman range. We drove through the small cantonment area, finally stopping at the British-built stone fort, constructed in the 1890s as the headquarters of the Kurram Militia. It was a place straight out of Kipling. After being welcomed by the colonel in command, we ate a quick dinner and played a game of billiards in the dark, wood-paneled room that had once been the commander's bar during British times, before retiring for the night in the officers' guest quarters.

The following day, we stepped outside into the clear, cool morning air to see spectacular, snow-capped peaks towering above us. The commander provided us with a comprehensive briefing on his manpower and force structure, as well as the positions of all his border posts and checkpoints, and the schedules and patterns of combat patrols being conducted all along the border for which he was responsible. It was an earnest and credible presentation, and made it appear, when viewed on a map, that the entire area south of Tora Bora—from the tip of the Parrot's Beak at the western end of the Safed Koh, all the way to the Tirah Valley in Khyber Agency to the east—was well covered. One look at the difficulty of the terrain, however, made it clear that sealing this area would be nearly impossible. The problem was compounded by the fact that the slopes, ravines, and foothills leading up to the high peaks were a so-called "no-go" area, where even the troopers of the Kurram Militia could not patrol, by agreement with the tribes. It seemed clear to me that as and when al-Qa'ida "squirters" fled through the high passes, the best hope of intercepting them would be immediately on the Pakistani side, where the topography would naturally channel them into corridors that could be patrolled and surveilled. As things were, the Frontier Corps could only hope to capture the Arabs as they emerged onto the roads and tracks of the valley below—a much more difficult proposition, and one made nearly impossible by the modest forces at hand.

At the tip of the Parrot's Beak at the far western end of the Safed Koh is Peiwar Kotal, the mountain pass through which Major General Sir Frederick Roberts made his surprise attack on Kabul in the Second Anglo-Afghan War of the 1870s. It was there that we met the border guards who had shown so much equanimity over their close encounter with an American bomb. Crossing the border and marching several hundred yards up the road, our Pak Army and Frontier Corps escorts in tow, Jafar and I made an inspection of the wrecked Taliban border post, climbing up on the rubble of what had once been a large stone building. Looking down from this little promontory, Jafar spied a dark green plastic object on the ground; it had the shape of a large, rounded cakepan.

"That's the cover of an antitank mine," he said. We looked at one another. "Perhaps we should climb down," he continued. I agreed, suddenly far more observant of where I was stepping. Close by, we found a jagged hole, clearly made by an American penetrator. It had burrowed at a slight angle, deep into solid bedrock. One couldn't see the bottom. Jafar stared at it in wonder, eventually calling one of the Pak Army *jawans* over. He was to come back, Jafar ordered, with a long string, to which he was to tie a rock. Jafar wanted to know just how deep that hole was.

We climbed from there up the steep hillside where the Frontier Corpsmen were eager to show us the new fighting positions they had constructed overlooking the pass. They had taken advantage of the Taliban guards' departure to move several of their observation posts to higher ground, in effect moving the Pak-Afghan frontier farther west. Jafar smiled and looked on approvingly. "I probably shouldn't be witnessing this," I thought.

On the long drive back to Islamabad, I compared notes and shared my thoughts with the general, who would be filing a report immediately upon his return. I cannot say for certain whether our inspection trip and Jafar's report were the cause, but two days later, on December 1, the governor of the North-West Frontier Province, Lieutenant General Iftikhar Hussein Shah, flew to Parachinar for a grand *jirga* with all the *maliks* of the Upper Kurram area. The tribal leaders agreed that for the first time in Pakistan's history, they would permit Pakistani government forces to move up onto the slopes and into the high passes of the Safed Koh—provided that the government sent regular Pakistan Army troops, and not the Frontier Corps. Their rationale was that Pak Army troops would surely leave when their mission was completed, whereas the Frontier Corps, once permitted to move into that area, would be far more likely to stay.

The *maliks* agreed to organize *lashgars*, or local militia units, to guide and accompany the Pak Army troops in setting up watch posts high in the mountains. Each combined unit of militia fighters and Pak Army *jawans* was to include the son of a prominent *malik*, as a guarantee against betrayal by the tribes. The first Pak Army troops began to move in immediately, employing mules to transport their gear on the steep mountain tracks. In a matter of days, they had moved some six battalions—over 4,000 men—high above Parachinar. As the troops dug in to seek shelter from the frosty mountain winds, they could hear the rumble of huge explosions from across the peaks. The massive American bombardment of bin Laden's Arabs, trapped in Tora Bora, was beginning.

Chapter 33

TWIN REPRIEVES

I ARRIVED IN MY office, still tired from my late-night return from the Tribal Areas, to find the usual pile of overnight cables stacked neatly on my desk. I had only begun to glance at the top one when Dave came rushing in, holding yet another in his hand.

"They're in the air!" he said. I had no idea what he was talking about, but already it didn't sound good.

"*Who's* in the air?"

"The Director!"

Good God. Director Tenet would be in Pakistan to meet with President Musharraf in a matter of hours, and had neither an invitation nor an appointment. At the moment, I didn't even know where Musharraf was. I arranged to see General Ehsan ul-Haq, the ISI chief, immediately.

That evening, I was standing at the foot of the stairs as George stepped down from the plane, with his security detail, some seniors from the Near East Division, and a number of analysts from CTC/WMD following behind. As the visitors, baggage, and logistics were being sorted, he and I climbed into the backseat of an armored sedan, and sped off toward Islamabad. I still didn't know precisely why he was there.

"We have to get to the bottom of UTN [Ummah Tameer-e Nau]. We're operating on the assumption that they've given al-Qa'ida the means to build a nuclear weapon," he said grimly. I was startled.

"I didn't know that was our assessment."

"It's not," he replied. "This isn't an analytic judgment. It's an operational one. If there's any chance at all that it could be true, we have to pursue it as though there were a high probability that it *is* true."

The November 4 revelation concerning Dr. Bashir's nuclear discussion with bin Laden and his subsequent meetings with Abu Zaydan had certainly gotten Washington's attention, but hadn't generated quite the degree of panic I had anticipated. Perhaps Washington's relative sobriety reflected that so far, at least, all we knew about was talk and bad intentions, with no hard evidence that al-Qa'ida had either fissile material or any substantive nuclear knowledge or capability. Everything depended on determining whether the well of Bashir's knowledge about al-Qa'ida's nuclear aspirations had in fact run dry, or whether his cooperation with al-Qa'ida had gone further than he had admitted. Almost four weeks later, we still didn't know for sure.

In early November, at the end of his forty-eight-hour interrogation of Dr. Bashir, Barry McManus had felt that he had played out his string, at least for the time being. Bashir was exhausted, and would not budge beyond his current admissions. The polygraph indicated that he was still withholding some information, but it was Barry's professional judgment that Bashir's cooperation with al-Qa'ida, and his knowledge of their capabilities, was not significantly greater than what he had told us. In any case, in his current state he could not be usefully questioned further. During an evening video conference with a group of skeptical Washington WMD analysts, it was agreed that Barry and his colleague Dave would return home for consultations. It was time to regroup.

In subsequent days, the political pressure on the government of Pakistan greatly increased. Stories began to appear in the press that Dr. Bashir had been arrested by the ISI, and was being tortured by foreign interrogators. He and his family made renewed claims of ill-health. We had no other leads to pursue, and no new information with which to confront either Bashir or his ISI minders: none of Bashir's colleagues in UTN appeared to know anything. ISI, feeling the heat and wondering how much longer this could go on, was beginning, again, to make noises about releasing him.

In the meantime, unsubstantiated clandestine reports began to appear that al-Qa'ida was actively planning weapons of mass destruction attacks in the United States. Fear and tension were rising palpably in Washington. On November 29, George briefed President Bush, Vice President Cheney, and national security advisor Condoleezza Rice on our state of knowledge as to al-Qa'ida's efforts to acquire WMD. Reacting to information on Dr. Bashir and UTN, the vice president asked if we thought al-Qa'ida had a nuclear weapon. A senior analyst accompanying George stated that we did not, but that we couldn't exclude the possibility. Thus was born Dick Cheney's "one percent doctrine": If there is a 1 percent chance it could be true, he said, we have to pursue it as though it were true. Given the stakes involved, that was hard to argue with—particularly at a time when the crushing fear of another, infinitely more devastating attack on the homeland hung like an incubus over every moment, waking or sleeping. The president directed George to leave immediately for Pakistan and to get from President Musharraf whatever help we needed to determine absolutely whether or not al-Qa'ida had gained from Pakistan the ability to hit us with a nuclear weapon. This was why Tenet had appeared, so suddenly that some of his security people didn't even have a change of underwear.

I dropped George at the ambassador's residence for the night, with plans for a preparatory meeting early in the morning. The director did not look good: he was obviously exhausted. The next morning, he looked worse. I had serious doubts as to how this would go. His big advantage, I told George, was that he definitely had the Pakistanis' attention. They had no idea why he had arrived with almost no notice, and given all that was happening, both across the border and on their own streets, they were highly concerned at what this might mean. If he was trying for a dramatic entrance, he had succeeded.

Just before 9:00 AM, we were joined by Wendy Chamberlin, and then whisked off at high speed to the old prime minister's residence, on a bougainvillea-draped hillside overlooking the city behind the presidency. As we walked down the long carpet toward the reception room, I could see a transformation coming over George. He suddenly had a bounce in his step. It was showtime, and I could sense the trouper in him rising to the occasion. He shook hands with Musharraf and exchanged a few pleasantries, the president motioning him to take a heavy, ornate chair just to his right. Ambassador Chamberlin, George's retinue, and I fell in alongside Tenet, across from a parallel row of Musharraf's senior staff and some of the army brass, a grim-faced General Ehsan among them.

George began by thanking Musharraf for seeing him on such short notice, and conveyed greetings from President Bush, on whose orders he had come. The U.S. president was seized with the continuing threat posed by al-Qa'ida, which we knew to have a strong interest in developing nuclear weaponry. Dr. Bashir and UTN had admitted attempting to provide nuclear expertise to others in violation of their solemn commitments, and Bashir had admitted discussing such assistance with bin Laden and al-Qa'ida. Now the president was seeking Musharraf's commitment to do everything necessary to determine whether UTN's involvement with al-Qa'ida might have gone further. We had to know whether al-Qa'ida might have a nuclear bomb.

Musharraf nodded. He had obviously been briefed on UTN, and was prepared. He understood the president's concerns, he said, but we were talking about Afghanistan. Whatever bin Laden's aspirations, he would need access to a large, industrialized infrastructure to build a nuclear weapon—an infrastructure that Afghanistan lacked. Pakistan knew quite a lot about what was required, having taken many years to produce a nuclear weapon itself. Our fears, he said, were surely misplaced.

George leaned forward and looked Musharraf in the eye. What the general had said was true of efforts to produce fissile material; this did indeed require a large-scale effort and considerable industrial capacity. But if terrorists were able to gain a supply of such material, the situation was completely different. We had checked with the best informed experts in the United States, and they had assured us that with recent advances in available technology, a terrorist group with access to a small supply of highly enriched uranium or plutonium could build a nuclear device in a garage. All they would need was access to the necessary brainpower, the necessary technical expertise. With the dissolution of the Soviet system, the opportunities for criminals and terrorists to acquire nuclear materials had greatly expanded. It was possible that bin Laden could have gained access to these materials from these or perhaps other sources. Given the courageous stand which Pakistan had taken against terrorism, it now could find itself at least as vulnerable to an unconventional nuclear attack by al-Qa'ida as we. Could we count on Musharraf's assistance in dealing with this mutual threat?

It was a brilliant performance. The DCI had not come to browbeat the Pakistanis to do something against their will. Instead, with reason and empathy, he had explained a mutual vulnerability of which they had been insufficiently aware, and had sought mutual cooperation to deal with it. Musharraf was won over. He glanced at General Ehsan. We could count on Pakistan's complete cooperation, he said. We could bring any experts we required in order for us both to get to the bottom of any threat these Pakistani scientists might pose. His solidarity in confronting terrorism, he said, was unshakable. Was there anything else we could do to improve our cooperation?

Tenet looked over at me. I had not anticipated this. With a glance toward General Ehsan, I looked back at Musharraf.

"Mr. President," I said, "our cooperation with ISI has been excellent. We have been working very closely with our liaison contacts as ISI has conducted investigations of al-Qa'ida. However, I think it would be more efficient and effective if we could work directly with those who are actually conducting those investigations on ground." To date we had had to work through General Jafar's staff, which played an intermediary role, making operational requests and proposals on our behalf, and passing back to us the fruits of the resulting investigations. But responsive as Jafar and his people were to our needs and desires, they were essentially acting as a post office. It would be far more efficient for us to deal directly with the investigators themselves. Musharraf glanced at Ehsan. The latter nodded. We would have what we wanted.

There was a buoyant atmosphere that afternoon in the "bubble," our bug-proof room, as the station conducted a full briefing for the director. I invited Wendy Chamberlin to sit in on the first part of the briefing, which gave her the opportunity to lobby George for "deliverables" she wanted from Washington, including compensation for the Pakistanis for war-related expenses they were incurring, border security equipment, and U.S. market access for Pakistani textiles. I knew George was unlikely to get into policy recommendations back in Washington, especially concerning textiles, when CIA was already so far out of its normal lane, but it was a gesture that the ambassador appreciated.

We discussed follow-up with the Pakistanis on Bashir, and on other WMD-related challenges. Just three days before, documents related to anthrax had come into our hands from a house previously used by UTN in Kabul. There were a large number of operational leads which would have to be followed up on, and I was already overstretched. Between the newly intensive effort on Bashir and these new leads, I would need more help from CTC/WMD. George looked at the CTC people with him.

"How about it?" he asked them, pointing at me. "He's got a war to run." After we conferred a bit, they agreed that three of the analysts would remain behind.

In addition to briefing on the progress of the war across the border, we spent considerable time describing what we were doing with ISI to dismantle the support infrastructure al-Qa'ida had painstakingly built to facilitate the movement of people, money, and things in and out of Afghanistan. We described the Joint Operations Center, the "Clubhouse," we'd set up with ISI, where every lead we forwarded was being followed up quickly by the Pakistanis. Having just returned from Tora Bora, I described the role General Jafar Amin was playing in trying to get Pak Army forces arrayed to intercept the Arabs we expected to start fleeing south. Asked what information we were passing the Pakistanis to give them advance warning as to where and when the Arabs might start moving through the passes, I had to tell him, "None." Our requests, I explained, had been denied. Asked what we expected to do with those we captured, I described my proposal for a joint detention and interrogation center.

"Good idea," George enthused, only to hear from me that that proposal, too, had been refused by headquarters. A look began to come over George's face. "These guys are doing a lot for us," he said. "They've done everything we've asked. What are we doing for them? They're incurring expenses on our behalf. Have we given them anything?"

This time a look came over *my* face. "No," I replied.

George sat back and looked directly at me. "There's a problem here, isn't there?"

A senior Near East Division officer who had accompanied the DCI as part of his delegation spoke up quickly. "No, George, we're working these issues with CTC. We're handling it. There's no problem." I looked at him for a couple of beats. If the Near East Division was handling anything with CTC on my behalf, I sure couldn't see any sign of it. But the tradition in the Clandestine Service is that we settle our problems internally. In the context of the DO, even the director is an outsider. I looked back at George.

"Yes, there's a problem," I said. "There's a big problem." Before 9/11, as George well knew, the Paks had been the enemy, refusing to provide us any assistance against al-Qa'ida or the Taliban. Now, I said, they had demonstrated that General Musharraf's abrupt shift in policy was not a sham. Not only were they providing basing rights and support to U.S. military operations, but ISI was providing us everything we asked for in terms of on-ground investigations and intelligence cooperation. They had facilitated the movement of Afghan oppositionists across the border to attack the Taliban. It wasn't important whether we liked the Pakistanis, or whether we considered them friends. They were going to continue to pursue their national interests as they saw fit. But we needed to be able to take yes for an answer: where they were willing to provide us help, we should take it. And if providing them with money would give them the means to help us more, we should do it. After a bit more discussion, Tenet suggested that we provide the ISI with a modest subvention.

I had my own reasons to be enthusiastic about this idea. I still owed the ISI over half the sum Tenet had proposed, and couldn't get authorization to pay them. Having been told on November 24 that the director's verbal authorization to procure weapons from the Paks was not valid, and that I should renegotiate the price in any case, I had sent a response a couple of days later, on the 26th. I explained that the matter of the badly used weapons was all my fault, but that our refusal to pay the agreed price was leaving General Jafar in a badly exposed position within the Pak Army. He was being told by the Supply Corps that the weapons were perfectly serviceable, and he had no compelling proof to the contrary. They were dunning him for the payment and making him look bad. For us, the amount of money at issue—the difference between new and reconditioned weapons—was negligible compared with what was being spent even on an hourly basis in Afghanistan, and yet for this we risked undermining the one individual who, perhaps apart from Musharraf himself, was our most important Pakistani ally. I thought the logic unassailable, but days passed without even the courtesy of a headquarters response. In the meantime, Jafar was inquiring about the money practically on a daily basis. The man had gone well out of his way to help me, and here I was embarrassing him. By the eve of Tenet's visit, I had had enough.

"I'm bringing you the payment tomorrow," I said. The general stopped and looked at me with genuine alarm. He knew me well enough to sense a hint of self-destructiveness in my demeanor.

"Do you have authorization?"

"No, but that's my problem, and I don't want you to pay the price for it." He could see that I was serious. From the look on his face, I surmised this would be as serious a breach in his system as it would be in mine.

"Well," he said slowly, "I suppose a few more days wouldn't hurt." With that one remark, he saved my career. It's very hard to get fired outright in the federal service. Even in CIA, manifest incompetence will simply get you shuffled off to some obscure sinecure where, with luck, you will do no harm. But financial malfeasance will get you fired, and nothing and no one can save you. Working on little sleep and high daily doses of adrenaline, furious with headquarters, I was beyond caring. Jafar saved me from myself.

Now Tenet was providing me a way out. He, too, believed that he had authorized the Pak weapons purchase during the November 13 video conference, but couldn't get in the middle of a fight over financial regulations. What he could do was arrange a reward for the ISI's good behavior. Suddenly seeing that the director was on our side, the Near East Division officer excitedly arranged a meeting to finalize signed authorization for the payment after their return. Walking alone with George toward the ambassador's residence on the embassy compound that evening, we discussed some of the internal obstacles I was facing.

"I understand what's going on here, but I can't solve this for you," he said. "It's just not my role." He was right. I told him I understood.

Some days later, I carried a heavy duffel bag stuffed with neat bricks of hundred-dollar bills into the ISI Headquarters. I insisted upon conveying it myself. In a long CIA career, I had never been a bagman; this was my one opportunity. The carefully worded receipt, signed by Jafar, stipulated that with this payment all outstanding financial obligations between CIA and ISI had been met. I never did get authorization from headquarters to pay for those weapons.

Within days of Tenet's departure, Barry McManus was back in Islamabad, and he and the nuclear specialists were back at work on Dr. Bashir. After two days—December 5 and 6—they were bogged down again. Bashir simply could not get through a polygraph exam without showing clear signs of deception. McManus and I sat down alone.

"We're getting close to the point where we can't run a valid test on this guy," he said. "His stress levels are getting so high that he's reacting just to being hooked up to the machine." The polygraph is actually a simple device. It simultaneously tracks heart and respiration rates, blood pressure, and perspiration levels, and charts them on a graph. It doesn't measure lies. What it actually measures is a person's fear response. It will only work if the subject being questioned fears getting caught in a lie. Clearly, Dr. Bashir was hiding information from us, and feared the consequences of our discovering the truth. Whatever he was hiding mattered to him. What we didn't know was whether it mattered to us.

"Maybe we need to go about this a different way," I said, thinking aloud. "Bashir obviously has a lot to hide, and we could spend years wandering around the fever swamp of his mind trying to figure out what it is. But there are only a few things we really need to know. We need to know whether, to his knowledge, al-Qa'ida has a nuclear device, fissile material, or a working bomb design. We need to know whether there is anyone else in touch with them who could advance their WMD capabilities. Apart from those, we can live with anything. We don't need to know the whole truth about Bashir's activities or what he was intending. Instead, we should start with what we absolutely need to know, and work backward from there."

After another intense day of interrogation, we had satisfied ourselves that if bin Laden's people had any of the three things we most feared—a nuclear device, fissile material, or a weapons design—Bashir didn't know about it. He had not introduced such knowledge or materials, nor did he know of anyone else in touch with al-Qa'ida who could advance their capabilities. Whatever his past intentions, he had not succeeded in bringing them to fruition, and did not know of anyone else who had. Our work with him was done.

That still left the matter of the anthrax documents from the UTN house in Kabul. And a couple of weeks later, my officers would find a cache of documents and supplies related to efforts to produce biological toxins, poisons, and chemical weapons—including a formula for atropine, used to counteract the effects of chemical warfare nerve agents—in bin Laden's abandoned compound at the Tarnak Qila, just outside Kandahar. The documents at the Qila were associated with an effort led by bin Laden's deputy, Ayman al-Zawahiri, to generate a biological weapons program. Months of subsequent investigation would show that these programs were at an embryonic stage when halted; but as indications of intent, they were unmistakable.

The thought of terrorists—accountable to no one and nothing beyond their warped conception of religious obligation—in control of a nuclear weapon or other implements of mass terror, is the ultimate nightmare scenario. UTN and its bizarre link with al-Qa'ida gave such fears a tangible face. Now, as a nuclear-armed Pakistan continues its gradual dissolution in a growing tide of Islamic radicalism, a flood which our Afghan adventure has done much to promote, the nightmare remains very much with us.

Chapter 34

THE CONVERGENCE

T HE SCENE WOULD HAVE been comical, if it weren't dangerous. From where Mark stood, Highway 4 sloped upward to the west where it crested a few hundred yards away. There he could see Gul Agha apparently wrestling with three members of the ODA, as rockets roared over their heads to explode in the desert beyond. Most of his men had sensibly taken cover, but not their chief: He had continued to stand in the open, shouting to them and trying to direct their fire on the Arabs hiding in the dry irrigation canals bordering the airfield below. Seeing him exposed to enemy fire, the Special Forces troopers had ceased directing close-air support to pull their principal charge out of harm's way. They eventually succeeded. "Say what you will about Shirzai," Mark said, "but he's a warrior."

It had been twelve days since the battle of Takht-e Pol, eleven days since Gul Agha and Team Foxtrot had succeeded in cutting Highway 4. As soon as they had done so, they set up roadblocks to screen traffic heading in either direction. The following day, Gul Agha's men intercepted five Arabs traveling down the highway toward Spin Boldak. After a brief firefight, they killed three and captured two, and a cousin of Gul Agha was shot in the abdomen. Gut wounds are always the worst. Although they were reluctant at first, we convinced the military to medevac the young man to Germany. It went a long way in further cementing our relations with Shirzai.

A couple of days after Takht-e Pol was taken, and after several rescheduled flights, Foxtrot finally received its second airdrop. When the bundles were broken open, they revealed considerably less weaponry and ammunition than expected: much of the precious volume had been taken up with bales of hay. Apparently, the packers had thought the shipment was bound for the horse-mounted team accompanying General Dostum in the north. Mark provided a sober, thorough accounting of the supplies received, including the number of hay bales, adding a comment: "We have no fucking horses."

The Directorate of Operations, the Clandestine Service, does not tolerate profane or abusive language in cable traffic. I had once seen a senior officer formally reprimanded by the deputy director for operations when he failed to adequately proofread a colorfully worded cable dictated in anger to a literal-minded secretary. The station officers supporting Team Foxtrot brought Mark's message to me.

"Should we send it like this?" they asked. The cable would bear my station's site line, and I would be held responsible.

"You saw Headquarters' instructions," I replied. "Send it out as received."

On November 28, we got a striking report from Kandahar. Mullah Omar had instructed his commanders to allow Gul Agha to move westward unimpeded until he reached the Shurandam bridge on the eastern outskirts of the city. They were then to attempt an ambush from the rear, using a combined Taliban-Arab force staged at the airport, just to the south. Rather than moving into the trap with his main force, on the night of December 1, Gul Agha sent a sixty-man advance party well ahead of the main body of his army to seize the Shurandam bridge and cut off reinforcements to the airport from the west. Taliban troops withdrew from the area west of the bridge, leaving only some Arabs, who subjected Gul Agha's men to a mortar and artillery barrage for an hour. The Taliban then staged a small attack on the bridgehead from the south, but were easily beaten off.

The following day, Gul Agha moved forward with his main force to seize the Arghistan bridge located east of the airport, cutting off the area. By December 3, there were few if any Taliban remaining at the airfield, leaving a substantial number of Arabs to fight on alone, using irrigation canals as cover. Gul Agha was growing increasingly impatient.

As soon as the Arabs had been sufficiently weakened from the air, he planned to attack them with 500 men. They were the last obstacle. In the near distance, he could see the prize: the ancient city founded by Alexander the Great, whose name it bore; the glorious former capital of Ahmad Shah Durrani, father of modern Afghanistan; the center of the Pashtun world. Kandahar, which Shirzai once had ruled, lay tantalizingly just ahead.

DECEMBER 5, 2001

I can no longer remember who brought word, perhaps because the message was so shocking: "Greg's team has been hit by a bomb. They've all been wiped out."

Before I could come to grips with the news, the first thing to enter my mind was that I needed to speak with Cindy. Greg's wife had been working in the station since being evacuated from her home along the Afghan border. I didn't want her to get the news in the hallway; I thought she should hear it from me. First reports from the field, they say, are never correct. Thank God, this was no exception. Within minutes, new information came across: catastrophic as the strike had been, most of the team, including Greg, had survived. Now I wanted to get to Cindy with the welcome news before someone told her that her husband was dead.

The CIA team was filing brief sitreps (Situation Reports), from which we could begin to piece together what was happening. The ODA, Team Echo, and a number of Afghan fighters had been skirmishing with Taliban troops intermittently since late on December 3 at the village of Shawali Kowt, which controlled the northern access point to a key bridge over the Arghandab River, about 20 kilometers north of Kandahar. By late on December 4, with liberal application of airpower, they had effective control of the village and, with it, the bridge. On the morning of December 5, the remainder of Lieutenant Colonel Fox's battalion headquarters element joined the band, and began directing further airstrikes. One of the new controllers made a devastating error, calling in a GPS-guided 2,000-pound JDAM (joint direct attack munition) "smartbomb" on his own location. The first several casualty estimates were contradictory, but as the dust cleared and the initial shock of the concussion wore off, we were told that three Americans had been killed, and many more severely wounded. Afghan losses, both killed and wounded, were far heavier—perhaps forty in all. In addition to losing two of its number, several members of the original ODA 574, including its commander, Captain Jason Amerine, were seriously wounded and quickly evacuated by helicopter. The unit had been decimated. Miraculously, none of the CIA officers was killed or seriously wounded. Karzai, standing inside a small building with Greg by his side, had suffered a minor cut when a mirror fell from a wall; Greg had immediately thrown himself on top of the insurgent leader when the initial blast hit.

The desultory fighting of the previous thirty-six hours north of Kandahar had been mirrored at the outskirts of Kandahar Airport, where Gul Agha continued his efforts to root out its Arab defenders. The reason for the Taliban's mysterious disappearance from the airfield had become apparent on December 3, when I had another long conversation with Mullah Jalil. Dadullah-Lang had finally returned to Kandahar from the north, he said, but was not exerting his influence in the direction he had hoped. Most of the Taliban leadership were posturing and claiming they would fight to the end, but Jalil could see their hearts were not in it. Many were secretly hoping Omar would change his mind if there was a consensus. Some 600 or 700 Arabs remained in and around Kandahar, he said, many of them at the airport, where some of the Taliban commanders were strongly encouraging them to press on with the fight.

"We are telling them it is *jihad*," he chortled; they were hoping to see as many Arabs killed as possible. Their presence in the city, he said, was impeding the negotiations.

Before ringing off, Jalil had another request. Could I arrange safe passage for him to Pakistan? It was too late for that, I said. The situation was too chaotic and uncertain. His best course would be to surrender to Karzai.

"Do you think so?" he asked.

"Yes, I do." He seemed skeptical. We never spoke again.

On December 5, the Arabs were continuing to block Gul Agha's progress. The irrigation canals just outside the airfield were of an unusual, semi-enclosed design, with a horizontal flange extending inward from either side to reduce evaporation loss. Working from within these partial tunnels, the Arabs were able to constantly change their positions while remaining mostly invisible to the aircraft and to those guiding them. They would emerge briefly to fire unguided rockets at Gul Agha's positions, and then dive back in again and change location. This made targeting them difficult work, but it also made their rocket fire inaccurate, as such rockets normally have to be "walked" onto their targets by firing a series from the same position, making gradual aiming adjustments each time.

On the morning of December 6, the day after the fratricidal bombing incident, Karzai received word that the Afghan representatives at the UN Bonn Conference had selected him to be chairman of Afghanistan's Interim Administration. He would serve for six months until a *Loya Jirga*, or "Grand National Assembly," could form a legitimate transitional government which would, in turn, write a new constitution and organize national elections. His first instinct was to leave immediately to go to Bonn. Could Greg arrange helicopter transport? Greg strongly advised that he do no such thing until Kandahar was liberated.

"The reason you have credibility with these people is because you're leading the Pashtun uprising against the Taliban. You need to finish the job," Greg said. They were still at Shawali Kowt, 20 kilometers from the southern capital. At that point, we still had no idea how long finishing the job might take, but events were moving quickly.

Later on that morning of the 6th, sitting in a hut with four Taliban representatives under the watchful gaze of Greg and Jimmy, Karzai hammered out the outlines of a surrender agreement. The Taliban *Shura*, he told Greg, had agreed to surrender the city and to recognize the Interim Administration. Mullah Naqib would have responsibility to secure the city proper, while Gul Agha would secure the airport and the southern and eastern approaches to the city. Once Karzai had entered Kandahar and assured himself that the situation was stable, he would appoint Jan Muhammad, a loyal supporter and former *mujahideen* commander from Uruzgan, to command his forces while he himself would depart immediately to see about organizing a national government.

That was the plan. Not everyone was happy with it. Shortly after, Karzai reported again to Greg that Gul Agha was objecting strongly to the prominent role being given to Naqib, his old antagonist and a Taliban ally, while Gul Agha himself, despite having led armed opposition to the Taliban, was locked out of the city. Citing Shirzai's ambition to be governor, he complained that the Barakzai leader's "greed and ego may continue to present us problems." This was not going in a good direction.

Greg got on the phone with me. I strongly seconded his admonition to Karzai that he should see through the final liberation of Kandahar, or risk a serious loss of credibility with the other factions in Kabul. We talked over the dispute with Shirzai. I should speak with Hamid, we agreed.

As I went to take the call, I considered how I should address our newly elevated friend. "Hamid," it seemed, would no longer do. "Mr. Chairman" seemed bloodless and stilted: a very un-Afghan title. I drew on my past experience in the francophone world, where they excel at diplomatic forms of address.

"Your Excellency," I began cheerfully, slightly concerned that I was overdoing it. "I want to congratulate you on your appointment." Hamid thanked me warmly and modestly, and made a few remarks about the important work ahead. I shifted to the reason for the call. My first mention of Shirzai brought a litany of complaints, most having to do with the former governor's bluster. When Karzai paused, I cut in:

"Your Excellency, Gul Agha is a simple man. He lacks your sophistication. He can't play the sort of role that you can. But he is a good man; he has a good heart. If you will put your trust in him, I know for a fact that he will accept your leadership, and will be very loyal to you." In fact, Mark had told me that Shirzai had been quite enthusiastic about Karzai only days before, and quite willing to follow him until the recent unpleasantness. Karzai saw immediately where I was going.

"Well . . ." he hesitated. "Well, I suppose he can be Governor," he said petulantly. From his tone, one might have thought that Gul Agha was demanding much more, and that this was a reluctant compromise. Once more, I'd gotten Hamid's agreement more easily than I had anticipated. I moved to consolidate.

"Your Excellency, that's wonderful. An excellent idea. I know you won't regret this." I recall having slight misgivings over the arbitrariness of what we were doing. As chairman of the Interim Administration, could Hamid be appointing governors? Was this legitimate? What sort of precedents were we setting? I put my misgivings aside. We could worry about governance issues later. Right now, I had to make sure that Karzai's and Gul Agha's forces wouldn't start fighting each other even before Kandahar was secured.

That out of the way, we moved on to a broader discussion, with Hamid recounting the events of the day. He had met with Taliban defense minister Obeidullah and former interior minister Abdul Razzak, both senior and influential members of the Taliban. Minister of Aviation Akhtar Muhammad Mansur was not present, but he had been strongly associated with the talks. It was agreed that Mullah Naqib would begin at the western end of the city, moving from checkpost to checkpost, disarming the Taliban and collecting their weapons. At the eastern end of the city, Taliban forces were to go to the airport, where Gul Agha would disarm them.

I didn't say so, but this all sounded too simple and orderly to be realistic. I wondered if Karzai believed things would unfold this way. He had promised amnesty for low-level Taliban members who agreed to be disarmed. I didn't even ask about the disposition of the Taliban leadership. Everything we were discussing was dependent upon the voluntary compliance of the Taliban. Between Karzai and Shirzai, there were not enough forces to ensure compliance with anything, and Karzai's men were still well outside Kandahar. Although there was regular bombardment of Taliban targets within the city, which was increasing as our intelligence and targeting improved, it was not as though we had the area surrounded and could block anyone's escape. With Karzai having reached nominal agreement, we would have to see how things unfolded.

When I expressed some misgivings about Naqib, Karzai said he shared our wariness. He fully understood that the reason the Taliban wanted to use Naqib as an intermediary was that they trusted him. That was useful for the moment, he said, but it also meant that Naqib should be watched carefully. In any case, given that the Popalzai, Barakzai, and Alikozai were the principal tribes represented in the city, it was important to include Naqib, as a respected Alikozai elder, to reassure his people that their interests were not being overlooked. It all made eminent sense.

Finally, the Taliban representatives had assured Hamid that the Arabs were in the process of leaving. Hamid had responded that the bombing of the city would continue as long as the Arabs remained.

I thanked Hamid and congratulated him again. I then lost no time in informing both Mark and Greg what had been agreed regarding Shirzai. It was up to them to facilitate things from there.

As light dawned on the morning of December 7, the streets of Kandahar were in chaos. Mark sat on a hill just beyond the eastern outskirts of the city, monitoring developments. He and an Arabic-speaking member of Gul Agha's family listened on a walkie-talkie captured from an Arab west of Takht-e Pol as leaders of the fleeing Arabs tried to organize their departure. It was almost like listening to a group of tourists preparing for an excursion. They heard someone say, "Be sure you have your passports!" As the convoy emerged from the city, Mark could count fifty vehicles. A single massed airstrike might have wiped them all out, but there was no one close by who could call it in. They watched as several hundred Arab followers of bin Laden drove off, disappearing to the north on the Kabul-Kandahar highway.

Meanwhile, Gul Agha led a large force in an attack on the airport, only to find that the Arabs and the Taliban had left. The way into Kandahar was open. Grabbing a portion of his force and piling them into a handful of vehicles, he dashed into the city, with Mark and part of the ODA in tow. Finding no opposition, they went straight to the Governor's Palace, and immediately occupied it. This was not quite in accordance with Karzai's carefully laid out plan. While Gul Agha was thus engaged, the newly appointed chairman was unsuccessful in his attempts to contact him by sat phone. Hoping to mediate between Gul Agha and Naqib, he planned to formally name Shirzai governor, but only if the latter would accept the Alikozai master of Arghandab as a partner in the liberation of the city. The deal would have to wait.

Mark's reports throughout Shirzai's campaign, for all that they were usually written in haste, often in appalling conditions and while their author was on the verge of exhaustion, frequently had a lyrical, understated, almost haunting quality. Now, having reached his objective, he paused to write a sitrep in which he described the first concrete sign of the city's liberation. Much has been written since then about kite-flying, and the symbolic place it holds in Afghan culture. The Taliban, who had banned kite-flying as a sinful frivolity since their takeover in 1994, had been gone for only a few hours. But as Mark stood looking out a window of the Governor's Palace, he could see, high above the darkening rooftops, that the last rays of sunset were illuminating a handful of kites as they swooped and darted in a bright azure sky.

It had been eighty-eight days since a series of attacks in a strange country many thousands of miles away had somehow unleashed a war for which no Afghans had been prepared. Now, this ancient city, traditional capital of an ancient land, would have the chance of a new beginning.

DECEMBER 8, 2001

I suppose it was inevitable. The dispute between the Afghan liberators of Kandahar was spreading to their American mentors. On the morning of December 8, Mark called to complain. He had contacted Greg to work through some remaining points of contention between their respective principals regarding the role of Naqib in securing the city. Some of Karzai's people had allegedly begun throwing their weight around, generating considerable resentment in Gul Agha's ranks, and now Mark was concerned that it could lead to violence. Greg, apparently, had been less than sympathetic.

"Hamid's just been named leader of the country. I think that makes him just a little bit more important than your guy, don't you?" he was supposed to have said. I winced. This was no time for Greg to be Greg.

"Look, Greg," I said, when I got him on the phone. "Mark doesn't know you like I do. He doesn't know how to take you, and he doesn't know when to ignore what you say." This was my lead-in to what I expected to be a counseling session, but the ex-Marine immediately burst out laughing.

"Okay, Chief, I got it. I hear you, five by five." He was still laughing. "You won't have any more trouble from me." We talked over the need to mediate between the two leaders; otherwise, we risked having our Afghan allies at war with each other, and it was entirely too soon for that.

When I got back to Mark, he explained that for his part, he'd had to get pretty rough with Shirzai. When our voluble friend had threatened, in a fit of anger, to attack Karzai's men, Mark had left him in no doubt of the consequences:

"Shirzai, if you attack, you won't just be attacking Karzai's men. You'll be attacking us, because we're with them. That will make you an enemy, and we will have to treat you accordingly." That got the big man's attention. It was something he could understand: "If my friend attacks my brother, I must attack my friend." There was no more talk of fighting with Karzai.

Later that day, I sent out a strongly worded message to both teams. Karzai, who was still moving south from Shawali Kowt, would be entering Kandahar for meetings at the Governor's Palace on December 9. On the margins of those meetings, CIA was to broker a private session between the new chairman and Gul Agha, at which both Echo and Foxtrot teams were to be present, and all outstanding issues were to be worked out. The two could bicker later, I said, but for now, with the situation in Kandahar still so unsettled, nothing must be allowed to interfere with our counterterrorism objectives. To that end, we would need immediate manpower and assistance from both men. Specifically, Echo and Foxtrot were to set up a joint counterterrorism "pursuit team" of the sort advocated by headquarters to round up any Arabs in the area and to follow up on all counterterrorism leads. We would need a dedicated detention and interrogation facility for any al-Qa'ida or senior Taliban officials captured, where they could be held pending a determination as to their disposition. A special security force should be established to control access to all designated sites associated with al-Qa'ida or with the Pakistani-based Ummah Tameer-e Nau, which was suspected of providing assistance to al-Qa'ida in developing weapons of mass destruction. And finally, a joint committee should be formed to oversee the equitable distribution of humanitarian aid in the city and the surrounding area.

The December 9 meeting went better than we could have hoped. Thanks in part, I'm sure, to American preparation, everyone was on his best behavior. Karzai, Gul Agha, and Mullah Naqib met, with both Gul Agha and Naqib pledging their fealty to their new leader. At Karzai's direction, it was agreed that during an interim period, Shirzai would take charge of security in the southern part of the city, south of the main highway, and that a senior lieutenant to be named by Naqib, though not Naqib himself, would assume responsibility for the northern part of the city. Once the situation had been stabilized, Shirzai would assume his full duties as provincial governor. It was a masterly stroke by Karzai, and it greatly eased the tensions between the Barakzai and Alikozai chiefs.

A cloud of suspicion still hung over Naqib because of the effective escape of both the Arabs and the Taliban leadership, which had occurred under the cover of a surrender agreement he had brokered. Realistically, even if Naqib had given the Taliban political cover to negotiate a handover of the city, political cover was about all he had been in a position to provide. No one could have prevented the Taliban's escape from Kandahar. The American failure to strike the fleeing Arabs, though, was a costly error for which we could blame no one else, and for which we would eventually pay a heavy price.

If Naqib had played a role in "saving" the Taliban leadership, he was no more complicit than Karzai. I was not entirely comfortable with the chaotic way in which the war had ended, but the Taliban had done us a great favor in abandoning the city. Had they and the Arabs decided to make a last stand in Kandahar, we would not have had sufficient Pashtun forces to root them out. Employing some combination of Northern

Alliance and American troops and U.S. airpower to do the job would have wrecked the city, generated heavy casualties, and completely changed the whole political character of the war in the south, probably precluding any chance of an effective peace. As it was, both Afghans and their foreign benefactors would have the opportunity, at least, for a new beginning, a chance to build a unified nation that would no longer serve as a base for international terrorists.

The question was whether they, Afghans and foreigners, would have the wisdom and the patience to succeed.

Chapter 35

THE ESCAPE

MID-DECEMBER 2001

T HE OFFICE DRAPES HAD been drawn, shielding us from prying eyes in the apartment block several hundred yards away. Once again, I sat on the threadbare couch, feet propped up on the blond wood coffee table, rubbing my eyes to ward off exhaustion as "Kate," the senior communicator, fussed with the video connection.

A strong, broad-shouldered, handsome woman in her mid-thirties, Kate had always been something of an enigma to me. She was highly competent, reliable, and devoted to her job, which she performed in the obscurity of her stoutly vaulted spaces. It is one of the great ironies that communicators occupy one of the lowest social rungs in their organization, and yet theirs is perhaps the most sensitive position. They are the keepers of the secrets. Everything flows through them.

Kate was perhaps more sensitively aware of her caste, and more affected by it, than most communicators. Among other things, it made her all the more fiercely loyal to those who served under her. She wore her chip quite clearly on her shoulder. Unless it was a professional necessity to enter my office, she would not do so. It soon became apparent that she would not pay the boss a call unless summoned. If I wished to interact less formally, I would have to come to her. I was more than happy to do so. And if such visits were not as frequent as they might have been, Kate was gratified at the mark of professional respect they implied.

After 9/11, things changed a bit. Where once Kate would have established the video link and returned to her office, after 9/11 she lingered to view the goings-on. The reason soon became apparent: she fixed me one day with an appraising eye during a series of particularly politically charged sessions. "It's interesting to watch the way you maneuver," she said. "It's pretty neat." I remember it as one of the best compliments I have ever received.

On this occasion, the screen before me was filled with boxes, most representing the various military entities—in Tampa, Qatar, Uzbekistan, and Afghanistan—involved in sharing information and coordinating actions for the Tora Bora campaign, which was now getting under way in earnest. This was the first of a series of virtual conferences with CTC/SO acting as host, and determining CIA participation, which meant that shortly I would be cut out, as CTC was eager to get me out of Afghanistan and restrict me to my Pakistani lane. But for some reason I was included in this one.

The key CIA field participant in the conference was Gary Berntsen, leader of Team Juliet, successor to the original Jawbreaker team led by Gary Schroen in the Panjshir Valley, and now directing the effort in Tora Bora. I had never met Berntsen, but had heard about him. He was reputed to be a bit of a wild man, which colored my perceptions. It would be fair to say that he made a very energetic presentation, punctuated with descriptions of complicated, synchronized movements of attacking forces, blocking forces, and so on. Apart from the handful of CIA paramilitary officers and SF troopers with him, he had only loosely organized rump Afghan militias at his disposal. It was hard for me to judge the soundness of his plans, as I lacked sufficient knowledge of precisely what was happening on the ground, but I do remember thinking that what he was describing was well beyond the capabilities of any group of Afghan militias I had ever heard of.

Hank was the senior CIA participant at the headquarters end. He said surprisingly little, and when he did speak, it was in a halting and hesitant manner. The meeting broke up in mild confusion. The whole thing struck me as bizarre, so much so that I contacted Pat Hailey at CENTCOM, who had been sitting in, to ask.

"What was going on with Hank?" I inquired. "Is he up to this?"

"Don't get me started," he said. His theory was that Hank was upset that CENTCOM had allowed an Australian liaison officer into the proceedings. He had therefore said the minimum necessary and shut the conference down as quickly as he could.

Throughout the first half of December 2001, the heavy bombing of Tora Bora continued. Following the message traffic from across the border, I was getting a rather sketchy and confusing picture of how the situation was evolving. My hope was to get some degree of advance warning as to when and precisely through which passes the al-Qa'ida fighters might flee the American bombardment. As I read the map, there were five passes that were the most likely avenues of escape, the lowest of which had an elevation around 11,000 feet. I was absolutely forbidden by CTC, however, to provide the Pakistanis with any sort of advance warning, as this might provide them an indication of the key points of U.S. attack, information which might then be shared with al-Qa'ida elements in the mountains. This was the sort of unhelpful paranoia with which I routinely had to deal. Nonetheless, the Paks were fully expected to capture any al-Qa'ida members who eluded our grasp, despite not being given any assistance in doing so.

I *was* told by CTC/SO that if any Americans or allied Afghan forces were about to cross the Pakistani border in hot pursuit, I was to have a mechanism in place for informing the Pakistanis so that we and our allies would not be fired upon. I reached Jafar at his office at 1:00 AM one morning to ask him to work out the modalities for channeling such a warning to Pakistani troops in the mountains, in the event a warning was necessary. Conveying a rapid message to Pak troops in the mountains would not be a problem, he said.

"If any Americans approach the border, please let me know right away," he added. "But if any Afghans try to cross the border, we will shoot them regardless." On the subject of Afghans, he was very consistent. This sounded like an argument in the making, but I decided to save it until it was needed.

By December 15, after two solid weeks of heavy bombardment, the Arabs had been driven well up onto the snow-covered north face of the Safed Koh. Soon the Pakistanis were picking up half-frozen, half-starved Arabs stumbling down the other side. On December 17, I paid a call on a then little known major general, Ashfaq Pervaiz Kayani, the director-general for military operations of the Pak Army, at the Pak Army General Headquarters in Rawalpindi. I didn't know it then, but he would have an illustrious future. He reported that the Pakistanis had detained some forty Arabs in the past two days. Many more would follow in the days to come, some 130 in all.

This raised the question of what to do with them. I had been left in no doubt as to CTC's views when I had proposed in writing, back in mid-November, a joint international detention and interrogation center for al-Qa'ida captives on Pakistani soil, the proposal to which Hank referred so unfavorably during our chat of November 18.

"We will not agree to Pakistani detention of any al-Qa'ida prisoners," the cable stated. "Appropriate arrangements for their internment are being made with our loyal Afghan allies."

CTC got a better idea what those Afghan detention arrangements might look like in late November, when Berntsen sent three of his people back up into the Panjshir Valley to inspect a Northern Alliance prison where a large number of captured Arabs were already being held. They were not prepared for what they found. Large groups of prisoners circulated freely in and out of the camp, while their guards frequently could not be found. The "inspectors" were horrified.

"You'll want to look at this," Dave smiled, as he handed me their report during one of our morning meetings. All I could compare it to was the scene in *Lawrence of Arabia* when an uninitiated British officer enters a captured Turkish military hospital in Damascus for the first time. Staring in shock at the filth and gore around him, the red-faced man can only shout, *"This is outrageous!"* again and again at the top of his lungs. The tone of this cable was not dissimilar.

"There is simply no question of our placing al-Qa'ida prisoners in Northern Alliance detention," it concluded. I was curious what CTC would come up with now.

Faithful to our directives, as the Tora Bora escapees fell into Pakistani hands, we arranged for the Pakistanis to move the captured Arabs, Chechens, Turks, Chinese Uigurs, and others in groups down to Chaklala Airbase in Rawalpindi, where they were loaded onto U.S. Air

Force C-17 transports. They were flown first to Bagram Airbase north of Kabul, where the U.S. military was quickly establishing a base of operation, and then immediately onward to Kandahar Airport, which the Marines had occupied after al-Qa'ida and the Taliban had fled. A temporary, open-air prisoner holding facility had been set up. We heard later on television that the Department of Defense had decided to ship the detainees from there to facilities being hastily built in Guantánamo Bay, Cuba.

Given the subsequent controversy over "Gitmo," CIA "black sites," interrogation policy, and all the rest, which together have caused the United States to bear alone the opprobrium that comes of implementing unilateral solutions to what are really global problems, or where alternatively America has stood accused of "outsourcing torture" by selectively repatriating al-Qa'ida captives to repressive allied regimes, it seems to me that my modest idea of a joint international facility might have had some merit after all. It would have harnessed the talents, and gained the support and moral complicity, of many of the nations that have in fact benefited from U.S. actions, while taking little of the responsibility.

In early December, I received a cable from the office of John McLaughlin, the deputy director of Central Intelligence, Tenet's number two. It informed me that McLaughlin had met with Arnaud de Borchgrave, the longtime journalist, who had a lead as to where bin Laden might be hiding, and would be arriving shortly in Islamabad. It asked that I provide him assistance.

As we finished shaking hands at the Islamabad Marriott Hotel, Arnaud got to the point. He would be meeting with a well-known and politically prominent Pakistani tribal figure. This man claimed to have precise information about bin Laden's whereabouts. Due to political sensitivities, he would meet in Pakistan only with de Borchgrave, and no other American. As had been agreed in Washington, Arnaud reported, I was to arrange for the Pakistani's immediate, discreet air transport to an aircraft carrier in the Arabian Sea, from which he would then be conveyed to Washington. He would reveal his information in George Tenet's office, and to Tenet alone.

I was dumbstruck. McLaughlin had somehow neglected to mention any of this. I had considerable respect for de Borchgrave, but there was no way I was going to suggest a scheme like this—even if the Pakistani gentleman in question could back up his assertion, whatever it was, with compelling evidence, which I was reasonably certain he could not. A glance at my face told Arnaud that I was entirely in the dark. He was miffed.

"Well, I don't think McLaughlin was just trying to humor me." I was reasonably certain that in fact he was. Perhaps McLaughlin had been a shade too polite.

"Look," I said, "if this gentleman has reliable information on the whereabouts of bin Laden, it will surely be very perishable, and something on which action will need to be taken immediately. We won't have time to bring him halfway around the world to meet with George Tenet in order to hear it. If he is really motivated by the desire to help us find bin Laden, and will only speak with you, surely he should tell you immediately what he knows. The fact that he insists only on revealing his information to Tenet suggests to me that he has some other agenda."

It was still Ramadan, the month when devout Muslims fast during daylight hours. Over *iftar*, the post-sunset breaking of the fast, de Borchgrave found that his contact's previously firm convictions on the whereabouts of bin Laden softened with scrutiny. Within a couple of days, Arnaud's plans had changed. Now he would journey out to the Tribal Areas with one of his contact's kinsmen to meet with other members of the tribe, and see where the path led from there. He wanted to get as close to Tora Bora as possible from the Pakistani side. Unable to dissuade him, I offered him the use of a sat phone. I had some trepidation as he set off; he was not a young man.

A little over twenty-four hours later, I returned to the office from a late-afternoon meeting at ISI Headquarters to find a red light blinking on my "black" or unclassified phone: a voicemail message. Arnaud had been turned back at the Chapri Post on the road to Parachinar, in the Pakistani Tribal Areas. Darkness had fallen, and he and his companion had nowhere to stay. Perhaps they would have to sleep in the car. As the message ended, his voice trailed away: "It's getting cold. . . ."

"Swell," I thought. "A high-profile Washington journalist is going to freeze to death in Pakistan, and it's going to be on my watch." I phoned General Jafar to seek his help. Jafar, unfortunately, was quite familiar with Arnaud's recent work.

"He criticizes us at every opportunity," he grumbled. Ah, I pointed out, but that's what would make this a great opportunity. If the Pak Army garrison at Thall would take him in, they could brief him on all that was being done to stiffen the borders. If a skeptic like de Borchgrave could be shown all that had been done in recent days to guard against incursions by bin Laden's Arabs, Jafar could turn this into a PR coup. The general was still less than enthusiastic as he rang off, but within a few hours, de Borchgrave was being fed and housed at Thall.

A bit later on, Jafar called again. "It's all set," he said. General Ali Jan Aurakzai, the bluff, imposing Pashtun commander of XI Corps in Peshawar, would stop in Thall by helicopter the following morning to pick up Mr. de Borchgrave before beginning an airborne inspection tour of the army's newly established border positions in Upper Kurram. This was turning out better than I could have hoped.

There's a saying in the military that in any operation, there's always someone who doesn't get the word. In this case, unfortunately, it was the young lieutenant who had been placed in charge of de Borchgrave. Rather than putting Arnaud on General Aurakzai's helo in the morning, he instead escorted him to the gate and sent him on his way. Perhaps he thought the journalist would be chastened and head back to Islamabad. If so, he was wrong: with help from his friend, Arnaud disguised himself in local dress, reentered the tribal agency, and traveled for a full day on local jitneys and shuttle buses all over Kurram.

The following Sunday I was surprised to glance up at the television, only to see Arnaud on the screen, sitting with a group of his colleagues on one of the Sunday morning news talk shows. I turned up the volume in time to hear him describe his post-Thall journey around the Tribal Areas near Tora Bora. Despite his transparent disguise, he said, he had been able to travel all around the area unmolested, and hadn't seen so much as a police officer. As far as he could detect, the Pakistan-Afghan border was a sieve, he frowned; precautions to intercept bin Laden and other al-Qa'ida escapees from Afghanistan were nonexistent.

I shook my head. "I hope Jafar doesn't hear about this," I thought. At least no one could say I hadn't tried.

It was not until over a month later, in late January 2002, that I learned what had happened when the al-Qaida cadres fled south from Tora Bora. Jafar and I traveled again for discussions with army and Frontier Corps commanders in North Waziristan and Kurram. This time, our concern was the threat of infiltration from the west rather than the north. But I was still curious about what had happened at Tora Bora. Unsurprisingly, each Kurram unit commander with whom we spoke claimed credit for the majority of the captures of the previous December. Not only were their stories contradictory, but none struck me as credible. It was not until the night of January 28, at a dinner hosted for me by the political agent in Parachinar, that I began to piece the story together. After Jafar had retired early with an oncoming case of the flu, I sat with the political agent and a number of local notables, including the bearded, fundamentalist ISI sector commander, all of whom seemed to regard me at the outset with a good deal of suspicion. It took a while to jolly them up, but soon we were all talking and laughing, and they began to lay out the recent events in considerable detail.

Although a significant number of bin Laden's followers had fallen into Pakistan Army hands, as reported to me by General Kayani on December 17, it was later, on the night of the 18th, that the majority emerged from the peaks above. In the darkness, most managed to avoid the army outposts on the high slopes, and arrived undetected near the base of the mountains. It was there, in small groups, that they encountered the *lashgars*, the local temporary tribal militias set up under agreement with the governor of the North-West Frontier. Exhausted, dehydrated, half-frozen, and lacking any food, they were persuaded by the *maliks* to give themselves up and to turn over their weapons, in the apparent hope that once their immediate needs had been met, they might be turned loose. The *maliks* instead turned them over to the army, as promised.

One group of about forty militants, fed, watered, and loaded onto an army bus for the trip south, revived sufficiently to attempt to seize control of the vehicle. In the fracas, the driver ran off the road and the bus overturned in a ditch. A number of the militants were badly injured, but the majority made off with weapons stolen from their guards. Once informed of the escape, the Kurram Militia organized local tribesmen into yet another *lashgar* and followed after them in hot pursuit. The militants were eventually located and surrounded at the village of Arawali in Lower Kurram, just south of Sadda, a town long known as a hotbed of sedition and religious extremism. It's not clear how many weapons the militants commanded at that point, but they managed to keep up a firefight for the better part of a day before the survivors among them were recaptured. I told the group that on the trip north I had seen a large field just below Sadda dotted with what appeared to be fresh graves, decorated with a large number of prayer flags.

"Yes, yes!" several shouted. As soon as the battle was over, the townsfolk had come out to bury the dead, and the women had decorated their graves with prayer flags to honor them as *shouhada*: martyrs. "Now you see what we're up against," the political agent noted, with a wry smile.

In the years since, of course, I have seen the reports that bin Laden himself was with the fighters at Tora Bora, and somehow escaped from the area. It was a confused and chaotic period, with decent intelligence very hard to come by. As we consider the reliability of the fragmentary reports of bin Laden's presence at Tora Bora, it's worth remembering some of the other wild stories given credence at the time—tales of vast, multistory al-Qa'ida cave complexes, complete with a hotel and massive storage areas, connected with elevators, no less—all of which turned out to be fantasy.

Perhaps the most compelling evidence of bin Laden's presence at Tora Bora came from CIA and SF personnel at the scene, who were directing airstrikes and marshaling the efforts of local Afghan militias against the militants. On two occasions, reportedly, bin Laden's voice was heard over the radio, alternately exhorting his men and apologizing to them for having led them into their hopeless predicament. I have no reason to disbelieve these reports; but even if we take them at face value, it is still not clear whether bin Laden would have been co-located with the militants under bombardment, or just close by. There have been a small number of reports attributed to militants present at Tora Bora, supposedly confirming bin Laden's presence. None strikes me as definitive. Taken together, the available evidence leads me to believe that bin Laden most likely was present at the battle of Tora Bora, but that he was not reliant upon the fighters trapped there for his security. He had independent arrangements for his own departure.

Some claim that bin Laden's escape, if such it was, was proof of his cowardice. I do not agree. I do believe, however, that Osama bin Laden was sufficiently convinced of his own importance to believe that his survival was vital to the future of his movement, certainly more than that of any of his men, whom he could not save in any case. I think he realized that he had a greater chance of survival if he were traveling with a very small group, rather than with a more easily detectable band of fighters. My suspicion—and it is only that—is that if he fled Tora Bora, he would have moved farther east through the mountains, crossing the Pakistani frontier into the Tirah Valley, in the Khyber Agency, just east of Kurram. Tirah Valley in those days was the ultimate "no-go" area, a place where the inhabitants were so fiercely jealous of their autonomy as to forbid any roads to be built, lest they serve as a conduit for government influence. There was certainly no means of intercepting bin Laden there. Once safely in Pakistan, given even a modicum of support, he could have gone virtually anywhere undetected.

It is still a point of contention whether a vigorous U.S. troop deployment at Tora Bora might have resulted in bin Laden's capture. Gary Berntsen, the CIA leader on the scene, has long made this claim, stating that if his requests for a modest number of troops had been granted, bin Laden would surely have been killed or captured. I am skeptical. It seems to me that any one of the many deep ravines on the north side of the Safed Koh could easily have swallowed up a whole battalion of troops; the modest numbers requested by Berntsen, and which otherwise might have been available, would have been inadequate to the task.

One tactic that might have succeeded in interdicting a greater number of those fleeing Tora Bora would have been to airlift U.S. Rangers up into the high passes on the crest of the Safed Koh. Success in capturing al-Qa'ida members fleeing through those passes would still not have been assured by any means, but an armed U.S. presence in those natural channels might have made a difference.

I was not present at any of the meetings where troop requests were discussed and, reportedly, rejected. Having had considerable contact with the military, though, my strong suspicion is that Berntsen's requests were rebuffed because they ran contrary to the prevailing doctrine that had been agreed for the conduct of the war. This was to be an Afghan campaign, with the United States merely acting in support. For U.S. troops suddenly to have been in the lead at Tora Bora would have been a sharp departure from established practice. It may well be that in this case, too slavish and literal-minded an adherence to an otherwise sensible doctrine had serious negative consequences. That's often the problem with doctrine.

Still, I strongly suspect that even effective American action to block the southerly passes into the Kurram Agency would not have resulted in bin Laden's capture, if indeed my theory about his escape into the Tirah Valley is correct. We will simply never know: the one man who could tell us is now dead.

Part Four

PAKISTAN, AL-QA'IDA, AND THE WIDER WAR

Chapter 36

THE CZAR

YOU HAD TO GIVE the brigadier his due, though whether he was courageous or merely stubborn, it was hard to tell. The villa we were touring seemed perfect for our purposes. Located on a quiet, leafy, residential street in Islamabad, it was shielded from view by high walls and tall, dense shrubbery. Inside the stout metal gate there was room in the tiled courtyard for several automobiles, so visitors would not have to park in the street and be exposed to the curiosity of neighbors. On the upper floor was a large kitchen and dining area, as well as a comfortable parlor for casual meetings, with several bedrooms for officers resting from watch duty. Below, on the ground floor, there were spaces for work areas, copy machines, faxes, and the like, as well as a formal briefing room and several small rooms for interviewing detainees.

General Jafar was insisting that the villa be ready within ten days, and the brigadier charged with supporting him was holding just as firm: This would not be possible, he said. But the glowering general was adamant. He walked through each element of the project. Why couldn't this be done right away, or that? What would be necessary to get a particular project done immediately? More money, more people, what? Dubbed the counterterrorism "Czar" by General Mahmud in September, during that sunny Sunday meeting with me and Wendy Chamberlin, Jafar was in no mood for delay.

Ten days later, our joint intelligence center was up and running. Quickly dubbed the "Clubhouse" by the Pakistanis, it was staffed by them twenty-four hours a day, and became the venue for daily meetings with my officers. The division of labor quickly became clear:

CIA's global intelligence system would develop and provide leads to al-Qa'ida-connected people and locations, and the ISI would conduct investigations on the ground to confirm whether the leads were valid, taking action jointly with us when they were. Infamous al-Qa'ida facilitators whom we had been tracking for years suddenly went to ground, or fled. Safe locations used for sheltering al-Qa'ida trainees transiting to or from Afghanistan were shut down. Every week or so, General Jafar and I would take our places in the front row of the Clubhouse briefing room, flanked by our respective officers, while Brigadier Adnan reviewed the latest statistics and summarized ongoing operations.

"To date," he would say for example, "we have received one hundred thirty-six inquiries from CIA. One hundred twenty-three have been processed and assigned for investigation. Eighty-one have been resolved. Forty-two are pending resolution." And on it would go, day by day, week by week. We would never reveal the sources of our information, of course, whether it came from human "assets," or technical intercepts of global communications, or from some allied service on the other side of the planet; but all this information would flow into Islamabad Station, where it was processed, analyzed, and pieced together into coherent investigative leads by targeting officers "forward-deployed" from CTC, and then funneled through the Clubhouse for follow-up by the ISI.

Our system of cooperation rested on a tacit suspension of the usual rules between representatives of sovereign governments. Under normal circumstances, the first reaction one would expect from the Pakistanis would be to inquire just how it was that *we* knew so much about what was happening in *their* country. But the exigencies of the situation did not permit this: the Pakistanis had professed that they would work with us to root out al-Qa'ida, and would not do anything that might call their commitment into question. To them, all that mattered was whether the information we provided was accurate. Our Pakistani friends would not ask where the information came from, and we would not tell. This was bound to lead to recriminations eventually, but that would come later; now was not the time.

A regular participant in the daily séances was Jenny Keenan, the

FBI special agent assigned as the assistant legal attaché, or ALAT, in Islamabad. Diminutive and fit, with cropped brown hair, piercing blue eyes, and a streetwise manner, Jenny was initially a source of startled wonder to our Pakistani colleagues, who didn't know quite what to make of an assertive young woman poking brazenly into their operations. Her knowledge and energy quickly won them over.

Her boss, Chris Reimann, the FBI legal attaché, had been assigned to Islamabad at the same time as I, and had already become a great friend. Large and jovial, he was the sort of person one couldn't help but like, and he quickly cut a wide social swath among both Pakistanis and foreigners in the capital city. Chris just wanted to see the right things get done. If he came across a lead of little potential use to himself, or one his tiny office didn't have the resources to deal with, he would turn it over to me. His ecumenism was often not appreciated by FBI Headquarters, and he sometimes paid a price for it: we would have to conspire together to keep unhelpful information on his activities from making its way to the J. Edgar Hoover Building in Washington.

Chris understood that he and I had different roles: mine was gathering intelligence, and his was seeing bad guys, specifically those indicted in the United States, put in jail. We put aside the rivalries that too frequently mar relations between the FBI and CIA. In the years before 9/11, it was nearly unimaginable, at least to me and my CIA colleagues, that the information we were gathering on al-Qa'ida would ever see the inside of a U.S. courtroom. Our job was to track al-Qa'ida and to try to disrupt them so that they couldn't repeat the success they had enjoyed against the U.S. embassies in Nairobi and Dar es-Salaam in 1998. Our information generally did not meet a legal standard. But as much as Chris was helping me to succeed, I wanted him to succeed, and so I was more than willing to see to it that whatever information we acquired would also be put to use to build legal cases against the militants we were pursuing.

In pre-9/11 days, when Pakistani cooperation was an unrealized dream, my station was gathering intelligence entirely on its own. Whenever we met with sources close to terrorists, we took elaborate precautions to protect our officers, fearing that on any given day one of these sources might be "turned" by al-Qa'ida to work against us. But in each of those so-called "high-threat" meetings, if a source turned over a terrorist's passport, or an al-Qa'ida document, or some other object which could be used as evidence, my case officer would motion for the source to turn the item over to an FBI special agent standing by, usually Mike Dorris, Jenny's predecessor.

For the FBI to be able to use an item as evidence in a court of law, it has to have a clear "chain of custody." Once received, the item cannot leave the FBI's control. FBI would keep the original or, when the original had to be returned to the source, it would make a duly certified copy. That way, both our needs would be met. It wasn't always smooth or pretty. My own officers sometimes didn't understand why they had to jump through hoops to preserve an FBI chain of custody that would probably never be used. There were inevitably annoyances, misunderstandings, and occasional hard feelings. But I made it clear to them this was how things were going to be, and Chris and I would consult to make sure irritants were smoothed over and everyone behaved.

The habit of cooperation we created stood us in good stead after 9/11 and the establishment of the Clubhouse, when al-Qa'ida evidence gathering became a wholesale business. Now, rather than just Chris and Jenny, there was a parade of FBI special agents and others from the law enforcement world who cycled through Islamabad to work with us. The division of labor remained clear. We provided the intelligence, the Pakistanis provided the on-ground investigations and the muscle, and the FBI catalogued and established a clear chain for the mountains of evidence all this activity generated as it was sent off for analysis in Washington.

Through it all, Jafar and I remained in near-constant touch. On a typical day I would be awakened at 7:30 or 7:45 AM by a phone call from the deep-voiced general, having typically gone to bed at 3:00 AM. We would always observe the same ritual.

"Bob," he would intone, reacting to the sleep in my voice, and smug at having been at the office since before six, "I wish I had your job."

"General," I would respond, "you're welcome to it." We would then get down to business. Having read as a boy how Winston Churchill began his days as wartime prime minister by working from bed, I flattered myself that I shared one thing in common with the great man. Later in the day, Jafar and I would speak on the phone two or three times more, frequently conducting a face-to-face meeting at ISI Headquarters as well.

I think Jafar took it personally when I asked, and President Musharraf agreed, that the station could meet directly with those responsible for on-ground investigations.

"I thought things were going pretty well," Jafar said, a hint of petulance in his voice. He enjoyed being at the center of the action.

"They are," I said, "but your president asked if there were anything at all we could do to improve our cooperation. I couldn't very well say no, could I? It's obvious that dealing directly with the investigators will make our operations faster and more efficient." He couldn't disagree. Bringing the investigators into our orbit didn't diminish the importance or the frequency of my contacts with Jafar, but it definitely brought a new dynamic to bear on CIA's cooperation with ISI, just as the recent exodus from Tora Bora was about to bring the work of the two services to a new stage.

Chapter 37

DISTRACTION IN THE EAST

I T WAS DEATHLY QUIET. I awakened with a start, and found myself slumped forward, sitting in front of my computer screen. As I regained some consciousness, I refocused on the paragraph before me: three lines of absolute gibberish. I had been typing in my sleep again; this was the second time tonight. I looked up at the clock marked "Islamabad:" It was after 2:00 AM.

Suddenly the phone rang on the table behind me. On the other end was the deep, familiar voice. "I thought I might find you there." It was General Jafar. "Bob," he went on, pausing for effect. "The Indian Army is mobilizing."

I was not entirely surprised. For months now, the Indians had been a recurrent distraction and a nuisance, at least as far as I was concerned. Since 9/11, I and the rest of the U.S. government had been focused on prosecuting the war against the Taliban and al-Qa'ida, a war in which Pakistan was an indispensable ally. Competing issues were unwelcome. But the view from New Delhi was quite different. As always in South Asia, to understand why, one had to go back in history.

Since 1989 and the start of an indigenous insurrection against Indian security forces on the eastern side of the Line of Control, Pakistan had been generally alleged by many international observers to be providing lethal aid to militant Muslim dissidents in Indian-held Kashmir. Over time, these Kashmiri dissidents had been progressively supplanted by Pakistani-born religious extremists eager to engage in *jihad* against the Indian "occupiers" of the former princely state, often

306

with the (again alleged) support of the ISI. Throughout the 1990s, as Pakistan flirted with placement on the State Department's official Terrorism List and was sanctioned as a nuclear proliferator, U.S. policy progressively tilted in favor of India. Where for years the State Department had deplored both the militant violence in Kashmir and the Indian repression that inspired it, the passage of time and frustration over Pakistani sponsorship of terrorism caused the second half of that equation to fade away. To Washington, Pakistan looked more and more the provocateur in Kashmir.

To say that the Indians were then frustrated by the sharp turnabout in post-9/11 U.S. policy toward Pakistan would be a considerable understatement. Here was their age-old nemesis, considered by many a state sponsor of terrorism, whose coddling of the Taliban and tolerance of al-Qa'ida had materially contributed to the disastrous attacks of 9/11, profiting from its past behavior. Like a returned prodigal child, Pakistan was not only avoiding punishment but was being rewarded, embraced as an ally and a front-line state in the global "War on Terror." Meanwhile, the ISI, it was presumed in New Delhi, carried on as a nexus of the violence against Indian security forces in Kashmir.

Soon after 9/11, the Indians launched a series of ground probes, artillery barrages, and other provocations along the Line of Control. It was as though they were trying to tempt the Pakistanis into an overreaction that would disrupt their new "strategic alliance" with the United States. I had no patience with any of this. From my perspective, it was imperative that Pakistan remain focused on common goals, dealing with the threat of Islamic extremism at home and in Afghanistan, and not constantly looking over its shoulder at the traditional menace to the east.

Now a bad situation was becoming immeasurably worse. On December 13, militants had launched a suicide attack on the Lok Sabha, India's national Parliament, producing twelve dead and twenty-two injured. Anyone would have thought it more than likely that these militants were somehow tied to the *jihad* in Kashmir, but the Indians could not wait to seize on this event as an opportunity to excoriate Pakistan and try to disrupt its resurrected alliance with the Americans. Even before any of the militants killed on the Parliament grounds could be identified, Indian security officials were pronouncing them Kashmiris because, they said, several were found with dried fruit, a favorite in Kashmir, in their pockets. That may have been laughable, but more compelling evidence was soon to follow.

India's immediate demands of Pakistan had little to do with its investigation of the attack on Parliament. Instead, the Indians' response was blatantly political, as they publicly demanded that Pakistan hand over an old list of "usual suspects"—alleged terrorists and criminals they had been seeking for years, but who had no clear connection to the latest outrage.

More menacingly, it was clear that domestic politics was driving the Indian response, and that pressure was building rapidly on the government to teach the Pakistanis a lesson. If the Indian Army were indeed mobilizing, it could mean that war was imminent. Just before Jafar's call, I had seen an unclassified State Department telegram from New Delhi, reporting uncorroborated news from Indian journalists that the feared mobilization was beginning.

"Yes, I saw something about that as well," I said on the phone distractedly, as these thoughts raced through my head. There really wasn't much I could say. Even if I knew that the Indians were mobilizing, which I did not, I couldn't confirm it for the Pakistanis at this early stage without authorization. In fact, I couldn't even promise to pass on any information I might get in future, for the same reason. As a policy matter, to avoid miscalculation, Washington might soon direct the embassy to inform the president of Pakistan, but I certainly couldn't do so on my own.

Jafar rang off with surprising haste, leaving me to ruminate. Suddenly, it struck me what had just happened.

"Oh, my God," I said aloud. I rang Jafar back.

"General," I said, trying to maintain an even tone in my voice. "I hope you didn't take what I just said as confirmation the Indians are mobilizing."

"That's exactly how I took it," he said, "and I've so informed my president." I had a sick feeling in the pit of my stomach.

"Well, you've got to call him back! What I saw were unconfirmed reports from the Indian press."

"It's too late," he said. I knew exactly what was happening. Given what he thought he knew about CIA technical capabilities, Jafar had to assume that we would know instantly if the Indians were mobilizing. He must have thought that I had confirmed the mobilization, then realized I'd done so without authorization, and now was trying to walk it back. I'd never convince him otherwise.

I repeated my message, with some disgust, and rang off.

I was wide awake now, trying to assess the possible damage. I couldn't be sure the Indians were in fact mobilizing; I hadn't seen anything from overhead reconnaissance or signals intelligence. If those in Washington were aware, they hadn't shared it with me. But the Pakistanis were convinced—I had helped see to that. They weren't about to launch a preemptive strike, though—not when the Indians would be on full alert and had a head start on mobilization, and when they themselves were not yet ready to deal with the expected retaliation. I knew it would take the Pakistanis days, perhaps over a week, to mobilize and move their forces into forward positions. By then, both sides would know precisely what the other was doing.

No, I hadn't inadvertently triggered the next South Asian war, but it was still a foolish lapse, the price to be paid for working to exhaustion. "You've done enough harm for one night," I thought, as I prepared to leave. This would be an especially busy day, I knew.

Chapter 38

DAYS OF HOPE AND PROMISE

LATE JANUARY 2002

A N INDISTINCT VOICE WAS crackling over the radio, just above the roar of the prop engines.

"Roger, Tailhook. You're cleared to land to the north."

My eyes widened, and I began nervously to scan the sky, looking for other planes. Seeing none, I turned to the pilot to my left. "But we're landing to the south," I said.

Tailhook smiled and shrugged. "Marines," was his one-word explanation.

This was my introduction to our station pilot, a former Navy F-14 aviator who, with the end of active hostilities, had been assigned to us, along with his beloved twin-engine Beechcraft, to ferry supplies across the border to our teams inside Afghanistan. It was a pleasure to associate with someone who so loved his work.

This was also my first real look at Afghanistan, which I had hardly seen except from across the Pakistani border, despite having devoted much of the previous two years of my life to it. From the co-pilot's seat I stared in rapt attention at places I had only read about in field intelligence cables and British history books. As the runway of Kandahar Airport emerged from the dust haze, I could see, off in the sepia distance to my right, the clear, pale blue of Kajaki Lake, a favorite camping place of bin Laden and his close associates, and, much closer, the squat mud buildings of Kandahar itself.

The domed terminal building at Kandahar Airport was a glass-and-concrete monument to 1960s architecture. Inside, I found the one-star Marine commander of the force that had caused us such concern when it arrived in the southern Registan Desert some weeks before. Fortunately, rather than moving north to create mayhem as we had feared, the Marines had sat on their haunches at Camp Rhino and done nothing. But now, with the Taliban and al-Qa'ida having fled Kandahar, they had quickly moved up to seize control of the airport. As I arrived, they were being replaced by troops of the Army's 101st Airborne Division, though the Marine commander was still in charge.

Marine Brigadier General James Mattis was tall and lean, with a pink face, neatly parted gray hair, and kindly blue eyes. But for his uniform, he looked like the model of a country parson, straight out of a Normal Rockwell painting. That impression did not survive his first few sentences. General Mattis was the most flamboyantly profane man I have ever met, before or since. He gave me an appraising look, taking in the tweed blazer I had worn against the winter chill. "You must be the best-dressed man in Kandahar," he said.

"Well, sir," I replied earnestly, "I was planning to pay a call on the Headmaster at Kandahar Prep, and thought I should dress appropriately."

The general invited me outside for a tour of the makeshift holding pen—and it was just that—which he had constructed for the al-Qa'ida Arabs whom the Pakistanis had captured after the flight from Tora Bora. I didn't know it yet, and Mattis probably didn't either, but they were shortly to depart for Guantánamo. The enclosure in which they were held had no walls, but was encircled by dense coils of silver razor wire. A few small, free-standing corrugated tin roofs, mounted on wooden poles, provided the only available cover from a merciless sun; there was nothing to break the cold wind sweeping across the flat surrounding desert. The pale skin of the Arabs' faces and necks had been burned raw, and they openly exposed themselves to urinate into tin basins, in full view of their newly arrived U.S. Army guards, a surprising number of whom were female.

I had had a mental image, based on my years in the Arabian Peninsula, of the typical al-Qa'ida militant as a callow youth from Yemen who had gotten fired up one day by his village mullah and gone off to join the *jihad* in Afghanistan. Weeks of bombardment from American B-52s on the Taliban's northern front lines, I reasoned, would have been far more than they had bargained on. Give them a pat on the head and a chocolate bar, and they would gladly return to their fathers. I couldn't have been more wrong. Their recent experiences had no doubt further coarsened them, but these refugees from Tora Bora were the toughest-looking bunch I had ever seen. According to Mattis, a U.S.-based mullah had shown up on his doorstep a few days earlier, asking to speak with the militants. After a few minutes with them, he fled in shock. "These people are irredeemable!" he had said.

By this time, I could no longer pretend to have any authority in Afghanistan. My two small teams, Echo and Foxtrot, had returned home. The tribal leaders they had supported had become, respectively, de facto interim president of the country and governor of Kandahar. A new station had been set up in Kabul, led by "Rich," another Africa Division officer with extensive experience in senior jobs in CTC. I had already sent him a personal message welcoming him to the region and making clear that I would transfer all of our Afghan sources and any other cross-border capabilities I had to him and his station.

This trip to Kandahar was part of that good-faith effort. I had brought Mark, former leader of the Foxtrot Team, and a number of other Afghan hands to make introductions and get our colleagues off to a decent start. I was concerned about them. One fellow, appointed to a senior position, had been plucked unawares from a posting in Central America. He seemed like a solid and sensible fellow, and had some paramilitary experience as well, but knew nothing about Afghanistan or South Asia. He was fated to learn quickly.

Gul Agha insisted upon receiving me when we arrived at the Governor's Palace. I had hardly recovered from his smothering embrace when he led me into a large public hall filled with visitors—eager petitioners for his favors—and invited me to address them. Completely unprepared and quite innocent of Pashto, I began with a religious invocation in Arabic and then went on, with Engineer Pashtun, Shirzai's

uncle, translating. I strung together what I hoped were a few grace-
ful words to congratulate them on having liberated themselves from
Taliban oppression, and professed a desire to learn how best America
could support them. I was then whisked outside to a waiting motorcade of ragtag vehicles, most filled with heavily armed men. We raced
out of the central city into the countryside to the west for a tour of
Mullah Omar's compound, surprisingly intact despite General Franks's
promise to turn it into a smoking hole, its walls incongruously decorated with colorfully painted flowers. Shirzai and I posed side by side
for a formal photo portrait, sitting a bit awkwardly on the edge of Mullah Omar's bed.

I would deliver two more, rather longer speeches that evening, and
take questions from two more delegations: one a group of characteristically dour and sullen Pashtuns led by Sher Mohammed Akhundzada,
the surprisingly young scion of a leading family of Helmand, elevated
by Karzai to be governor of that province; and the other an enthusiastic
crowd of Hazaras, Shiites of distinctly Asiatic appearance, long abused
by the radical Sunni Taliban, who had journeyed from Bamiyan Province looking as if they had just wandered out of the thirteenth century.
Unlike the silent Pashtuns, they murmured their approval of my religious incantations in Arabic, and clapped enthusiastically at my promises of American support. Word had obviously spread far and wide
that Shirzai had the favor and the ear of the Americans, and thus was
the man to see for assistance. It seemed to me that for the time being
at least, we would be best served by allowing Shirzai to take political
credit for that assistance, building him up as the just and beneficent alternative to Taliban rule in the Southern Zone of the country.

But already simple, fundamental questions were arising regarding
governance. Within a few weeks, Gul Agha had slipped comfortably
into his old role as provincial governor. He was generating significant revenue by imposing tolls on commercial truck traffic along the
Quetta-to-Kandahar highway, one of only two key transportation por-
tals for the entire eastern half of the country. In a nation as poor and
primitive as Afghanistan, such transit tolls were *the* key source of public funds. Gul Agha was greatly motivated to build up political support

by using that money for good works, but there were no controls over its disbursement. And what of the rest of the country? Shouldn't those funds be shared as a national resource with provinces not so favorably situated? What would be the mechanism for dividing those revenues with the center?

Gul Agha's accession as governor had been an essentially arbitrary move by Karzai; I had played a role in it, but where was the local legitimacy and accountability in that? Sooner rather than later, short-term expediency would have to be replaced. Long-term stability required that Shirzai, as leader of the Barakzai, be willing to share power and benefits with the other tribes in the area—the Popalzai, the Alikozai, and a host of others. My strongly held view was that someone, preferably from CIA, should remain closely engaged with Shirzai to help ensure that this key regional figure pursued policies which would redound to his long-term benefit and ours. That was fine and probably necessary for the time being, but was it sustainable? America was hardly set to be a colonial power for very long. How could appropriate checks and balances be institutionalized in a place in which American notions of democracy were foreign, and where traditional means of tribally based accountability had broken down, perhaps irretrievably? Surely a new Afghan constitution would have some influence over these matters, but who was going to influence that? I was certainly in no position to do so.

While staying at the Governor's Palace, I saw evidence that perhaps the Taliban surrender had not been so abject as it had appeared. A CIA bomb expert from our Office of Technical Service whom we had fortuitously sent over a couple of weeks previously had made an important discovery. He showed me a thin, partially concealed wire running down the side of the palace, which had been pointed out to the governor's staff by an old man in the neighborhood. Our expert had traced it up to the top of the building, where he and his colleagues had found some twenty land mines buried in the mud roof, set to fire downward. We could only speculate, but the theory was that the Taliban had planned to detonate the mines during the upcoming *Eid al-Adha*, the main religious holiday of the year, when the governor traditionally receives large numbers of supporters. Had the Taliban succeeded, our joint Afghan-American experiment in building a post-Taliban order might have begun very differently. I saw this attempted attack as the last-gasp effort of a dead-end movement. In fact, it was a premonition of what was in store if we and our Afghan friends were not prudent.

The speeches I gave to Afghan audiences in Kandahar were full of good intentions, but not being in a position to implement them, they were more like a prayer for constructive American engagement in Afghanistan. My visit to Kandahar gave me some ideas about how we, and particularly CIA, should use our newfound influence; but now, relegated back across the border, my ideas were not being sought, and understandably so. It would be up to the new team to figure things out for themselves. If I had a sinking feeling that a great opportunity was being lost, I could not dwell on it. I had more than enough work of my own in Pakistan.

Several weeks later, I looked up from my desk to see television coverage of the *Eid al-Adha* celebrations in Kandahar. I could see Gul Agha, smiling and laughing, mobbed by well-wishers, looking like a Chicago ward politician who had just won a landslide victory. In his left hand he held a large stack of bright red Pakistani hundred-rupee notes. With his right he pressed one into the palm of every person who approached him. He was the happiest man I had ever seen.

Chapter 39

THE POET

I T WAS SUPPOSED TO be a formal gathering, but there they were, joking together off in a corner, their heads inclined, like a couple of sniggering schoolboys. They made an unlikely looking pair. The American, trim and athletic, kept brushing a hank of sandy-blond hair from his pale blue eyes. His Pakistani companion, balding and rotund, was sunk deeply into the white settee. One might have thought they had broken off to confer on some urgent operational matter—if they weren't so obviously enjoying themselves.

Sitting at the head of the long, ornate reception room at the ISI mess, I tried to keep up my end of the polite conversation among Deputy Director John McLaughlin, Ambassador Wendy Chamberlin, and ISI director-general Ehsan. The members of McLaughlin's traveling CIA delegation and General Ehsan's senior staff sat across from one another in roughly descending order of seniority, listening politely as their elders conversed. But my attention was drawn to the antics of the two outliers. I couldn't have been more pleased to see the way they got on. The fact was that my country's interests relied to a significant degree on the relationship between these two men.

The following day, during a lengthy briefing for McLaughlin in the "bubble," Dave, my deputy, laid out the fruits of his collaboration with "General Imran Zaman." These occasional briefings for senior Washington visitors were as useful for us as for the recipients, probably more so. Operating at full throttle, constantly improvising, we seldom had occasion to stop and consider what we were doing, or how.

As Dave explained, with al-Qa'ida fighters filtering across the Afghan border in significant numbers, Imran and he had worked out a "template" for their capture. The process began with data the CIA and the American intelligence community collected from sources—human, technical, and otherwise—around the world. Reports from CIA's human sources concerning movements of al-Qa'ida fighters and operatives fleeing Afghanistan were funneling in to CIA Headquarters, where they joined streams of intercepted technical data and all manner of other esoteric information. Some came from satellites, some from lonely technical collection stations on mountaintops, some from drones, and some from allied intelligence or security services.

"Targeters," the headquarters analysts in CTC whose job it was to immerse themselves in this flood of data and try to make sense of it, winnowed and sifted it, using complex algorithms and keyword searches. Information of any significance would be forwarded to other targeters working with us in Islamabad. There, a phone number thought to belong to an al-Qa'ida operative would be matched to a residential address in a teeming Pakistani city; or the name of a Pakistani militant thought to be harboring al-Qa'ida fighters fleeing from Afghanistan would be connected to an obscure business establishment. Slowly, from a daunting mass of almost unintelligible bits of data, physical targets—places that could potentially be raided—would emerge. The addresses would be forwarded by the station to Imran's operators at the Clubhouse, who parceled out these locations to ISI sector commanders around the country. They and their operatives would carry out ground investigations. An address that turned out to be a public location might be placed under intermittent surveillance; but an apartment belonging to a known militant would be placed under direct observation; or a rented villa from which unknown young men were constantly coming and going would be flagged for an immediate raid.

Night after night, the operations unfolded according to a script refined and perfected by Dave and Imran. An ISI sector commander would arrange for a large number of local police armed with Kalashnikovs to appear on short notice at a particular spot and an appointed time, usually late at night. The police would be told nothing in advance. Once assembled, they would pile into their beat-up Toyota pickups to be led by ISI to their target address, which they would surround. The door would be forced, and the police, accompanied by a handful of ISI operatives, would rush inside to arrest all the males. Women and children would be sequestered, isolated, and supervised by female police.

Waiting across the street, invariably, were a few of my CIA officers, accompanied by one or two FBI special agents, usually on temporary assignment, sent to reinforce Jenny and Chris in the Legal Attaché Office. Once the building or apartment was secured, its occupants disarmed, and the premises searched for explosives, the Americans would be invited inside. The male detainees would be screened by my officers. Any Pakistanis, often members of radical *jihadi* groups such as *Lashgar-e Taiba*, were remanded to Pakistani law enforcement. Their fate was not our business. The foreigners, on the other hand—Yemenis, North Africans, Turks, Chechens, ethnic Uigurs from western China, fighters from all over the Islamic world—were ours. They would be searched, identified where possible, and transported to Pakistani jails pending disposition.

The Americans present would seize any materials found on the premises—passports, documents, cell phones, computers, hard drives, disks, thumb drives, and the like. With FBI agents ensuring that all the materials remained in a proper law enforcement "chain of custody," everything would be copied or downloaded. The originals, whether documents or equipment, would go to FBI as potential criminal evidence; the copies would be forwarded to CIA Headquarters to join the mass of exploitable data being fed into the process. Night after night, data streams from hard drives deemed of priority value would be shot skyward from our roof to satellites overhead.

Generally, the raids went well: the militants and their hosts would be taken by surprise, usually in their beds, and several foreign fighters would be taken into custody. Generally, but not always. On one occasion, General Imran received a panicky phone call from one of his sector commanders. During that night's raid, the commander and his men had burst through the heavy wooden door of a substantial house, but rather than a group of foreign militants bivouacked on mattresses, they had discovered the large sleeping family of a highly respected local physician. Imran reacted quickly. The commander was to apologize to the doctor and inform him that he, his wife, and their family would be personal guests of the general that evening. Ice cream was to be brought immediately for the children, and the physician and his wife were to be transported to the best hotel in town, where they would be offered tea and cakes until their door was fixed and everything put right. That incident passed.

Imran and the ISI were taking much of our information on faith, and trusting us not to embarrass them. Usually, it was rewarded. In return, they maintained our moratorium on inconvenient questions as to where our intelligence was coming from.

Imran had an unusual background. His father was a literary figure, revered in Pakistan as a humorist. There were few situations we encountered together so tense that General Imran could not find a vein of humor. He and Dave made a perfect pair, and were soon inseparable.

In short order, they would account for much of the prisoner population of Guantánamo Bay. When time was available, the foreign fighters picked up in our raids would receive preliminary questioning by my officers at the Clubhouse. But as fast as possible, they would be loaded aboard C-17 transports at Chaklala Airbase in Rawalpindi, just south of Islamabad, and flown first, briefly, to Bagram Airbase north of Kabul, and then to the open-air detainee holding facility crudely constructed at Kandahar Airport. There they would be held until transported to Guantánamo. The detention facility had opened on January 11, 2002.

Our detainee airlift program also involved some quick lessons. A prisoner in one of the first groups to be turned over to the Air Force at Chaklala was discovered to be hiding a large knife inside his *shalwar*, the traditional baggy trousers worn in Afghanistan and South Asia. It had been missed by his Pakistani guards. Thereafter, all prisoners were strip-searched by Air Force security personnel, and given U.S.-issue prison garb. In another early incident, a particularly energetic prisoner was caught attempting to bring down an aircraft in flight, despite his hand restraints and shackles, by gnawing on a high-pressure hydraulic hose. From then on, all prisoners were restrained in the middle of the cargo deck.

Our briefing finally completed, McLaughlin looked at me. "This is quite an operation you've got here." In fact, I was pleased with what we had managed to accomplish. With active hostilities in Afghanistan ended, at least for the time being, and most, if not yet all of al-Qa'ida fled, the main counterterrorism focus was now centered on Pakistan, where we continued to dismantle al-Qa'ida's infrastructure and arrest a steady stream of its rank-and-file members and close associates. We had made a good start. But the most important thing we had done was to establish an effective tactical working relationship with ISI. Now we would be ready for the far bigger fish yet to swim into the net.

Chapter 40

THE PUBLIC AND THE PERSONAL

Then out spake brave Horatius,
The Captain of the Gate:
"To every man upon this earth,
Death cometh soon or late.
And how can man die better
Than facing fearful odds,
For the ashes of his fathers,
And the temples of his gods?"

—Thomas Babington Macaulay, *Lays of Ancient Rome*

MARCH 17, 2002

WE STOOD, YAWNING, AT the far western end of the shopping square, warily surveying the area. There seemed little to arouse our concern. The faded storefronts were shuttered, their tattered awnings hanging listless in the damp, post-dawn air. A few Pakistanis, mostly older men in stained *shalwar khamises*, milled about on the raised concrete sidewalks in groups of two or three. At the open, northern end, where the square fronted on the road, a slight, dark-skinned sweeper stood in the gutter, languidly pushing dust to and fro with a large palm frond. Close by, next to the bus stand, were a group of eight or so Westerners, men and women of various ages, clad in hiking gear. Across the street we could see two more, venturing over to join them. My wife Paula and I would soon

321

join as well, but not right away. Only when the low-slung coaster bus approached would we dash over to climb aboard. If the group should become a target, we wanted to limit our exposure.

Such precautions had long since been a way of life in a country where a measure of latent hostility always lurked just below the surface for Westerners, and particularly Americans. Large crowds, especially those gathered for Friday prayers, were to be strictly avoided. And any concentration of Westerners that had been advertised or could be anticipated, such as that at the Sunday morning pickup point for our hiking group, was a potential invitation to tragedy for the unwary.

For the two years before 9/11, on every schoolday morning, I would stand before the heavy, solid metal gate at the front of our house, waiting for the school bus while my son Doug stayed inside. Mr. 'Abdul Qadir, the guard, knew everyone in the neighborhood. I would scan up and down the block, and quiz him about any loiterers, anyone who seemed out of place. Anybody unknown would be confronted by Qadir, in his green-and-khaki uniform with the outsize brass buckle, a stout stick tucked under his arm, and asked to explain his business.

None of this diminished our enjoyment of an exotic and fascinating country. We traveled widely, especially in the mountainous north, hiking in the Kagan Valley and along the rushing torrents of Kafiristan, near Chitral. Doug and I would go on weekend jaunts to experience the sights and smells of the ancient bazaars of Lahore and Peshawar. While I was chained to a desk, Paula joined groups to scale the heights of Nanga Parbat, ninth highest mountain in the world, and to float down the Indus River on pole barges.

When 9/11 struck, Doug had been devastated to leave his school and head off, with his mother, to exile in America. He had also been mystified by the attitudes of some of his Pakistani schoolmates: though closely acquainted with the West, and from families who had opted expressly for an American-style education for their offspring, many displayed satisfaction at seeing Americans as the victims, rather than the agents, of violence. "Now you see what it's like," one had said.

With families away and a huge crisis to deal with, I and my colleagues had been consumed in a blur of eighteen-hour days and seven-day workweeks. But with the fall of Kandahar, I encouraged them to carve out a little time, at least, for personal relaxation. Beginning in February, Dave and I began to indulge ourselves in a weekly round of golf, which became a Sunday morning ritual.

Golf in South Asia is something of a communal undertaking. On a reference from a friend, I sought out Sulayman as my caddy. A tall, slender, laconic young man, and an excellent golfer, Sulayman took on additional duties as my instructor/coach and, golf being golf, occasional spiritual advisor as well. He soon recruited the rest of my golfing entourage. This included a bag carrier, two or three ball-spotters, and various other hangers-on of indeterminate role.

We would meet at the Islamabad Golf Club. Upon my arrival, my various satraps would set about industriously cleaning balls and scrubbing clubs as Sulayman and I went through our prescribed warm-ups on the practice tee and at the putting green. As we made our cumbersome way around the course, the spirits of my golfing claque would rise and fall sharply with the vicissitudes of my game. A blistering drive of 250 yards down the right-center fairway would be cause for euphoria. Player, caddy, and bag carriers would march off the tee smartly, while the ball-spotting outliers would converge in the fairway to marvel at the prowess of their patron. An outright duff would produce despondency: shoulders would slump, and my followers would scuffle dejectedly along the turf in their ill-fitting sandals.

Having long been away from the game, and months of overwork having done nothing to improve upon my modest skills, a significant number of my drives would sail beyond the boundary stakes in the direction of deep eucalyptus groves, where a loud report would signal the impact of ball with trunk. It was the duty of the ball-spotters to find these errant missiles. Not infrequently, I would arrive on the scene after such mishaps in a foul humor, only to find my spotters loitering nonchalantly near a ball—mine—in the first cut of the rough. I would raise an eyebrow. "Good bounce, sir," was the assessment. I would look at them skeptically, but what was one to say? Far be it from me to subject my good fortune to excessive scrutiny. It had characterized most of my career.

Over the weeks, my game improved under Sulayman's patient tutelage, though I sometimes failed to appreciate his wry humor. On one occasion I sent a drive on a wide parabola to an area beyond the ability even of my ball-spotters to penetrate. A drop in the fairway was followed by a pathetic miss-hit of 50 yards or so. A fourth strike sent the ball into a deep sandtrap. It required three more swings, accompanied by some imaginative oaths, to propel the ball from the trap and onto the green, a good 80 feet from the pin. I was sufficiently disgusted by this time that I didn't bother to line up the putt, instead knocking the ball haphazardly in the general direction of the hole. It struck the back of the cup and went in. Still seething, I stalked silently toward the next tee, Sulayman matching me stride for stride. "Putting good," he said.

On Sunday, February 3, I was about to get up for my weekly round with Dave when I received an unexpected call from Paula. My father had just died of a heart attack, collapsing on the tennis court. I had known he wasn't doing so well, as the symptoms of congestive heart failure were creeping back ten years after quadruple bypass surgery. I rushed home to my mother and my siblings.

After the funeral, there were important decisions to be made. Dependents of official Americans were being allowed to return to Pakistan. Doug very much wanted to rejoin his classmates and resume his old life, but Paula was skeptical: there were only six months left in our tour, and she and Doug had put down roots in Virginia. Like Doug, I felt strongly that they should return to Pakistan. There were dangers, yes, but we had always managed them before. We were devoted to service, and to overseas living; this is what we did.

The decision to allow dependents to return was not without controversy. CIA, and specifically CTC, were leery. For my part, I had argued strongly that the threat was manageable. In the weeks and months after the start of the U.S. military campaign in Afghanistan there had been mass demonstrations in Pakistani cities, and public outrage at the United States had been feverish. And yet, there had been no attacks on Americans; other Western embassies, though on heightened alert, had allowed their dependents to remain. Now, with hostilities in Afghanistan effectively ended, the atmosphere was becoming more normal.

CTC had wondered about the effect of al-Qa'ida militants fleeing Afghanistan into Pakistan. Most of these, I pointed out, were simple fighters. They were disoriented, on unfamiliar ground, and most
were attempting to transit Pakistan as quickly as possible for less hostile regions. We and the Pakistanis were capturing them in wholesale
numbers. Yes, al-Qa'ida would have both motive and some means to
strike us, but that was true in many other places; there was no reason,
I said, to believe that we could not, with prudence, mitigate the threat
to our safety. Most of the dependents returned to post, Paula and Doug
among them.

We and our fellow hikers had stopped for a break on a mountain
path when I received a call from the Marine standing guard at Post
One, the principal security monitoring center of the embassy. Details
were sketchy, but there had been a number of explosions at the Christian church located in the diplomatic quarter. There were dead and
wounded. The church was regularly attended by Americans from the
mission and NGOs.

When Ambassador Wendy Chamberlin saw me rushing down the
hall toward her office two hours later, her eyes widened in shocked
surprise. It was the first of several such encounters I would have that
day. Initial reports from the church had listed me among the dead, and
Chamberlin had so reported to her senior staff.

It took some time to piece the facts together, but it appeared a
slight, dark-skinned young man had run down the center aisle of the
half-full church, thrown several grenades, and then blown himself up.
Among the seventy or so Pakistani Christians and Westerners present, five were killed and forty-six injured. That evening, Paula, keeping
vigil, as one of the embassy nurses, over the Americans lying wounded
at the hospital, sat down quietly with the embassy physician as they
explained to young Zachary Green that his mother, Barbara, and his
half sister Kristen Wormsley, were dead. Kristen was about to graduate from high school; her college plans had been set. Zachary's father
Milton, like Barbara a member of the embassy staff, had also been hurt.
Ten Americans had been wounded in all.

Within days of the church attack, the wife of a French diplomat discovered a bomb attached to her car. The January abduction in Karachi and execution of Daniel Pearl, the *Wall Street Journal* reporter, could no longer be considered an unfortunate aberration. There was now no question of official American families remaining in Pakistan. Doug said his final goodbyes at school, and he and Paula left.

Pakistan continued its descent into violence. It had long been a turbulent place, where civic tensions could spawn vicious mobs at a moment's notice, and where religiously inspired attacks against Shia, Christians, and other minorities were common. Now the list of targets would increase. On May 8, eleven French naval engineers and two Pakistanis were killed by a car bomb outside the Sheraton Hotel in Karachi. On June 15, I journeyed to Karachi to visit colleagues who had escaped serious harm when a car bomb detonated just outside the U.S. Consulate.

Post-9/11 Pakistan is not alone in succumbing to greater levels of violence. We have seen similar events throughout the region. But in my view, America has often greatly overreacted. Experiences such as that in Pakistan have made us gun-shy. Far too many posts, including those in countries where terrorist violence has been relatively infrequent, have been declared "unaccompanied," with no non-employees allowed. Rather than *managing* risk, the U.S. government has sought to *avoid* risk. There is a price to be paid for such timidity. Unaccompanied posts eventually suffer greatly in their performance when employees, the vast majority of whom have family responsibilities that our culture, rightly, takes more seriously than ever, avoid them. Even in places to which it is not appropriate to bring children, at least permitting adult dependents would be an improvement.

Worse yet, in all too many cases, those employees who are assigned to dangerous posts are not permitted to do their jobs properly by traveling freely and maintaining local contacts, instead being confined to fortified installations. Yes, greater openness will inevitably produce more official American casualties, in an environment where recriminations in Congress and elsewhere make sensible risk-taking greatly hazardous to the careers of senior bureaucrats. But if America is to meet its responsibilities, courage, both physical and political, will be required. Like Horatius at the gate, American spies and diplomats will accept the risks associated with their calling, but only if permitted to do so.

Chapter 41

THE RECKONING

MARCH 29, 2002

I T HAD BEEN A particularly late night, but I had a spring in my step as I strode across the sun-dappled lobby of a luxury hotel in Islamabad. I found my delegation, several members of the Senate Select Committee on Intelligence and their wives, sitting in the breakfast room. This was not the sort of meeting I would normally hold, and certainly not the normal venue for it. I had held my formal briefing for the legislators the previous afternoon, but had promised to stop by before their planned departure that morning to update them regarding a certain ongoing matter. They looked up as I ambled over to their table. I held the suspense for a bit longer as I settled into a chair and greeted them confidently. I looked about for some coffee. "I have good news," I said finally. "We've captured Abu Zubayda."

Zayn al-Abidin Muhammad Husayn, aka Abu Zubayda, had been an obsession for me for two and a half years. For months even before the February night in 2000 when former Ambassador Bill Milam and I met with President Musharraf to seek his help in capturing the man, I had watched with growing frustration as this master terrorist logistician traveled repeatedly through Pakistan to and from al-Qa'ida's Afghan training camps. He maintained a sort of underground railroad, facilitating the movement of young Muslim men to and from their courses of instruction in the dark arts, providing them with tickets, guidance, lodging, and assistance with their travel documents. We couldn't generate information precise or immediate enough to force the government of Pakistan to capture him on his jaunts through their country. And in spite of President Musharraf's assurances and my own importunings, General Mahmud of the ISI would not help us.

All that changed at the precipice of 9/11, but in the months thereafter Zubayda went to ground. In February 2002, reliable reporting placed him in Waziristan, in the Pakistani Tribal Areas. By that time, hundreds of foreign fighters were fleeing Afghanistan, trying to make their way through Pakistan, which they now considered hostile territory, into Iran, from where they hoped to return to the Arab countries most of them had come from. We presumed Zubayda was arranging travel or safehaven for fugitive Arab fighters in the Tribal Areas, but could not be sure, and our sources did not want to look for him there. Zubayda was a professional, and highly suspicious. If our agents were to search for him without a transparently good reason for doing so, they would immediately fall under sustained, and perhaps lethal, suspicion.

In early March, we had clear indications that Abu Zubayda was somewhere in Faisalabad, in the "settled areas" of Pakistan, and that a significant number of his fleeing Afghan Arab fighters were with him. This initially came as a surprise. Faisalabad had never been on our screen, but on examination it proved to be a likely place for our quarry to hide. A gritty, sprawling industrial town in northeast Punjab Province, it was the third largest metropolis in Pakistan, after Karachi and Lahore, though with nowhere near the prominence or social cachet. Located at a major road and rail junction about 75 miles westsouthwest of Lahore, it was an easy place to travel quietly to or from, a perfect place to get lost in.

Our targeting system went into overdrive, and we began generating multiple sites for General Imran and his operators—many more than we would be able to handle at one time, even if only a portion of the suspected targets proved viable. Until then, we had done a maximum of two or three raids on a given night, but since we couldn't pin Abu Zubayda to any particular one of the targeted locations, we determined that we would have to hit every identified site simultaneously, in hopes that Zubayda might be in one of them. Manpower would of course be no problem for the Pakistanis, but we would not have nearly enough Americans—CIA or FBI—to go around; both had to be present at each target location. We deployed a number of our officers to Faisalabad, with a senior visiting ethnic-Arab CIA case officer in charge—a first-rate fellow dubbed "Detroit" by the FBI—to work with the Pakistanis under Dave's supervision and set the raid plan. I went to work getting us more resources.

The one source of readily deployable people, not otherwise productively occupied, that I knew of was the Incident Response Team (IRT) in CTC. This unit had a long and undistinguished pedigree. It had been created with much fanfare back in the 1980s, given a dedicated aircraft, highly skilled operational and technical officers, and the most sophisticated gadgetry available at the time. The idea was that any time there was a terrorist incident anywhere in the world, such as a plane hijacking or hostage taking, the IRT would be sent in to provide advice, guidance, and technical assistance to the host government. It was a wonderful idea, with a small wrinkle: No country would have it. Any time there is a terrorist incident, the government of the concerned country wants to demonstrate that it is competent to deal with it. Inviting foreigners to handle a high-profile situation is a political impossibility, and bringing in such a team surreptitiously, directly under the glare of world media, would be unfeasible. Add to that the fact that many governments will want to have the flexibility to deal with such incidents in their own way—perhaps to include paying ransom or striking some other deal the United States is likely to disapprove of—and you begin to understand why the Incident Response Team may not have been such a good idea after all. As the years of inaction mounted, the team became something of a refuge for misfits and problem children.

I got a bad feeling when I held a video conference with the unit's chief. I made clear that I was only looking for people who could passively observe detentions and make copies of any materials seized: all the muscle would be provided by the Pakistanis. The IRT, bristling with guns and pent-up testosterone, was looking for validation and a larger role. They would prove problematic, but I'd gotten the bodies I needed.

On the afternoon of March 28, 2002, Dave laid out the plan for the visiting senators. After ground investigations led by the ISI, we had winnowed the number of targets in Faisalabad to fourteen. We had identified another three related locations well outside town. All would be hit simultaneously. I rated the chances of capturing Abu Zubayda at fifty-fifty. We had also identified another "safe" location quite some distance from Faisalabad to which we thought Abu Zubayda might flee if we missed him in the first wave. We would allow for reasonable travel time, and then hit that one, too.

The raids were to be launched late that night. Two hours beforehand, I got a call from "Detroit." The ISI had detected a "squirter": one of the militants had left a target villa under surveillance, and boarded a train south. Surely we should not have him arrested right away, Detroit advised. He might alert others with a cell phone. Should we just let him go?

"No," I said. "For all we know, it might be Abu Zubayda." We had not told the ISI about our main target. "Have the Pakistanis break off surveillance so as to avoid alerting him. They can relay a full description ahead and have him picked up at a scheduled stop after the start of the raids." I lost all track of this fellow in the subsequent excitement; I have no idea if he was ever picked up.

At most locations, the raids went smoothly. Dozens of foreign militants were captured. The teams at at least two locations claimed initially to have captured Zubayda, based on identification from outdated photographs, but just as quickly concluded they were in error. There was firing at one location not far from the safehouse in Faisalabad where our officers were staged. A militant had attempted to escape across the roof of the villa in which he was trapped, but was shot several times in the thigh and lower abdomen by a member of the Punjab Rangers, a paramilitary force pressed into service by the ISI. Badly wounded and bleeding profusely, the man was dumped onto the rear bed of a police pickup truck. Dave Falco, a visiting FBI special agent, took a look at him. The man in the truck appeared quite different from the one in the photograph. He was considerably heavier, and had no facial hair. "It's him," Dave said.

Chris Reimann, the legal attaché, rushed to the scene. He shook his head. "I don't think so," he said, but Falco was adamant. They took a picture at the scene, which was sent by sat link to CIA Headquarters. Within a few minutes, after some technical analysis, CTC returned its assessment: an over 85 percent likelihood that this was, in fact, Abu Zubayda. That was encouraging, but in the meantime the wounded captive was bleeding to death. He had to be gotten to a hospital. A Pakistani police driver leapt behind the wheel of the truck. It wouldn't start. A mixed group of Pakistanis and Americans pushed to jump-start it; finally, the engine caught with a lurch, and the truck raced off, with several other vehicles following.

Detroit reached me in my office. I directed that there was to be an American with Abu Zubayda every minute, 24/7, until we could get him out of the country. I didn't relish the thought of trying to explain how we had let him escape if he went missing. Detroit set up a round-the-clock watch at the hospital. All the IRT members, notably, declined to participate. The raids over, they were eager to return to a safer locale. Soon, Detroit was back on the phone. He was with Zubayda.

"There's firing outside the hospital," he said. He hadn't seen anything penetrate the building, but feared they might be under attack. Dave, my deputy, immediately phoned Imran. The general called back ten minutes later, laughing.

"It's just celebratory firing," he said. "There's a wedding in the neighborhood."

I arrived home at three in the morning. Four hours later, I was driving myself in an armored SUV to a breakfast appointment in town.

As is now well known, Abu Zubayda survived his wounds. After a day and a half in that hospital in Faisalabad, he was sufficiently stable to be moved by helicopter to a hospital in Lahore. A day later, he was loaded aboard a CIA plane and taken to a third country where he was treated, and then interrogated. He was the first senior member of al-Qa'ida to be captured. It was his apprehension which triggered—one might say forced—CIA back into the business of interrogation, after a hiatus of many years.

There remains much confusion about what Abu Zubayda represented. Some say that we erred in considering him a senior leader. I don't think they understand the way we perceived him. After tracking the man for two and a half years, I did not believe he was a senior *leader*; he was merely a *senior*, and a very important one. The distinction is significant. If al-Qa'ida were an army, Abu Zubayda would certainly not be a commander, or even an executive officer. He was more like a sergeant major. He wasn't hatching plots and giving orders: he was the guy who got things done. I did not expect that he would know the time or place of the next attack; in fact, I would have been surprised if he did know such things. I had little doubt, however, that he would know the names, the aliases, the phone numbers, the points of contact that would enable us to find and capture the operatives who would be involved in those future attacks.

That was what we, the entire U.S. government, and indeed the American people most feared in those days: the next attack. CIA was supposed to make sure it didn't happen. Given the importance of what we were sure was in Abu Zubayda's head, extracting it was not a responsibility we could delegate to someone else. We would have to do it ourselves, and quickly. This was the thinking and the unbearable pressure which led us, starting with Abu Zubayda and continuing with the even more important captures made subsequently, down the road that led to CIA "black sites" and coercive interrogation techniques. I couldn't know it in 2002, but it would someday fall to me to deal with that legacy.

Chapter 42

THE SAGE

T HE MOST SURPRISING THING about the man was the softness of his voice. The timbre was deep, but the volume was barely above a whisper. Sitting a few feet away, I had to lean forward to hear him—to the point where I thought this must be a ploy to gain advantage. It was hard to argue with someone when you were devoting all your energies simply to hearing what he had to say.

The post of Director-General for Military Operations, or DGMO, in the Pakistan Army is only a two-star slot, its occupant nominally on a par with all the divisional commanders in the Pakistani armed forces, of which there are many. The leaders of Pakistan's Army, the three-star Corps commanders, are far more prominent than the DGMO, their support carefully cultivated by the four-star chief of Army Staff. But in this case, rank is deceiving, even in the ultra-rank-conscious Pakistan Army. In fact, the DGMO has enormous power, essentially controlling the day-to-day operations of Pakistan's military, and exercising great influence, even if from behind the scenes. That was why I was sitting across a desk from this slight, chain-smoking army officer inside a brick bungalow flanking the central courtyard at the General Headquarters of the Pakistan Army. Major General Ashfaq Pervaiz Kayani, I would soon learn, was the ultimate behind-the-scenes operator. What he clearly lacked in command presence he more than made up for in intelligence, clarity of thought, and deftness of maneuver. To me, he was the Sage. The truth was that I was caught, once again, in the fog of mutual incomprehension between Washington and Islamabad. I was looking for an ally, and badly needed his help.

Ironically, in view of CTC's distrust of the Pakistanis, the first reports I was aware of concerning al-Qa'ida fighters in the area of Afghanistan's Shahi Kot Valley came to us from Brigadier Suhail Majid, the ISI Afghanistan expert. According to his sources, as of late January 2002, Arabs were regularly descending from the mountains near Zormat, in Afghanistan's eastern Paktia Province, to buy food from villagers in the valleys below. They appeared well equipped, and had money to spend. These reports were followed by others from American sources, and soon it was clear that there were at least several hundred foreign fighters in and around Shahi Kot. One had to wonder how many had escaped Kandahar, from under our noses.

By early February 2002, CIA and the U.S. military command in Afghanistan were collaborating on a strategy to attack them. The plan, as I understood it, appeared intended as a refinement of the one that had largely come to grief in Tora Bora. Again, an Afghan militia organized by CIA, guided and supplemented by U.S. Special Forces, was intended to be the main fighting force. It would sweep into the Shahi Kot Valley from the west. But this time, the expected escape routes at the northern and southern ends of the valley, and through the mountains to the east, would be blocked by a combination of U.S. conventional and Special Operations forces. That was the plan.

In subsequent weeks, as Afghan forces were being trained and U.S. units moved into place, I received a pair of cables from CTC, describing the evolving battle arrangements for "Operation Anaconda." Both expressed the peculiar view that the key to our success—and the chief weakness in the plan—would be the Pakistanis' ability to seal their border and interdict foreign fighters fleeing the Shahi Kot battle zone. Given my past history with CTC, it was hard not to be paranoid about this. It seemed to me an obvious and gratuitous effort to shift the blame for possible failure onto the Pakistanis and, by extension, onto me.

I shot back immediately to both cables. The Pakistani border, I pointed out, was a minimum of 50 kilometers distant from the area where we hoped to hem in the al-Qa'ida fighters. The further out one projected from the battle zone, the wider the area in which "squirters" could disperse, and the greater the consequent difficulty in intercepting them. There should be no illusions about the Pakistanis' ability to control infiltration across their border, I said.

In January, when General Jafar and I had made our second foray into the Tribal Areas, Colonel Wajahat Chaudry, the Tochi Scouts' commander, had taken us to their elevated observation post at Ghulam Khan, northwest of Miram Shah. From there, we had an unobstructed view over many miles of the Afghanistan-Pakistan frontier opposite Khost, Zormat, and the Shahi Kot Valley. The low, brown, treeless hills to our west offered little impediment to would-be infiltrators. Though Colonel Wajahat provided a spiritedly optimistic appraisal of his ability to control the area, it was obvious that with the few resources at his disposal, the border was essentially wide open, particularly at night. Lacking any sort of electronic sensors or other means of technical observation, the colonel's system of static checkposts and infrequent foot patrols could be easily circumvented.

I shared CTC's reluctance to provide an advance indication to the Pakistanis concerning the timing or location of our intended attacks on al-Qa'ida. We had no assurances that the information would be protected as we would wish, and the risk of a leak to the enemy would be intolerable. But even my modest proposal to wait until after the battle was well under way, and then merely to make suggestions to the Pak military as to which sections of the border we would wish them to reinforce, was met with cold silence. Under the circumstances, I said, if we intended that the foreign fighters in and around Shahi Kot should be entrapped, we had better make sure we were in a position to do it ourselves.

Others far closer to it than I can better describe the extended battle which took place over the first half of March 2002, but the results would have to be described as mixed. Battle plans, it is said, never survive contact with the enemy, but this one fared worse than most. A key U.S. blocking force in the valley had to be evacuated under fire, and two others in the mountain passes to the east were essentially overwhelmed. If the plan was to encircle and eliminate these foreign fighters, it failed.

American losses were rather heavy, at least by the standards of the war up to that point: eight killed and over forty wounded. Post-contact tallies of the al-Qa'ida presence at Shahi Kot were bumped up sharply to between 500 and 1,000; U.S. commanders variously estimated enemy losses in the hundreds, although scarcely over 20 bodies and no graves were discovered after the fighting ended.

Whatever the results of Operation Anaconda, the upshot was that now, America's antiterrorism focus shifted in the direction of Pakistan's Tribal Areas. The consensus was that the foreign fighters had fled east, across the Pakistani border. Various "special mission" forces of JSOC, anointed by the Pentagon with the counterterrorism lead in Afghanistan, were roaming about the countryside in search of al-Qa'ida "high-value targets." I was never quite sure which targets would qualify as "high value," but in any case, they weren't finding any. I began getting indications from the JSOC reps in Islamabad that our military brothers across the line were growing impatient. Convinced that their prey lurked just beyond their grasp, JSOC commanders looked at the international frontier between Afghanistan and Pakistan as a mere abstraction. They were eager to expand their search to the other side.

While my station and the ISI were doing a land-office business in rounding up escaping foreign fighters in the urban areas of Pakistan, there were growing indications that the combination of our success and the hospitable environment for fleeing Islamic extremists in the Tribal Areas were causing some of these fighters, at least, to reassess their options and to collect in the wild areas just east of the Durand Line. The escape from Shahi Kot added measurably to that impression. The question was: If they were there, then precisely where were they? Much of the intelligence that gave us such an edge in the Pakistani settled areas was unavailable to us in the remote tribal territories. And most of what little we had concerning the goings-on in the Pakistani Tribal Areas was from Afghan sources across the border.

During this time, Secretary Rumsfeld made one of his periodic visits to Islamabad. Again, I was summoned for a private consultation, with Steve Cambone, then the principal deputy under secretary of defense for policy and one of the defense secretary's closest acolytes, sitting in. I described the "post-conflict" intelligence beginning to come out of Afghanistan during that period as the worst I had ever seen.

Congress had reacted to the supposed intelligence failure behind 9/11 not only with recriminations but with an avalanche of new money and people. Already, inexperienced graduates of the Farm were being issued carbines and rushed, on their first assignments, into Afghanistan. It normally takes years to learn the art of espionage, and early mentoring is crucial, but now the Afghan intelligence-scape was being overwhelmed with raw novitiates, operating with woefully insufficient supervision.

It's fair to say that a large number of wily Afghans were getting rather the better of their overeager CIA contacts. In just one example, an Afghan intelligence "source" of no particular account, with natural access to practically nothing, was able nonetheless to demonstrate for his new American friend a great nose for intelligence and a positively uncanny sense of timing. While wandering along the Pakistan border, he happened upon a large group of armed men, among whom he noted Ayman al-Zawahiri, Osama bin Laden's second in command, speaking furtively with a Pakistani Army colonel in full uniform. Some days later, he fortuitously came upon this same Pak officer, and even managed to espy his credential, which identified him as a senior ISI operative. Within days, he succeeded in getting himself recruited by the ISI as a source. This went on for a couple of weeks, each story more outrageous than the one preceding it, all of it reported breathlessly in CIA channels by this credulous young man, who no doubt counted himself an intelligence prodigy rivaling Allen Dulles himself.

When at last I'd seen enough, I sent out a personal message addressed not only to the officer concerned but to his management in both Afghanistan and Washington. This chain of reporting, I noted drily, would be highly significant if true. If indeed the ISI were in league with bin Laden and Zawahiri, we needed to get to the bottom of it, and as quickly as possible. I proposed that this source be brought to a secure location where he could be properly questioned by an experienced counterintelligence specialist from outside, and possibly polygraphed.

Thus confronted, our young paragon from eastern Afghanistan informally indicated to one of my officers that he had no intention of doing any such thing. I was curious how he would propose to justify such an incorrigible stand, but before he could be obliged, CTC came to his rescue. Islamabad's preoccupation with counterintelligence was all very well, their message read, but one could not impose the standards of classic Soviet-era espionage on rough Afghan sources. Headquarters' response was doubly unfortunate, I then wrote: not only was it embarrassingly wrongheaded on its merits, but it would have a pernicious effect on the development of any junior officers exposed to it.

In this environment, one might have been excused for a bit of skepticism about reports emanating from Afghanistan alleging that al-Qa'ida fighters in groups of up to 1,500 strong were being spotted in South Waziristan, on the Pak side of the border. Even when allowing for Afghan math—to begin, one should divide by ten—one could not dismiss these reports out of hand. There were too many strong indications from several quarters that we had a serious problem in the Tribal Areas.

For the JSOC colonel in Islamabad who had replaced Marco, the solution was simple: I should convince the Pakistanis to allow a squad of JSOC operatives, in American uniforms, to patrol with the Frontier Corps throughout Waziristan, thus inuring the locals to their presence. Once this pattern was established, small groups of JSOC operatives could begin dropping out of these patrols, unseen, to reconnoiter the reported al-Qa'ida hiding places. I did what I could to advocate for the military, usually with their representatives in tow, but I knew what they were asking was a non-starter for the Pak military, understandably so. The mere presence of uniformed American military personnel patrolling in an area where Osama bin Laden was considered a hero would set off unrest among the tribals.

Convincing the Pakistanis to take risks to address a problem was all the more difficult when they would not acknowledge the problem's existence in the first place. I arranged for senior U.S. military to meet with Lieutenant General Ali Jan Aurakzai, the commander of XI Corps, responsible for the security of all northwest Pakistan, including the Tribal Areas. Well known for his aggressiveness and outsize personality, the strapping Pathan argued vociferously that our intelligence was simply wrong. If there were al-Qa'ida in his area he would know about it, he said. His comments were no doubt influenced by the consideration that if our reports were true, they would constitute a very inconvenient fact.

At length, I did convince General Kayani to arrange for a JSOC unit to join my friend Colonel Wajahat of the Tochi Scouts, in North Waziristan. In the interim, in an attempt to provide Washington with a little perspective on the problem, I invited one of Hank's deputies to join me on a tour of both North and South Waziristan, where the alleged al-Qa'ida armies were reported by our imaginative Afghan sources. As we were escorted about the area by the commander of the South Waziristan Scouts, the local Frontier Corps unit, it was obvious that a dozen or so militants could be easily accommodated in any of the fortresslike reddish mud compounds that dotted the high plateau surrounding Wana, the South Waziristan capital, but that the presence of hundreds of outsiders would be impossible to hide.

Assigning JSOC to join the Tochi Scouts proved a near disaster. I had once heard General Franks say that the reason he liked his JSOC people was that they were "asocial." Indeed they were, and properly so. Their job was to operate as an efficient, narrowly targeted, unilateral killing machine, designed to find, fix, and finish the enemy, operating in stealth and entirely on their own. I contemplated their dealings with Colonel Wajahat and the Frontier Corps with some trepidation.

Sure enough, the American commandos were highly mistrustful of their Pak colleagues. Wajahat's reluctance to take actions which might stir up local resentment they took as evidence of complicity with the terrorists. They declined the tented on-base accommodations offered by the Pakistanis in favor of an abandoned brick school, which could be more easily defended against their hosts. Although they were to adopt Frontier Corps dress and otherwise blend in, they were easily distinguished among the tribal levies, and refused to forsake their distinctive, high-tech weapons in favor of AK-47s. Despite the valiant efforts of the CIA operative I had assigned to liaise between them and Colonel Wajahat, the experiment was short-lived.

This failure was all the more frustrating as I had argued with the military in vain that this mission should be assigned to the Green Berets, the so-called "white" Special Operations Forces, who had collaborated with us so successfully in support of the anti-Taliban Afghan tribals. Their job, unlike the "black" SOF of JSOC, was to work with indigenous forces. My hope was that over time they would build trust with their Frontier Corps hosts, and provide them with training and mentoring that would permit the Scouts to operate more effectively in a counterterrorism mode. When I reported on all this to headquarters, I described JSOC as "the wrong force, in the wrong place, at the wrong time."

This was the sad history which then brought me, alone this time, to General Kayani's door. As seemed so often to be the case, I had no friends: the Pakistanis were in denial about the al-Qa'ida presence in the Tribal Areas, and the Americans were asking for all the wrong things. I pointed out to the general that the al-Qa'ida presence would manifest itself over time. And as it did, the Pakistanis would come under overwhelming American pressure either to do something about it themselves or permit unilateral U.S. means to deal with it. If CIA provided precise information, including satellite imagery, of the suspected al-Qa'ida hide sites, could not the Pakistani Special Services Group, their respected special forces, do something against them?

Kayani looked at me coolly and empathetically. With the lucid logic that would always characterize my dealings with him, he replied that yes, they could. "But consider this," he said. "If we operate as you suggest, within a short period of time, we will have a major tribal uprising on our hands." That would be all right, he said; the Pakistan Army had dealt with such uprisings before. "But if an uprising comes, it will require three brigades of troops to put it down, and there is only one place those brigades can come from."

The Indian Army mobilization reported to me by General Jafar back in December had been quickly matched by the Pakistanis. Now, with the punishing South Asian summer about to descend, the two armies still confronted each other toe-to-toe, and every available unit of the Pakistan Army was deployed on the eastern frontier. "I cannot afford to reassign those brigades," he said. "And if I lack the means to deal with the problems I might cause, I simply cannot afford to invite them."

Sending in the Special Services Group to mount JSOC-style commando raids against terrorist targets might be all well and good, he said. There was no doubt they could successfully attack any compound we might designate. But likely as not, once they had succeeded in taking their objective, they would find themselves surrounded by a howling mob of well-armed tribals, and a large force would be required to rescue them.

Still, Kayani was prepared to answer our concerns, but only using the traditional means employed by the Frontier Corps. The Urdu code name he gave to the ensuing campaign spoke volumes: "Operation Tewazen—Operation Balance." The job of the political agents and the Frontier Corps, at the end of the day, was to maintain a rough equilibrium in the Tribal Areas. Lacking sufficient force to impose their will on their own, they could nonetheless police the area according to established tribal norms, relying on the implied threat of a punitive campaign by the powerful Pakistan Army if their authority were challenged by the tribes or the situation otherwise got out of hand. Lacking the means to exercise that implied threat, Kayani gave them the task of investigating the reported presence of al-Qa'ida, but without upsetting the delicate political balance in the wild buffer zones along the Afghan border.

A pattern took hold in the subsequent weeks. We would pass the Pakistanis an unconfirmed report alleging the presence of al-Qa'ida militants in a compound in some remote part of North or South Waziristan. A day or two later, troops from the concerned unit of the Frontier Corps would noisily fire up their trucks at dawn, and sally forth in cumbersome fashion. Approaching the target area, they would fan out to establish an extensive cordon, designed to keep the alleged "miscreants" from escaping. In the meantime, the political agent and several concerned tribal *maliks*, or elders, would be summoned. They would join a Frontier Corps officer to present themselves at the gate of the alleged al-Qa'ida hideout, where they would request permission to conduct a search, albeit one where any areas housing women were strictly avoided. Such searches predictably revealed nothing out of the ordinary. Foreign militants with any wits would have disappeared long before the Frontier Corps arrived.

Not only was Operation Tewazen inadequate to the task at hand, but it was interpreted within CTC as a manifestion of Frontier Corps complicity with the militants. Why else would they so blantantly telegraph their moves? To Washington and the station in Kabul, the whole exercise was a pantomime designed to warn off al-Qa'ida and thus avoid having to do anything about their presence. In fact, Tewazen was not a conspiracy; it was just the unfortunate local way of doing business in a place where tribal sensitivities had to be respected, and where normal law enforcement did not involve the capture of alleged criminals, but instead negotiation with tribal authorities, who would hand over the suspects themselves under the threat that the hamlets of the concerned families would otherwise be destroyed. Speed and subtlety were foreign to the Tribal Areas.

Still, despite the limitations of the tactics used, as the months progressed beyond my scheduled rotation out of Pakistan in June 2002, these Frontier Corps searches would produce a number of firefights with foreign militants, who in turn gained the growing assistance of local extremists, operating under the influence of radical mullahs inflamed by the continuing American presence in Afghanistan. Soon, Frontier Corps convoys would be ambushed, and Pakistani casualties would mount. By the time I returned to South Waziristan three years later as director of CTC, the tribal insurrection originally feared by General Kayani had taken place, and South Waziristan had been occupied by the Pakistan Army. Not wishing to repeat this history in North Waziristan, the Pak Army would negotiate with local mullahs and tribal strongmen there, this time from a position of weakness, producing results clearly unacceptable to the Americans, who would turn increasingly to the use of drone strikes as the only effective means of attacking the al-Qa'ida militants operating beyond Islamabad's reach. As Pakistani-based support for the insurgency inside Afghanistan increased, so too did the breadth of the American target set. Rather than a limited counterterrorism tool, focused on significant international terrorists, drone strikes would become a broad-based counterinsurgency tool, employed against large groups of Pakistan-based militants. Collateral casualties would rise commensurately, producing greater radicalization. In time, the tribally affiliated Islamic extremists of the *Tehreek-e Taliban Pakistan*, the Pakistani Taliban, would be in open warfare with a Pakistani government seen as fully complicit with the Americans.

Now, from the vantage of thirteen years later, it is perhaps instructive that much of this sorry history was seen and predicted from within a little bunglow at the General Headquarters of the Pakistan Army in the early spring of 2002. General Kayani, who would become the most powerful man in his country, was right. But as I look back, I fail to see how the history of the past dozen-plus years could have been different. Given American interests, the nature of the Tribal Areas, and the limitations—both physical and moral—of the Pakistan Army and its nominal civilian masters, the course of subsequent events seems inevitable. So long as America remained in Afghanistan, Pakistan was condemned to erupt in flames, and then as now, there was nothing to be done about it.

Chapter 43

FLIRTING WITH ARMAGEDDON

RICHARD ARMITAGE, THE VOLUBLE and energetic deputy secretary of state, strode confidently into the dark-paneled White House Situation Room. A bald-headed, barrel-chested weightlifter, he looked as if he might burst out of his suit. No sooner had he entered, though, than he was fixed by Stephen Hadley, the slight, bookish deputy national security advisor, sitting at the head of the table. Had the deputy secretary not seen the latest from CIA? That representatives in both New Delhi and Islamabad were jointly predicting war between India and Pakistan? And if so, just what was State doing about it? Armitage was taken up short; if he was momentarily discomfited, he had me to thank for it.

As of early May 2002, tensions between India and Pakistan, already high, were growing markedly higher. The armies of the two great South Asian rivals remained fully mobilized along much of their 1,800-mile border; some 500,000 Indian troops, including three armored strike corps, stood ready to invade. They were opposed by the most capable elements of the Pakistan Army, numbering 300,000 strong. Neither side could maintain this posture indefinitely. With the summer heat coming on, the speculation, widely circulated in the press, was that India would either have to go on the attack or stand down.

The war hysteria would rise further. On May 14, three Muslim gunmen disguised as Indian soldiers and later reported to be Pakistani nationals infiltrated an Indian Army camp near Kaluchak, killing thirty-one people and wounding forty-seven others, many of them the wives and children of Hindu and Sikh troopers serving in Kashmir. The country exploded in outrage. On May 18, India expelled the Pakistani high commissioner (ambassador), as villagers in both Indian- and Pakistani-occupied Kashmir fled exchanges of artillery fire. Further clashes on the 21st left six Pakistani soldiers and one Indian, as well as a number of civilians, dead. On May 22, the Indian prime minister, Atal Bihari Vajpayee, toured the Line of Control, the tense, "temporary" mountain border along which the Indian and Pakistani armies had confronted one another since its formal creation in 1949. At a neighboring Indian military base, he announced: "The time has come for a decisive battle . . . and we will have a sure victory in this battle." For its part, and as if to underscore the point that it could compensate for its relative deficits in conventional arms through resort to nuclear weapons, Pakistan began a series of long-range missile tests on May 24.

Observing the situation from Islamabad, I was convinced that U.S. counterterrorism policy was encouraging and emboldening the Indians to deal with the problem of Pakistani-supported terrorism once and for all. The whole point of the American "War on Terror," after all, was to set new international norms, rejecting terrorism as a means of redressing grievances. After it was struck on 9/11, the United States had taken quick military action. India had been menaced by Pakistani-supported terrorism in Kashmir for many years: if America could deal with its terrorism problem in such summary military fashion, why shouldn't India do the same?

During a visit to Islamabad by Secretary Rumsfeld in April 2002, some of his closest military aides, quite uninstructed on South Asian history, had begun to ruminate in my presence. "Say," one said, "isn't this stuff going on over there in Kashmir terrorism?" The United States had long decried outrages against civilians in Kashmir, of course, and had exerted pressure on the Pakistanis for years to do something about it, several times coming close to sanctioning them as a formal state sponsor of terrorism. The implication here, though, was that consistency in the War on Terror would demand far more muscular action on our part. I was aghast.

"Hold on," I said. "There's a long history behind this, which dates back to 1947 and beyond. It would be a big mistake to try to deal with terrorism in Kashmir in isolation from the underlying dispute. We can't think about addressing the terrorism unless we're willing to seriously address the dispute." They all looked at me. "And no one in the U.S. government has ever been willing to do that," I added. There was little doubt in my mind that the U.S. government's counterterrorism zeal was leaking out in all sorts of other ways, and having unanticipated effects in New Delhi.

The American ambassador in New Delhi at the time was a highly ambitious former State Department officer and sometime Harvard academic named Robert Blackwill. Since his arrival in Delhi, he had been aggressively pushing the line that despite a few decades of unpleasantness during the Cold War, the United States and India were natural strategic allies. Blackwill seemed determined to foster such a strategic alliance through sheer force of personality, if necessary. His missives from Embassy New Delhi touted the importance to the United States of our "common strategic interest" in counterterrorism, among other things. I was highly skeptical. As a career intelligence officer from the Near East and South Asia Division, I knew we had never gotten much of anything from the Indians, least of all on counterterrorism. "If they really want to help us on terrorism," I told our political counselor in Islamabad, "they should stop abusing the Kashmiris."

Now, in the aftermath of the December 2001 terrorist attack on the Indian Parliament, Blackwill was beating the drum of Indian-American solidarity. I closely followed the accounts of his private meetings with senior Indian officials and his public pronouncements. He never precisely said so, of course, but I thought his statements suggested that the United States would be very understanding, at a minimum, if India felt compelled to use military force to end Islamabad's support to Kashmiri militants. I had little doubt that his words would be so interpreted by those in India inclined to read them that way.

By late May, I was convinced that India and Pakistan would in fact go to war, and initiated an informal exchange with John Ferguson, an old friend, now in India, under whom I had served years before, to see if he agreed. To my great alarm, he asserted that the Indians would launch at least a limited attack. It was clearly time, I felt, for an Aard-wolf—a chief of station field appraisal.

It occurred to me, though, that such a field assessment would be far more powerful if issued as a single document from either side of the potential conflict. The fact that to my knowledge a joint assessment had never been done before made it all the more appealing. I broached the idea with John, offering to compose the initial draft. He enthusias-tically agreed. I then informed my division leadership. As I expected, the senior division reports officer wasted no time in responding: there was no provision for such a joint document, she said. The Aardwolf was to be issued only by an individual station chief, providing his or her own view of the situation.

The chief of staff to deputy director for operations Jim Pavitt was another old friend. I sent him a note, informing him of my idea and the current state of play. Perhaps, I suggested, if the DDO himself were to *request* a joint field assessment, this might be enough to overcome the opposition of the Vestals. I got an amused reply: "Go ahead," it said.

I didn't mince words. Recounting past history, recent events, the evolving views, and the underlying political imperatives, both inter-national and domestic, of all concerned, I predicted that India would launch a military strike on Pakistan within weeks. In addition to air-strikes in Pakistani-held Kashmir targeted against alleged terrorist training camps, which would probably be ineffective, the primary in-tent of the Indian campaign would be to make a limited incursion de-signed to seize territory and force the Pakistanis to negotiate. From such a position of strength, the Indians would expect to have the whip hand in coercing concessions from Islamabad. However, there should be no illusions with regard to the possibility of a nuclear exchange. Knowing the Pakistanis as I did, I had no doubt that they would em-ploy nuclear weapons if they became convinced that the continued vi-ability of Pakistan as an integral, contiguous state were imperiled. It would not be the intent of the Indians to dismember Pakistan, I said, but Pakistani judgments as to Indian intent would be highly subjective, and made rapidly in the heat of battle. Both sides could be seriously prone to miscalculation. I did not think the coming conflict would go nuclear, but one could certainly not exclude the possibility.

My other main point was that U.S. policy, as enunciated both in Washington and in New Delhi, was making an Indian attack more, and not less, likely. It was a point I had to make carefully. This document, unlike the one I issued after 9/11, could not be policy prescriptive. As I explained in an accompanying internal CIA message, I was being very careful neither to criticize current policy nor to suggest an alternative. I was merely offering an analytic view as to how statements emanating from Washington and New Delhi were likely to be interpreted by the Indian government.

John and his senior reports officer offered a number of excellent suggestions and refinements, tightening up the analysis considerably, especially regarding politics in Delhi, which they understood far better than I. I was pleased with the result. As required, I gave my newly arrived ambassador, Nancy Powell, the opportunity to comment. Having arrived only the day before to replace Wendy Chamberlin, she was at a great disadvantage. Here was her station chief predicting war between India and Pakistan—no small pronouncement—and she was supposed to indicate whether or not she agreed, with little personal basis on which to make such a judgment. She delegated the task to her deputy chief of mission, also newly arrived, who shared her concerns and offered a few mild caveats, but otherwise commented little.

The effect of the document, when it reached policymakers in Washington, was electric. As recounted to me later by Rich Armitage, his arrival the next day at the White House for a Deputies' Committee meeting precipitated an onslaught from his interagency colleagues.

Action was soon in coming. On May 31, 2002, the American Embassy in New Delhi declared an evacuation of dependents and non-essential staff, and issued a Travel Advisory warning Americans against travel to India. Other Western countries immediately followed suit. American businesses, ever alert to signals from the State Department, immediately announced plans to remove staff. According to Indian accounts, the abrupt American order came as something of a shock, and was interpreted by many as an implicit threat of economic punishment if India did not seek a negotiated solution to the crisis. That seemed to induce a bit of stocktaking in New Delhi.

I immediately arranged a meeting with ISI chief Ehsan ul-Haq for the following day, June 1, a Saturday. The ISI normally worked only a half-day on Saturdays, and things were ordinarily quiet. I arranged to meet in the early afternoon, wanting to make sure we would have an extended chat. Armitage would soon be traveling to both Islamabad and New Delhi for a round of shuttle diplomacy, and I knew the discussions would revolve primarily around the activities of just one Pakistani government entity—the ISI.

Armitage's discussions with Pakistani leaders, I realized, would fall within the context of the peculiar dysfunction that has long beset U.S.-Pakistan relations. Since the 1980s, and especially since the early 1990s, Pakistan has promoted a number of policies of which Washington has disapproved—development of nuclear weapons, construction of long-range missiles, and support to Kashmiri militants principally among them. When not otherwise constrained, the United States has excoriated and sanctioned Pakistan. But when Pakistani support has become necessary, as during the anti-Soviet *jihad* of the 1980s, America finds a way to overlook Pakistani misdeeds and focus instead on common interests. After 9/11, we found ourselves in another such cycle. Now our other concerns would have to be set aside once again, so that we could focus on the joint task of ridding the region of al-Qa'ida.

Although the Pakistanis would often complain of U.S. inconstancy, neither they nor the Americans would admit to the mendacity underlying relations on both sides. The unwritten rule for Pakistan has been never to admit engaging in activities of which Washington disapproves; and in fact, such duplicity is tacitly welcomed by the Americans during times, such as the one in which we then found ourselves, when the United States too would not want to admit that it was looking the other way on banned Pakistani activities.

That was why, I knew, President Musharraf had been so outraged the previous December when, in the aftermath of the attack on India's Parliament, Ambassador Chamberlin had pressed him on Pakistani support to the militants. At first, Musharraf had engaged in the usual, ritual denials. But when Chamberlin refused to be put off, he had become enraged. In effect, she was breaking the tacit rule: "You *must* understand our compulsions," he had complained. After all, wasn't he giving us everything we wanted in the War on Terror?

General Ehsan, I feared, would not be so candid. At this point, I was already focused not on the present crisis, but on the next. Now that the United States was finally engaged, and had put both Pakistanis and Indians on notice, I thought there was a fair chance that the deputy secretary could gain Pakistani agreement to cut off infiltration of Kashmiri militants across the Line of Control, and that this would be enough to satisfy New Delhi—at least for the nonce. But I didn't believe for an instant that the Pakistanis would make the cutoff permanent, and feared that once the Indians realized this, as they would, they would not be dissuaded from attacking in response to the next, inevitable terrorist outrage.

On January 2, President Musharraf had delivered a much-anticipated address to the nation dealing with religiously inspired militancy in their midst. Extremism, he stated forthrightly, was destroying Pakistan from within, and had to be opposed. We had hoped, in the process, that he would clearly and permanently forswear support to those engaged in violence in Kashmir, many of whom, we knew, were Pakistani nationals. Sitting at home that evening, I had listened carefully to the coded language he employed—and came away disappointed. The following morning, Ambassador Chamberlin and Chat Blakeman, the political counselor, were exultant, but I was depressed. Yes, the president had forsworn any Pakistani support to terrorism, but how could he do otherwise? It was all a matter of definition, I knew, and unless Musharraf placed his words in the context of a change in policy on Kashmir, those words would be meaningless. On the issue of Kashmir, Musharraf had been implacable; absent any other means of exerting pressure on New Delhi, I felt certain, sooner or later support to militants would inevitably continue.

That Saturday, June 1, I sat alone with Ehsan for well over an hour. I approached the topic carefully. I reviewed the past history of U.S.-Pakistan relations, noting the layered, institutionalized duplicity which had always characterized them. I pointed out that it is the habit, and indeed the duty, of diplomats, and spies for that matter, to lie to one another. That was how they protected their national interests. He smiled in wry recognition. I fully expected more such ritual duplicity, I said, when Mr. Armitage came to town. But at a certain point, duplicity would no longer serve either of our interests.

"Please don't misunderstand me," I continued. "I fully support my country's policy. I believe Pakistan should immediately and permanently end its support to armed militancy in Kashmir and cease militant infiltration across the Line of Control. That is what we will want to hear when Mr. Armitage arrives. But if that is not what you actually intend—if other things must happen before you will actually make the cutoff permanent—then saying otherwise will not serve your longterm interests, or ours. If there is in fact more that must happen to achieve a permanent cutoff, then you must tell us." Ehsan looked at me thoughtfully. I had gone as far as I could go, and probably further than I should.

On June 6, Rich Armitage arrived in Islamabad and held highprofile meetings with Abdul Sattar, the foreign minister, with Foreign Secretary Inam ul-Haq, and with the chief secretary for Kashmir. He sat for two hours with President Musharraf, and came away with at least vague assurances. He had one other scheduled meeting before departing for New Delhi.

The three of us sat on a long, low couch, with the late-afternoon sun pouring over our shoulders through the plate-glass window directly behind us. Lieutenant General Ehsan sat between Armitage and me, slim and dapper as always. He had abandoned his uniform in favor of a well-cut dark suit. He bore the uncomfortable look of a smooth and clever man who has suddenly found himself cornered. Normally, a discussion like this would have taken place in General Ehsan's offices but, given the sensitivity of the situation, all had thought it best to keep the meeting as low-key as possible. We were meeting in the residence of the American ambassador.

As we sat together, General Ehsan repeated the assurances newly provided by General Musharraf; Ehsan would be the one charged with carrying them out. A beat passed in awkward silence, as I waited to hear a "but . . ." It was not forthcoming. At last, I put the question to him directly: "Will you need some reciprocity from the Indian side to make these assurances permanent?" The general looked at Armitage furtively for a moment, and then managed a tentative, equivocal "Yes."

But the opportunity, such as it was, had passed. Ehsan did not press the point. Deputy Secretary Armitage had what he needed. The following day, June 7, he presented the Pakistani assurances, such as they were, to the Indians as a firm commitment to cut off militant infiltration into Indian-held Kashmir. The Indians were guardedly mollified. Soon they would see a drop in infiltration across the Line of Control. It would take several months more before the two armies would end their mobilization and pull back completely from the frontier, but the point of greatest danger had passed.

I had hoped, perhaps naively, that Armitage's shuttle diplomacy would lead to concerted U.S. engagement to deal with the underlying dispute over Kashmir. I thought this close brush with open warfare between two nuclear-armed powers would convince us that the status quo was unacceptable. I had stressed to Rich that difficult as that might be, a resolution of Kashmir was necessary if we were to achieve our regional objectives, including in Afghanistan.

But the deputy secretary didn't need guidance from me, and my concerns did not change the objective circumstances. Despite a UN Security Council resolution dating from 1948 demanding a plebiscite in the disputed territory, India had always refused any outside involvement in Kashmir, considering it an internal matter. And the United States was not about to put its potential strategic relationship with India at risk in deference to a negotiation that would probably never get off the ground.

And yet, as we would shortly see again, the key to our objectives in Afghanistan, to say nothing of our other regional interests, depended on a genuine peace between India and Pakistan, a peace they were manifestly incapable of achieving on their own; and that peace, if we were to have it, would rest in turn, then as now, on a resolution of Kashmir.

Part Five

———————————

POSTSCRIPT: ONCE AND FUTURE WARS

Chapter 44

PREMONITIONS

I T WAS ONE OF those perfect days which lingers in the memory. Standing on the grounds of the Arg Palace in Kabul, I could take it all in at a glance: the bright emerald green of the carefully manicured lawns framing the understated, traditional elegance of the palace, and the tall, stately pines that drew the eye upward toward the Afghan flag, which snapped smartly in the wind before the backdrop of a cloudless, crystalline azure sky.

It had been nearly three years since I had left South-Central Asia. Now I was returning on a week's visit to the region that had once been my home. My courtesy call on Hamid Karzai, the president of Afghanistan, which had taken place minutes before, had seemed surreal. We chatted amiably, but there was little reference to the struggles and adventures of the past. Surrounded now by the trappings of position, if not power, I had the impression that the humble, parlous circumstances of Hamid's rise were perhaps an embarrassment best not spoken of. From the many current, pressing problems which I had been prepared to discuss, the president had seemed to me strangely detached. His mind that day was working on a grander scale. If one hadn't known better, one might have thought it was within his power to unite all Pashtuns under the Afghan flag, to obliterate the hated, British-imposed Durand Line, and to fix the border with Pakistan at the Indus River.

As I strolled about outside, the air of unreality persisted. I marveled at the improbability of it all. In the fall of 2001, when Karzai was being chased from hill to hill by the pursuing Taliban, it would have been impossible to imagine a day such as this. Now our courageous if somewhat impractical friend was the duly elected president of his country. It was like a dream. How could things have turned out so well? I should have remembered the age-old admonition about things that seem too good to be true . . .

I had failed to understand the nature and the limits of our victory over the Taliban in December 2001. Having been so concerned at the outset that we would reprise the experience of the British and the Soviets, I was seduced by the deceptive ease with which the Taliban had been driven off in a period of only eighty-eight days since the attacks of 9/11. Rather than fighting on in a twilight guerrilla struggle, the Taliban had simply disappeared as Afghan-American forces closed in on their final redoubt in Kandahar. I concluded, prematurely, that my grave misgivings had been misplaced.

There was so much we all failed to realize. First, for all that I had preached that ours must be a political more than a military victory over the Taliban, I had not quite grasped the underlying politics of the Taliban's collapse. Very few Pashtun leaders had actively risen up against the Taliban, and yet it had become clear—to the Taliban, if not fully to us—that they had thoroughly worn out their welcome among the Pashtuns who comprised their natural base of support. As defeat piled upon defeat for the Taliban, and as it became apparent that Hamid Karzai and Gul Agha Shirzai would converge on Kandahar, the insurgent leaders were tacitly accepted, if not enthusiastically welcomed, by a population transparently happy to see the Taliban depart. They were simply tired: tired of the Taliban's fundamentalist repression, tired of relentless taxation, tired of seeing their young men press-ganged into military service, tired of incessant war. It strikes me now that it was the realization of their own political weakness, more than American bombs, which convinced the Taliban that their time in power had passed. American bombers, for all their effectiveness, could not have secured the two dissident Pashtun chieftains from an angry and hostile populace. Similarly, we did not realize how evanescent, or how reversible, this tacit popular support could be.

History, viewed in hindsight, takes on the trappings of inevitability.

The victory of the anti-Taliban opposition in the south was anything but. Much was written at the time, and much has been written since, some of it by former colleagues, about how, in combining rude indigenous forces with small numbers of SF troops and CIA operatives, and supporting them with precisely targeted airpower, we had somehow set a brilliant new template for how future wars would be fought. That will depend very much on the war. The tactics we employed in 2001 were simply an adaptation to the unique circumstances in which we found ourselves. They fit our political need to keep Afghans in the fore and to keep the American footprint small, while taking full advantage of our technological superiority. The approach we took was a function of political necessity as much as military prowess. There was hardly any genius at work in defeating a primitive army, employing primitive tactics, with uncontested airpower and precision-guided munitions. An old nineteenth-century London music hall chorus celebrating the success of British colonial armies against benighted tribesmen summed it up nicely:

> *For whatever happens we have got*
> *The Maxim gun, and they have not.*

And yet . . . and yet, it had still been a close-run thing. Even with the full benefit of U.S. air forces on their side, Karzai and his band had come within minutes of annihilation at Tarin Kowt on November 17, 2001. Throughout the southern campaign, the Taliban's repeated tactical stupidity—rushing headlong, again and again, in truck-mounted attacks over open ground in the face of American airpower—was as much a factor in their defeat as was the sophistication of the weapons they faced. The Taliban have since shown themselves to be a "learning enemy." We were merely fortunate at the beginning that they were a *slowly* learning enemy.

Had Karzai been lost, the political tenor of the war in the south would have been radically changed. If the U.S. Marines, who fortunately stayed isolated in the trackless southern Registan Desert and out of the fight, had instead been the ones to drive the Taliban and al-Qa'ida out of Kandahar, the Taliban would have seen their defeat in very different terms. They would not have accepted the legitimacy of the new Interim Administration, and Afghanistan would most likely not have had the window of opportunity which it did, in fact, enjoy for some years to create a stable, peaceful political environment.

Although I did not realize it yet, that opportunity had ended by the time of my presidential courtesy call in the spring of 2005. Its demise was the result of many factors, but to understand what happened, one has to go back to the rise of the Taliban as a political force in 1994. It began as a movement of clerics in the Kandahar area with rather modest goals: to stamp out the rampant crimes and abuses of the many petty, feuding warlords besetting their region and, in the process, to bring some measure of unity and stability. Adherence to *sharia*, Islamic law, would be their weapon and their guide. But as so often happens, success caused the Taliban to expand upon their core aspirations. Shortly after Kabul fell to them in 1996, and with most of the opposition having been consolidated under the leadership of Ahmad Shah Masood, some sort of power-sharing agreement could almost certainly have been reached to bring peace to the country. But by now the Taliban leadership, carried away with power, could only conceive of national unity under its direct control.

The multiple, crushing defeats of 2001, in combination with the loss of grassroots political support in the south, brought the Taliban back down to earth. Theirs was a religious *movement*, never a political *party*. In their many confused interactions with Hamid Karzai as he made his way south from Uruzgan, they were not so much seeking a political settlement as assurances of personal safety for themselves. During his negotiations, Karzai tried to wend his way through a political minefield, attempting to reassure the Taliban leadership so as to secure their de facto surrender, without alienating his foreign patrons. In the process, he made promises he could not keep, which would ultimately undermine his credibility.

With the prominent exception of Mullah Omar himself, many in the Taliban leadership were quite willing to accept Karzai as head of the interim government established and blessed at the UN Conference in

Bonn. As the self-styled "Commander of the Faithful," Omar was not about to bow down before any secular authority, but he did not object if others chose to. He merely advised them not to trust Karzai, and fled—most likely to Pakistan, where he probably remains to this day. There were never, to my knowledge, any clear discussions, let alone any agreement, between Karzai and any American authority concerning the status or potential reintegration of senior Taliban members into Afghan political life. To the Americans, and particularly to the Department of Defense, which acted as an independent authority in Afghanistan after the Taliban's defeat, most if not all senior members of the Taliban were necessarily connected to al-Qa'ida, and their detention therefore an imperative of the "War on Terror." Still other Taliban commanders were wanted under UN war crimes' auspices for the massacres previously visited on the Shiite Hazara minority during the civil war.

Given the ambiguity of their circumstances immediately after the surrender and evacuation of Kandahar, senior Taliban were no doubt paying close attention to the actions of the victors. Mullah Abdul Salam Zaeef, a founding member of the Taliban and the Taliban ambassador to Pakistan, was arrested by the ISI and turned over to the U.S. military immediately after the Taliban government's collapse in December 2001. He would soon find himself in Guantánamo, and remain there until 2005. In my contacts with him since his release, Zaeef has claimed that he had firm assurances from Karzai that he would not be touched following the Taliban's surrender. Regardless of what he might actually have been told, Zaeef, who despite having withdrawn from the struggle against the Americans and the Afghan government remains a respected figure among the Taliban, still denounces Karzai's role in his treatment. He does so while splitting his time between Kabul and Doha, Qatar. His attitudes may be representative of others in the Taliban leadership: either he was actively deceived, he says, or else Karzai had no real authority, and thus was a puppet of the Americans.

Wakil Ahmed Muttawakil, the former foreign minister, approached people associated with Gul Agha Shirzai in Quetta in early February 2002, seeking their intercession with the Americans. He was escorted by Gul Agha's men to Afghanistan, and turned over to the U.S. military at the Kandahar Airport, where he was detained. Although by that time I no longer had any direct role to play in Afghanistan, I believed Muttawakil's imprisonment to be a gross mistake. It seemed clear that there would have to be some process of reconciliation with the rank-and-file of the Taliban, and that to be credible, reconciliation would have to extend to members of the leadership who were neither under indictment for crimes nor had any continuing relations with al-Qa'ida. Surely, I thought, Muttawakil, who was no terrorist and who had little real authority within the Taliban, should not be seen as a threat. I feared that others, who might otherwise be willing to reconcile with the government, would draw lessons from his arrest. It took several years and strong lobbying to get Secretary Rumsfeld, whose personal authorization was required, to agree to his release. By then, the harm had been done.

From the collapse of the Taliban government in December 2001 until my departure from Pakistan in June 2002, I neither sought nor received any sort of policy guidance regarding senior Taliban figures, many of whom were thought to have fled to Pakistan. On the Pakistani side of the border, we were focused on one thing: finding and capturing as many fleeing al-Qa'ida members as possible, preferably to include Osama bin Laden, Ayman al-Zawahiri, and their senior lieutenants. Virtually all of our intelligence collection was geared in that direction. We would see the occasional report to indicate that members of the Taliban *Shura* were pitching up in Quetta or Karachi, and we sought ISI help in investigating these leads. Somehow, though, the effectiveness which characterized the ISI's pursuit of al-Qa'ida did not apply where the Taliban was concerned.

By early 2002, it was obvious to me that the Pakistanis had no interest in pursuing these people. And no wonder: already one could see that the new government in Kabul would be dominated by the former Northern Alliance, and that it was forging close ties with India. Pakistan's past relationship with the Taliban had always been wary and mistrustful, and its active aid to the forces which attacked and overthrew the clerical regime had surely done little to improve it. Nonetheless, the Taliban was the only Afghan entity capable of serving as a counterweight to the despised government in Kabul, and Pakistan was not about to gratuitously foreclose future dealings with it. I tried to make that clear to every visiting American official who would listen.

I refused to allow Pakistani hedging regarding the Taliban to become an issue between us. We were focused as a laser beam on al-Qa'ida. Countries will not act in ways which they believe detrimental to their interests. Knowing that I would get no traction on the Taliban, I wasn't about to let a moot issue complicate or undermine the success we were enjoying against al-Qa'ida, whose members were being snatched up on an almost nightly basis with the ISI's help. I believed the Taliban were spent. To the extent I was concerned over their capacity to make a political comeback, I felt that the best means of foreclosing that possibility lay not in Pakistan but in Afghanistan. The Afghans had been given a chance at a new beginning. If they succeeded in governing themselves, there would be no need of, or political space for, a Taliban.

It would be hard to overstate how surprised and encouraged many of us were, in the wake of the Taliban defeat, at how Afghans were behaving. The Afghan national mood reflected a strong desire to avoid repeating the abuses that had brought the country low. Where one might have expected the sweeping Northern Alliance victories in the north and their conquest of Kabul to precipitate an orgy of vengeance on the minority Pashtun communities now under their sway, such outrages were relatively few. It felt as though the country were embarking on an "era of good feelings," that the past was in the past, and that everything was possible.

But if Afghans were ready for a new national beginning, the United States proved unready and unwilling to do what was necessary to encourage it. As early as January 2002, I could see the relevant elements of the vast U.S. government bureaucracy, which would have to combine and coordinate efforts in new ways if we were to achieve our goals in Afghanistan, reverting to old instincts. People naturally gravitate toward the prescribed and the habitual, to stay in their comfort zones. Bureaucrats never welcome interference from outside their own organizations.

Shortly after my return to Islamabad from Kandahar in January 2002, Andrew Natsios, the administrator of the U.S. Agency for International Development (AID), stopped in en route to Kabul. I desperately wanted to speak to him about how CIA's relationships with key leaders around the country could serve his interests. Somehow, his traveling staff and my local AID contacts couldn't get me on his schedule. I'm sure they felt they didn't need advice from me as to how they should do their jobs.

A few weeks later, I met with a couple of senior Drug Enforcement Agency managers from Washington. They paid a call on me before going to Afghanistan to survey what DEA ought to be doing there. I pointed out that the Taliban had had more success in wiping out narcotics production than we, or any future Afghan government, could ever hope for. I said they should work with the State Department to reinforce and extend the Taliban's success with value-added crop-substitution programs. I could see their eyes glaze: their job was to pursue narcotraffickers.

Even within my own organization, I could already see my colleagues reverting to normal practice. In Kandahar, I had advised a colleague to stay as close as possible to Gul Agha and his people. A small Special Forces contingent had set up shop in the palace to help with security. "Stay with them," I said. "Gul Agha is a decent sort, but he needs guidance. The best way to meet our counterterrorism goals is to ensure that Gul Agha retains political support." My advice was ignored. CIA officers typically do not want to be in the business of political mentorship: they want to collect intelligence and chase terrorists. This was as understandable as it was regrettable; it was the natural order of things, even if it meant we would be thoroughly unequal to the needs of the hour.

When I returned to Washington in June 2002, it wasn't clear at first what I would be doing. Tenet wanted me around on the seventh floor, and so Jim Pavitt created an associate deputy director position for me as a placeholder while they figured out what to do with me. I wrote a long memo for George laying out the role I thought the agency *ought* to be playing in Afghanistan. CIA had relationships with many of the major political players around the country. We should take the lead in leveraging those relationships. We could bring together teams comprised of Special Forces, the State Department, the Agency for International Development, and others, who would lead the regional engagement of their respective agencies in the physical and political reconstruction of Afghanistan. In my suggested scheme, CIA and the Special Forces would work with the regional warlords hosting us to raise and train militias, which would be responsible, among other things, for protection of the American teams. The name hadn't yet been coined, but the interagency units I was describing were a more robust version of what would later be called Provincial Reconstruction Teams (PRTs), which unfortunately included neither the Special Forces nor CIA.

There would have been many pitfalls in my suggested approach, had it been adopted. If we were not careful, American support could be misused. Militias, if they were not again to become the scourge they had been in the past, would have to be tied, even loosely, to some national authority. Regional warlords would have to be subject to local accountability, through representative *shuras* or otherwise. But political power in Afghanistan has always been highly decentralized. If we hoped to realize our goals there, it would have to be through Afghans and on Afghan terms, and not by trying to make the country something other than what it is. Provincial Reconstruction Teams, when they were eventually set up, generally failed because of their isolation and estrangement. They pointedly did not include an organic Afghan component, and lacked local political support. Operating alone, they were not reinforced by the greater U.S. military presence.

The memo returned with a note from Tenet. "This is excellent," it said. "But what do I do with it?"

I had thought the director would forward it to Dr. Rice for consideration by the National Security Council, which might then adopt a plan to be implemented by the various agencies of government. Tenet's comment reflected a tacit recognition that a detailed operational plan was unlikely to be successfully imposed from Washington. Concepts half-understood at the cabinet or subcabinet level were unlikely to be coherently communicated downward through the separate bureaucracies. The hope of success was based on those in the field coming together to agree on a sustainable way forward. No one should have understood that better than me. But if the true path lay in making Afghan warlords the best warlords they could be, the international mission in Afghanistan would fail to realize it.

Taliban commanders and fighters did not flee immediately en masse to Pakistan following the fall of Kandahar. Although much of the senior leadership left, most cadres—many of them local mullahs—returned to their villages, particularly in the south. In many cases, they faced harassment and abuse from the dominant tribals whom the Taliban had previously neutered. The extent of such harassment may never be precisely known, but there was enough—accompanied by oft-repeated stories concerning the alleged abuse of respected Taliban figures—to have convinced many in the Taliban by 2005 that there was no place for them in the new Afghanistan. A number of them joined their seniors in Pakistan. As men who were literate and knowledgeable of religion, though, they retained respect and influence in the rural areas, and were ready to come back when the opportunity presented. Some less prominent tribes, previously favored by the Taliban but now shut out of power and unable to share in the business opportunities generated by reconstruction spending, were drawn by the mullahs into insurgency. There was no general template. Each Pashtun district had its own dynamic, and its own story. But by spring of 2005, as I strolled the palace grounds in Kabul, the Taliban was well on the way to reconstituting itself in many areas, though we were only just becoming aware of the threat.

Within weeks of my return to Washington, a new job began to take shape. In August 2002, Tenet emerged from a beach vacation to meet with Jim Pavitt and me. "Start studying up on Iraq," he said.

For the next two-plus years, through war preparations, the invasion of Iraq in March 2003, and the first year and a half of counterinsurgency warfare, I served as CIA's Washington-based Iraq Mission manager. Although I lacked the rank, John McLaughlin persuaded the National Security Council to allow me to represent CIA on the Deputies' Committee. I traveled widely throughout Mesopotamia. In over two years of thrice-weekly meetings in the White House Situation Room, I had a front-row seat on some of the most disastrous foreign policy decisions in our history. It was a deeply disillusioning experience.

My disillusion was all the greater in that I genuinely believed in the mission to topple Saddam. It never mattered whether he had chemical, biological, or nuclear weapons on the shelf, ready to deliver in March

2003. What mattered was that his regime had the documented capacity to build them, thoroughly catalogued by UN inspectors, and surely would do so again in future, once the UN sanctions regime was ended. Saddam had had every opportunity to make a clean breast of all his programs and to fully account for all his weapons and precursors, but in over ten years of cat-and-mouse with UN inspection regimes, he had failed to do so. We couldn't know all we needed to know about the Republic of Fear, but what were we to think? I would have thought it criminally irresponsible if the United States had been willing to stand aside while a regime that had launched two regional wars and murdered many thousands of its own citizens, in a position to control a majority of the world's traded oil, were allowed to rebuild its WMD programs at its leisure. The world could tolerate an Iraq equipped with WMD, or an Iraq ruled by Saddam Hussein and his sons, but not both. If the United Nations would no longer forcefully uphold its own resolutions, America should be prepared to do so.

There was never any question that the U.S. military would rapidly defeat Saddam's army. But the signs that we lacked the collective wisdom to deal with the aftermath were manifest from the start. Where Iraq was concerned, the national security apparatus was completely dysfunctional, its rival elements so far apart that they could not have an honest discussion of the issues. The meetings I attended at the pinnacle of the foreign policy bureaucracy were notable for what wasn't said, rather than what was: mendacity and indirection were the orders of the day. A rough coalition of the NSC, the State Department, and CIA were able to prevent Rumsfeld's Defense Department and the vice president from naming an Iraqi government-in-exile and then arbitrarily installing it after the invasion. They wouldn't say so, but I and others were convinced that Deputy Defense Secretary Paul Wolfowitz, Under Secretary Doug Feith, and their subordinates in the Office of the Secretary of Defense, as well as the neoconservative stalwarts in the Office of the Vice President, intended to put Ahmed Chalabi, a brilliant but duplicitous longtime Iraqi émigré oppositionist with a Svengali-like influence over them, in charge of that government. We were just as convinced that such a government would never be accepted by Iraqis.

On the other hand, Defense and the vice president quashed the idea of identifying clean, respected figures at the local and regional levels and bringing them together in a sort of constituent assembly to form an interim Iraqi government after the invasion. The United States would be able to influence the selection of such leaders, but could not—and should not—control it. In one critical meeting on the subject, Vice President Cheney was very explicit: Given the choice between political legitimacy and control, he said, we should opt for control. The upshot was that as the U.S. invasion began on March 19, 2003, the U.S. government was internally at loggerheads, unable to agree on a plan for Iraq's political reconstruction.

As soon as the shooting stopped, Zal Khalilzad, still at the National Security Council, was sent to Iraq by Condoleezza Rice to break the impasse. In what some of us hoped would be the first of several such meetings around the country to identify local leaders with legitimate support, Zal and retired General Jay Garner, designated to be head of the Iraq reconstruction effort, met with local notables from southern Iraq at Nasiriya on April 16. Secretary Rumsfeld intervened before a second such meeting could be held and Zal was ordered home. On May 11, in a move that took me and most of those supposedly in the know completely by surprise, President Bush named Paul "Jerry" Bremer, a former State Department official who had long since left government and had no Middle East experience, to head what would soon be called the Coalition Provisional Authority (CPA). He would be absolute dictator of Iraq, empowered to rule by decree. He would report directly to Secretary Rumsfeld. Defense and the vice president's office had won. Now the political reconstruction of Iraq would proceed according to their wishes.

The immediate focus was on the Iraqi Ba'ath Party and the army. Bremer, under Pentagon influence, banned the former ruling party and instituted a "de-Ba'athification" program, designed to purge its members from senior jobs in the public sector. His decree may have seemed fairly moderate on paper, but with the vengeance-minded Ahmed Chalabi, still the darling of Wolfowitz, Feith, and Cheney, overseeing its implementation, it went far deeper than originally intended. Hundreds of schoolteachers, for example, forced earlier to join the Ba'ath for reasons of career advancement, were thrown out of work.

Rather than calling elements of the regular Iraqi Army back to their barracks and employing them in reconstruction projects, as the departed Jay Garner had planned to do, Bremer formally dissolved it. The army would be rebuilt from scratch, from the bottom up. No senior officers would be retained. The Sunni minority, which had dominated both institutions, got the message: There would be no place for them in the new Iraq. By fall 2003, I was organizing a series of formal CIA briefings, first for Condoleezza Rice and the NSC, then for Vice President Cheney, and finally for the president, to explain that a genuine insurgency was under way in the Sunni-dominated center and west of the country, and that U.S. policy was largely to blame. Religious extremists from all over the Muslim world were flocking to Iraq to join the next *jihad*. Civil war loomed just over the horizon.

Our briefing for the president, called on short notice for November 11—Veterans Day—was more dramatic than I anticipated. Cheney, Rice, secretaries Powell and Rumsfeld, and the rest of the senior foreign policy team from the White House, State, and Defense packed the Situation Room to hear what Tenet, McLaughlin, three of our senior analysts, and I had to say. After the analysts provided a description of the situation on the ground, I launched into a broader summation of the reasons for the insurgency, with much implied criticism of current policy. No sooner had I finished than the president, looking grim, swung his gaze across the table toward a surprise participant just in from Baghdad. "What do *you* say, Bremer?"

The presidential envoy seemed resigned and depressed. He had searched in vain, he said, for effective Sunni leaders who could appeal to their community. The Iraqi army had in effect dissolved itself and could not be recalled. And as much as the Sunnis might wish a rollback of de-Ba'athification, powerful leaders in the Shi'a community would not permit it. In short, there was nothing to be done but to continue on the basis of current policy.

Robert Blackwill, the former ambassador to India during my Pakistan days and now the NSC's point man for Iraq, asked me to accompany him on a fact-finding trip over the 2003 Thanksgiving holiday. After several days spent with the Coalition Provisional Authority and deployed U.S. Army elements in the field, we agreed that the CPA was beyond redemption. The only hope was for CIA and the military to somehow stem the insurgency on their own. Blackwill so reported to the White House. President Bush would not countermand the policies pushed by Rumsfeld and Cheney, but he did decide to accelerate the handover of power to an interim Iraqi government the following spring.

In the meantime, as Iraq descended further into violence, CIA reported forthrightly on the worsening situation, in sharp counterpoint to the hopeful reports being conveyed by the military. Day after day, to my great admiration, George Tenet entered the Oval Office to bring the president the truth, long past the point when his message was no longer appreciated. On one occasion he took our Baghdad station chief into the oval to brief the president directly on a particularly stark field appraisal he had prepared.

In senior policy councils, we went through the motions of debating whether the de-Ba'athification process should be revised. In a paper solicited by Blackwill, I argued as persuasively as I could for a rollback. But the outcome was a foregone conclusion. Doug Feith carried the message from the only parties who would have a vote: a change in policy regarding the Ba'ath Party, he said, would "undermine the whole moral justification for the war."

Meanwhile, the effort to create a "New Iraqi Army" to replace the one we had disbanded was a disaster. Responsible Iraqi military leaders with whom CIA was in touch pleaded for creation of a unifying national institution of which Iraqis could again be proud. There were plenty of clean, capable, and respected officers, both Sunni and Shiite, they said, who could organize proper army divisions and re-create a national command structure under civilian control, along with a national academy to train the next generation of officers along democratic lines. Iraqis, they said, should be taking the lead in fighting an insurgency rapidly falling under the sway of foreign terrorists. Instead, the U.S. Army was training disaggregated, battalion-size militias, with no senior command and no organic support, utterly dependent on their American masters, to serve as cannon fodder for the occupation.

I was able to make some headway in persuading Condoleezza Rice of the merits of reestablishing the "core divisions" of the Iraqi Army.

But she was in no position to overcome DoD opposition, particularly when their opposition was seldom stated forthrightly. The Defense seniors found it much more convenient to obfuscate and throw up roadblocks. But if they were coy, their underlings often reflected their thinking more openly. I recall a lower-level Defense Department official putting it succinctly: "If we ever bring back the Iraqi Army," he said, "it will be to shoot them."

When Ayad Allawi, the secular nationalist politician and longtime exile oppositionist, became Iraq's interim prime minister on June 1, 2004, a DoD delegation led by Paul Wolfowitz journeyed to Baghdad to ensure the new Iraqi leader understood the limits within which he would be working. Allawi made the case for reconstituting elements of the army. Wolfowitz conceded that it was an interesting idea; but just how did the prime minister propose to pay for it?

In December 2004, Dr. Rice called a meeting of the Principals' Committee specifically to discuss a pair of papers authored by Charlie Allen, the assistant director of Central Intelligence for Collection, and me. Allen was a legend, having begun his career as an analyst in 1958 and having dealt with many of the most difficult and controversial intelligence issues in the decades since. He had just returned from a visit to Iraq. He described his shock at the deterioration in the situation over the previous few months. In my analysis, I predicted—correctly, as it turned out—that the upcoming January 2005 national elections, which the Sunnis were boycotting, would lead to a worsening of the civil war. I still thought the elections should go ahead, but argued again that Allawi should be allowed to take the forceful measures necessary both to deal with the insurgency and to encourage national reconciliation. Again, the suggested course corrections were dismissed by Defense.

Back before the invasion, colleagues at CIA Headquarters had sometimes stopped me in the hall: How was planning going for after the invasion? "They don't have a clue," was my stock response. "But they'll learn." I had gotten it half right.

My despair over Iraq was further compounded by what I was able to gather about our policy in Afghanistan. For reasons I could not fathom, economic reconstruction there had been very slow to start.

Early on, the United States pledged itself to rebuild the section of the "ring road," Afghanistan's great circular highway, between Kabul and Kandahar, but the project suffered from inattention and lack of funding. It became a symbol of the U.S. government's lack of commitment. There seemed little interest in Washington in expending resources in Afghanistan, and what resources were available were indifferently administered. Yes, there was a lack of command attention from Washington, distracted as it was by the conflict in Iraq; but surely, I thought, a global power should be able to do two things at once? Afghanistan was being left to drift.

Meanwhile, seeds of future instability were being sown. The Afghan Constitution was drafted largely in secret in 2003 by a thirty-five-member panel of Afghans and foreign constitutional experts, all appointed by interim President Hamid Karzai. Unsurprisingly, the product of their work, approved by a *Loya Jirga* (Grand National Assembly) in January 2004, provided for a great concentration of power in Kabul, and specifically in the hands of the president. Not only were cabinet ministers and other national-level officials appointed by the chief executive, but all provincial, and district governors were as well, along with police chiefs and even customs inspectors. The ability to appoint local officials from Kabul was not unique to the Karzai regime—it had been the rule going back to the days of King Zahir Shah. But with foreign reconstruction money beginning to flow into the country, along with the ability to steer lucrative contracts to favored parties, centrally approved local government appointments were becoming licenses to steal, the ill-gotten gains shared back up the line with those whose influence had facilitated them. With little or no local accountability, good governance at the provincial and district levels was seldom a priority for those in power.

Worse, the Pashtun areas were beset by a lack of security. In my analysis for Tenet, I had assumed that local security would be provided for locally, as had been traditionally the case, and that the challenge for a new Afghan government and its foreign benefactors would be to encourage local accountability for militias and police forces organized by traditional tribal leaders, to ensure against their being misused by the powerful against the weak. I hadn't thought U.S. and Afghan government policy would be to try to do away with such locally raised forces altogether. But that was precisely the attitude of the U.S. military. To them, local militias equated to warlordism, responsible for the rise of the Taliban in the first place, and were to be discouraged and avoided at all cost. Their views were reinforced by the Karzai government, which did not want to see local rivals for power.

The two things the Taliban had been able to dispense effectively were security and justice. Their notions of justice may not have been pretty by our lights, involving amputations and summary executions, but when administered by them it was swift, sure, generally impartial, and welcomed by a population beset by crime and violent disputes. The Taliban had established a relative monopoly of armed force by disarming the tribes. When they withdrew, there was little to replace them. With a nascent, ill-led, ill-trained, and ill-equipped national army and police force, and virtually no system in place to resolve disputes impartially or to dispense justice, there was a glaring vacuum of power, particularly in rural areas, that was begging to be filled. The Taliban was waiting in the wings.

By the end of 2004, with the situation in Iraq growing worse by the day and no reason to believe I could be even remotely helpful, I was more than ready to leave that account. With the CIA leadership in chaos, I had my chance. George Tenet had resigned the previous summer and been replaced some weeks later by Porter Goss, the longtime Republican congressman from Florida and former chairman of the House Permanent Select Committee on Intelligence. As a young man in the 1960s, he had been a case officer in CIA's Clandestine Service. On paper, he might have seemed an ideal choice. He wasn't.

Though a decent and unassuming fellow, Goss had brought with him from the Hill a number of abrasive, hyperpartisan young Republican staffers whose past relations with the agency had been adversarial. It was hard for them to put old habits aside. A number of senior agency staffers who worked directly for George Tenet and were closely associated with him expected to be replaced, and were. Jami Miscik, the deputy director for Intelligence (Analysis), was both closely asso-

ciated with Tenet and publicly identified with the flawed analysis on
Iraqi WMD that had occurred on her watch. She negotiated a smooth
departure.

Steve Kappes, the new deputy director for operations, and an old
friend with whom I'd worked overseas, had expected he might be asked
to leave as well. If he had been, as he told me at the time, he would
have accepted his fate gracefully and tried to assure a smooth transition. I'm certain that's true. But no axes fell on the DO, at least not immediately. Instead, a sort of subterranean warfare broke out between
the DO front office and Goss's people, quickly dubbed the "Gosslings."
There were apparently a number of midlevel DO officers, mostly disaf-
fected types not held in high esteem by their peers, with whom Goss's
staffers had cultivated relationships over the years, and whose careers
they now sought to champion. The Gosslings were told that the DO's
promotion panel system, a source of considerable organizational pride,
was not going to be subverted. There followed a series of petty disputes
and misunderstandings which ought to have been easily avoided, and
in other circumstances would have been, but in the atmosphere of distrust and animosity prevailing on the seventh floor quickly spiraled out
of control. When Steve Kappes's deputy, Mike Sulick, clashed with Pat
Murray, Goss's chief of staff, calling him a "Hill puke," Murray reacted
by demanding that Kappes fire him. His order was met with incredu-
lity: from time immemorial, the director's chief of staff had worked for
the director alone; he was not in the chain of command, and could not
issue orders. Except that Murray *was* in the chain of command. Goss
had simply failed to tell anyone other than Murray. Informed that this
was not the way things were done, Goss quickly agreed to rescind Murray's executive authority. But that would be from then on; the former
order would stand.

There was a larger context to these disputes. In the latter half of
2004, the atmosphere between CIA and the White House was toxic.
With Iraq threatening to go up in flames, and CIA seen as a dissenter
from current policy, the vice president's office, in particular, suspected
that CIA was behind a series of damaging press leaks that appeared
designed to embarrass the administration during the president's re-

election campaign. I never believed that to be true, but one could understand the White House's suspicion. By fall, it was getting to the point where senior analysts had to assume that the next piece of finished intelligence on Iraq would end up in the press, and that they would be blamed for trying to show up the administration. I never saw an instance where they pulled their punches or softened their analysis as a result, but it was not a healthy situation.

I vividly remember a post-election op-ed by David Brooks, the conservative *New York Times* columnist reputed to have close connections to the Bush White House. "Now that he's been returned to office," the column began, "President Bush is going to have to differentiate between his opponents and his enemies. His opponents are found in the Democratic Party. His enemies are in certain offices of the Central Intelligence Agency." Brooks went on to charge that the agency was waging "an unabashed effort to undermine the current administration," citing the serial leaking of "gloomy" reports on Iraq, ". . . . designed to discredit the President's Iraq policy," which amounted to "brazen insubordination." Now, he said, "C.I.A. officials are . . . busy trying to undermine their new boss, Porter Goss." In another time, said Brooks, "the ground at Langley would be laid waste and salted, and there would be heads on spikes." He advocated harsh but presumably updated measures to remind CIA employees "that the person the President sends to run their agency is going to run their agency. . . ."

It didn't take much imagination to suppose Brooks had been fed complaints from the White House, and that this was a pointed, if indirect, message from the administration to CIA "rebels." The director's excuse for allowing Murray to exert ex-post facto authority over Kappes, repeated many times, was that "I don't do personnel." Was Goss seizing the opportunity that had fallen into his lap to demonstrate to the president that he could bring a recalcitrant CIA to heel? I certainly don't know. But one would have difficulty convincing me otherwise.

As it was, Kappes, the former Marine, was faced with the unappealing choice between refusing to obey a direct order or being seen by his DO colleagues as a toady willing to sacrifice Sulick to save himself. His choice was no choice at all: he resigned instead. In days, both he and

Mike Sulick were gone. The Directorate of Operations was thrown into turmoil, and it seemed outright mutiny might ensue.

By this time, Goss had named Kyle "Dusty" Foggo as CIA's executive director. I had had a passing acquaintance with Dusty for years, and rather liked him. He had a high-living, larger-than-life persona and was reputed to be a bit of a rogue, but he knew how to get things done. Still, like others, I was dumbfounded when he was plucked from the relative obscurity of a midlevel logistics position in Europe and given the third-ranking job in CIA. With the Clandestine Service threatening revolt, Foggo made a panicky 10:00 PM call to Jose Rodriguez, the director of CTC, summoning him back to the office and offering him Kappes's job. The offer didn't seem to have involved a lot of deliberation. A couple of days later, when the dust had settled, Rodriguez accepted. In just over two years, Foggo would be indicted, and ultimately convicted, on federal corruption charges. This was not our finest hour.

The sudden departure of the two top DO leaders triggered a quick reshuffling of the chairs. With wholesale leadership changes at the top of the Clandestine Service under way, I expressed interest in becoming chief of the Near East and South Asia Division, but doubted I'd get it. I hardly knew Rodriguez, who had made his career in Latin America, and I had publicly crossed swords two years before with his newly named deputy, ultimately prevailing in a nasty Iraq-related dispute. Now that seemed like a Pyrrhic victory.

Around the same time, Condoleezza Rice, about to become secretary of state, approached Deputy Director John McLaughlin about my taking over the top counterterrorism job at the White House. McLaughlin demurred, saying CIA had other plans for me. I had mixed feelings when he told me, but I'm sure he did me a great favor. It would have been far too political a job for me; I wouldn't have survived long.

Suspecting there might be nothing for me in the DO at the end of the day, I approached the leadership of the National Intelligence Council. With the incumbent about to leave, they offered to make me National Intelligence Officer (NIO) for the Near East and South Asia. It was a job I had coveted for years.

But to my surprise, the new DO leadership did offer me a job—

director of CTC. There was more than a little irony in that, given the tenor of my past relations with the organization, but my disputes had been with a handful of leaders, never the organization as a whole. I had always recognized the Counterterrorist Center as a vital institution, indispensable if we were going to attack global terrorism on a global basis. If CTC hadn't existed, it would have had to be invented. It was by far the largest organization within CIA, combining the largest offices in the Directorate of Operations and the Directorate of Intelligence. Its budget ran into the billions. There was simply no more important job in CIA. I also felt that CTC needed change, both structural and cultural, and that I could lead it. It was an offer I could hardly refuse. Still, I asked for a bit of time to think it over.

"Tell me if I've got this straight," my wife Paula said. She could always cut to the heart of things. "Your job will be to make sure there are no terrorist attacks against the United States, anywhere. If you succeed, and there are no attacks, no one will notice. But if an attack happens, in spite of your best efforts, you'll be the one to take the blame."

"That's about it," I said. I accepted the following day.

Realistic as I thought I was, within weeks I realized that the challenges of running the Counterterrorist Center—which I would soon rename the "CIA Counter-Terrorism Center"—would be even greater than I had imagined. I had inherited an organization which undeniably was doing terrific work, supporting and coordinating a highly successful effort to capture or kill terrorists all around the world. It had done much to keep the country safe since 9/11. But its people had been going all-out for three years, and were paying a high price, personally and professionally. Many were exhausted and dispirited. With al-Qa'ida metastasizing around the globe and Iraq becoming a terrorist hub, the center's burdens would only increase, and markedly. Far from receiving the thanks of a grateful nation, it was beset on all sides. As public fear of al-Qa'ida waned, support for the counterterrorism methods mandated by the Bush administration was beginning to erode. Congress, in its wisdom, had created a rival organization in the National Counterterrorism Center (NCTC), which did no operations but was inexorably bleeding CTC of vital resources. The center had grown rapidly and chaotically, and was having difficulty managing itself. Its relations with the geographic divisions were still tense. Now, the problems, some of which I had complained of bitterly in the past, were all mine to solve.

As I stood in my new office in December 2004, I could see trouble everywhere, and precious few allies. I had never fully realized just how much I'd depended on Tenet, McLaughlin, and Pavitt for support, and sometimes protection, until now, when all of them were gone.

My senior lieutenants in CTC were all understandably preoccupied with their own parochial interests, and they all had them. Some were concerned with the lack of promotion or training opportunities for their people. The analysts were obsessed with their feud with the new National Counterterrorism Center. Targeters were concerned that cutting-edge technical tools being developed in our center were not being shared equitably. Operators were frustrated that we were not getting the support we needed from the military. Still others were worried that movement of priorities and resources was not keeping up with the evolution of the terrorist threat. By ensuring that everyone's needs were considered and addressed, I was able to get their buy-in and commitment for a strategic planning process designed to address all the center's problems comprehensively.

At the same time, I engaged a cleared outside contractor to conduct a thorough, impartial review of the organization, which I thought long overdue. The contractor staff conducted interviews in every office throughout the center. They visited field stations, and questioned our customers in the policy community. They polled attitudes in the workforce. Over the next few months, they issued a series of reports and provided several briefings to the management team. The results were fascinating, and extremely useful. We found our structure was working against us. Our customers in the field were confused, and often didn't know which office in the center they should look to for support. Some requests would languish without response; others would elicit two or more conflicting responses from competing offices.

The major culprit was Alec Station, sometimes referred to as the "Bin Laden Unit." That was a misnomer. Alec, named for the son of its founder and former chief, Mike Scheuer, was actually the al-Qa'ida unit, with a fascinating history dating back to the beginning of our preoccupation with bin Laden and his minions in Sudan in the early 1990s. But now, as al-Qa'ida members fled from the Pak-Afghan theater and associated groups began to crop up around the Muslim world, it was often difficult to determine who was al-Qa'ida and who was not. Alec was deciding that question for itself, its geographically based sub-units cherry-picking the most interesting and promising operations, and feuding with other geographically organized offices charged with pursuing non-al-Qa'ida Sunni extremists. Everyone agreed that we couldn't go on this way. Alec had become an anachronism in this new world; we had no choice, it was agreed, but to reorganize it out of existence. A couple of years later, after I had left government, charges appeared in the press that CIA had "abolished" the Bin Laden Unit, speculating that we had given up on capturing the leader of al-Qa'ida. That was nonsense. After our reorganization, the same people, in the same numbers, continued to pursue the same targets, very much to include bin Laden, but in a more rational structure.

Not surprisingly, some of CTC's cultural problems revolved around Alec as well. Its leaders were sometimes arrogant and obsessive, and regularly alienated the geographic divisions on whose support we depended. I did all I could to change those perceptions of the center, constantly preaching that our role was to support and enable operations, and telling people to remember that others, not we, were conducting them. I moved to embed some of our geographic subunits into the geographic divisions they were supporting. I joked with our "embeds" that they should salute the division chiefs, not me; the point was to *cooperate* with the divisions.

Many of the senior members of Alec, disproportionately women, were among the very best al-Qa'ida experts we had, with years of experience. Their devotion to the mission of hunting down al-Qa'ida was legendary. These were people who woke up in a cold sweat at three o'clock in the morning, fearful that they had missed something that put the nation at risk. Their expertise was critical to us, and their dedication heroic, but they were definitely a handful to manage. They were a tight, cultish group. Several had photos of Scheuer, their first boss, hung up in their offices, like shrines. Many, I knew, suspected that the structural reorganization which eliminated Alec was a sort of punishment, part of the cultural change I was promoting. It wasn't true, but some could not be convinced otherwise.

I vividly recall an occasion when one of the senior Alec people made a terrorist threat presentation to Director Goss at one of our regular five o'clock briefings. She started out calmly enough, but as she warmed to her subject, she began to rock, forward and back, rhythmically in cadence with her speech. After a few minutes she began punctuating each forward motion by addressing Goss as *sir*: "—and so, *sir* . . . we believe, *sir* . . . and therefore, *sir*. . . ." A few minutes later, still rocking, she began to embellish each *sir* with a sharp rap of her knuckles on the conference table. I wasn't sure what to do. I thought she must be coming unglued, and wondered if I should intervene. Mercifully, the presentation came to an end. As the meeting broke up I pulled my chief of operations aside. He had arranged the briefers.

"What the hell?" I said. "We can't put her in front of the Director!"

He smiled. "Don't worry about it, Chief. She's just a little wound up today. We'll get her back on her medication." I sighed. When you're making war on fanatics, it can be a great advantage to have a few fanatics of your own—so long as you keep them under close supervision.

Perhaps CTC's greatest contribution to the counterterrorism effort was its targeting—sifting through huge masses of data from many sources to identify and locate terrorists in the places they were hiding, just as it had done so masterfully in Pakistan. The targeters did not sit in one place, but were dispersed, as they should be, to work within the various operational units of the center. But that meant that new innovations in the state of the art being developed in one place were not necessarily shared elsewhere. We organized a new unit within CTC to serve as a home base for the targeters and a repository for technology and expertise, so that knowledge was shared, and innovations developed to confront one set of targets that could be applied to others.

Conducting a true war on terrorism, though, was not just a matter of finding and attacking targets. At base, the problem of violent extremism in the Muslim world was a broad social, political, and cultural phenomenon. It involved an internal struggle for the future of the Muslim world; it was a struggle in which we in the United States and the West had an important stake, even if it was essentially not our fight. That said, there was much the United States could do from the margins to influence the direction of change in countries of great concern to us. I was much encouraged by President Bush's second inaugural address, promising a renewed American commitment to democratic change in the world. If we meant to keep those who thought themselves oppressed from using violence and terrorism to redress their grievances, we would be wise to help give them a peaceful, democratic alternative. The primary reason Islamic militants were attacking us in the first place was to discourage U.S. support for what they regarded as impious, tyrannical regimes. I'm not sure the U.S. government has ever really gotten that; but by 2005 the nation was becoming more cognizant of the need to respond to negative perceptions of the United States and the distrust of American motives resulting from the War on Terror. To lead this global PR effort, Bush sent Karen Hughes, perhaps his closest advisor, to serve as under secretary of state for public diplomacy. Diplomacy and democracy promotion were outside our lane; but convinced there was much CTC could do in support of overt U.S. policy, I created a new department within the center, staffing it with the best cultural experts I could find. I gave them broad latitude to do whatever they could to help Ms. Hughes.

One of the more vexing problems to confront me when I took over CTC was the poor state of our relations with the military leadership at the Pentagon. CIA's cooperation with deployed military units in the field, now in Iraq as well as in Afghanistan, was excellent. That went especially for our intelligence support to the Joint Special Operations Command, whose leader, General Stanley McChrystal, became a valued friend. But things were not working at the Washington end. We had a number of fleeting opportunities, when a target we had been developing for weeks or months in the field would suddenly come into the crosshairs, and military assistance would be needed to launch a sensitive and risky operation. A secure video conference would be called to brief Secretary Rumsfeld and gain his approval. He would look to his senior uniformed military staff for advice—and find they knew nothing about it. The secretary would then begin to poke at the details of the operation, as was his wont, and ultimately defer a decision. Opportunities were being lost.

This couldn't go on. It was a problem of our own making, and I set out to fix it. We needed to ensure that the senior intelligence and operational leaders in the Pentagon's Joint Staff were aware of the operations which they might eventually be called upon to address, and well in advance, so that they would understand them and the intelligence picture behind them, and feel confident in advising the secretary to go ahead when and if they matured. We had a well-connected senior liaison to the Pentagon who had been generally ignored in the center and excluded from senior meetings. With his help, we set up a committee comprised of my most senior operational managers and members of the Joint Staff, to include General Ron Burgess, the director for intelligence, or "J-2." We met every two weeks, either in our building or at the Pentagon. At these sessions we circled the globe to keep the Joint Staff up to date on the developing intelligence picture on targets where military assistance might be required. They were extremely grateful. In time, our outreach would pay substantial dividends.

I also spent considerable time with General Jerry Boykin, Rumsfeld's deputy under secretary for intelligence, to develop a system whereby DoD personnel and capabilities, normally bound by the Title 10 legal authorities governing military operations, could be quickly and fluidly migrated to be employed under Title 50 authorities governing intelligence, and thus be eligible for use on short notice in CIA operations. In the CIA system, this would have been easy, but in the rigid bureaucratic environment at the Pentagon it was not, and required setting up elaborate protocols. In the spring of 2005, Boykin and I rolled out for John Negroponte, the newly created director of national intelligence, our legal and policy "template" for use of military forces in CIA operations. Again, the investment in time and patience would prove worth it. I'm not sure I can take even a small measure of the credit, but it's worth noting that when JSOC commandos killed Osama bin Laden in Pakistan in 2011, they did so while operating under the authority of CIA, not the Department of Defense.

When I took over CTC, there had not been a single town meeting or mass interaction between the center's senior leadership and the troops in over two years. Soon after my arrival, I inaugurated a series of briefings, alternating between auditoriums in the two buildings where the bulk of center employees were housed, using closed-circuit TV links to reach the rest of the widely dispersed workforce. I announced the strategic review, and provided regular updates on its progress, its conclusions and, finally, the progressive measures we were taking to implement it. I wanted our people to know where we were as an organization and where we were going, the reasons for the reorganization and the other measures we were taking to improve ourselves and, most of all, what we were doing to address their concerns over lack of training, lack of promotions, and lack of opportunity for overseas assignments. I wanted them to know that we understood that they were paying a high price for their devotion to counterterrorism, with few rewards beyond personal satisfaction. We couldn't solve our problems overnight, but at least we recognized them and were doing what we could. Since 9/11, we had been operating at an unsustainable sprint. Now we were preparing ourselves for the marathon to come.

I didn't share everything with them, though. As I and my key lieutenants sat in our conference room one day, awaiting the start of a briefing by our outside consultants, we silently leafed through the executive summary from an opinion poll taken of the CTC workforce. Among many, many other questions, the force was queried on its attitudes toward senior leaders in the Center. The CTC leadership team was viewed with some skepticism by the rank-and-file, it said, "with the exception of the Director, who is seen as a great improvement over his predecessor." I burst out laughing.

"This does *not* leave the room," I said, repeating it for emphasis. "If this gets out, Jose will assume that I'm behind it." It was already becoming obvious that things were not healthy between me and Jose Rodriguez, whom I had replaced and who had recently been given a new title: Director of the National Clandestine Service (D/NCS). I wasn't going to go out of my way to make things worse.

The most important part of the review, though, focused on the mission. My analysts prepared a thorough appraisal of the current evolution and future direction of the terrorist threat. This was the template on which all of our long-range planning and resource allocations would be based. We concluded that we needed to be poised to shift our resources rapidly to growing terrorist hot spots around the world—especially Iraq (which was already absorbing a lot of manpower) and a number of other badly underresourced regions—but that we couldn't shift them just yet, given the lingering threat from al-Qa'ida along the Pak-Afghan border.

The majority of our resources were still devoted to that theater, and we were achieving remarkable results. Even if bin Laden and Zawahiri were still at large, most of the organization's senior operational leaders had been captured in raids in Pakisan's settled areas. Those that remained were being forced to flee into the tribal badlands along the border. Within months, the post of al-Qa'ida's chief of operations was a revolving door; any new incumbent would have a brief life expectancy. But even as the state of the art for drone strikes was advancing, I knew that they were not a permanent solution. The safehaven in far northwest Pakistan would have to be ended. As I said at the time, the Tribal Areas were a romantic anachronism that the world could no longer afford. The only long-term answer would be to incorporate them fully into Pakistan and bring them under real government control. Even with the rising challenges in other regions of the world, we needed to finish the job in South-Central Asia, in part so that resources currently concentrated there could be migrated elsewhere.

By spring 2005, with our study complete and most of our strategic goals set, I concluded that we needed to make a major push over the remainder of the year to find, fix, and finish bin Laden, and to eliminate the remnants of the organization responsible for 9/11. I decided to carry that message to the field, on an extended visit to Pakistan and Afghanistan, in late April and early May 2005.

If I thought that it would be easy to finish al-Qa'ida in the Tribal Areas within the year, I would soon be disabused. In Islamabad, I paid a call on an old friend. Lieutenant General Ashfaq Kayani, the former director-general of military operations of the Pakistan Army, whose prescient warnings I had received three years before, was now director-general of the ISI. He would soon rise further to be the four-star chief of Army Staff, the most powerful man in Pakistan.

Kayani's fears of radicalization in the Tribal Areas had been realized. Armed probes to flush out foreign militants, launched in response to American pressure, had touched off a violent reaction from the tribes, just as the ISI chief had predicted. In response, the Pakistan Army had had to forcibly occupy South Waziristan. The al-Qa'ida militants who had been pushed out were now concentrated in North Waziristan, where CIA was feverishly trying to track them and learn their precise locations.

I made my pitch. The occupation of South Waziristan had been a great success, I said. It had forced al-Qa'ida and the foreign militants to converge on North Waziristan. We hoped Pakistan would make them uncomfortable there, just as it had in South Waziristan, perhaps to the point of shifting the army to occupy North Waziristan as well. As the militants were chased ever northward, they would eventually be hemmed in, and would become easier to track and to finish. We should set a goal, I said, of capturing or killing bin Laden within the year.

Kayani didn't need to say a word. I could tell in an instant what he was thinking. ISI, in my view, had few capabilities in the Tribal Areas. It had always been primarily a security service, not an intelligence organization in our sense of the term. Its officers could operate well in areas they controlled, but the tribal agencies were like foreign ground to them. To put pressure on al-Qa'ida in North Waziristan, the Pakistan Army would have to move in. Circumstances may have forced him to occupy South Waziristan, but it seemed to me that Kayani was not spoiling for another fight, especially in an area where the tribal structure had been thoroughly degraded and the influence of radical mullahs was far greater than in South Waziristan.

Capturing bin Laden, I knew, would be still more problematic. He remained popular in much of Pakistan. If the Americans were to quietly kill or capture him in some remote area, so much the better. But for Pakistan to kill or, worse yet, capture him and turn him over to the Americans, the domestic political consequences would be very unpleasant. Better to ignore the problem, and hope it would go away. ISI had shown considerable capability in capturing al-Qa'ida cadres in the settled areas. Kayani's steadfast silence signaled he thought it better to continue focusing efforts there.

As if to underscore the point, as we sat across from one another at breakfast the following morning, an aide entered the room to whisper urgently into the ISI chief's ear. His mouth curled into a tight smile. Abu Faraj al-Libi, the latest operations chief of al-Qa'ida, had been captured a few hours before, in a late-night raid on a graveyard in Mansehra, where he had been lured by Pakistani agents. I thanked and congratulated Kayani on the success.

A few hours later, I was looking down from a Pak Army helicopter at the high plateau surrounding Wana, the capital of South Waziristan. I couldn't believe the contrast from three years before. The Pak Army was deployed in full force, with tents, vehicles, and howitzers everywhere. When I sat down with the local Pakistani political agent, he provided a lucid briefing, complete with PowerPoint slides, on the government's overall plan. The agency would be pacified, he said, through a coordinated program of military force, economic development, and political reform. The military part we could readily see; he assured me that development projects were also in train, and that elections would soon be held for local councils. It was an impressive exposition. "This guy really gets it," I thought.

But if so, he was probably alone. What he was describing demanded a stark departure from the Frontier Crimes Regulation, the 1901 law governing the Tribal Areas since British times and scarcely amended since. The old regulation had never been rescinded. If the Pak government had a comprehensive plan to pacify the Tribal Areas along the lines this fellow had suggested, Kayani certainly hadn't mentioned it. In any case, it was obvious that if Pakistan were going to tame the Tribal Areas and end the terrorist safehaven, a lot of American assistance would be required, and not just for intelligence and weaponry.

Before finally heading over to Afghanistan, I sat down with the head of the Agency for International Development office in Islamabad. Economic development assistance in the Tribal Areas, I said, was at least as important as anything else we were doing in the War on Terror.

AID and the State Department were spending hundreds of millions per year in Pakistan. How much was going to the Tribal Areas? The answer: very little. AID had a few boutique projects along the western border, but nearly all development assistance was going elsewhere in the country. We were letting the Japanese, who had a very modest budget, take the lead in the Tribal Areas. I was appalled.

The U.S. government had been saying for years that we were leading a global "War on Terror," bringing all aspects of national power to bear. That was the rhetoric. What I could see now in Pakistan was the reality.

In Kabul, my colleagues were seized with yet another threat. Pakistani militants, based mostly in North Waziristan and outraged at what they saw as the long-term occupation of Afghanistan by a U.S.-led NATO army, were launching increasingly brazen attacks against American and Afghan troops across the Durand Line. The Pakistanis were doing little or nothing to stop them. There were stories about how heavily armed fighters were crossing the border within sight of Pak military checkposts, firing rockets, and then retreating. To my colleagues and to the U.S. military, this looked like complicity. I doubted the Pakistanis were actively aiding and abetting the militants, but was not at all surprised at the lack of Pakistani reaction. We might feel that Pakistan had a solemn responsibility to keep its territory from being used as a base from which to attack an ally. But I knew that to the Pakistanis, these cross-border attacks would look like someone else's problem. The Pakistanis had troubles enough in the Tribal Areas. They weren't about to invite more.

On the final day of my trip, as I stood looking up at the Afghan flag above Hamid Karzai's palace, I could yet take satisfaction in what we had accomplished on both sides of the Pak-Afghan border. But I was beginning to think that perhaps those successes, too easily achieved, could come undone.

Chapter 45

THE UNRAVELING

T HE GREATEST CHALLENGES I faced as director of CTC did not come from terrorists. You might have thought, given the importance of what we were doing for the security of the nation, and the fact that we had thwarted thus far all attempts to reprise 9/11, CTC would have friends everywhere. But you'd be wrong. In 2005 we were under attack from all sides, and our most formidable enemies included other elements of the executive branch, the Congress, and the press. If good fortune had given some people license to become complacent, I had no such luxury. Al-Qa'ida had not hit us again, but it was not for want of trying. Other nations had not been so lucky: Bali, Indonesia, was struck by a devastating attack in October 2002, and Madrid in March 2004, to name a couple. London would be hit in July 2005, and Bali again later that year. My job was to make sure that CTC's ability to protect us was maintained and enhanced. But as I surveyed the landscape on my return to Washington in May 2005, beginning at the seventh floor of my own headquarters and extending out across the Potomac to the capital city beyond, I could hardly find a single friend in a position to help me. This was the start of the loneliest but perhaps the most strangely exhilarating six months of my life.

Shortly before I took over CTC, Congress had passed legislation creating the National Counterterrorism Center. The reasons were obvious. After the report of the 9/11 Commission, documenting (among many other things) intelligence failures that had contributed to the disaster, Congress had to be seen to act in some way. The measures already taken to correct systemic problems involved improved information sharing and work practices, and were not readily visible to the public. Congress couldn't take credit for them. But creating a new government bureaucracy is highly visible.

At the same time, the framers of the Intelligence Reform and Terrorism Prevention Act of 2004, which created NCTC, were very well aware of the critical operational work CIA was doing around the world, and didn't want to interfere with it. They certainly didn't want to be blamed for the next terrorist attack. So they did something seemingly safe: They took the Terrorist Threat Integration Center (TTIC), a new organization created since 9/11 to improve information sharing between the domestic law enforcement and foreign intelligence communities, and gave it a new name and a new, important-sounding mandate. The National Counterterrorism Center would henceforth have "primary responsibility" for intelligence analysis, though CIA and the other intelligence agencies could continue to do it as well. NCTC could expressly *not* do counterterrorism operations overseas. That risked creating havoc. But by creating another government entity to "connect the dots" that CIA and others had failed to connect in the past—well, Congress must have thought, what was the harm in that? The law of unintended consequences took over from there.

The vast majority of the federal government's best terrorism analysts were in the Directorate of Intelligence's Office of Terrorism Analysis, which was the analytic wing of CTC. The acting head of NCTC was John Brennan, a good friend of over twenty years' standing, highly ambitious and a talented bureaucratic infighter. Years later, he would hold the senior counterterrorism job in the Obama White House, and then become director of CIA. Trying to bring federal intelligence and law enforcement to cooperate more closely with states and localities was important, but it was difficult, thankless work. Now Brennan seized the opportunity to take over preparation of high-profile terrorism analysis for the president and senior policymakers. Using the newly passed legislation as a stick, he successfully pressured the CIA leadership into giving up significant numbers of CTC's terrorism analysts, whom he organized, along with others from elsewhere in the intelligence community, into a structure mirroring that in CTC. We were taking the same analysts whom Congress saw as having failed, putting them in a different place, and pretending this would solve the problem.

It was an aggressively bad idea. Before long, analysts who had formerly been colleagues were in rival organizations, competing viciously for the right to take the lead on analytic pieces for the President's Daily Brief. It was a huge duplication of effort at a time when there simply weren't enough seasoned analysts to go around. It served the analysts themselves very badly. NCTC was in no position to effectively recruit, train, or develop career analysts in the way that CIA's Directorate of Intelligence could. For CTC, whose strength had long been in using the same analysts to support operations and to write finished intelligence, the loss of these people both weakened our analytic depth and threatened to hurt our operations. Worse, there was no end in sight. NCTC was constantly pressing for yet more of our analysts. My organization was being picked apart.

Less than a week into my tenure, I sat down with Brennan to make him an offer. Rather than progressively raiding CTC of its analysts to create a rival organization, I asked, why not just take all of it? All the key agencies—CIA, the FBI, and the Defense Intelligence Agency—had large, dedicated counterterrorism organizations. Why not create a *real* national counterterrorism center by bringing these units together? They would remain functional parts of their parent organizations, from whom they would continue to derive their legal authorities and to receive administrative and "back-office" support, but would be "matrixed" together into a coherent organization in which sharing of analysts and other resources would be facilitated, and cross-government activities far better coordinated. This was what CTC had done successfully on a smaller scale in bringing together elements of completely independent directorates within CIA. Now we could do the same thing, but on a much grander scale, this time under Brennan's direction. Rather than fighting for a place at the counterterrorism table with a nascent, immature organization, Brennan could instead have me and the chiefs of all the principal federal counterterrorism organizations sitting around his conference room every morning, answerable to him.

John was momentarily intrigued, but just as quickly seemed to sense a trap. From his questions, I could see he doubted whether he would be able to control people who still belonged simultaneously to independent agencies. For him, this might be like invading China: You would be enveloped and overwhelmed by those whom you had nominally conquered. A veil fell over his eyes; he had no interest.

Undeterred, I continued to promote the idea elsewhere. The head of CIA's Directorate of Intelligence indicated he would go along, but only if and when we were about to lose all our terrorism analysts. Other agencies were either opposed or apathetic; in any case, they saw no urgency. They weren't under attack by NCTC. Fran Townsend, the president's senior advisor on both counterterrorism and homeland security and a canny political operator, could see I was fighting an uphill battle. She expressed interest and encouraged me to continue—on my own.

When Brennan was passed over in his quest to be named the permanent director of NCTC, I made another pitch to his successor, retired Admiral Scott Redd. He responded very frankly. A long career in government had taught him that if you didn't have direct command of the troops you were leading, you had nothing. The immutable laws of bureaucratic survival had won out, again, over effective government. The debilitating rivalry between CTC and NCTC continued. It would fester for years to come.

As our terrorist adversaries around the globe fell victim to our close cooperation with other intelligence and security services, and retreated increasingly into ungoverned spaces beyond the effective reach of allied governments, use of Predator drones was becoming increasingly important. I am not at liberty to discuss much of this, but let us say that the U.S. government in this period was not putting a premium on the use of drones—by any government entity—in the global counterterrorism fight. In 2005, with Iraq going up in flames, every available Predator coming off the assembly line was being sent there. This seemed unwise to me, but with Tenet gone, there was no one at CIA of his stature with the respect or force of personality to make a case for even a modest reallocation of DoD resources elsewhere. I argued for it everywhere I could, in the executive branch and even with congressional committees. I found sympathy for my views, but nothing more.

Yet of all the challenges CTC faced during that fateful year of 2005, the controversies surrounding detainees, interrogations, and secret prisons were by far the greatest. When I first arrived, the CIA terrorist interrogation program had been in existence for nearly three years. It had begun just after our capture of Abu Zubayda in Pakistan in 2002, and evolved greatly since then.

Interrogation is not a core function, nor is it a traditional skill of the CIA. Yes, the organization did have a small number of experienced interrogators, most of whom were also polygraph operators. Barry Mc-Manus, who dealt with Dr. Bashir, the Pak nuclear scientist, was one of these. But there were only a few of them, and their skills and experience varied widely. Case officers, who reflect the traditional methods of the Clandestine Service, depend upon the willing collaboration of their sources; they are trained in manipulation, not intimidation or coercion. But it is a core aspect of CIA culture that it responds to the needs of the moment. Given direction from the president, it quickly becomes whatever its masters need it to be.

I was not involved in the interrogation of Abu Zubayda, or in the subsequent construction of a formal program to detain and interrogate the senior al-Qa'ida members whose capture would follow. Once Abu Zubayda was dispatched aboard a CIA plane, I and my station were back at work to capture more like him. But I could readily understand why CIA needed a controlled, disciplined interrogation program. The alternative was something like what I had in Pakistan.

All of those we captured in the early, pre-Zubayda days, the low-level operatives and fighters, we placed as rapidly as possible into U.S. military custody to be flown out of Pakistan. We could try to question only a relative few of them. Most, no doubt, knew little of value to us. But even if they did, we were ill-equipped to extract it. The detainees were being kept in regular Pakistani jails, where they had ready access to one another and could coordinate their stories. They were brought to the Clubhouse for debriefing for a few hours at a time. My officers did the best they could, but they were not trained to elicit information from hostile parties, and those being questioned had little incentive to cooperate. Those doing the questioning had a general idea of what we were looking for, and several spoke Arabic; but in addition to a lack of skills appropriate to an adversarial setting, they did not have the comprehensive knowledge of al-Qa'ida and its members that was critically important to the undertaking.

In presiding over this mess, it became obvious to me that if CIA were to be successful in rapidly gaining information from the so-called "high-value targets" whom we hoped to capture, we would need a serious, focused effort to do so. In short, we would need everything I didn't have in Pakistan. We would need to have complete control over the detainees, so that we could set the environment and determine the conditions in which they would be questioned. We would need to be seen by them as the sole determiners of their fate, whether we were or not. Most important, we would need to have the means of bringing all available information to bear on their questioning. The most powerful tool in a terrorist interrogation is knowledge. The detainee must be convinced that there is a distinct possibility that we already know the answer to any question put to him. If he has a compelling interest in convincing his questioner of his truthfulness, the questioner's knowledge is a powerful threat—often more so than any coercive methods we might name.

Two of the distinguishing features of CTC's program were the methods it was permitted to employ, and the secret locations where it was conducted. The bar to admittance was high: only so-called HVDs, "high-value detainees"—those strongly suspected of having information concerning future terrorist attacks—were accepted. In most cases they had been captured by cooperating foreign security services, the Pakistanis in particular, and turned over to CIA. The agency would then "render" them to a so-called "black site," a prison which a cooperating country would allow us to build and control entirely on our own. The reason for black sites was the perceived need for CIA to control all aspects of the detainee's incarceration and interrogation. We did not want a detainee to have contact with any outside persons or entities; he would have to deal with us. And we would not trust anyone else to deal with him. In any individual case the lives of hundreds or thousands of innocent people might be at stake.

The other distinguishing feature of the program was the use of what we euphemistically called "enhanced interrogation techniques," or EITs. Again, this involved methods we would not trust to anyone else, lest they go too far and we be accused of "outsourcing torture." At the beginning of the program, the EITs had famously included "waterboarding," which gave the sensation of drowning. Previously employed against many American servicemen as part of their counter-interrogation training, it was not physically dangerous but absolutely terrifying to most human beings. Only three of the detainees, Abu Zubayda, 'Abd al-Rahim al-Nashiri, and, most infamously, Khalid Shaykh Mohammed (KSM), the mastermind of the 9/11 attacks, were ever waterboarded. KSM was a particularly hard case. A man with the blood of over 3,000 Americans on his hands, his stock answer to any question regarding future terrorist attacks was, "Soon you will see."

Even so, as the interrogation program matured and methods were refined, the interrogators concluded that waterboarding was superfluous and unnecessary. The practice was abandoned in 2003, well before I arrived on the scene. The other EITs were not nearly so harsh. They were designed and administered so that the detainee would not be physically harmed, but would be frightened, humiliated, and psychologically worn down, especially through sleep deprivation. Still, it was a grim business at best.

Whatever else one might think of the program, and whether or not one agreed with its methods, it was an efficient, highly disciplined program by the time I inherited it. But the political climate it was operating in had changed markedly. It is striking now just how uncontroversial these interrogations were in the early years, at least for those few members of Congress who were briefed on the details. Among the general public, fearful of another devastating attack, there seemed little concern for the tender sensibilities of terrorists. The administration would have done well to have harnessed that latent public and congressional support early on. Instead, Vice President Cheney, who had the final say, restricted congressional notification to the minimum permitted by law, and nothing was revealed publicly.

But three years after 9/11, the fear which had gripped the nation was beginning to subside, and questions about Bush administration counterterrorism policies were being raised in various quarters, especially in Congress. This was probably a healthy thing. But what most affected public perceptions of detention and interrogation practices was the wave of revulsion, both at home and abroad, generated by public dissemination in April 2004 of shocking photographs of Iraqi detainees at Abu Ghraib prison being abused by leering American troops. Separate reports of abuse at Guantánamo only fed the fire. CIA's legally approved interrogation program may have had no connection to the brutal freelancing being conducted by untrained and ill-supervised U.S. troops in Iraq and Cuba, but all three were soon conflated in the public mind. As the military was called before Congress to publicly explain how such abuses could have been allowed to occur and how they would be prevented from ever happening again, it was natural to question what CIA was up to, particularly as rumors of aggressive CIA interrogations were cropping up in the press.

In early 2005, as congressional restiveness increased, Cheney belatedly agreed to bring more members of the oversight committees fully into the picture. I insisted on participating in these briefings myself. Never did I hear an objection to our practices, even from Democrats; reactions ran more along the lines of one Republican, who expressed surprise: "You mean that's it? That's all you're doing? They did worse to me in boot camp!" That sort of congressional feedback, though, only gave the illusion of support. Our erstwhile friends on the Hill would pull a disappearing act later, when the going got rough.

Whatever the moral, ethical, or political considerations involved, what made the enhanced interrogation techniques legally dicey was the international Convention Against Torture and Other Cruel, Inhuman or Degrading Treatment or Punishment, to which the United States was a signatory, and which therefore had the force of U.S. federal law. Anyone might agree in the abstract that "torture and other cruel, inhuman or degrading treatment or punishment" were abhorrent, and should not be allowed. The tricky bit was to define such treatment in practical terms. If, in questioning a known terrorist thought to hold information about an imminent terrorist attack, the American public might wish us to have the option to use means beyond what U.S. police might typically employ in a precinct house with a lawyer present, as they most certainly did, the question was: How far, precisely, can one go without violating the law? The EITs were spelled out in great detail for the Department of Justice, which approved their use in August 2002.

That initial answer from the Office of Legal Counsel at Justice necessarily involved a degree of subjective judgment, and that judgment was likely to be affected by the political environment, the degree of public fear of terrorist attack, and the beliefs of the individual lawyers concerned. Unsurprisingly, two years later, after some key personnel changes, the Office of Legal Counsel's practical interpretations of the law changed with them.

For CIA, the situation was doubly difficult. We were charged with preventing the next mass terrorist attack by al-Qa'ida. We knew by early 2005 that information we had extracted from the high-value detainees—including through use, in some cases, of aggressive interrogations—had prevented several such attacks at different stages of maturity. Of the approximately one hundred individuals interrogated by CIA during the seven-year life of the program, both before and after my tenure at CTC, only a minority were ever administered enhanced interrogation techniques; a majority of the captives willingly cooperated without resort to any extreme measures. Still, the techniques had been highly effective against a number of hard cases. With the fear of attack constantly hanging over our heads, no one wanted to be in the position of having to live with the thought that we had failed to employ all the legal means at our disposal to protect the country. Again, the question was: Where is the legal red line?

When I took over CTC, we no longer had a definitive answer. As my lawyers in CTC explained it, the Department of Justice had backed off its earlier interpretation of what was permissible under international law, but had not updated its specific judgment regarding whether use of the enhanced interrogation techniques was legal. Instead, they had given us a dodge: The law against torture would not apply in our case, because any signatory to the international convention was only responsible for actions taking place on its territory. CIA was operating outside U.S. territory, and so was not subject to the law. If that sounds flimsy, it's because it was. We insisted on a new legal judgment on the techniques to replace the one Justice had rescinded—one we could rely upon even if we were operating on U.S. territory. In the spring of 2005, we finally got the supportive legal guidance we wanted, but it would provide only fleeting comfort.

If I was facing enormous difficulties outside CIA, I wasn't getting much love at home, either. My relationship with Jose Rodriquez, the hastily elevated head of the Clandestine Service, had gotten off to a shaky start and had deteriorated steadily from there. By late spring 2005 the rift was an open secret, and the subject of many rumors.

As best I could intuit the problem, Rodriguez wanted me to run the center as he had done. His occasional questions of me usually involved the minutia of day-to-day operations, and that was where he wanted me to be focused. He couldn't understand why I was wasting so much of my time with the White House, with Congress, and with the Pentagon, to say nothing of my misbegotten strategic planning. In his time at CTC, he had avoided all of that.

Of course, I inevitably spent much of my time engaged on operational issues, especially those where we needed help from outside CTC. In the last half of 2005 alone, after my lengthy trip to Pakistan and Afghanistan, I traveled to Tampa and Doha, Qatar, for operational coordination with CENTCOM; twice to East Africa, where Somalia was becoming a worry; once to Europe for coordination with allies; and once to the Middle East. Ultimately, operations drove everything we did.

But I found my boss's attitude incomprehensible. Our operations were going extremely well. My senior operations managers were terrific—certainly at least as capable as I was. I didn't have the time to duplicate their efforts—not when our analysts were being hijacked, the government wouldn't devote the resources necessary to conduct a proper drone war, operations were being thwarted by poor relations with the Pentagon, my workforce lacked support, parts of my organization were working at cross-purposes and, worst of all, the legal basis of our detention and interrogation program was under multipronged attack. My ops guys didn't need kibitzing; they needed the support that only their director could give them. Rodriguez's views, though never directly expressed to me, were clear enough; I just didn't have time for them. In deference to his interests, I stopped going to his morning meetings, and sent my chief of operations, instead.

From the start of 2005, Steve Hadley, newly promoted to national security advisor after serving four years as deputy to Condoleezza Rice, understood that aspects of CIA's detention program were simply not sustainable. Already there were detainees in CIA's prisons who had long since outlived their usefulness as intelligence sources. We couldn't keep such individuals indefinitely; sooner or later they would have to come to light, be declared to the International Committee of the Red Cross, and be given some form of due process, whether they ultimately went to trial or not. As I said repeatedly in interagency meetings in those days, we couldn't simply "disappear" people. If we couldn't risk returning them to their home countries where they might well be set free, where could we send them? They would have to surface somewhere. When that happened, the U.S. government would have to say something publicly about where they had come from and where they had been since their capture, which in many cases had been publicized. Word about their interrogations would also get out. We would need something to say about that as well. There would be a huge "public diplomacy" aspect to what we came to refer to as the "end game."

The fate of CIA's detainees was also linked to Guantánamo. Public and congressional pressure was increasing to shut the place down and to adjudicate the status of inmates there—to release those who could be safely released, to repatriate those who could not be tried in court but whose governments could be trusted to incarcerate or monitor them, and to prosecute those who could be tried by military commissions. Throughout the early fall of 2005, I participated in endless meetings at the working level, as well as at the Deputies' Committee and Principals' Committee levels, all dealing with the "end game." There was much thrashing about, but nothing ever seemed to get resolved. Everything was dependent upon everything else, and the Department of Defense seemed reluctant to do anything. DoD had supposedly been preparing for years to hold military commission trials. They continued to go through the motions, but nothing ever happened. It was mysterious: Secretary Rumsfeld was a fierce taskmaster. If he'd wanted results, surely he'd have gotten them.

Early on in the interagency process, I was approached by Steve Cambone, the under secretary of defense for intelligence. Recognizing that our two agencies were the keys to the "end game," he proposed that he and I hold a series of meetings off-line to work out a strategy for "black site" detainees; if we could agree, he reasoned, the other agencies would fall in line. Steve was not much trusted in my building because of his close association with Rumsfeld. It was true he could be very clever in advancing his secretary's agenda; that was his job. But I always found Cambone to be decent and reasonable. He soon came to realize that there was no alternative but eventually to move CIA's detainees to Guantánamo, and he helped to work through a strategy designed to get us there. I believe he worked in good faith to convince Secretary Rumsfeld to agree to it. He would fail to deliver his boss in the end, but I'm sure it was not for want of trying.

When, in November 2005, Dana Priest of *The Washington Post* came out with a series of articles exposing the fact that CIA was interrogating terrorist suspects in a string of "black sites" in foreign locations, the pressure on us increased exponentially. The reaction of those hosting these secret prisons was about what one would expect. Their cooperation was based on our ability to maintain the secret. Even if they themselves had not been exposed—and of course they could not be sure how accurate the *Washington Post* stories were about others— the fact that the program had come to light at all undermined their confidence. Several asked us to pack up and leave as quickly as possible. This further ratcheted up the pressure to decrease our detainee population and shift those we still needed to hold elsewhere. Again Guantánamo came into the conversation. Still Rumsfeld refused. He was trying to decrease the population at Gitmo, he pointed out, not increase it. Left unsaid was that he was already tarred with Abu Ghraib. He saw no reason to be connected to CIA prisons and interrogations as well. If CIA had a problem, he saw no reason why he should have to take responsibility for it.

If all that were not bad enough, another large shadow loomed on the horizon that fall, threatening the legal underpinnings of the CIA interrogation program so recently won in June. Senator John McCain of Arizona was one of the most powerful and influential members of the Republican Party. As a former prisoner of war and survivor of brutal mistreatment at the hands of the North Vietnamese, he also spoke with unparalleled moral authority on the issue of torture. He was loudly uncomfortable with what he understood to be administration policy on interrogation, and indicated he would introduce new legislation to deal with it. It wasn't clear at first if McCain was solely concerned with the military, but even if so, it appeared that CIA's interrogations might be an unintended victim of whatever legislation he introduced.

Again, Vice President Cheney took the lead. Convinced that CTC's use of enhanced interrogation techniques was critical to national security, he set out to persuade McCain to provide a "carve-out" that would exempt CIA from his legislation. I thought it a very bad idea, and said so in a meeting with Goss and the acting general counsel. The legislation simply banned "cruel, inhuman or degrading treatment or punishment." That was already the law. Did we want exemption from that? The point of potential disagreement did not regard the principle, but the way it was interpreted. Nonetheless, Cheney and Goss met alone with the Arizona senator to brief him on our program. After sitting in on Goss's "pre-brief," I felt uncomfortable. He seemed not to have a good grasp of the details of the program; but in the end it didn't matter. From Goss's account of the meeting, Senator McCain was not prepared to listen to anything he had to say anyway. No one was going to convince him that our methods didn't amount to torture. His legislation passed the Senate in October as an amendment to a supplemental military appropriations bill.

Things got worse from there. Expecting to get greater support in the House, the National Security Council continued negotiations with McCain's people to win protections from future prosecution for CIA personnel who were acting in good faith on the basis of Justice Department legal approvals. It became obvious that McCain didn't trust Bush's Justice Department to interpret the law, and so would not provide CIA employees such assurances. He wanted them to be potentially subject to prosecution by a future administration if it decided, after the fact, that Justice's legal rulings had been incorrect. On the other hand, he wouldn't specify what CIA would be permitted to do; instead, he chose to leave them in doubt as to their legal standing if they went beyond what the military was permitted. Now we were in an even deeper hole: these discussions would become part of the "legislative history" of McCain's bill, and determine how its intent would be interpreted by the courts.

Confronted with the twin threats of exposure of the black sites and House passage of the McCain Amendment, the interagency process kicked into high gear. Beginning in early November, J. D. Crouch, the deputy national security advisor, chaired a feverish series of so-called "Tiger Team" meetings, comprised of senior representatives from State, Justice, Defense, and CIA. Our charge was to work out the "end game" for terrorist suspects in both CIA and DoD custody, and to explore how the CIA interrogation program might be adapted and saved in light of McCain. Tiger Team recommendations would go up for consideration by the Principals' Committee. I and my senior lawyer, Bob Eatinger, represented CIA. As the late-evening meetings churned on, I had a growing sense of despair. In mid-December, Rumsfeld was still adamant that he would not accept CIA detainees at Guantánamo, and it was even clearer that there would be no protections for CIA in McCain's pending legislation. His amendment limited the military strictly to interrogation methods prescribed in the *Army Field Manual*, which did not allow anything more aggressive than various forms of the "good cop, bad cop" routine. It did not address CIA explicitly, but provided no exception for it, either. CIA officers could follow Justice Department guidance, but would do so at their peril. The pressure from all sides was becoming suffocating.

At a meeting in the White House Situation Room on December 20, again chaired by Crouch, he reminded me that it was CIA that had made such a strong case for the importance of the EITs. For the safety of the country, we would have to carry on. "Can't you convince the interrogators to continue?" he asked.

"I probably could," I said. "These people are highly dedicated. I'm sure they would continue if I let them. But I won't. If McCain passes, they will have no legal protections. If I allow them to continue under those circumstances, where is the leadership in that?" I told him that if the bill passed, we would do nothing beyond what was permitted in the *Army Field Manual*.

I was out on a limb, and he knew it. He looked at me steadily. "Is that the CIA position?"

Though we hadn't discussed it—we were barely speaking—I felt confident that Rodriguez would back me up; he was all about protecting our people. But I honestly didn't know where Goss stood on this. "It's the DO [Directorate of Operations] position," I said. I hoped to get Goss's support as well, but in the end it really wasn't going to matter. Without appropriate legal protections for our officers, we weren't going to continue as though McCain hadn't happened.

Back at Langley, I reported to Goss on what I'd told the NSC and the interagency. "You did?" He sounded pleased. By his account he'd been excusing himself at the White House for some time, protesting that he couldn't order us to move forward with coercive interrogations if we refused. "This isn't the military," he'd said. Now, to his relief, I was substantiating his warnings.

On December 23, Andrew Card, the president's chief of staff, paid a visit to CTC on short notice. I gave him a walking tour of our Global Response Center, and then ushered him into a small conference room to meet with the managers of our detainee program. Card thanked them and stressed the importance of what they were doing for the safety of Americans.

Finally, he said, "I'd like to know if there is anything I can say that would increase your confidence. Is there anything you would like to hear from me? You should know that I begin every day the same way: I walk into the Oval Office, and say, 'Pardon me, Mr. President.'" There was a moment of confused silence. His words rolled out on the table, as though daring someone to pick them up.

Quick calculations ran through my head. Was Card suggesting what I thought? Could the White House really provide preemptive pardons to protect against something a future administration might do? Surely the president would only do it at the end of his term. But a promise now to do something then would be worthless; could one get such a commitment in writing? And was it even worth exploring? This sounded like the pardon former President Ford had provided to Nixon. How would that look? Wouldn't it appear like a tacit admission that we were violating the law? Anyway, how could we trust these people? If they were really concerned about protecting us, wouldn't they be standing up more forcefully to McCain? Instead, they were claiming confidently that a compromise would be reached, when in fact there was none in sight. No, I concluded; we wouldn't go down that road.

Card and I chatted amiably as I walked him out to his waiting car. Nothing about pardons was ever said again.

In the end, my suspicions were confirmed. The opportunity for a last-second reprieve in the House came and went a few days later. Duncan L. Hunter, the Republican chairman of the House Armed Services Committee, threatened to withhold the supplemental Defense Appropriations bill from a floor vote unless he received firm assurances from the intelligence community that passage of the McCain Amendment would not harm counterterrorism efforts. The administration wanted that legislation; the appropriate assurances were arranged. The bill, with the McCain Amendment attached, passed on December 30, 2005. The White House had caved, disingenuously claiming success in its negotiations. The president was even photographed shaking hands with McCain.

———

I believe it is a reasonable view, perhaps the correct one, to argue that Americans should never engage in any form of coercive or abusive interrogation. It seems to me that those making that moral argument also need to be prepared to follow their principles in all circumstances, and to accept a higher degree of risk, even if it means their fellow citizens may be killed, in order to uphold them. Unless they're willing to say that—and in my experience, very few are—I have trouble taking them seriously.

For me and others, this was not an academic question. It involved hard decisions, with real consequences either way. When I headed CTC, I did not consider what we were doing to be torture; nor do I think so now. As I reflect, putting myself where I was then, knowing what I did about our past success, having the concerns about imminent attack that we all did, and with the legal assurances we had, I still come out in the same place I did then.

CIA has borne a considerable degree of opprobrium for its part in what once was called the global "War on Terror." It still does today, especially in the context of targeted killings. But it seems to me that if people have problems with policy, they should bring their concerns to the policymakers; and if they disagree over legal interpretation, they should complain to the U.S. attorney general. That doesn't absolve CIA people from personal responsibility. Individuals in CIA, as elsewhere, can and should make decisions for themselves about whether they feel morally justified in doing as they are ordered, irrespective of its legality; they should decline, as individuals, to follow those orders, and even to resign, if they do not. But it is manifestly not in the interest of the American people to foster an institutional climate that encourages their national intelligence service to decide for itself which of its legal orders it will follow, and to decline to carry out those assignments it deems risky or inconvenient to itself. I had seen this tendency earlier in my career, when some had ducked the dicey effort to overthrow Saddam Hussein. I had disapproved of their behavior then, and I disapprove of it now. If we are not careful, institutional insubordination will be the unwanted legacy of our collective moral ambiguity on the difficult measures which have been taken, and are still being taken now, to deal with vicious, committed non-state actors who hide in the shadows, and plot to do us harm.

I did not then, and do not now have any problem with Senator McCain's views concerning interrogation. My problem with him, perhaps ironically, was a moral one. His legislation could have directly addressed the matter of CIA, as well as military interrogations. Rather than publicly clash with the administration, he chose not to. Instead, he tried to achieve the same result indirectly by putting the troops—my troops—at legal risk. I did not consider that a highly principled stand. Nor was the senator entirely consistent. Around this time, McCain was asked in an interview how he would deal with a classic conundrum: There is a nuclear bomb set to go off somewhere in the United States, and we have a limited amount of time to learn its whereabouts from a terrorist in our custody. What do we do?

"You do what you have to do," he said.

———

In January 2006, the Tiger Team continued its deliberations. I made clear, again, that we would not continue interrogations as though nothing had happened, but that we would adapt to the new post-McCain reality. A Principals' Committee meeting was scheduled for CIA to report on its strategy. I and my staff drew up a set of briefing slides, and I met on January 13 with Rodriguez and Goss to discuss them. In the brief I stated that though loss of the enhanced techniques would make our program less effective, we could still continue to question terrorist suspects, limiting our interrogation to those techniques specified in the *Army Field Manual*. Both Goss and Rodriguez dismissed the brief out of hand.

"Without the EITs, we can't continue the program," Goss said. "We're out of the interrogation business." Rodriguez strongly agreed. I thought they were both being irresponsible and childish. Yes, we had to protect our people and make sure we were on the right side of the law, but we still owed it to the country to do what we could with what we had. We hadn't had to use EITs on a majority of our detainees, and the most powerful interrogation weapon we had, still, was our ability to bring knowledge to bear. No one could do that as well as we could. Instead, these two wanted to pick up their marbles and go home. That sort of posturing might sound good in the safe confines of one's own conference room, but I knew it wouldn't travel well. When I protested again, they cut me off.

"Change the briefing," Goss said. I would accompany him to the Principals' Committee, and I would make the presentation to the cabinet secretaries.

Returning to my office, I dutifully made Goss's changes, but did not want to be associated with them. I called Pat Murray, Goss's chief of staff. "Look," I said. "I've been thinking about this. The ideas in this briefing are the Director's. He feels strongly about them. He would be far more effective in presenting them than I would."

"The Director wants *you* to deliver the brief," he said.

There was nothing for it, as the British would say, but to brass it out. Early on in the presentation, I came to the critical line. Summoning all the confidence I didn't feel, I said, "And so, CIA will have to end its interrogation program . . ." I tried to move quickly on to the next slide, but Secretary Rice, who had been listening with growing impatience, cut me off.

"Wait just a minute," she said. Looking balefully at Goss, she continued: "This isn't the meeting I thought I was coming to." She then went on to verbally eviscerate him, in effect telling him that he should come back with a responsible plan. He didn't have much to say for the rest of the meeting.

As we gathered our papers to leave, Steve Cambone, who had accompanied Secretary Rumsfeld, leaned over to me, shaking his head at the debacle. He fully understood my position; he'd no doubt been in similar situations, carrying water for his principal. "I felt for you," he said softly.

It was a fitting cap to an extremely frustrating year. And yet I took some satisfaction in the fact that, somehow, I was still standing. In the latter months of 2005, rumors of my imminent demise had ebbed and flowed. Rodriguez had tried to ease me out gracefully, even offering through his chief of staff to give me a highly prestigious European posting typically reserved as a retirement tour for former chiefs of the Clandestine Service. I turned it down. There were still things I wanted to finish at CTC. If Jose wanted to get rid of me, I wasn't going to make it easy for him.

A big part of that unfinished business was to finalize the strategic plan for the center, which would require directorate-level support. I knew the newly styled "Director of the National Clandestine Service" would never accept it if it came only from me, so I organized a command briefing, with all my senior lieutenants gathered around, many of whom had worked previously for Jose, and let them take turns arguing for the reforms that mattered most to them. It worked. Rodriguez wouldn't say no to them. He approved the full strategic plan, though he had transparently little enthusiasm for it. He had only two questions: In light of our reorganization of the center, where would the former head of Alec Station, a favorite of his, end up? Pointing to a box in the new organigram, I explained that the reorganization amounted to a promotion for her. His second question: "When are you going to get bin Laden?"

Winston Churchill once said that "Nothing is so exhilarating in life as to be shot at with no result." For months on end, I had awoken each day feeling like I was the last man standing on the roof of the Alamo, alone and surrounded. It was exciting. Survive long enough in that position, and you begin to think you can do so indefinitely. But on February 3, 2006, I got the summons to the seventh floor. I was pensive as I rode down alone in the elevator afterwards. This was definitely a new and different feeling. I'd never been fired before. Still, I had to smile at Jose's last words to me: "We'll have to figure out what we're going to say to people."

"Why not the truth?" I thought.

It was a Friday afternoon. We had planned a dance party at our home for that Saturday night to celebrate Paula's birthday. I didn't say a word to her until Sunday, so as not to put a damper on the festivities. That night I went to the office, as usual, and composed a message to the CTC workforce. I explained that the D/NCS had lost confidence in my leadership, and that I was being dismissed. I thanked them for all they'd done to combat our enemies and to make us better, and asked their assistance to ensure a smooth transition to my successor, whoever that might turn out to be. The following morning, I made the announcement personally to my senior staff, and then released the general notice via e-mail.

I treated my last week as director of CTC as a victory lap. I visited each of the units in the center, delivering at least a dozen speeches in a five-day period. I was warmly received, and presented with lots of plaques and mementos. I was gratified by the many supportive messages from inside and outside CIA. That week was the most fun I'd had since before 9/11.

In the weeks that followed, I pondered my next move. I received a couple of fairly attractive offers for intelligence community jobs outside CIA. One friend memorably suggested that my position was like that of an imperial legate who had fallen out of favor with Caesar. Such leaders, he said, would typically go off to govern some distant province, and wait for a change in power that would permit them to return to Rome.

But the more I thought about it, the more I realized I'd been done a favor. I'd been in CIA for twenty-seven years, and it had been a great run. I had served at the heart of the greatest national security challenges of my generation. I'd seen and done nearly everything I'd wanted. Given the seductiveness of our work, I had feared that I would never be able to detach from it, that I would wake up one day on the far side of sixty-five never having done anything else. Because of my years of service and the number of years spent overseas, I qualified for early retirement. I'd just been handed a golden opportunity to see what else life had to offer. I decided to take it.

There was also something else at work. The two great foreign policy challenges of my career had been Iraq and Afghanistan. I felt that we had failed utterly in Iraq, and that I shared the blame. I believed that as a government, perhaps as a nation, we had been unworthy. Not to be too dramatic or maudlin about it, I felt we had not been equal to the role that history had given us to play.

I still hoped that Afghanistan would be different. The one, the only job that might have lured me to come back into government would be a field assignment in Afghanistan. Given my seniority and my family circumstances, though, I knew that was just not a realistic possibility. Now it would be up to others. I retired in June 2006.

By then, the signs of a concerted Taliban comeback were no longer subtle. The terrorist/insurgent methods of the Iraq War—car bombs, improvised explosive devices, and suicide bombers—had migrated to Afghanistan and Pakistan, where they had been unknown just a few years before. The levels of violence and terror, with the Taliban targeting individuals associated with the government or foreign forces, were rising appreciably. The Bush administration responded with increased spending and the incremental addition of troops.

Far from questioning the political model of a highly centralized state, the administration reinforced it. Warlords and militias would still be resisted. The emphasis would be on developing a strong national army and police force. Although once chary of nation building, the Bush administration now embraced it. If lack of development was contributing to the Taliban's rise, the United States would increase funding for infrastructure. If want of fair and impartial courts was driving rural Afghans to the Taliban, judges would be trained and the Ministry of Justice reinforced. If narcotics cultivation was generating funds for the insurgency, poppy eradication would be stepped up. The effort was mostly top-down, piecemeal, ill-coordinated. At no point did the Bush administration ever articulate a set of strategic objectives for Afghanistan, or a coherent plan for how they would be achieved.

That would change, nominally, in the Obama administration. After campaigning on the accusation that the Bush administration had ignored and underresourced the "good war" in Afghanistan in favor of the "bad war" in Iraq, the newly elected Obama set out to demonstrate a clean break with the past. At first, the break was more apparent than real. The new administration's plan for Afghanistan, formally rolled out in March 2009, was ambitious. Al-Qa'ida, the president said, would be disrupted, dismantled, and defeated, both in Afghanistan and Pakistan; and to ensure against a future safehaven, the Taliban insurgency, too, would be defeated outright. The Afghan National Army would be made a capable fighting force some 134,000 strong—much larger than any future Afghan government would conceivably have the means to support—and the Afghan National Police would be increased to some 82,000. While waiting for the Afghan Army to show up, the U.S. military would take the fight to the Taliban in the highly contested areas in the south and east of the country. Counterinsurgency (COIN) doctrine was the rule of the day; its role in the relative stabilization of Iraq during the "surge" of 2007–08 having been largely misunderstood, it was believed that the same "population-centric" approach would produce benign results in Afghanistan.

At the same time, Obama announced that foreign assistance to the Afghan economy would be increased, and the government made capable of delivering basic services, to undermine support for the Taliban. With American help, Afghanistan would crack down on corruption, eliminate narcotics, and establish full gender equality for women and girls. And although the president gave a nod to those advocating a locally based, bottom-up approach to rebuilding Afghanistan, it was clear that the main thrust of the U.S. effort would still be top-down, through the same hopelessly inept, corrupt, and unaccountable central government which had helped bring the situation to the current pass. If the goals Obama was pursuing and the methods he was employing were not so distinguishable from those pursued by Bush, the president stressed that the difference this time was that they would be pursued systematically, with adequate resources, and with a commitment sufficient to accomplish the goal.

The president's "commitment," in fact, would not survive his exposure to the price tag associated with it. In the summer of 2009, General Stanley McChrystal, the former JSOC commander, now newly named as the overall chief of American and international forces in Afghanistan, embarked on a thorough "commander's review" of the situation. Having been away from the fight in Afghanistan for two years, he was shocked at just how badly the war was going. According to some accounts, he believed that reversing the momentum of the Taliban would require an additional 60,000 U.S. troops; in the end, he requested 40,000. Rhetoric aside, this was not what the president was counting on, particularly when he had already dispatched an additional 21,000 troops to Afghanistan in the first days of his administration. The conflict, the president concluded, would require a complete rethink.

The thrust of President Obama's second Afghan strategy speech, delivered at West Point on December 1, 2009, could not have been more different from the one he had delivered nine months earlier. There would be no "open-ended" escalation in Afghanistan, he said. Nor would America take on a nation-building project there "of up to a decade." No goals would be set beyond those needed to secure core U.S. interests, and those that could be achieved at "reasonable cost." There was no more talk of defeating the Taliban. Instead, the goal would be to arrest their momentum and deny their ability to overthrow the Kabul government. All of this was sensible enough, and if the announcement of these objectives had been accompanied by a far more modest, sustainable strategy to achieve them, Obama would have been on solid ground.

But the president's speech was an exercise in misdirection, and the military failed to grasp it. Obama was signaling a strategic withdrawal from Afghanistan, but would not say so in as many words. The warfighters had target fixation, convinced that a COIN strategy could still succeed, if only they were given more troops. Obama, apparently more seized with politics than with substance, did not want his shift in favor of far more modest goals in Afghanistan to seem like a product of failure. So he did two completely incompatible things. He partially acceded to the military by agreeing to a "surge" of an additional 30,000 U.S. troops to drive the Taliban from areas under their control, but demanded that the surge only last eighteen months. By July 2011, he said, U.S. forces would begin to depart Afghanistan. The leaders of the uniformed military had to know that a year and a half would not be enough to achieve success, but they convinced themselves that the troop withdrawal would be "conditions-based." They were wrong. The civilian leadership made clear that once begun, the troop withdrawal would be inexorable. Obama, more disposed than most politicians to believe that his words were indistinguishable from facts, sought to reconcile the incoherence at the heart of his policy by asserting that the plan to create a huge Afghan army, never realistic or sustainable in the first place, could in fact be accelerated even further, so that Afghans could consolidate the anticipated gains to be made by U.S. troops.

The whole enterprise, in my view, was criminal: Hundreds of U.S. servicemen lost their lives, their limbs, or suffered debilitating head injuries to IEDs while on patrol in Kandahar and Helmand, taking territory that their superiors should have known could never be held by Afghan forces. COIN, as practiced in southern and eastern Afghanistan, was doomed to failure from the outset: it demanded greater local knowledge and cultural understanding on the part of very junior officers operating at their own discretion than could be expected of conventional forces. More fundamentally, a genuine counterinsurgency campaign cannot be won by a proxy army. Had the Americans in Afghanistan been like the French in Algeria—that is, if they had considered Afghanistan theirs, and intended to stay—our COIN strategy might at least have had some coherence and a plausible rationale. In fact, it had little. Predictably, once U.S. forces had cleared an area of the Taliban, installing Afghan "government in a box," in Stan McChrystal's infelicitous phrase, would not prove feasible.

As part of an accompanying "civilian surge," U.S. experts tried to reform a recalcitrant Afghan bureaucracy, ignoring the fact that a structure built to facilitate corruption was unlikely to be reformed from the margins. They threw huge quantities of money at high-profile and often unsustainable infrastructure projects in an attempt to demonstrate progress. I sat bemused at dinner parties where old State Department and military colleagues debated the relative merits of their initiatives. What struck me most was how seldom Afghans figured in these discussions. Afghans had become an afterthought or an annoyance. It was as if the Americans had concluded that the fate of Afghanistan was far too important to allow Afghans a hand in it. The principles of the plan that had guided us during the First American-Afghan War and the lessons we had learned from that time had been progressively, and by now completely, forgotten.

From the outset, the Obama administration had pointed out with pride that theirs was an integrated, regional policy, falling under the purview of Richard Holbrooke, the special representative for Afghanistan and Pakistan. India would by rights have been included as well, had the Indians not taken such umbrage at being associated with the other two. With the war in Afghanistan going so badly, the need for an "integrated regional approach" took on a special meaning, and special urgency: Pakistan came under unrelenting pressure to find and arrest the Taliban leadership sheltering on its soil, and particularly to stop homegrown Pakistani militants' use of the Tribal Areas—especially North Waziristan—as a base for attacks on NATO and Afghan forces.

The Americans were to be constantly frustrated. Pakistan's concern over the Kabul government and Indian inroads there remained unchanged and, with it, their motivations regarding the Afghan Taliban. Religiously based militancy in Pakistan had taken on new and more malignant forms. The U.S. government might have thought that Pakistani efforts to control militants engaged in cross-border attacks were woefully insufficient, but the militants themselves took rather a different view. In late 2007, a number of Pakistani militant groups, having concluded that their government was in league with the Americans and must be opposed, formed the *Tehreek-e Taliban Pakistan*—the Pakistani Taliban—under the leadership of the charismatic *jihadist* Beitullah Mehsud, and began launching attacks against government forces. In subsequent years, their operations would spread well outside the Tribal Areas. In the process, religious extremists elsewhere in the country were energized, leading to a cycle of mass-casualty terrorist attacks, assassinations, and assaults on government installations throughout Pakistan.

Islamabad responded with a mix of policies, from violent counterinsurgency operations in which millions of civilians were displaced, to negotiated cease-fires, to traditional divide-and-conquer tactics in which certain militant groups would be bribed or suborned into temporary neutrality so that the government could focus on others. In the midst of these maneuvers, for years the United States could not induce Pakistan to invade and occupy the militant safehaven in North Waziristan, which provided a base for groups whose primary targets were in Afghanistan. The Pakistanis lived in fear that to do so might drive those groups to join forces with others primarily focused on Pakistan, with potentially disastrous consequences to themselves. They had their own challenges, and were not about to take risks to defend foreigners, who—the Pakistanis reasoned—could take care of themselves. Over time, the efforts of Pakistan's ISI to maintain links and to try to manipulate all these groups in defense of its own interests looked progressively to U.S. observers more and more like active Pakistani collusion with those who were killing Americans.

In response, the employment of armed drones in the Pakistani Tribal Areas, which had once largely been limited to pinpoint strikes against foreign militants with operational ties to al-Qa'ida, was expanded, if press accounts and those of organizations dedicated to the subject are to be believed, to include attacks against groups of armed men apparently engaged in cross-border insurgency. Out of frustration with Pakistan's unwillingness or inability to police its own territory, what once had been primarily a limited counterterrorism tool became a broad-based counterinsurgency tool. As the number of cross-border attacks increased, so did the number of drone strikes. The fact that such "signature strikes" were aimed at local, as opposed to foreign militants, and had a much greater propensity to generate collateral casualties among non-combatants, had the effect of greatly increasing public outrage in Pakistan, and encouraging yet more militancy.

By 2013, U.S. policy in South-Central Asia had conspired not only to generate a losing war in Afghanistan but in the process to fundamentally destabilize neighboring Pakistan, a nuclear-armed state of some 180 million people. After a span of a dozen years, the longest war in American history, we had succeeded in killing Osama bin Laden and degrading the organization responsible for the attacks on our shores. But regarding arguably our most important objective—to deny South-Central Asia as a future safehaven for international terrorists—a combination of unwise policies, inept execution, and myopic zeal had produced a situation arguably worse than the one with which we started.

Chapter 46

ACCEPTANCE

A MERICA IS LEAVING AFGHANISTAN. Plans may call for a minimal, non-combat military presence for another year or two beyond 2014, but we should not be fooled. The trajectory of American policy in South-Central Asia has been clear since President Obama's West Point speech of December 1, 2009. However deliberately, we are headed inexorably for the exit.

Core American interests in Afghanistan and Pakistan have been, and remain, simple: to drive al-Qa'ida from both countries and to end the terrorist safehaven. The first goal has proved largely achievable. The second has not.

Immediately after 9/11, in decisions in which I played some role, we sensibly limited the means we would employ in pursuit of our goals to those that would and could be achieved by Afghans, knowing that only those could be sustained. Our current abandonment of Afghanistan is the product of a subsequent colossal overreach, from 2005 onward, which ultimately saw the deployment of 100,000 American troops, supplemented by another 40,000 from NATO and allied nations, and the expenditure, at our peak, of some $100 billion per year.

In the process, we overwhelmed a primitive country, with a largely illiterate population, a tiny agrarian economy, a tribal social structure, and nascent national institutions. We triggered massive corruption through our profligacy; convinced a substantial number of Afghans that we were, in fact, occupiers; and facilitated the resurgence of the Taliban. For all the billions spent and lives lost, there is little to show, and most of that will not long survive our departure. If there is a principal reason for that catastrophic lapse in collective judgment, it is that

415

we decided, in typically American fashion, that failure was not an option. If Afghans were transparently unable to make of their country what we believed it needed to be in order to achieve our notion of victory, then by God we would do it for them.

In fact, failure is always an option. That was true in Vietnam; we are finding it true of Afghanistan today.

The American reaction to the failure of our imperial overreach in Afghanistan is unfortunate. Rather than adapt our timeline and our notions of an achievable victory to reality, we are simply going home. Having failed by trying to do too much, we are set to compound our failures by doing too little.

Prediction, they say, is difficult—particularly concerning the future. But there are some things we can foresee with confidence. Afghanistan has been in the grip of civil war almost continually since the Soviet withdrawal in 1989. The three years following the defeat of the Taliban was but a respite, and the civil war will likely grow more acute following the departure of American and NATO combat troops. The religio-ethnic divide between the Taliban and the former Northern Alliance, combined with a lack of governance and the ruthlessness of the Taliban's domestic terror tactics, ensure that large parts of the country, particularly rural areas in the south and east, will be subject to Taliban rule.

To remain viable and capable of resisting the Taliban, the Kabul regime will remain dependent upon U.S. and other foreign support, probably to the tune of several billions per year. Financial support will mean more to its survival than foreign troops. The fall of the Najibullah regime in 1992 was the result not of the Soviet military withdrawal three years before, but of the cutoff of Soviet aid. The few non-combat American troops set to remain in Afghanistan for a year or two will be useful primarily as hostages. As long as they remain, some level of American financial support will continue. But it is crystal-clear from past history that there will be no substantial foreign assistance to Afghanistan in the absence of foreign troops. Without the vital need to protect their own forces, it is most unlikely that either the United States or other Western governments will follow through on their pledges of assistance. What happens to the Kabul regime thereafter is anyone's guess, but the prognosis is not good.

Some would argue that none of this matters. Even if the Taliban were to return to power, they say, surely the clerics would have learned a lesson from the misfortunes that befell them post-9/11. They point to the assurances long given by the Taliban leadership, that theirs is a national movement, nothing more, and that they will not allow Afghanistan to be used as a platform from which to attack other countries.

We should not be assuaged. True, the Afghan Taliban is not an organization devoted to global *jihad*. The Taliban did not encourage and certainly did not participate in the terrorism sponsored by al-Qa'ida. But they will not turn their backs on, still less cooperate with infidels against, those whom they consider devoted and pious Muslims resisting the oppression of America and the regional governments it supports. Their thinking tends to be binary: Is a particular course required by Islam, or not? There is no reason to believe that those we regard as international terrorists will be turned away if they seek the future support of the Taliban.

In fact, the future threat posed by an Afghan safehaven has increased. Pakistan is beset by a religiously motivated insurgency. That insurgency will not go away, even after the U.S. withdrawal from Afghanistan. Pakistani militants have already shown a penchant for maintaining safehavens in Afghanistan and launching attacks toward the east. Given their religious sympathies and close, longstanding affiliation with Pakistani religious extremists, not to mention their own latent antipathies toward Islamabad, it is simply not credible that the Afghan Taliban would refuse to permit the Pakistani Taliban to operate from areas under their control.

It is one of the great ironies of the current situation that although the insurgency in Pakistan is largely an unintended consequence of the American occupation of Afghanistan, and despite Pakistan's conviction that the government in Kabul is antagonistic toward it, the survival of an anti-Taliban regime in Afghanistan is in Islamabad's critical national interest. And given Pakistan's nuclear capabilities, the survival of moderate, secular governance there is in *our* interest. If the Taliban were to prevail in Afghanistan and establish unfettered control, the results for Pakistan would be serious, if not disastrous. Despite appearances to the contrary, the Pakistani state is not on the verge of collapse. But the future undoubtedly holds surprises for us all, and in Pakistan those surprises are unlikely to be pleasant.

A wise American policy would see continued, open-ended U.S. engagement in the region. A small but effective American force designed to train and equip a sustainably small Afghan army would be supplemented by a limited number of specialized CIA officers and Special Forces troops whose job would be to identify, train, and organize Afghan tribals in areas beyond the effective reach of Kabul who have the desire, the ability, and the indigenous leadership to resist Taliban domination. In effect, the United States would aid counterinsurgency in areas within the ambit of Kabul and promote insurgency in those areas outside it. The American presence also would provide the platform from which to strike groups of international terrorists as and when they appear on either side of the Durand Line.

A limited American engagement could not produce the sort of victory Americans are comfortable with. Its near-term results would be most unsatisfying. It would be designed to ensure that potential terrorist safehavens, which might otherwise be uncontested, would at least be contested. Americans don't like playing for a tie. But in time, politics on both sides of the Pak-Afghan border would find its own level. The Taliban, denied the possibility of ultimate victory, would eventually find its place in Pushtun society, not as a conventional power-sharing party among parties—its absolutist leaders are not capable of or interested in such a role—but as a regulatory influence enforcing fundamentalist religious norms on the local level.

Open-ended American engagement in South-Central Asia would be well within the capabilities of a global power. But there is little point in perseverating on what will not and cannot be. The only sort of victory achievable even for a superpower in Afghanistan would require a degree of wisdom and steadfastness not seen in the United States since the end of the Cold War, and one of which the current generation of American leaders seems manifestly incapable.

It remains to be seen whether and when the United States will again be drawn into South-Central Asia. Notwithstanding our failure of recent years to meet the challenges which history has thrust upon us, we remain a global power, with global responsibilities. The forces of global *jihad* which Osama bin Laden did so much to inspire are stronger than ever. Now, and perhaps for some time to come, their efforts will be concentrated in the Middle East, where opportunities to advance their millennial goals abound. But in the long-term struggle for the soul and future of Islam, the battlefield will inevitably shift. The fertile ground of Islamic extremism in the Asian subcontinent may beckon them yet again. We may think we are finished with Afghanistan. But Afghanistan may not be finished with us.

ACKNOWLEDGMENTS

To those whose important contributions to this book are catalogued and acknowledged in the Author's Note, I must add a number of others.

First, I owe a great debt of gratitude to David McCormick of McCormick and Williams, who saw potential in a single *New York Times* op-ed and who pursued me with a patience and persistence without which the long-term aspiration represented by this book might have remained permanently unrealized.

I am similarly grateful to Webster Younce, then of Simon & Schuster, who first decided to take a chance on an untried author.

To the entire team at Simon & Schuster I owe much. The legendary Alice Mayhew, muse to many eminent writers, must have wondered frequently how she could have been saddled with me. This book would never have achieved its current form but for her guidance. Jonathan Cox and Stuart Roberts were both patient and efficient in guiding me through the publication process. Ann Adelman, my copy editor, was nothing short of brilliant.

Lists of acknowledgments always include ritual recognition for the forbearance of the author's all-suffering family. In this case, though, neither the degree of my family's forbearance nor the extent of my thanks can be adequately expressed.

Special thanks go to Daniel Markey of the Council on Foreign Relations, every inch the scholar and intellectual that I am not, who was so generous with his time in making sure that I did not do violence to the truth in the historical sequences of this book. Any lapses, needless to say, are mine.

And finally, I would be remiss if I did not extend thanks to "C," who cannot be identified even in alias, but whose long-ago, offhand comment convinced me that this book simply had to be written.

PHOTO CREDITS

INDEX

Names entirely in quotations refer to aliases or partially true names.
Page numbers in *italics* refer to maps.

ABOUT THE AUTHOR

Robert Grenier is a highly decorated twenty-seven-year veteran of CIA's Clandestine Service. He played central leadership roles in the greatest national security challenges of his generation—as CIA station chief for Pakistan and Afghanistan during 9/11, as CIA mission manager during the invasion of Iraq, and as the head of CIA's global counterterrorism operations. Today he is chairman of ERG Partners, a strategic and financial advisory firm. A noted lecturer and television commentator, he is also a life member of the Council on Foreign Relations and a member of the board of the CIA Officers' Memorial Foundation. When not sailing, he resides with his family in the Washington, D.C., area.